Managing the Sustain

11/5 4, 12   wk 11
11/19 13   ethics exercise
              wk 13

10/22   9/10   wk 9
10/29   11, 14 wk 10

We hear the term "sustainability" everywhere today. In the context of city management, the term often refers to environmental concerns, both locally and globally. *Managing the Sustainable City* examines not only how cities can prepare to weather the local effects of climate change, but also how urban centers can sustain themselves through other modern management challenges, including budgeting and finance, human resource management, public safety, and infrastructure. This clearly written and engaging new textbook provides a comprehensive overview of urban administration today, exploring the unique demographics of cities, local government political structures, intergovernmental relations, and the full range of service delivery areas for which cities are ever more responsible.

Throughout the book, two important components of city management today—the use of technology and measuring performance for accountability—are highlighted, along with NASPAA accreditation standards and competencies. Particular attention is paid to incorporating Urban Administration standards to provide students with a thorough understanding of:

- The ethics of local government management
- The roles and relationships among local and elected/appointed government officials, as well as what makes local institutions different from other institutions
- Strategies for engaging citizens in local governance
- The complexities of intergovernmental and network relationships to develop skills in collaborative governance
- How to manage local government financial resources as well as human resources.

Public service values such as accountability, transparency, efficiency, effectiveness, ethical behavior, and equity are emphasized throughout the text, and discussion questions, exercises, and "career pathways" highlighting successful public servants in a variety of city management roles are included in each chapter. *Managing the Sustainable City* is an ideal textbook for students of public administration, public policy, and public affairs interested in learning how cities can be sustainable—in their management, their policies, and their interactions with their citizens—as well as in preparing for and managing the impacts of climate change.

Genie N. L. Stowers is Professor of Public Administration at San Francisco State University, USA.

Albert C. Hyde is currently Visiting Professor of Public Administration at Northern Ilinois University, USA.

M. Ernita Joaquin is Associate Professor of Public Administration at San Francisco State University, USA.

"*Managing the Sustainable City* provides a unique and useful approach to the business of managing cities. Organized around NASPAA accreditation standards, the reader is provided with a breadth of topics on how cities work from the perspective of the professional managers."

Robyne Stevenson, *University of Central Florida,* USA

"The focus on sustainable urban management, full coverage of issues facing urban managers, and excellent exercises that link theory to practice make this the ideal text for undergraduate and graduate students and a great resource for urban managers."

Ronald K. Vogel, *Ryerson University,* Canada

"Stowers and her collaborators offer a concise overview of core topics in city management and provide questions that help students structure an exploration of their own community. Rich in data about American cities, this book provides students with a unique overview of local government management."

Eric Zeemering, *Northern Illinois University,* USA

Managing the Sustainable City

GENIE N. L. STOWERS

with Albert C. Hyde and M. Ernita Joaquin

Routledge
Taylor & Francis Group

NEW YORK AND LONDON

First published 2018
by Routledge
711 Third Avenue, New York, NY 10017

and by Routledge
2 Park Square, Milton Park, Abingdon, Oxon OX14 4RN

Routledge is an imprint of the Taylor & Francis Group, an informa business

Library of Congress Cataloging-in-Publication Data
Names: Stowers, Genie N. L., author.
Title: Managing the sustainable city / by Genie N.L. Stowers.
Description: New York, NY : Routledge, 2017. | Includes bibliographical
   references and index.
Identifiers: LCCN 2017015252 | ISBN 9781138102521 (hardback : alk. paper) |
   ISBN 9780765646293 (pbk. : alk. paper) | ISBN 9781315717401 (ebook)
Subjects: LCSH: Municipal government—United States. | Municipal finance—
   United States. | Municipal services—United States. | Public administration—
   United States. | Sustainability—United States.
Classification: LCC JS331 .S768 2017 | DDC 352.160973—dc23
LC record available at https://lccn.loc.gov/2017015252

ISBN: 978-1-138-10252-1 (hbk)
ISBN: 978-0-765-64629-3 (pbk)
ISBN: 978-1-315-71740-1 (ebk)

Typeset in Sabon
by Apex CoVantage, LLC

Thank you to Ernita Joaquin and Al Hyde for participating in writing this textbook, through their respective chapters. With gratitude to all the many M.P.A. students in my classes at San Francisco State over the years—for your willingness to share your ideas and engage, and for making teaching fun and rewarding.

Thanks also to those friends, colleagues, and former students (Bob S., Christine J., Christine L., Danelle C., Diane M., Emily D., Jill R., Jim G., Jim P., Mai-Ling G., Megan O., Michael P., Rod G., and Tina O.) who agreed to give me their work-life history for the career pathways in this book. And finally but most importantly, to my family Marissa and Gabriela, for sharing me with this book. Much love always.

CONTENTS

BOXES

FIGURES

TABLES

FOREWORD

We hear the term "sustainability" everywhere today; in the context of city management, the term is most used to mean environmental sustainability or being able to thrive in a world facing climate change. In this book, however, we posit the term means something more extensive, more holistic—how cities can sustain themselves during climate change but also through the many other challenges facing the modern world. Every area of city management faces sustainability changes. In the area of budgeting and finance, the meaning is clear—a city must prepare for difficult times and sustain itself through putting funds away in reserve, having sound internal controls to prevent embezzlement and losses, and conducting effective monitoring to ensure funds are spent as approved. For human resources management, sustainability can mean effective hiring and training of personnel then working within the organization to retain those highly skilled individuals; the city then is better able to sustain its most valuable resource—its workers. What sustainability does *not* mean is to just add the word and "stir."

The sustainability approach is a meaningful approach to city management, and this textbook provides an overview of this field in today's challenging world strategy. As such, it provides a comprehensive overview of urban administration today, from the demographics of cities to local government political structures and why those make cities different from other levels of government, to intergovernmental relations and, then, to the full range of service delivery areas for which cities are responsible today.

We first explore the urban context with Chapter 1: Today's Diverse Cities; Chapter 2: City Structure, Leadership, and Elections; and Chapter 3: Cities and the American Intergovernmental Structure.

The next section covers core managerial areas, beginning with Chapter 4: Engaging Urban Residents, then focusing on Chapter 5: City Budget and Financial Management, and Chapter 6: Employees as Human Resources. The remainder of this section is Chapter 7: Data, Information, and Communications and Chapter 8: Urban Service Delivery, both highlighting the importance of data and technology in today's city governments.

The final section on delivering urban services covers a wide range of urban service and policy areas, from Public Safety and Emergency Management (Chapter 9), Urban Planning (Chapter 10), and City Infrastructure and Transportation (Chapter 11), to Housing and Community/Economic Development (Chapter 12), and Parks, Recreation, and Libraries (Chapter 13). Last in this section is Chapter 14: Sustainable Cities, which covers air and water pollution, climate change and its impact on cities, and strategies for managing the environmental challenges of our cities.

Throughout the book, three important components of city management today—the use of technology, measuring performance for accountability, and sustainability strategies—will be highlighted.

And—as a book for public administration and public policy students, NASPAA (formerly the National Association of Schools of Public Affairs and Administration, now the Network of Schools of Public Policy, Affairs, and Administration) accreditation standards and competencies will be highlighted. As a text for public affairs, public service values such as accountability, transparency, efficiency, effectiveness, ethical behavior, and equity will be highlighted throughout. The NASPAA standards are:

- To lead and manage in public governance;
- To participate in and contribute to the policy process;
- To analyze, synthesize, think critically, solve problems, and make decisions;
- To articulate and apply a public service perspective; and
- To communicate and interact productively with a diverse and changing workforce and citizenry.

Particular attention is also paid to incorporating the additional content relevant to NAS-PAA's Urban Administration elective emphasis standards (see below) so that students using the text will have a basic understanding of each area:

1. Demonstrate an understanding of the ethics of local government management, emphasizing the role of the professional chief executive.
2. Understand the roles and relationships among key local and other government elected and appointed officials as well as what makes local institutions different from other institutions.
3. Articulate the purposes of and processes for communicating with citizens in local governance.
4. Develop strategies for engaging citizens in local governance.
5. Lead, manage, and serve the management of local government core services and functions.
6. Apply the management of local government financial resources.
7. Apply the management of local government human resources.
8. Understand the complexities of intergovernmental and network relationships and develop skills in collaborative governance.

Cities *can* be sustainable, in all definitions of the word: in their management, their policies, their interactions with their citizens, as well as in preparing for and managing the impacts of climate change. Becoming knowledgeable about city issues and how they can best be managed in today's world is one important step toward ensuring that future.

Today's Diverse Cities

Chapter 1 is an introduction to the diversity and range of cities in today's America. Today's cities are sites of exciting activity, diversity, and people engaged in all kinds of endeavors, and sites full of interesting challenges for public sector managers. They are critical to Americans because they are where, in 2010, 82 percent of the United States lived (World Health Organization 2014). They are where citizens notice potholes, go to the park, find a place to live or work, exercise, send their kids to school, and, otherwise, live their lives. As professionals in city management, we need to learn how to keep the processes of city government working—and try to solve our cities' ongoing problems. In 2015, the mayors of the nation's top 100 cities identified their most significant challenges as economic development, infrastructure, public safety, budgets, and education (National League of Cities 2015). This chapter will introduce students to the exciting sites that are cities today, as well as to the issues that they face, and will discuss the role of city management as a profession. In terms of NASPAA standards, this chapter will introduce students to the "diverse and changing workforce and citizenry" in America's cities today.

More and more, the United States is a country of cities; ten states have more than 90 percent of their populations living in their urban areas (Figure 1.1). Beyond those, there is disparity across states; four states (Mississippi, West Virginia, Vermont, and Maine) have less than 50 percent of their populace living in cities (World Health Organization 2014).

As might be expected, there is quite a lot of difference across the nation in city and urban area size. The ten largest metropolitan statistical areas (MSAs) in the 2010 Census are listed in Table 1.1. The New York, Los Angeles, and Chicago MSAs are the three largest in the country. Note that of these ten areas, eight of them lie on the coasts, one indication of how many people live in coastal zones.

There is also quite a bit of difference across the country in urban growth and decline. In general, the North and Midwest have more cities in decline while the West and Sunbelt regions have more cities that are growing. This trend can be seen in Table 1.2, which shows two cities in Texas, three in California, one in Arizona, and one in South Carolina among the MSAs with the most growth from 2000 to 2010.

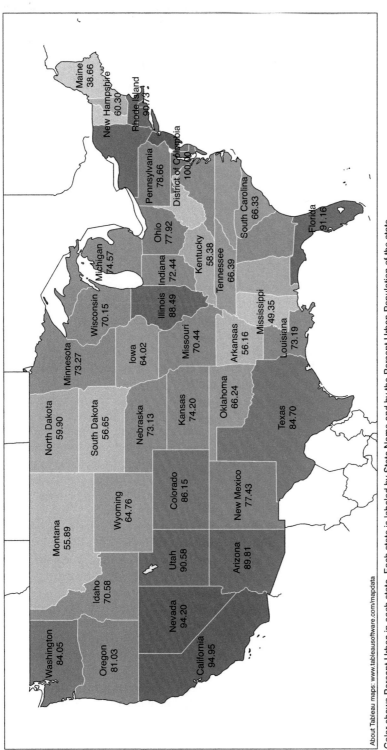

About Tableau maps: www.tableausoftware.com/mapdata

Color shows Percent Urban in each state. Each state is labeled by State Name and by the Percent Urban Population of the state.

POPPCT_URBAN

38.66	100.00

FIGURE 1.1
Percent Urban Population by State, 2010

Source: Developed from PctUrbanRural_State Excel file accessed on March 12, 2014. March 12, 2012, release of analysis and data found at https://www.census.gov/geo/reference/ua/urbar–rural-2010.html, based upon US 2010 Census.

◤ BOX 1.1   URBAN DEFINITIONS

A **Census Designated Place** is a "densely settled concentration of population that is not within an incorporated place, but is locally identified by a name" (U.S. Census Bureau 1994, p. G-9).

Metropolitan and Micropolitan Statistical Areas are areas created to be used for collecting and publishing statistics. A metropolitan statistical area "contains a core urban area of 50,000 or more population. A micropolitan statistical area contains an urban core of at least 10,000 (but less than 50,000) population. Each metro or micro area consists of one or more counties and includes the counties containing the core urban areas, as well as any adjacent counties that have a high degree of social and economic integration (as measured by commuting to work) with the urban core." (U.S. Census Bureau 2014a)

A **Consolidated Metropolitan Statistical Area** is a metropolitan statistical area with a population of one million or more (U.S. Census Bureau 1994, p. 12–12).

Urbanized Areas (UAs)—"A UA is a continuously built-up area with a population of 50,000 or more. It comprises one or more places—central place(s)—and the adjacent densely settled surrounding area—urban fringe—consisting of other places and nonplace territory" (U.S. Census Bureau 1994, p. 12–1).

An **Urban Place outside of UAs** is "any incorporated place or census designated place (CDP) with at least 2,500 individuals" (U.S. Census Bureau 1994, p. 12–1).

◤ TABLE 1.1

The Ten Largest Metropolitan Statistical Areas, 2010

	Metropolitan Statistical Area	2010 Population	Population Change, 2000 to 2010
1	New York, NY—Newark, NJ—Connecticut	18,351,295	3.1
2	Los Angeles-Long Beach-Santa Ana, CA	12,150,996	3.1
3	Chicago, IL—Indiana	8,608,208	3.6
4	Miami, FL	5,502,379	11.9
5	Philadelphia, PA—New Jersey—Delaware—Maryland	5,441,567	5.7
6	Dallas-Fort Worth-Arlington, TX	5,121,892	23.6
7	Houston, TX	4,944,332	29.4
8	Washington, D.C.—Virginia—Maryland	4,586,770	16.6
9	Atlanta, GA	4,515,419	29.0
10	Boston, MA—New Hampshire—Rhode Island	4,181,019	3.7

Source: Developed from PopAreaChngeUA Excel files. Accessed on March 10, 2014 from www.census.gov/geo/reference/ua/urban-rural-2010.html. Data is based on a March 12, 2012 release of analysis and data from the U.S. 2010 Census.

TABLE 1.2

Ten Metropolitan Statistical Areas with the Most Increase and the Most Decline from 2000 to 2010

	MSAs with the Most Increase			MSAs with the Most Decline		
	Metropolitan Statistical Area	*2010 Population*	*% Increase*	*Metropolitan Statistical Area*	*2010 Population*	*% Decline*
1	McKinney, TX	170,030	211.8	Parkersburg, WV—Ohio	67,229	−21.5
2	Avondale, AZ	197,041	190.3	Lodi, CA	68,738	−17.9
3	The Woodlands, TX	239,938	168.3	Charleston, WV	153,199	−16.3
4	Lady Lake, FL	112,991	122.8	Uniontown-Connellsville, PA	51,370	−12.1
5	West Bend, WI	68,444	105.6	New Orleans, LA	899,703	−10.9
6	El Centro, CA	107,672	103.3	Saginaw, MI	126,265	−10.4
7	Hilton Head Island, SC	68,998	100.6	Johnstown, PA	69,014	−9.3
8	Temecula-Murrieta, CA	441,546	92.1	Anderson, IN	88,133	−9.2
9	Concord, NC	214,881	86.8	Seaside-Monterey-Marina, CA	114,237	−9.0
10	Visalia, CA	219,454	82.8	Pine Bluff, AR	53,495	−8.7

Source: Based upon PopAreaChngeUA Excel file. Accessed on March 10, 2014 from www.census.gov/geo/reference/ua/urban-rural-2010.html. Based on the March 12, 2012 release of analysis and data from the U.S. 2010 Census.

The Midwest and North's decline is likewise illustrated by the five MSAs from West Virginia, Ohio, Pennsylvania, and Michigan. Also of note is the 10.9 percent decline in the New Orleans MSA, a result of the devastating Hurricane Katrina in 2005.

As an example of growth and decline, we view Williston, North Dakota (population of 14,716 in 2010 [American FactFinder 2016]), which became an oil fracking boomtown in 2011 and continued enormous growth for five years, until the price of oil started declining. At the peak of its boom in 2015, there were 26,977 people officially living in Williston (U.S. Census Bureau 2016), although the city says it grew to more than 36,000. When the boom began, people arriving for jobs in the oil industry put up tents in the city's parks, and moved to backyards and then to "man camps" after those parks were closed for habitation. The city then set up mobile homes for workers that the city is also now trying to close. However, during the boom, the city built a new $70 million high school, a

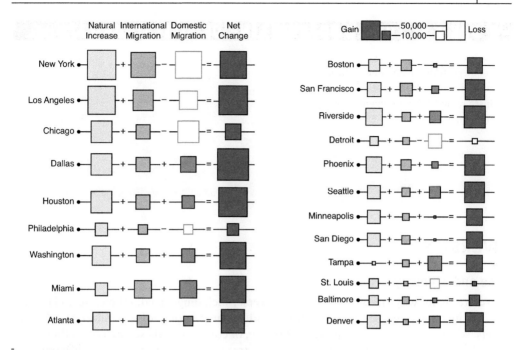

FIGURE 1.2
Components of Metro Area Change, 2010–2011

Source: U.S. Census Bureau Data Visualization Gallery. Accessed February 14, 2014. https://www.census.gov/dataviz/visualizations/040/.

recreation center almost as expensive, new water and sewer systems, and widened streets. Builders developed almost 10,000 new homes and apartments. Now, the city has already lost 6,000 people, and more are leaving. The city is trying not to become a "bust" but is struggling (Yardley 2016).

The components of urban population change are nicely illustrated in Figure 1.2's data visualization from the U.S. Census Bureau. The components of urban growth are Natural Increases (i.e., births), International Migration and Domestic Migration; the size of each box indicates how much population growth came from that component, and the Net Change box indicates how much the city has grown, in this case from 2010 to 2011. Filled boxes indicate increases, while boxes that are not filled indicate declines in population.

Thus, we can see that all of the cities represented here had positive increases in their birth rates and from international migration (this trend was led by international migration into New York City). However, seven cities had declines in their domestic migration patterns; i.e., some of their residents left the city and moved to other places. The city losing the largest number of residents in this fashion was New York City, followed by Los Angeles, Chicago, Detroit, and then Philadelphia, St. Louis, Baltimore, and Boston. The result is that only Detroit experienced a net loss in population; St. Louis grew the least of the others, and Dallas, Houston, and Miami had the most net growth in the 2010–2011 period.

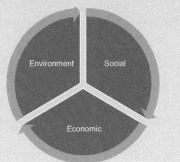

> **BOX 1.2 TRIPLE BOTTOM LINE OF SUSTAINABILITY**
>
> Planners in the sustainability field refer to the Triple Bottom Line (TBL) of Sustainability: Environment, Social, and Economic.

DIVERSITY

Race and Ethnicity

There are many ways in which cities are diverse, including racial, ethnic, age, class status, and income levels, sexual orientation, and a whole variety of groupings based upon beliefs, social activities, and interests. Moreover, of course, it is these differences that make cities different and interesting. For city administrators, being aware of these differences is important so that City Hall knows how to provide services appropriately to groups that might have very different needs and cultures but also how it can work to ensure these differences are recognized and respected.

Beginning with race and ethnicity, in 2012 metropolitan and micropolitan statistical areas across the country were about three-quarter white, 13.7 percent African-American, about 7 percent Asian and Pacific Islander, and not quite 1 percent American Indian or Alaska Native (Figure 1.3). The latest Census (2010) and other data from the U.S. Census Bureau allow respondents, for the first time, to claim membership in more than one racial

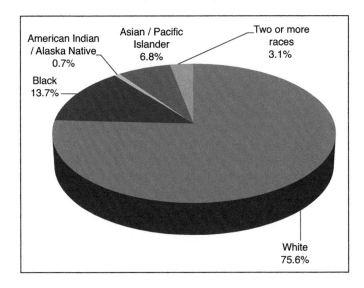

FIGURE 1.3
Race as a Proportion of Total Population in All Metropolitan and Micropolitan Statistical Areas, 2012

Source: Calculated from U.S. Census Bureau, American Fact Finder ACS Demographic and Housing Estimates, 2012. American Community Survey 1 year Estimates.

TABLE 1.3

Top Ten Cities in Proportion of African-American Population, 2010

	Total Population	Rank	% of Total
Detroit, MI	713,777	1	84.3
Jackson, MS	173,514	2	80.1
Miami Gardens, FL	107,167	3	77.9
Birmingham, AL	212,237	4	74.0
Baltimore, MD	620,961	5	65.1
Memphis, TN	646,889	6	64.1
New Orleans, LA	343,829	7	61.2
Flint, MI	102,434	8	59.5
Montgomery, AL	205,764	9	57.4
Savannah, GA	136,286	10	56.7

Source: Rastogi, Sonya, Johnson, Tallese D., Hoeffel, Elizabeth M. and Drewery, Jr., Malcolm P. 2011. Table 6: Ten Places with the Largest Number of Blacks or African Americans: 2010 in *The Black Population: 2010 Census Briefs.* Issued September 2011. Accessed on March 16, 2014 from www.census.gov/prod/cen2010/briefs/c2010br-06.pdf.

group. So in 2012, approximately 3 percent of Americans self-identified as members of more than one race.

Of course, racial groups are not equally distributed across all cities. As Table 1.3 shows, some cities are majority African-American (Detroit, Jackson, Miami Gardens, and Birmingham are roughly three-quarters or more African-American); most of these cities are in the South or Midwest. Likewise, in some regions of the country, some cities have relatively few African-Americans.

The same pattern is true of ethnic background—18 percent of Americans are of Hispanic ethnicity (Figure 1.4), but those Hispanics are not evenly distributed around the country.

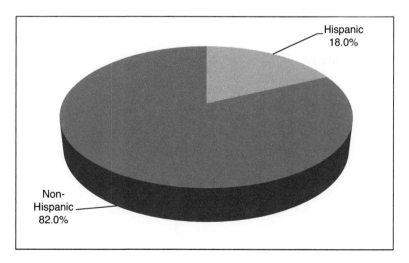

Hispanic
18.0%

Non-
Hispanic
82.0%

FIGURE 1.4

Proportion of Hispanic and Non-Hispanic Ethnicity in All Metropolitan and Micropolitan Statistical Areas, 2012

Source: Calculated from U.S. Census Bureau, American Fact Finder, ACS Demographic and Housing Estimates, 2012 American Community Survey 1 year Estimates.

Figure 1.5 is composed of a series of "spider" charts, so named because they tend to look like spider webs. These particular charts have six axes (one each for percent white, percent Hispanic or Latino, percent African-American, percent American Indian or Alaska Native, percent Asian, and percent Pacific Islander). The very center of the chart represents

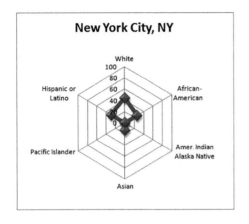

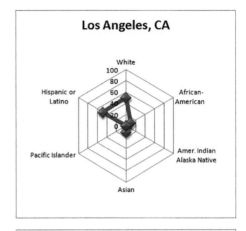

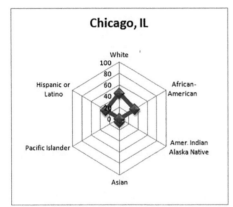

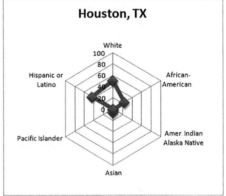

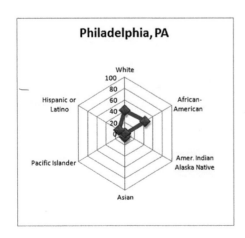

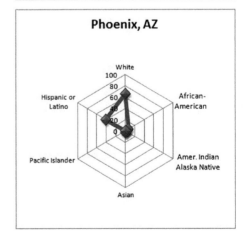

FIGURE 1.5

Comparisons of Ethnic and Racial Diversity among Selected American Cities, 2012

Source: Developed from U.S. Census Bureau, Population Division, Vintage 2012 Population Estimates.

0 percent for each of these variables. For each city, the percent of each of these variables is represented by how far out from the center the marker is placed. For instance, 44 percent of New York City's population is white, so the marker goes on the 44 percent spot on the percent white axis. It is 25.5 percent African-American, so the marker goes to the 25.5 percent spot on the African-American axis, and so on. Putting the data on a spider chart not only allows the user to see and compare the relative amounts of each group within one city—but also allows the user to see each city's diversity compared to that of other cities.

So, from Figure 1.5 we can see that New York City has large populations of African-Americans, Hispanics, and whites, but Philadelphia is mostly white and African-American, and Phoenix is mostly white and Hispanic.

Table 1.4 presents the ten cities with the highest proportion of the Hispanic population; all of these cities are in either California, Texas, or Florida. For eight of these cities,

BOX 1.3 SUSTAINABILITY PLAN STRATEGIES FOR DIVERSITY

Throughout this text, strategies from city sustainability plans around the country will be presented, in the relevant chapters. Here, we see strategies to enhance diversity.

- "Conduct a City-wide equity assessment." St. Louis, Missouri, p. 132
- "Create two additional diversity festivals to recognize, celebrate, and promote the diversity in Grand Rapids by June 30, 2018." Grand Rapids, Michigan, p. 7

- "Engage seniors in civic and volunteer programs." St. Louis, Missouri, p. 123

Sources: City of Grand Rapids, MI. 2016. Sustainability Plan FY 2017–2021. Accessed on February 22, 2017 from http://grcity.us/Documents/2016-07-22%20 Sustainability%20Plan.pdf.
   City of St. Louis, MO. 2013. City of St. Louis Sustainability Plan. Accessed on February 22, 2017 from www.stlouis-mo.gov/government/departments/ planning/documents/city-of-st-louis-sustainability-plan.cfm.

TABLE 1.4

Top Ten Cities in Proportion of Hispanic Population, 2010

Place	Total Population	Rank	% of Total Population
East Los Angeles, CA	126,496	1	97.1
Laredo, TX	236,091	2	95.6
Hialeah, FL	224,669	3	94.7
Brownsville, TX	175,023	4	93.2
McAllen, TX	129,877	5	84.6
El Paso, TX	649,121	6	80.7
Santa Ana, CA	324,528	7	78.2
Salinas, CA	150,441	8	75.0
Oxnard, CA	197,899	9	73.5
Downey, CA	111,772	10	70.7

Source: Ennis, Sharon R., Rios-Vargas, Merarys, and Albert, Nora G. 2011. Table 5: Ten Places with the Highest Number and Percentage of Hispanics or Latinos, 2010. U.S. Census Bureau. *The Hispanic Population: 2010. 2010 Census Briefs.* Accessed on March 16, 2014 from www.census.gov/prod/cen2010/briefs/c2010br-04.pdf.

at least 75 percent of their population is Hispanic. It is important to realize, however, that the Hispanic population is made up of individuals whose heritage emerges from various nationalities (Mexican, Cuban, Salvadoran, Nicaraguan, Guatemalan, for instance). These groups have different histories with different customs and cultures and speak slightly different versions of Spanish with different accents.

The diversity of cities has an enormous impact on city management and how city programs should be delivered to various communities. Often, diversity means that residents do not speak English and that city managers need to consider language when delivering services. Examples of this diversity abound; Turkish is one of Dayton, Ohio's top five languages, and New York City's school system has more than 160 languages represented. Languages used for service delivery could include Spanish, Somali, Vietnamese, Tagalog, Chinese, or Japanese. Some strategies for cities include having signs in languages other than English, having staff who can speak something other than English, and having websites and written materials in other languages. Diversity of language often means cultures are different, as well (Nemeth 2016). Different cultures can mean that services delivered based upon traditional models might have to be reconsidered. Asian cultures have different attitudes toward mental health services, for instance, than Anglo cultures, so services to the Asian-American community need to take these differences into account.

IMMIGRANTS

Immigration has become an important issue in the 2016 presidential election. In 2013, the immigrant population in the United States was 12.8 percent of its total population (40.1 million people). Of these, 18.2 million were naturalized U.S. citizens. Most immigrants to the United States come and reside in its cities—particularly in its larger and more knowledge-based cities. For four American cities (Miami, San Jose, Los Angeles, and San Francisco), immigrants comprise 30 percent or more of their total populations. There, immigrants make significant contributions to many industries, particularly high technology (U.S. Census Bureau 2013).

Age

Another element that is important to cities is the distribution of age of its citizens. In 2012, 6.4 percent of the United States was less than 5 years old, 23.5 percent was under 18 years of age, and 13.7 percent was 65 years or older (U.S. Census Bureau 2014b). For city administrators, a large proportion of very young citizens means a very different set of services is required than in cities with a large proportion of much older citizens. Having more young children means a need for more schools, more parks, and more day care; having more elderly citizens means the need is for senior centers, libraries, and easy transportation (Ortman, Velkoff, and Hogan 2014).

Cities with the most growth in the number of families with children are affordable suburbs in the South and Intermountain West; examples are Austin, Las Vegas, Phoenix, and Salt Lake City (which has the largest share of children at 16.2 percent). These cities have crucial features to attract families with children: affordable housing and good schools, which can mean a large and, perhaps, growing labor force and a good economy.

Large coastal cities like Los Angeles, New York, and San Francisco, on the other hand, have had the largest declines in the population from ages 5 to 14. It is not an accident that these cities tend to be less affordable, with higher housing costs, and so are more difficult for families with children. These trends can become self-reinforcing, as cities with fewer children sometimes make choices that further reduce the chances of families with children living there (like not investing in parks with up-to-date play equipment, summer camps, and good schools). In many of these cities with fewer children, there is also a trend of families living in the city until their children become school age; at that point, the families often move to suburbs with more affordable housing and, sometimes, better schools. Cities with large immigrant populations also tend to have more children, as many immigrant families have more children (Florida 2015b).

Differences in economies and urban cultures can cause extreme differences in age groups between cities. Richard Florida refers to the "barbell demography" of cities, where young single people, married without children, and older people whose children have left home (empty nesters) comprise large groups in cities because of cultural opportunities and amenities. Those in the middle part of the barbell, age-wise, have left to go to the suburbs (Florida 2015b).

As Table 1.5 indicates, the top ten cities for older residents have 16 to 20 percent of individuals 65 years or older; it is not surprising that six of these cities are in Florida or Arizona—both with large retirement communities. There are two main types of cities

TABLE 1.5

Top Ten Cities with Most and Least Proportion of Population More Than 65 Years Old, 2010

	Cities with Most Population 65 Years and Older			Cities with Least Population 65 Years and Older		
	Place	Total Population	% 65 and Older	Place	Total Population	% 65 and Older
1	Scottsdale, AZ	217,385	20.0	West Jordan, UT	103,712	4.6
2	Clearwater, FL	107,685	19.8	Killeen, TX	127,921	5.2
3	Hialeah, FL	224,669	19.1	Frisco, TX	116,989	5.4
4	Surprise, AZ	117,517	19.0	Fontana, CA	196,069	5.7
5	Honolulu, HI	337,256	17.8	Provo, UT	112,488	5.8
6	Metairie, LA	138,481	17.1	Gilbert, AZ	208,453	6.1
7	Cape Coral, FL	154,305	17.0	Enterprise, NV	108,481	6.2
8	Warren, MI	134,056	16.1	Moreno Valley, CA	193,365	6.3
9	Independence, MO	116,830	16.1	Aurora, IL	197,899	6.5
10	Miami, FL	399,457	16.0	Thornton, CO	118,772	6.5

Source: U.S. Census Bureau. 2011. *The Older Population: 2010 Census Briefs.* Accessed on January 6, 2015 from www.census.gov/prod/cen2010/briefs/c2010br-09.pdf.

with older populations—cities that are retirement communities and cities with declining populations, as in the Rust Belt, with large populations of older citizens who stay put where they have lived for years. Cities in Florida or Arizona, long-time retirement communities, also have large populations of older residents. Other retirement locations are cities that may be less expensive, like Austin, Raleigh, Charlotte, Portland, and Denver. Sometimes, older people are following their children to other areas to live near them and grandchildren. Other retirees, more affluent, often plan to stay where they are or move to the suburbs. There is not much support for a recent meme that retirees are relocating to urban areas (Kotkin 2016).

The cities on the right side of the table have the fewest percentage of those who are 65 years or older; they all have only slightly less than 5 percent to 6.5 percent groups of citizens 65 years or older.

Moreover, the American population is aging as Baby Boomers grow older. In 2010, 13 percent of the U.S. population was 65 years or older, but by 2030, that percentage is projected to be more than 20 percent—fully one in five of all Americans (U.S. Census Bureau 2011).

Lesbian/Gay Households

Until recently, it was impossible to determine much of anything about a largely hidden population in the United States, the lesbian and gay community. However, the U.S. Census questions have changed, so more information is available. Also, more lesbians and gay men are willing to self-identify as lesbian or gay on a U.S. Census questionnaire.

In the 2008 to 2012 American Community Survey (ACS), the percentage of total households that were unmarried partner households (male and male partners, and female and female partners) was very small. There are many reasons that these numbers could underrepresent the reality in today's cities. One, there is still a threat for lesbians and gay men to self-identify, particularly if they have children. Two, the period of this questionnaire was one of a great deal of turbulence in the question of same-sex marriage across the American states. While the U.S. Supreme Court did rule same-sex marriage legal in all 50 states, same-sex marriage was already legal in some way in more than one-half of all states. So, the undercount could be because many couples were in fact already married and would not show up in a U.S. Census questionnaire asking about unmarried couples. Still, the ACS provides researchers some information at the city level.

Many of the cities in Table 1.6 with the highest percentage of same-sex unmarried partner households are sites of institutions of higher education (Cornell University in Ithaca, Oregon State University in Corvallis), arts communities (Santa Fe, New Mexico), or high-income areas like the Napa/Santa Rosa/Petaluma areas, the location of much of California's wine industry. For instance, the MSA with the most of these households is the Ithaca, NY, MSA, in which 1.4 percent of the total was male/male and female/female.

INCOME AND POVERTY

According to the U.S. Census Bureau, income is composed of any sources of revenue received by a household and is expressed as per capita personal income (total income divided by the number of residents) or median household income. Income (measured as real median household income) increased by 5.2 percent to $56,516 from 2014 to 2015, an upward trend after the continued decline from the effects of the Great Recession (U.S. Census Bureau 2015).

TABLE 1.6

Top Ten Metropolitan Statistical Areas of Same-Sex Unmarried Partner Households as a Percentage of Total Households

Rank	Metropolitan Statistical Area	Same-Sex Unmarried Partners as a Percent of Total Households
1	Ithaca, NY Metro Area	1.40%
2	San Francisco-Oakland-Fremont, CA Metro Area	1.22%
3	Santa Fe, NM Metro Area	1.17%
4	Barnstable Town, MA Metro Area	1.09%
5	Napa-Santa Rosa-Petaluma, CA Metro Area	1.07%
6	Kingston, NY Metro Area	1.03%
7	Corvallis, OR Metro Area	0.99%
8	Portland-South Portland-Biddeford, ME Metro Area	0.98%
9	Springfield, MA Metro Area	0.93%
10	Portland-Hillsboro, OR—Vancouver, WA Metro Area	0.92%

Source: Developed from U.S. Census. 2012. 2012 ACS 5 year estimates B11009 table, Unmarried Partners. Accessed on January 5, 2015 from https://censusreporter.org/tables/B11009/.

While median household income has slowly increased for all groups, the rate of increase and the median household income itself are different across groups. In 2015, the median household income for African-Americans was only $36,898; for Hispanics it was $45,148. Above the average for all Americans, the median household income for white, non-Hispanics was $62,950, and for Asians, it was $77,166. Inside metropolitan statistical areas (cities), the median household income was $59,258, very close to the national average. Outside MSAs, it was significantly lower, at $44,657 (U.S. Census 2015).

Women are making proportionally more compared to men than ever before but still are making only 80 percent (79.6) of what men are making. The median income for men was $51,212, but for women, the median was only $40,742 (U.S. Census 2015).

The per capita personal income for the entire United States in 2015 was $48,112. Table 1.7 illustrates the ten cities with the highest per capita personal income in the country. Bridgeport-Stamford-Norwalk, Connecticut, in the suburbs of New York City, is the highest ($106,382), with a per capita personal income more than double the national figure (U.S. Census Bureau 2015). Obviously, there are great differences in income across the states and cities—and across gender, race, and ethnicity.

These per capita and median household estimates mask the reality that today, a great many Americans live in poverty. The definition of poverty includes having less income than a threshold of "money income before taxes or tax credits and exclud[ing] capital gains and non-cash benefits (such as Supplemental Nutrition Assistance Program

TABLE 1.7

Top Cities in Per Capita Personal Income, 2015

Rank	Metropolitan Statistical Area	2015 Per Capita Personal Income
1	Bridgeport-Stamford-Norwalk, CT	$106,382
2	Midland, TX	104,714
3	San Jose-Sunnyvale-Santa Clara, CA	81,592
4	San Francisco-Oakland-Hayward, CA	79,206
5	Naples-Immokalee-Marco Island, FL	78,473
6	Casper, WY	68,692
7	Boston-Cambridge, MA—Newton, NH	68,292
8	Sebastian-Vero Beach, FL	67,978
9	Washington, D.C.—Arlington-Alexandria, VA—Maryland—West Virginia	64,882
10	Barnstable Town, MA	64,730

Source: Developed from U.S. Bureau of Economic Analysis. 2016. Data Table lapi1116msa.xls. Accessed on November 21, 2016 from www.bea.gov/newsreleases/regional/lapi/lapi_newsrelease.htm.

benefits and housing assistance). The thresholds do not vary geographically." They are, however, adjusted each year for inflation (U.S. Census Bureau 2015, p. 41). So, a family is considered to be living in poverty if their combined income falls below the poverty threshold for their family size and the number of children under 18 years of age. Table 1.8 illustrates this concept; if a family of five together makes less than $28,741, they are living in poverty.

TABLE 1.8

Weighted Average Poverty Thresholds in 2015 by Size of Family

Number of People in Family	Dollar Threshold in 2015
One	$12,082
Two	15,391
Three	18,871
Four	24,257
Five	28,741
Six	32,542
Seven	36,998
Eight	41,029
Nine	49,177

Source: U.S. Census Bureau. 2015. Appendix B: Estimates of Poverty: Weighted Average Poverty Thresholds in 2015 by Size of Family. In *Income and Poverty in the United States: 2015 Current Population Reports.* Washington, D.C.: U.S. Census Bureau.

Across the United States, the official poverty rate in 2016 was 13.2 percent, slightly down from the previous year and several years beforehand, as well. This means that 43.1 million people live in poverty today. Inside MSAs, this is 13.0 percent, or 35.7 million people. Inside principal cities within those MSAs (central cities), the rate is even higher, at 16.8 percent, or 17.37 million people. Many of the people living in poverty are elderly; the poverty rate among those 65 and older is 8.8 percent. The group with the most living in poverty is children under age 18; in this group, 19.7 percent live in poverty (U.S. Census Bureau 2015).

The starkest differences in poverty rate are due to family type. Married couples with both parents present have only a 5.4 percent poverty rate, an artifact of having two adults present to work and bring in income to the family. The male heads of household with no wife present have a 14.9 percent poverty rate, lower because of only one adult but still showing the impact of men's higher income levels. The highest level of poverty is, of course, found among female-headed households. Already disadvantaged by having only one breadwinner in the family, a female-headed household then has a wage earner who earns, on average, only 80 percent of what men earn—so more than one in four of every female-header household (28.2 percent) lives in poverty (U.S. Census Bureau 2015).

CONCLUSIONS

The information in this chapter illustrates the wide diversity of American cities today—in population, race, ethnicity, income, class status, and other characteristics. These differences make cities the interesting and vibrant places they are but can also present challenges for city managers as they strive to deliver effective and equitable services to all residents. As the NASPAA standards challenge students to do, we must learn to communicate with the "diverse and changing workforce and citizenry." But first, we must learn about that diversity, as we have done in this chapter.

EXERCISES AND DISCUSSION QUESTIONS

Know Your City: There will be Know Your City (KYC) exercises in almost every chapter. In these exercises, students will find data about their city and will write brief descriptions and summaries using this information. These are designed both to allow students to get to know their community and how it is managed, but also to help students become familiar with urban data sources and how to find data about cities. Students should choose a city in which they are interested and should use it for the KYC exercises in the chapters.

1. **Know Your City:** Using U.S. Census Quick Facts (www.census.gov/quickfacts/table/ PST045215/00), find the following data for a city of your choice.

- 2015 population estimates
- Percent persons 65 years and more (2010)
- Percent persons fewer than 18 years (2010)
- Percent white (2010)
- Percent African-American (2010)
- Percent American Indian and Alaska Native (2010)
- Percent Asian (2010)
- Percent Native American and other Pacific Islander (2010)
- Percent two or more races (2010)
- Percent Hispanic or Latino (2010)
- Percent white alone, not Hispanic or Latino (2010)

- Percent foreign born persons (2010–2014)
- Median household income (2010–2014)
- Percent persons in poverty
- Percent persons without health insurance, less than age 65
- Percent Bachelor's degree or higher of persons 25+ years (2010–2014)
- Average number of persons per household (2010–2014)
- Percent language other than English spoken at home (2010–2014)

  Does anything in particular strike you about the data from your city? Anything that appears to be higher or lower than most other cities? What could be the consequences of those differences for city managers and leaders?

2. **Learn from visualizing data:** Find the U.S. Census Bureau's Islands of High-Income interactive data visualization in its Data Visualization Gallery at www.census.gov/dataviz/visualizations/019/. Run the animation by clicking on the Play button at the bottom. Then, work the slider at the bottom of the visualization, starting with the lowest median household income (at the left side of the visualization) then slowly moving the slider to the right in order, to see when your county goes gray at the point of its median household income. When do the last of the counties in your state still show green, i.e., still have islands of high income within them? What do you know about these islands of high income, and where they are found?

3. **Learn from visualizing data:** The U.S. Census Bureau's data visualization on languages spoken at home, "Top Languages Other Than English Spoken in 1980 and Changes in Relative Rank, 1990–2010," shows several patterns in languages spoken in the American home. What are some of these patterns?

4. What are the benefits of the kinds of diversity that cities possess today? What is the relationship between innovation and creativity and diversity?

5. How diverse an environment do you and your friends live within? Do you live around others like you, or are some neighbors different? Are your friends alike or different from you?

SELECTED WEB RESOURCES

- U.S. Census Bureau www.census.gov/
- U.S. Census Bureau Quick Facts www.census.gov/quickfacts/
- American Fact Finder https://factfinder.census.gov/
- Interactive Maps www.census.gov/geography/interactive-maps.html

- American Community Survey www.census.gov/programs-surveys/acs/
- 2010 Census www.census.gov/2010census/
- Data Visualization Gallery www.census.gov/dataviz/

REFERENCES

Berube, Alan, and Nadeau, Carey Anne. 2011. "Metropolitan Areas and the Next Economy: A 50 State Analysis." *Brookings Institution.* Accessed on February 25, 2014 from www.brookings.edu/research/papers/2011/02/24-states-berube-nadeau

Florida, Richard. 2015a. "America's Leading Immigrant Cities." *CityLab.* Accessed on October 31, 2016 from www.citylab.com/politics/2015/09/americas-leading-immigrant-cities/406438/?utm_source=nl__link4_092215

Florida, Richard. 2015b. "Where Kids Live Now in the U.S." *CityLab.* Accessed on November 29, 2016 from www.citylab.com/housing/2015/04/where-kids-live-now-in-the-us/390243/

Kotkin, Joel. 2014. "Baby Boomtowns: The U.S. Cities Attracting the Most Families." *Forbes,* November 29, 2016.

Kotkin, Joel. 2016. "America's Senior Moment: The Most Rapidly Aging Cities." *Forbes,* February 16, 2016.

National League of Cities. 2015. *2015 State of the Cities Report.* Washington, D.C.: National League of Cities.

Nemeth, Karen N. 2016. "Extreme Diversity in Cities: Challenges and Solutions for Programs

Serving Young Children and Their Families." *Young Children* 71 (5). Accessed from http:// www.naeyc.org/yc/extreme-diversity-cities.

Ortman, Jennifer M., Velkoff, Victoria A., and Hogan, Howard. 2014. *An Aging Nation: The Older Population in the United States.* Washington, DC: U.S. Census Bureau.

Rastogi, Sonya, Johnson, Tallese D., Hoeffel, Elizabeth M., and Drewery, Jr., Malcolm P. 2011. "Table 6. Ten Places With the Largest Number of Blacks or African Americans: 2010." *The Black Population: 2010 Census Briefs*, Issued September 2011. Accessed on March 16, 2014 from www.census.gov/prod/ cen2010/briefs/c2010br-06.pdf

U.S. Census. 2016. *American FactFinder.* Accessed on November 28, 2016 from http://factfinder. census.gov/faces/nav/jsf/pages/index.xhtml

U.S. Census Bureau. 1994. "Chapter 12: The Urban and Rural Classifications." *Geographic Areas Reference Manual.* Accessed on March 24, 2014 from www.census.gov/ geo/reference/garm.html

U.S. Census Bureau. 2011. *The Older Population: 2010 Census Briefs.* Accessed on January 6, 2015 from www.census.gov/prod/ cen2010/briefs/c2010br-09.pdf

U.S. Census Bureau. 2013. *Foreign Born: Table 1.1- Population by Sex, Age, Nativity, and U.S. Citizenship Status: 2013.* Accessed on

January 28, 2017 from www.census.gov/ data/tables/2013/demo/foreign-born/cps-2013.html

U.S. Census Bureau. 2014a. *Geographic Terms and Concepts.* Accessed on March 24, 2014 from www.census.gov/geo/reference/terms. html

U.S. Census Bureau. 2014b. *People QuickFacts.* Accessed on March 26, 2014 from http:// quickfacts.census.gov/qfd/states/00000.html

U.S. Census Bureau. 2015. "Appendix B. Estimates of Poverty: Weighted Average Poverty Thresholds in 2015 by Size of Family." In *Income and Poverty in the United States: 2015 Current Population Reports.* Edited by Bernadette Proctor, Jessica L. Semega, and Melissa A. Kollar. Washington, DC: U.S. Census Bureau.

World Health Organization. 2014. *WHO Global Health Data Observatory. WHO Region of the Americas: United States of American Statistics Summary (2002-present).* Accessed on March 17, 2014 from http://apps.who.int/ gho/data/?theme=country&vid=20800.

Yardley, William. 2016. "In North Dakota, an Oil Boomtown Doesn't Want to Go Bust." *Los Angeles Times.* Accessed on November 28, 2016 from www.latimes.com/nation/la-na-sej-north-dakota-oil-town-20160111-story. html

City Structure, Leadership, and Elections

City government structures have an influence on what happens in cities, as does the elected and non-elected leadership of those cities. Moreover, politics and political power always matter—prominent early political scientist Harold Lasswell (1962) defined politics as "who gets what, when and how." In cities, as in other arenas, political power and economic, social, and other resources determine these processes of "who gets what, when and how." This chapter will introduce readers to city structure and authority, city leadership and elections, the policy process within cities, and management tools that city managers can use to deliver effective services. This is an important chapter for understanding the information behind NASPAA standards, as this chapter covers the process of policy-making in cities (NASPAA standard "To participate in and contribute to the policy process"), tools that managers and leaders need to effectively manage cities (standard "To lead and manage in public governance"), and the ethics of local government management (standard "Demonstrate an understanding of the ethics of local government management"). In addition, some of the tools discussed in this chapter will allow students to think more critically about relationships with stakeholders in cities (standard "To analyze, synthesize, think critically, solve problems and make decisions").

In the late 1800s, the United States was undergoing three important sets of changes: immigration, industrialization, and urbanization. As cities grew, those where many immigrants landed were governed by political machines. Political machines were organized geographically by blocks and wards with each geographic entity represented by someone within the local machine. These ward or block leaders helped to organize the residents in that area for the machine in elections. In turn, the machine helped people, including immigrants, get housing and jobs. Voters voted for those who were going to represent their district on the city council, as well as the mayor. Because candidates were associated with political parties, voting ballots included the party membership next to each; this identification made it easier to immigrants who could not read to elect the machine's entire group, or slate, of candidates.

During the Progressive Era (the late 1880s–1920s) in many cities, however, the middle and upper classes fought back against immigrants to take back control of cities. Eventually, in some cities but particularly in the suburbs, reformers made elections non-partisan to remove political machines and easy party labels from ballots—and to keep urban parties from directly benefitting from elections. They made elections for city councils city-wide rather than districtwide, arguing that the interests of the entire city, rather than the parochial, narrow interests of a single district, would be served. In reality, this allowed white majorities to win most, if not all, city elections and left minorities with little representation on city councils.

The middle class created the civil service and civil service examination requirements; this meant that only those with education would be able to pass the examinations and get city jobs. In turn, this led to less educated immigrants being much less likely to be able to get those city jobs; this removed the political machines' ability to give away city jobs as an incentive when asking for voters' support. The political reformers developed city budgets to get control over city spending, arguing that scientific management should be used to manage cities more efficiently—but, in reality, further removing the political machines' ability to use city government as a vending machine for jobs. These developments led to the creation of city managers being selected to manage cities to achieve efficient and effective administration. City managers were well-educated individuals—typically engineers, in the beginning—who would specialize in cities and how they worked. Job requirements automatically ruled out immigrants due to the education and experience needed. Together, these changes led to the beginnings of the field of public administration, forged from political science, and taught that politics should, and could, be removed from the administration of public agencies.

CITY GOVERNMENT STRUCTURES TODAY

Today, city government structures are still connected to that early history. City governments consist of the council-manager structure, formed out of the Progressive Era, the strong mayor structure, commission forms, or hybrids of these. Typically paired with government structure are types of elections (non-partisan, partisan) and electoral areas (district, at-large, or entire city): council-manager usually with non-partisan and at-large elections, and strong mayor with partisan and district elections. City structures follow the federal form in that there is some sort of executive who manages the city and can set priorities, some form of legislative branch that considers legislation or policies, and a court system in the state if not at the municipal level.

Council-manager cities are led by an elected city council. The council typically contains five to seven members with a revolving mayor whose tasks are ceremonial; it collectively serves as the legislative policy body for the city and hires, fires, and supervises the professional city manager. The city manager, then, manages all the agencies in the city. Figure 2.1 illustrates this type of city government structure in Winston-Salem, North Carolina. The citizens of the city are at the top of the organizational chart; citizens elect the city council. Directly below the city council is the city manager, who is appointed by the city council. In fact, the city council appoints and can fire the city manager, who serves "at the pleasure" of the city council. The city manager has some central functions (Human Resources, for instance) directly reporting to him (in this instance) but also has three assistant city managers. Each of these assistant city managers, in turn, has from five to seven agencies reporting to them. This structure is not an arrangement found everywhere, but in this case, it is obviously an attempt to effectively manage a large number of departments within this city government.

Under the strong mayor or mayor-council structure, it is the mayor rather than the city council or city manager who has the power and authority to manage city departments

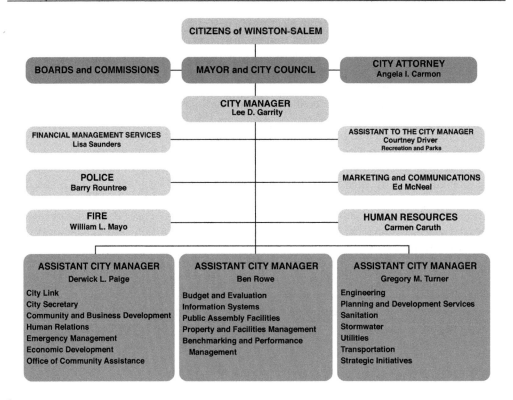

FIGURE 2.1

Organizational Chart of City of Winston-Salem, North Carolina City Manager Form of Urban Government

Source: City of Winston-Salem, North Carolina. 2016. City of Winston-Salem Organizational Chart. Accessed July 26, 2016. http://www.cityofws.org/Portals/0/pdf/city-manager/Winston-SalemOrganizationalChart_july-2015_www.pdf.

and set the agenda for the city. The city council acts as the policy body, but the mayor submits the budget to it and acts as the chief executive and administrator. Cities with this form are typically bigger, older cities, usually in the Northeast and Midwest.

Figure 2.2 illustrates the strong mayor form of government in Boise, Idaho. Once again, the citizens are shown at the top, electing both the mayor and the city council. The city council is shown as equal in power and authority to the mayor, but all the city agencies are under the control of the city's mayor. The mayor initiates policy, helps set policy with the city council, and then manages its implementation in various programs in city departments.

Finally, there are just a few cities today that continue to use the commission form of city government structure. Portland, Oregon is one of these—the only city among the 30 largest cities to do so. Under this structure, the mayor and four to five commissioners are all elected. The mayor controls and manages some agencies, but each of the commissioners does, also. As Figure 2.3 indicates, the Position 1 commissioner in Portland manages the Public Utility agencies, the Position 2 commissioner manages Public Works, the Position 3 commissioner manages Public Affairs (including Fire and Rescue), and the Position 4 commissioner manages Public Safety (which includes emergency management but not fire).

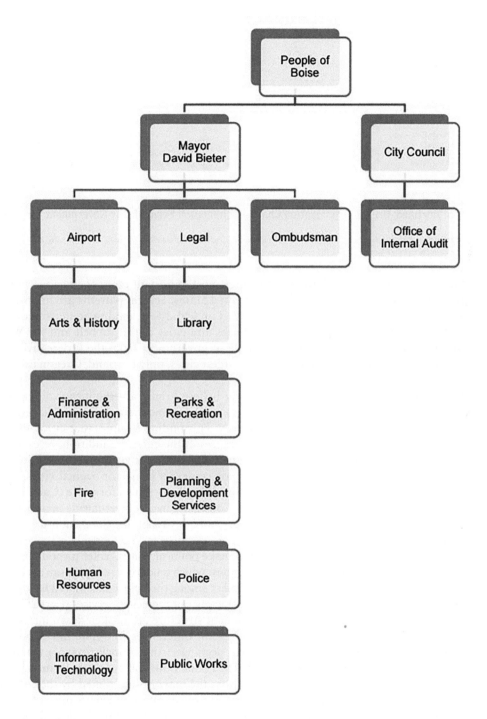

FIGURE 2.2
City of Boise, Idaho Strong Mayor-Council Form of City Government

Source: City of Boise. 2015. *Comprehensive Annual Financial Report.* City Organization Chart, p. 6. Accessed July 26, 2016. http://dfa.cityofboise.org/media/272265/boise-city-2015-cafr_final.pdf.

City of Portland Government Structure

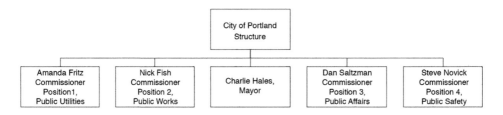

FIGURE 2.3

City of Portland, Oregon Organization Chart—Commission Form of City Government Structure

Source: Developed from City of Portland. 2016. City of Portland Structure as of January 2016. Accessed July 26, 2016. https://www.portlandoregon.gov/oni/article/41381.

Table 2.1 shows the distribution of the three most important types of city government structure among the 30 largest cities in the United States. Several patterns are important; the oldest cities, typically those in the Northwest and Midwest, tend to be mayor-council forms of government. The newer cities—suburbs and cities in the Sunbelt and the West, have mostly adopted the so-called reform type of government from the Progressive Era, the council-manager form. Among the top 30 largest cities, only Portland, Oregon uses the commission form, which has mostly died out.

Researchers in city management have long believed there are significant differences between the cities that use each different type of government structure and have done many studies to investigate proposed differences. This finding assumes that cities' preference for one or the other shows inherent differences in the cities. In addition, researchers believe city management professionals leading council-manager governments will impact their cities in different ways than the mayor and councils in mayor-council cities, who have incentives that are much more political, since they have to run for office (Carr 2015).

In some cases, these assumptions are true. Council-manager governments appear to be less likely to adopt policies that are purely symbolic or highly visible development projects that would bring only very local benefits. Mayor-council governments are more likely to seek that kind of project, supposedly seeking these out to make political points. Voter turnout appears to be lower in council-manager government elections, which tend to be non-partisan in nature. Council-manager governments also have less conflict among their city councils and have more incentives to adopt innovative practices like contracting out municipal services (Carr 2015).

In practice, the two main forms of government structure are broken down into seven variations (Nelson and Svara 2010), depending on differences in appointment powers or elections, but three of the seven structures dominate: the council (mayor) manager, mayor-council-manager, and mayor-council. The council (mayor) manager form exists in 21.0 percent of all cities in 2010. In this variation, the mayor is appointed by the council, whereas, in the most common form (35.4 percent of all cities and 61.5 percent of the council-manager cities), the mayor-council-manager, the mayor is directly elected (Nelson and Svara 2010). Under each of these, the council appoints the chief administration officer.

The third most common form of city government structure, the mayor-council, was found in 21.3 percent of all cities. Under this form, there is no chief administrative officer, because the elected mayor does that job.

> **▶ TABLE 2.1**
>
> **Form of Government Structure for 30 Largest American Cities, 2016 (Population Rank in Parentheses)**

Mayor-Council	Council-Manager	Commission
• New York, NY (1)	• Phoenix, AZ (6)	• Portland, OR (29)
• Los Angeles, CA (2)	• San Antonio, TX (7)	
• Chicago, IL (3)	• Dallas, TX (9)	
• Houston, TX (4)	• San Jose, CA (10)	
• Philadelphia, PA (5)	• Austin, TX (14)	
• San Diego, CA (8)	• Fort Worth, TX (16)	
• Indianapolis, IN (11)	• Charlotte, NC (18)	
• Jacksonville, FL (12)	• El Paso, TX (20)	
• San Francisco, CA (13)	• Las Vegas, NV (30)	
• Columbus, OH (15)		
• Louisville-Jefferson County, KY (17)		
• Detroit, MI (19)		
• Memphis, TN (21)		
• Nashville-Davidson, TN (22)		
• Baltimore, MD (23)		
• Boston, MA (24)		
• Seattle, WA (25)		
• Washington, D.C. (26)		
• Denver, CO (27)		
• Milwaukee, WI (28)		

Source: Adapted from National League of Cities. 2016. The Form of Government in the Thirty Most Populous Cities. Accessed on July 26, 2016 from www.nlc.org/build-skills-and-networks/resources/cities-101/city-structures/forms-of-municipal-government.

Through election referenda, cities can change the form of their government and types of elections, under the banner of seeking reform. A 2010 analysis concluded that nine cities of more than 100,000 population changed from council-manager to mayor-council forms of government, many of them reasoning that the council-manager form worked best for smaller cities. However, once those cities grew larger, the structure was less effective. Another nine cities tried but turned down a change in form. Further, three cities went from the mayor-council to the council-manager form. Among the factors that led to efforts to change structure were growth politics in the community or an unsettled political environment, shortcomings of city managers, pressure by the media and the business community, and changes in other types of structural features (Svara and Watson 2010).

CITY MANAGERS

City managers are critical leaders in council-manager cities. While the city council sets policy, city managers are responsible for implementing it. City managers have a great deal of responsibility (see Box 2.1) and are expected to show strong leadership, work well in teams

▶ BOX 2.1 DUTIES OF A CITY MANAGER

An administrator in a Council-Manager Community is expected to:

1. Meet with the elected council to determine the policies set by the council and to inform council members and citizens about the operations of the local government. The manager may discuss problems and recommendations, propose new plans, or discuss issues that affect the community and its citizens.
2. Hire department heads, administrative personnel, and other employees, and supervise top appointees.
3. Prepare the annual budget, submit it to elected officials for approval, and implement it once approved.
4. Solicit bids from government contractors and select or recommend the appropriate individual(s) or organization(s) to perform the work.
5. Ensure that laws and policies approved by elected officials are enforced equally throughout the city.
6. Investigate citizen complaints and problems in the administrative

organization and make recommendations for changes to elected officials.
7. Manage the daily operations of the city or county by completing administrative reports, corresponding by mail and telephone, and performing many other duties needed to meet community needs.
8. Work with elected officials and citizens to plan for the future of the community. The manager will set goals and establish strategies for reaching the community's goals.
9. Meet regularly with legislators and citizens to discuss current problems and future initiatives.
10. Identify, understand, and address specific problems that face the community, such as crime, homelessness, or deteriorating infrastructure.
11. Deal with federal and state mandates, population and demographic shifts, and other changes that affect public service demands, including fluctuations in the economy.

Source: International City/County Management Association. 2016. What Does a Local Manager Do? Accessed on December 5, 2016 from http://icma.org/ Wiki/Careers_in_Local_Government_Management.

▶ BOX 2.2 ATTRIBUTES OF A CITY MANAGER

- Communication
- Budgeting
- Accounting
- Appreciation for Diversity
- Creativity
- Public Speaking/Presentation Skills
- Passion
- Integrity
- Story Telling
- Technology
- Listening Skills

- Strategic Planning
- Principled/Moral Compass
- Media Relations
- Self-Motivation
- Vision
- Creativity and Innovation

Source: International City/County Management Association. 2016. Attributes of a City Manager? Accessed on December 5, 2016 from http://icma.org/Wiki/ Careers_in_Local_Government_Management.

(like the city council), set an example of ethical behavior, be innovative, and be problem-solvers. As the Career Pathways throughout this text indicate, there are different paths to being a leader in a city. Most students will begin as an intern or as an entry-level analyst. They might then move into a department or be an assistant to the city manager, then move up to a deputy city manager position. City managers might start working in small cities, then move to other small cities. Many can then move up as manager in larger cities.

Most city managers (59 percent in 2012) have master's degrees like the Master of Public Administration (M.P.A.) degree from an M.P.A. program accredited by NASPAA, the accrediting association for public administration or public affairs degrees. In 2012, most (39.5 percent) were between 51 and 60 years of age, with another 23.8 percent more than 60. Across the nation, city managers' average salary was $110,972. City managers' average tenure was estimated to be 7.3 years; one reason for the short tenure is the difficulty of working for up to seven people at a time on the city council with the power to hire and fire (International City/County Management Association 2016).

City managers as a profession are still overwhelmingly white and male, although this is changing gradually. In 2012, 19.8 percent of city managers were women, but only 4.5 percent were not white. The pipeline of talent from entry level to the top position is filled with women, but it is taking time for them to move up. The current increase in retirement bodes well for both women and people of color in being able to move into leadership positions (Voorhees and Lange-Skaggs 2015; International City/County Management Association 2016).

POWERS OF CITIES

According to legal tradition, most cities have only the powers granted to them by their individual states. This situation is due to Dillon's Rule, suggested by John Forrest Dillon, an Iowa Supreme Court and United States Circuit Court justice in the mid-1800s. In a case brought by the City of Clinton, Iowa over whether it could block a railroad approved by the state, Dillon stated cities could have only:

1. Powers specifically granted to the city;
2. Powers implied in those powers specifically granted to the city; and
3. Those powers that are indispensable to the existence of the city.

The practical meaning of Dillon's Rule is that cities are "creatures of their states" and that cities need to have their states grant them power to accomplish specific functions. Under Dillon's Rule cities have limited, narrow authority.

However, in states with "home rule" statutes, cities can have broader, more expansive authority ("home rule authority") because the state legislature has passed packages of powers for their cities. Cities in states without home rule statutes have to go to the legislature to get authority to complete many functions or tasks. Having to go to their state legislatures can be particularly difficult in states with very bifurcated population—a few cities with little representation in the legislature and most of the state represented by rural legislators. In these states, cities and states often have very conflictual relationships, which can make having to request extra authority very difficult. Grants of home rule powers, or charters, were another reform that emerged from the Progressive Era of the late 1880s/ early 1920s. Home rule statutes gave cities powers to accomplish whatever they needed to do to function, without state intervention (Spitzer 2015).

▶ **TABLE 2.2**

Application of Dillon's Rule across States

Dillon's Rule States Applied to All Cities (30)			Dillon's Rule Applied Only to Some Cities— Others Have Home Rule	Dillon's Rule Applied to Selective Powers
Arizona	Nebraska	West Virginia	Alabama	Florida
Arkansas	Nevada	Washington	Indiana	
Connecticut	New Hampshire	Wisconsin	California	
Delaware	New York	Wyoming	Louisiana	
Georgia	North Carolina		Colorado	
Hawaii	North Dakota		Tennessee	
Idaho	Oklahoma		Illinois	
Kentucky	Pennsylvania		Florida	
Maine	Rhode Island			
Maryland	South Dakota			
Michigan	Texas			
Minnesota	Vermont			
Missouri	Virginia			

Source: Adapted from National League of Cities. Local Government Authority. Accessed on August 9, 2016 from www.nlc.org/build-skills-and-networks/resources/cities-101/city-powers/local-government-authority.

The National League of Cities separates the discretionary powers of cities into four categories: structural, functional, fiscal, and personnel. Structural powers are those that enable a city to select and change their form of government. Functional powers are those allowing cities to govern themselves and take on specific functions. Fiscal authority allows cities to control their finances—taxing, spending, and borrowing. Personnel authority gives cities the power to bargain with employees and set their salaries and wages (National League of Cities 2016).

According to the National League of Cities (2016), 39 states apply Dillon's Rule in some way: 30 for all their cities and eight for only specific cities (Table 2.2). Florida has home rule but, still, keeps taxing authority for the state government itself.

PUBLIC POLICY IN CITIES

Public policy is defined as those things that government does. There are several different ways, or models, of explaining how public policies are created by cities.

The first is an institutional model, which helps us understand how urban policy is made by understanding the various institutions and their roles in local government. The different urban government structures are discussed previously. As in any other American government, the legislative body makes the policy decisions, which are then implemented by the executive. In cities, the legislative body is the city council. The executive is either the mayor or the entire city council acting as an executive, then delegating implementation authority to the city manager.

Another set of models are the group, or pluralism, model and the elite model. These two models explain public policy as the result of two different patterns of political power. The pluralism approach says that groups and networks rule and share power; in cities, this would mean that groups like developers, neighborhood groups, or environmentalists bargain between themselves until they reach a compromise. These groups thus often decide the results of conflicts over city policy. No side gets everything it wants, but they all get some of what they want.

The elite theory approach says that societal elites (the people with the most money, bankers, business people, owners of important institutions in the city) have the most power in cities. Elites might not be the ones holding elective office, but they are still determining the outcomes of public policy, according to this theory. Public policy outcomes, under elite theory, are those desired by the elite. For example, new developments get approval because they benefit the elite; or, sports teams are brought to the city because elites think it would benefit them and their interests in the city.

A theory of policy change can also help explain the power and public policy outcomes in cities. Theories of change suggest that most change happens very slowly, and in small bits (increments); this part of the theory is called incrementalism. This theory explains how little change occurs during most periods, which can explain how it can be very difficult for change to happen. However, the theory also explains how some events can produce greater change—like changes in leadership, new societal problems emerging, or sudden events or tragedies. When these events occur, often at the same time, greater change can happen, at a faster pace. For example, city budgets change very little, at a very slow pace, over time. However, newly emerging problems or sudden crises, like homelessness in the 1980s, for instance, can create new programs and increase parts of the budget.

Finally, one more approach can be used to explain public policy outcomes in urban settings—game theory. Game theory tries to understand interactions between actors, based on rational self-interest, in situations of conflict and cooperation. For instance, one famous "game" is that of the prisoner's dilemma. In this situation, two prisoners have been arrested after allegedly committing a crime together. Only one prisoner will get to plea bargain and not go to jail—but only if they are the one who asks for a plea first, and tells the story of the crime. The other prisoner will go to jail. Each prisoner has an equal opportunity to have that plea deal. Alternatively, if both prisoners stay quiet and say nothing, neither goes to jail. The dilemma lies in having to make the decision under conditions of uncertainty for both.

In cities, a similar situation could occur when city governments go after new business, promising them tax breaks and other benefits for locating in their city. Both the city government and businesses seeking to relocate in a city operate in a competitive environment under uncertain conditions—not knowing whether the other is bargaining in good faith. Say that two different businesses are considering relocating to a city. The city wants to keep negotiations going with both of the companies, and would like to have both in its community, but has limited resources to offer. So, the city has two possible packages of tax breaks and other incentives—Package B, which is good but not great, and Package A, which is much better. Only one business gets A. The other business is left without A and must settle for Package B. Both businesses want to relocate to the city. Business C comes in and tries to strike a hard bargain, demanding tax concessions and many more incentives than the city is able to offer, even more than is being offered in Package A. Business D would settle for Package B because its founder is from the area; C would rather go somewhere else. How does the city negotiate this deal, with imperfect information and in a competitive environment?

URBAN ELECTIONS

Local elections are substantially different from state or national elections. Local voters tend to have more personal contact with candidates and, often, more personal connection with issues being discussed. In fact, so-called home voters, or homeowners, often have great motivation to vote in local elections when issues affect their home values or taxes. Election campaigning is also different, for most voters, in that there is more reliance upon door-to-door campaigning, passing out flyers and using other face-to-face techniques rather than the use of media. Local elections involve less money since, by definition, they involve smaller geographic jurisdictions. Oliver (2012) contends that many of the models and research on local elections and power are not entirely accurate because they are based upon a few larger cities and most Americans live in smaller communities without powerful "growth machines."

Voter choice in national elections is determined by candidate charisma, how voters view the economy, some issue stances, and connections to a political party. There is very little known about what drives voter choice at the local level, however. As will be seen, most local elections are non-partisan, so party choice is not relevant, and information about incumbent performance in office is often vague and difficult to obtain. In fact, most local elections are more managerial than ideological since the services provided by cities are typically straight-forward (Oliver 2012).

Local elections involve many fewer voters, with much lower turnout than in state or national elections. The actual numbers vary from community to community—and also differ by whether the elections occur during the same year as presidential elections or important state elections (on-year elections) or are off-year elections, and whether they are held in the same month and day as these other elections. There is also evidence that electoral turnout in council-manager cities is lower than that in other systems (Caren 2007). Oliver (2012) points out that up to 25 percent of a community cannot vote because they are too young or don't meet other requirements, so a typical local turnout rate of between 20 and 25 percent means that often only a few thousand voters are making decisions for a whole city. In 340 elections from 144 cities during the period from 1996 to 2011, the average turnout for mayoral elections was 25.8 percent. Over the ten-year period from 2001 to 2011, the average voter turnout swung from 26.6 percent down to 20.9 percent (Maciag 2014).

There are several defining characteristics of each city's electoral structure: whether candidates run with a party affiliation or not (partisan or non-partisan) and whether candidates run from a district or compete citywide (district versus at-large). Also, each election can be a primary where candidates from parties run against each other to determine who will be the party nominee or whether or not it is the general, or final, election.

At-large elections are those where all voters within a city run for each office. In the Progressive Era, at-large elections were labeled as a reform because candidates were thinking of what would benefit the entire city, not just their section of the city. In reality, this was a way to disenfranchise machine voters, including minorities. Because people largely lived together with others who were like themselves, geographically contiguous neighborhoods that formed electoral districts could have a majority of Italian voters or Polish voters and so a person of that group could be elected.

However, once districts were eliminated by Progressive reformers, the power of that Italian or Polish vote was diluted by the White Anglo vote, which might have been a majority citywide. So under at-large elections, minorities were largely absent from city councils. Today, the same pattern exists as researchers continue to find that, when minority group residences are sufficiently concentrated, district elections do result in higher numbers of underrepresented groups like African-Americans and Hispanic-Americans being elected to office. There is, however, a gender effect in that women are more likely to be elected under at-large elections (Trounstine and Valdini 2008).

Cities are still working to reduce racial and ethnic disparities in the city councils; for example, after a lawsuit by Latinos and an eventual court settlement, the City of Anaheim, California (home of Disneyland) is just, in November 2016, moving to single member district elections from at-large electoral districts (Southern California Public Radio 2016).

Another feature of city elections is whether candidates run as identified members of a political party—i.e., partisan elections—or whether the elections are non-partisan. Non-partisan elections are yet another change from the Progressive Era to what reformers considered corrupt elections. At that time, political machines continued to be elected through partisan elections because many of their voters were illiterate immigrants; it was easy for political machines to use party label as a way to determine which were their candidates. Reformers were not able to overturn partisan elections in many cities, but as urbanization grew, non-partisan elections became partnered with council-manager forms of government as a package of reforms adopted in new suburbs and newer cities in the expanding South and West. Today, few cities still use partisan elections for city offices (Table 2.3); the National

TABLE 2.3

Type of Electoral System (Partisan versus Non-Partisan) in 25 Largest American Cities, 2016 (Population Rank in Parentheses)

Partisan	Non-Partisan
• New York, NY (1)	• Los Angeles, CA (2)
• Houston, TX (4)	• Chicago, IL (3)
• Philadelphia, PA (6)	• Phoenix, AZ (5)
• Indianapolis, IN (14)	• San Antonio, TX (7)
• Charlotte, NC (18)	• Dallas, TX (8)
• Baltimore, MD (20)	• San Diego, CA (9)
	• San Jose, CA (10)
	• Detroit, MI (11)
	• San Francisco, CA (12)
	• Jacksonville, FL (13)
	• Austin, TX (15)
	• Columbus, OH (16)
	• Fort Worth, TX (17)
	• Memphis, TN (19)
	• Boston, MA (21)
	• El Paso, TX (22)
	• Milwaukee, WI (23)
	• Denver, CO (24)
	• Seattle, WA (25)

Source: Adapted from National League of Cities. 2016. Election Type of the 30 Most Populous Cities. Accessed on September 6, 2016 from www.nlc.org/build-skills-and-networks/resources/cities-101/city-officials/partisan-vs-nonpartisan-elections.

League of Cities reports only 6 cities in the top 25 most populous cities use party labels for candidates. No matter whether the elections are non-partisan or partisan, Ballotpedia estimates that in 2016, 27 percent of the mayors in American cities were Republican and 67 percent were Democrat (Ballotpedia 2016c).

Referenda and initiative elections on policy issues are yet one more reform measure that emerged from the Progressive Era and are still used today in many states and cities. A ballot initiative is one where citizens or organizations gather signatures to place a proposed piece of legislation on the ballot to be voted upon by citizens; this is generally used to bypass the state legislature. A referendum is an election, also brought by citizens via collecting signatures, on a particular political or policy issue. These means of direct democracy are available in 27 states and the District of Columbia (Ballotpedia 2016b). Many of these states are in the West, with California seeming to be the leader in ballot initiatives, having more than 500 issues on the ballot in various locations throughout the state in 2016 (Ballotpedia 2016a).

The topics of initiative elections include many issues from state or national policy agendas, such as marijuana legalization, stopping the use of fracking, mandating a minimum "living wage," outlawing genetically modified organisms (GMOs) in food, local development issues, and voting for or against LGBTQ rights. Other common measures affect a city's fiscal status, such as increasing taxing, issuing bonds to pay for capital improvements, and reforming pension systems (Ballotpedia 2016a).

Specific ballot measures include initiatives to ban commercial marijuana in three cities in Alaska, a 2014 City of Pocatello, Idaho Sexual Orientation and Gender Express Discrimination Referendum (Proposition 1), and a 2016 City of Ferguson, Missouri Mandatory Body Cameras for Police Officers Initiative. Other recent initiatives were the 2014 initiative to ban fracking in Denton, Texas and the many initiatives during 2014 in Wisconsin cities to mandate a minimum wage of $10.10 per hour (advisory only).

BOX 2.3 KEY QUESTIONS TO BE ASKED BY NEW LEADERS TO LEARN ABOUT THEIR CITY GOVERNMENT

To Department Heads

- What are the key issues in each of your departments? What needs immediate attention?
- What are the strengths, weaknesses, opportunities, and threats to providing services from each of your departments?
- What are each department's priorities?
- What is the employee turnover rate in each department?

Key Issues

- What do employees think of their salaries and benefits packages?

- How does the pay and benefits package work?
- How many grievances have been filed in the last year?
- What kind of employee recognition programs are held?
- Are exit interviews conducted when employees leave the city?
- Can the city maintain its equipment and grounds with current funding levels?
- What issues emerged from the city's last audit that still need to be addressed?
- What is the ratio of General Obligation Debt to assessed valuation (should be no more than 8–10 percent)?

▶ BOX 2.3 (CONTINUED)

- What is the city's bond rating and when was it last rated?
- What is the city's tax collection rate?
- Is there any upcoming federal or state legislation that could impact the city?
- What are the population and demographic projections for the city for the next 10 to 20 years?
- How strong are the economic development and environmental feelings in the city? What are the feelings about growth?
- Who is most active in planning and zoning controversies? What have been the last five zoning battles? Who won?
- What is the crime rate for the city, broken down by types of crimes? What are the clearance rates for crimes?
- What are the high crime rate areas in the city?
- What are the current and five-year programs to reduce crime?

Source: International City/County Management Association. 2016. What Does a Local Manager Do? Accessed on December 5, 2016 from http://icma.org/Wiki/Careers_in_Local_Government_Management.

TOOLS FOR MANAGING CITIES

Public goods are those goods that are left to government to provide because private sector firms will always under-provide them. They include goods and services like public health and public education, which provide part of the structure and fabric of our society. A central role of any government, including city governments, is to provide public goods to residents. To accomplish this, the recognition of core public service values and a complete understanding of the ethics of the profession are critical tools. Other tools are a myriad of public management strategies; some of these are discussed in this section.

▶ BOX 2.4 CAREER PATHWAY TO CITY MANAGEMENT

Current Position

Semi-retired

Education

B.A. Economics and Political Science
Master's in Education
M.P.A.

Ongoing professional education and lifetime designation as a certified city manager by the International City/County Management Association (ICMA)

Career Pathway

Robert's career began as a Volunteers in Service to America (VISTA) volunteer and federal summer intern. He then took a job as assistant to the director of operations of the Boston Housing Authority and, from there, moved into consulting as a senior consultant of Deloitte Haskins & Sells. He specifically learned what he needed to know by serving as an assistant to the city manager and, then, as an assistant city manager to a small city.

Robert was city manager for four different cities. He began in a small city in 1991 then over the next 29 years served as city manager for three cities, ending his career as city manager for a mid-sized city.

How Did Robert Know He Wanted to Be a City Manager?

"I knew I wanted to become a public manager of some sort and in my late twenties

▶ BOX 2.4 (CONTINUED)

discovered city management by listening to a retired veteran city manager at an American Society for Public Administration (ASPA) dinner. I then interviewed six city managers and was hooked."

A Typical Day

"There is no typical day. The work is highly diverse, fast-paced and ever changing. Such are the needs of a modern city. Any day can include meetings with department heads and staff on all manner of operations, budgeting and finance, human resources and labor relations, council members, members of the public, business community and media, organizational development and intergovernmental relations and the crisis of the moment."

Professional Associations and Networking

Robert has been quite active in the International City/County Management Association (ICMA), serving as ICMA West Coast vice president and executive board member. He has also been president and served on the board of directors of the League of California Cities, City Managers Department; served on the board of directors of the Institute for Local Government; been a senior fellow of the Davenport Institute for Civic Leadership and Public Engagement; served on the editorial board of State and Local Review; and served as senior manager of training for the Center for Public Safety Management.

He networks by attending conferences of these organizations, volunteering for professional association work, and staying in contact with his peers.

What Has Been Most Helpful in Robert's Career

For Robert, having mentors who have taken personal interest in his professional growth as well as colleagues and friends to lean on and learn from has been most helpful.

Challenges and Overcoming Them

Robert says challenges have included: "Constant fiscal pressures, lack of public trust of government, resource constraints, divided or timid councils, rise of reckless speech through social media, tendency of organizations to do what they have always been doing regardless of whether it is effective."

These challenges have been overcome through: "Leadership by council members, community members, senior staff and my own efforts." He also believes that the "application of proven management techniques and willingness to innovate" has been effective, as well as just "plain hard work."

What Robert Finds Rewarding about Being a City Manager

Robert believes "the ability to improve the safety, quality of life and sustainability of thousands of people" is very rewarding. He says, "Community building is exciting and demanding. Municipal services are highly valued by most people. The effective, efficient and equitable provision of such services is essential for civic health and vitality. Making local representative democracy work is the highest honor." Moreover, he believes that, "Working with good people on councils, staffs, and communities for civic progress is a great reward."

Recommendations for Students

"Study public policy and public administration. Seek internships in well-run cities. Join professional associations like ICMA, MMANC (Municipal Management Association of Northern California) or MMASC (Municipal Management Association of Southern California). Do informational interviews with good city managers and assistant managers. Break into cities wherever you can make entry and then volunteer for everything and sponge it all up. Seek training to build skills for future responsibilities."

Core public values for city management include the traditional central values of equity, effectiveness, and efficiency, accompanied by other values like accountability, transparency, responsiveness, and participation. In general, the public service is about providing public goods to residents without bias in an effective, equitable, and efficient manner.

Ethics in the Profession

Living up to these public service values is part of the ethical code of the profession of public administration and city management. Boxes 2.5 and 2.6 provide the codes of ethics for the ICMA and ASPA. In these codes, there is much emphasis on advancing the public interest and upholding democratic principles, the U.S. Constitution, and the law. There are also admonishments to move toward fuller public participation and to ensure social equity for all groups and individuals. Moreover, finally, the codes also advise administrators to be honest and ethical and to serve the people and not themselves. Each of these professional association codes has supporting materials and guidelines that can be studied and addressed.

BOX 2.5 CODE OF ETHICS FOR THE AMERICAN SOCIETY FOR PUBLIC ADMINISTRATION

The American Society for Public Administration (ASPA) advances the science, art, and practice of public administration. The Society affirms its responsibility to develop the spirit of responsible professionalism within its membership and to increase awareness and commitment to ethical principles and standards among all those who work in public service in all sectors. To this end, we, the members of the Society, commit ourselves to uphold the following principles:

1. **Advance the Public Interest.** Promote the interests of the public and put service to the public above service to oneself.
2. **Uphold the Constitution and the Law.** Respect and support government constitutions and laws, while seeking to improve laws and policies to promote the public good.
3. **Promote democratic participation.** Inform the public and encourage active engagement in governance. Be open, transparent and responsive, and respect and assist all persons in their dealings with public organizations.
4. **Strengthen social equity.** Treat all persons with fairness, justice, and equality and respect individual differences, rights, and freedoms. Promote affirmative action

and other initiatives to reduce unfairness, injustice, and inequality in society.
5. **Fully Inform and Advise.** Provide accurate, honest, comprehensive, and timely information and advice to elected and appointed officials and governing board members, and to staff members in your organization.
6. **Demonstrate personal integrity.** Adhere to the highest standards of conduct to inspire public confidence and trust in public service.
7. **Promote Ethical Organizations.** Strive to attain the highest standards of ethics, stewardship, and public service in organizations that serve the public.
8. **Advance Professional Excellence.** Strengthen personal capabilities to act competently and ethically and encourage the professional development of others.

The Implementation Guide is available at www.aspanet.org/ASPADocs/Resources/Ethics_Assessment_Guide.pdf.

Source: American Society for Public Administration. 2016. Code of Ethics. Accessed on January 12, 2017 from www.aspanet.org/ASPA/Code-of-Ethics/ASPA/Code-of-Ethics/Code-of-Ethics.aspx?hkey=5b8f046b-dcbd-416d-87cd-0b8fcfacb5e7.

BOX 2.6 CODE OF ETHICS FOR THE INTERNATIONAL CITY/COUNTY MANAGEMENT ASSOCIATION

The mission of ICMA is to create excellence in local governance by developing and fostering professional local government management worldwide. To further this mission, certain principles, as enforced by the Rules of Procedure, shall govern the conduct of every member of ICMA, who shall:

Tenet 1

Be dedicated to the concepts of effective and democratic local government by responsible elected officials and believe that professional general management is essential to the achievement of this objective.

Tenet 2

Affirm the dignity and worth of the services rendered by government and maintain a constructive, creative, and practical attitude toward local government affairs and a deep sense of social responsibility as a trusted public servant.

Tenet 3

Be dedicated to the highest ideals of honor and integrity in all public and personal relationships in order that the member may merit the respect and confidence of the elected officials, of other officials and employees, and of the public.

Tenet 4

Recognize that the chief function of local government at all times is to serve the best interests of all people.

Tenet 5

Submit policy proposals to elected officials; provide them with facts and advice on matters of policy as a basis for making decisions and setting community goals; and uphold and implement local government policies adopted by elected officials.

Tenet 6

Recognize that elected representatives of the people are entitled to the credit for the establishment of local government policies; responsibility for policy execution rests with the members.

Tenet 7

Refrain from all political activities which undermine public confidence in professional administrators. Refrain from participation in the election of the members of the employing legislative body.

Tenet 8

Make it a duty continually to improve the member's professional ability and to develop the competence of associates in the use of management techniques.

Tenet 9

Keep the community informed on local government affairs; encourage communication between the citizens and all local government officers; emphasize friendly and courteous service to the public; and seek to improve the quality and image of public service.

Tenet 10

Resist any encroachment on professional responsibilities, believing the member should be free to carry out official policies without interference, and handle each problem without discrimination on the basis of principle and justice.

▶ BOX 2.6 (CONTINUED)

Tenet 11

Handle all matters of personnel on the basis of merit so that fairness and impartiality govern a member's decisions, pertaining to appointments, pay adjustments, promotions, and discipline.

Tenet 12

Public office is a public trust. A member shall not leverage his or her position for personal gain or benefit.

Source: ICMA. 2016. ICMA Code of Ethics with Guidelines. Accessed on January 12, 2017 from http://icma.org/en/icma/knowledge_network/documents/kn/Document/100265/ICMA_Code_of_Ethics_with_Guidelines.

Collaborative Management

Today's world is no longer one of hierarchical organizational structures and fixed boundaries between governments and sectors. Historically, much of the public sector was organized along geographic boundaries, but today, many problems exist across boundaries. Boundaries between the public, private, and nonprofit sectors have become "fuzzy," and cities, in particular, are no longer the direct provider of many services to their citizens. Instead, cities contract out to the private sector or nonprofit agencies or provide funding to support communities within their borders. Public administration and city management are finding it much harder to effectively solve and manage the increasingly more complex ("wicked") problems of using traditional, hierarchical, and bureaucratic structures (Kettl 2015).

As a response to these trends, networks across agencies and governments began forming, and collaborative management strategies began emerging. Managers work vertically, up and down their agencies, and horizontally, across agency lines, and even across government lines. McGuire (2006) identifies several types of collaborative structures, organized mostly by how often collaborations take place. Collaboration is defined as "a process in which autonomous actors interact through formal and informal negotiation, jointly creating rules and structures governing their relationships and ways to act or decide on the issues that brought them together; it is a process involving shared norms and mutually beneficial interactions" (Thomson and Perry 2006, p. 23).

One type of collaboration is intermittent coordination, which involves low levels of interaction and does not occur on a regular basis; an example is a response to a natural disaster. Another kind of structure is a temporary task force, which works on a limited problem and ends when the goal is completed. Permanent or regular coordination occurs on a much more regular basis, such as information networks or learning communities. Coalitions or networks are the most permanent collaborative structures. A network has several nodes with multiple connections across members and organizations McGuire (2006).

Networks, in turn, can take several forms. There can be informational networks with members sharing information, as well as developmental networks with information sharing but learning and training also going on. Outreach networks exchange strategies, but the most extensive type are action networks, which do all of the former but also take action together McGuire (2006).

Cities can have numerous collaborative networks operating, with connections between city departments, neighborhood groups, nonprofit advocacy organizations, and private sector companies. Skills, like conducting negotiations and being able to move toward compromise, are of immense value to collaborative organizations and network members.

BOX 2.7 LEADERSHIP STRATEGIES IN CITY SUSTAINABILITY PLANS AROUND THE COUNTRY

Presented here are the leadership-related strategies found in a selection of city sustainability plans around the country.

- "Increase the diversity (age, gender, race, ethnicity, socio-economic, etc.) on City boards and commissions by June 30, 2021 to mirror census data." Grand Rapids, Michigan, p. 7.
- "Engage more diverse members in community leadership roles at the neighborhood, local, and/or regional level." Longmont, Colorado, p. 6.
- "Strengthen communities by encouraging communication, partnerships and trust within and among residents, government,

and the larger community." Dover, New Hampshire, p. 5.
- "Promote the full enjoyment by individuals and groups of their political, social, and economic civil rights." Dover, New Hampshire, p. 5.

Sources: City of Dover, New Hampshire. Not Dated. City of Dover Sustainability Goals with Purpose Statements. Accessed on February 22, 2017 from www.dover.nh.gov/Assets/government/city-operations/2document/planning/outreach/sustainabilitygoals.pdf.

City of Grand Rapids, Michigan. 2016. Sustainability Plan FY 2017–2021. Accessed on February 22, 2017 from http://grcity.us/Documents/2016-07-22%20Sustainability%20Plan.pdf.

City of Longmont, Colorado. 2016. Sustainability Plan. November 2016. Accessed on February 22, 2017 from www.longmontcolorado.gov/home/showdocument?id=16700.

Stakeholder Analysis

Another critical tool in the city manager's toolkit is stakeholder analysis. Stakeholders are those people and groups across the city who have some interest in a particular issue. Not only is it helpful for the manager to be aware of whom those stakeholders might be for any particular issue, but it is helpful to understand their level of interest and how much power they might have to be able to intervene in a given situation or to affect policy outcomes.

One useful tool is the power versus interest grid (see Figure 2.4). In this grid, there are two axes: interest in the issue (low and high) on the vertical, y-axis, and power and influence on the issue (low and high) on the horizontal, x-axis. Analysts list their stakeholders then place them into one of the four cells in the grid:

- Low Interest, Low Power and Influence (Crowd);
- High Interest, Low Power and Influence (Subject);
- Low Interest, High Power and Influence (Context Setters); and
- High Interest, High Power and Influence (Player).

Once this analysis is complete and the analyst has determined which stakeholders belong in which cell, the analyst can then formulate strategies. If there are stakeholders

	High Interest	*Subject*	*Player*
Interest	**Low Interest**	*Crowd*	*Context Setters*
		Low Power and Influence	**High Power and Influence**
		Power and Influence	

FIGURE 2.4
Stakeholder Power versus Interest Grid

Source: Developed from Bryson, John M.; Cunningham, Gary L.; and Lokkesmoe, Karen J. 2002. "What To Do When Stakeholders Matter: The Case of Problem Formulation for the African American Men Project of Hennepin County, Minnesota" *Public Administration Review* Sep / Oct 2002 62 (5): 568–584.

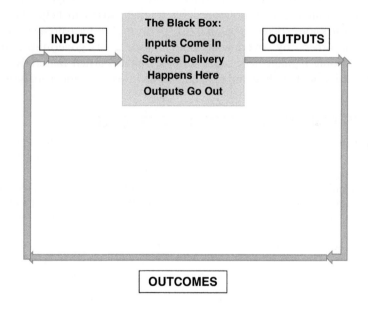

FIGURE 2.5
The Systems Model and Performance Measurement

Source: Developed by author.

who are in the Crowd or Subject cells, they might need help to allow them to develop more power and facilitate their movement into the Player cell (Bryson, Cunningham and Lokkesmoe 2002).

Performance Measurement

Another crucial tool for public managers today is performance measurement, which involves measuring what organizations use up, what they produce, and how they change their environment. (Figure 2.5). Organizations use "inputs" to produce public services;

inputs are resources like agency dollars or staff members. These inputs go into a "black box" that represents the organization itself; in this black box, services are produced. The direct results of these services are "outputs," which are the activities of the organization. An example of inputs and outputs for a public health department, for instance, would be inputs of public health nurse time and outputs of the number of vaccinations completed by the department. Then there are outcomes, which are what the department wants to change. An outcome in the case of a public health department would be a disease-free community. City administrators keep track of performance measures for various departments so they can monitor how well they are doing their job and can be accountable for their use of public resources.

CONCLUSIONS

Chapter 2 has presented an overview of city governmental structure and authority, city leadership, urban elections, ethics, and management tools that can be used by city managers. City managers must operate within the legal structure of their states and then are constrained further by state and federal rules. However, city managers have a variety of management and administrative tools available to them that can help: the ethical standards of their profession, stakeholder analysis, performance measurement, collaborative management, and others. By covering the policy process, city government structure and constraints, and some management tools, students have learned materials in important NASPAA standards about leading and managing, public policy, critical analysis, and ethics.

EXERCISES AND DISCUSSION QUESTIONS

1. **Know Your City:** City Leadership and Structure

   Using the website for the city you have chosen to study, find out the following:
   - The structure of the city (council-manager, strong mayor, etc.).
   - How many members are on the council and how they are elected (i.e., district or at-large)?
   - Whether there is a city manager or a strong mayor, how did they find their way into that office? What are their background and interests?
   - Is the city a home rule city or not?
   - What are three of the top public policy issues faced by the city in recent years?

   - Have there been ethical problems or scandals within the city? If so, what were the repercussions?
2. Who do you think holds power in your community, the people, groups in the city, or a power elite? Whichever one, do you think that is a good or bad situation?
3. How does your community handle important policy issues? Is there public discussion? How could you get involved and give your opinion or make a difference?
4. How responsive to citizens does your city council seem? How could you work to try to build that responsiveness?
5. How important are ethical standards in your community? What happens when there is an ethics scandal? Do the voters care about that? Why or why not?

SELECTED WEB RESOURCES

- International City/County Managers Association (ICMA) http://icma.org/
- American Society for Public Administration (ASPA) www.aspanet.org/
- National Association of Counties (NACO) www.naco.org/
- U.S. Conference of Mayors http://usmayors.org/

REFERENCES

Ballotpedia. 2016a. *Local Ballot Measure Elections in 2016*. Accessed on September 7, 2016 from https://ballotpedia.org/Local_ballot_measure_elections_in_2016

Ballotpedia. 2016b. *States With Initiative or Referendum*. Accessed on September 7, 2016 from https://ballotpedia.org/States_with_initiative_or_referendum

Ballotpedia. 2016c. *United States Municipal Elections*. Accessed on September 7, 2016 from https://ballotpedia.org/United_States_municipal_elections,_2016

Bryson, John M., Cunningham, Gary L., and Lokkesmoe, Karen J. September–October 2002. "What to Do When Stakeholders Matter: The Case of Problem Formulation for the African American Men Project of Hennepin County, Minnesota." *Public Administration Review* 62 (5): pp. 568–584.

Caren, Neal. 2007. "Big City, Big Turnout? Electoral Participation in American Cities." *Journal Of Urban Affairs* 29 (1): pp. 31–46.

Carr, Jered B. 2015. "What Have We Learned about the Performance of Council-Management Government? A Review and Synthesis of the Research." *Public Administration Review* 75 (5): pp. 673–689.

International City/County Management Association. 2016. *Why a NextGen Initiative?* Accessed on December 5, 2016 from http://icma.org/en/icma/priorities/next_generation/why_a_nextgen_initiative

Kettl, Donald F. 2015. *The Transformation of Governance: Public Administration for the 21st Century*. Baltimore: Johns Hopkins Press.

Lasswell, Harold D. 1962. *Politics: Who Gets What, When, How*. New York: Meridian Books.

Maciag, Mike. 2014. "Voter Turnout Plummeting in Local Elections." *Governing*, Accessed on September 12, 2016 from www.governing.com/topics/politics/gov-voter-turnout-municipal-elections.html

McGuire, Michael. 2006. "Collaborative Public Management: Assessing What We Know and How We Know It." *Public Administration Review* 66 (S1): pp. 33–43.

National League of Cities. 2016. *Local Government Authority*. Accessed on August 9, 2016 from www.nlc.org/build-skills-and-networks/resources/cities-101/city-powers/local-government-authority

Nelson, Kimberly L., and Svara, James H. 2010. "Adaptation of Models versus Variations in Form: Classifying Structures of City Government." *Urban Affairs Review* 45 (4): pp. 544–562.

Oliver, J. Eric with Shang E. Ha and Zachary Callen. 2012. *Local Elections and the Politics of Small-Scale Democracy*. Princeton, NJ: Princeton University Press.

Southern California Public Radio. 2016. *5 Changes for Anaheim Now that District Elections Are Coming*. Accessed on September 6, 2016 from www.scpr.org/news/2016/02/10/57366/five-changes-for-anaheim-now-that-district-electio/

Spitzer, Hugh. 2015. "'Home Rule' vs. 'Dillon's Rule' for Washington Cities. Legal Studies Research Paper No. 2015–11." *Seattle University Law Review* 38 (2015): pp. 809–860.

Svara, James H., and Watson, Douglas J. (Eds.). 2010. *More Than Mayor or Manager: Campaigns to Change Form of Government in America's Large Cities*. Washington, DC: Georgetown University Press.

Thomson, Ann Marie, and Perry, James L. 2006. "Collaboration Processes: Inside the Black Box." *Public Administration Review* 66 (S1): pp. 20–32.

Trounstine, Jessica, and Valdini, Melody E. July 2008. "The Context Matters: The Effects of Single Member versus At-Large Districts on City Council Diversity." *American Journal of Political Science* 52 (3): pp. 554–569.

Voorhees, Heidi, and Lange-Skaggs, Rachel. 2015. "Women Leading Government: Why So Little Progress in 30 Years?" *PM Magazine*. Accessed on December 5, 2016 from http://icma.org/en/Article/105323/Women_Leading_Government

Cities and the American Intergovernmental Structure

M. Ernita Joaquin

In the United States, cities operate within a federal system as just one layer of governments inside an intergovernmental structure. Cities are constrained from above, mainly by states, but also have to manage relationships with other cities and governmental units, like school boards and special districts. In today's environment, city managers are relying more upon collaborative management and networking to rise to these challenges. This chapter will explore these relationships around the city. In doing so, students will learn to understand the roles and relationships among key local and other government elected and appointed officials as well as what makes local institutions different from other institutions, understand the complexities of intergovernmental and network relationships, and develop skills in collaborative governance (NASPAA Student Learning Goals).

DILEMMAS OF ACTION

Cities navigate horizontal and vertical dimensions of action. They take account of the democratic forces arising from the people below, the authorities above, and the duplicative, consolidative, and collaborative arrangements they may have to enter to accomplish public service objectives. The American federal system places cities, or local governments, in a unique position for action, yet it constrains them in the kinds of authority, organization, or financial latitude they desire to perform their tasks.

On the one hand, local governments possess inherent efficiency: the short political distance between local administrators and their constituents allows for interests to emerge and consensus to consolidate more swiftly. If more targeting is necessary, local governments may reproduce parts of themselves in the form of special districts, or consolidate, or split into, new local government units.

On the other hand, the need to act quickly does not always entail capacity for action; other governments with more resources and powers may be needed. Creating more local units may not solve service problems, but merely fragment them. Consequently, intergovernmental (including inter-municipal) and regional arrangements can be viable alternatives, even preferable, to individual city action on thorny dilemmas. Many communities remain reluctant to cede resources and decision-making beyond their borders. Given a historical preference for anything local, political culture draws communities away from more centralized solutions.

Local governments number almost 90,000, each of them with differing capacities to address "wicked" problems (Rittel and Webber 1973). Studies have found that areas that are more highly fragmented exhibit larger disparities in revenue raising capacities (Atkins 2008, p. 75). In political theory, actors facing the greatest challenges or on the losing side of a conflict would want the scope of conflict expanded (Schattschneider 1960; Carr 2004). Smaller communities would theoretically be more willing to see problems and solutions brought up to the next level, or regionalized. Yet, barriers remain: localist impulses diminish public reception toward regionalism. Also, the transaction costs for local governments of entering into cooperative arrangements with other governments could sometimes be higher the potential benefits to individual localities (Feiock 2007). Collection action dilemmas attend even intergovernmental service agreements and contracting (Andrew 2009; Brown and Potoski 2003). More deeply, there has always been ambivalence about, or a tradeoff between, legitimacy and authority in the eyes of local communities whenever arguments arise for centralization, like regionalization, of decision-making and action (Wallis 2008).

Regions are not the natural environs of cities; it is important to understand them first in their historical habitat—the federal system. American federalism is complex but adaptable, but its long history and evolution cannot be done justice in one book, let alone a chapter, and therefore no attempt will be made here. Instead, the following discussion looks at intergovernmental relations (IGR), including regionalism, to the extent they drive cities toward more effective action.

DEFINING KEY CONCEPTS

In a *federal system*, power is divided between the central government and the constituent governments. In the United States, the Constitution divides power between the federal government and the states. As explained by Stephens and Wikstrom (2007, pp. 2–4), in this system:

- Both levels have substantial authority, whether residual or delegated, although the federal government is much stronger and pervasive today than it was at the birth of the nation;
- The distribution of authority between the federal and state governments usually cannot be changed by ordinary legislation;
- Both levels have the ability to draw their authority from and act directly upon individuals within their jurisdiction, for example, in tax collection and law enforcement;
- States have considerable leeway in devising their forms of government and procedures; and
- All states must have legal and political equality, as demonstrated by their equal representation in the U.S. Senate.

The central national government and the states dominate the vertical dimension of local government, for the states subsume the local governmental units under their power. Their dominance is reflected by the traditional "cake metaphors" of federalism:

Layer cake or dual federalism (approximately 1800 to 1930) suggests a central government and states having a discrete division of responsibilities and authority such that incursions into the other's domains would violate its sovereignty (Nathan 2008). National responsibilities would include national defense and interstate commerce; state responsibilities would be family law and education. A two-layer cake of intergovernmental relationships made local governments invisible; three layers would show them at the bottom.

Marble cake or cooperative federalism (the 1930s–1950s) was symbolic of the collaborative efforts between the federal government, the states, and local governments in the aftermath of the Great Depression, with the expansion of the administrative state. Federalism scholar Morton Grodzins described the three-layer cake metaphor as erroneous, advocating instead "the rainbow or marble cake, characterized by an inseparable mingling of differently colored ingredients, the colors appearing in vertical and diagonal strands . . . (as) functions are mixed in the American federal system.

(Grodzins 2013, p. 37)

After the war, the metaphors began to shift away from cakes. Deil Wright (1988) described the succeeding phases as *creative federalism* (the 1950s–1960s), *coercive/competitive federalism* (1960s–1970s), *calculative federalism* (1970s–1980s), and *contractive federalism* (1980s–1990s). This shifting framework captured the growth of interactions within the network of governments, including municipalities and the nongovernment sector, as substantial autonomy within their respective realms gave way to more cooperative, then contentious, and then coercive relationships.

With this brief background, the city's *intergovernmental environment* is what John Pelissero (2003, p. 9) refers to as:

The mix of government and governmental levels that are present in the area of a city. The typical city operates within an environment that includes the national government, state government, and other local governments, including counties, townships, school districts, special districts, and other cities.

The horizontal dimension of local government may be visualized here, dominated by the interaction among multiple forms of local government. As of the 2007 Census, almost 90,000 local government units were identified, broken down as follows:

- Counties—30,343
- Municipalities (cities)—19,492
- Townships—16,519
- School districts—13,051
- Special districts—37,381

Counties, in general, are administrative divisions of the states. There is no hierarchical relationship between municipalities and counties. However, in regionalizing service delivery, county leadership has grown over the last several decades (as discussed later in this chapter). Other local governments consist of municipalities (what we call cities and towns), townships, and villages, which are known as general-purpose authorities. Their special-purpose cousins, the special districts (discussed in more detail below), deliver services within defined boundaries. Local differences have also created unique types of local governments, or further subdivisions of counties and municipalities themselves, such as the boroughs of New York.

CREATURES OF THE STATE, CREATURES OF THE PEOPLE

Finding local governments' place in the intergovernmental structure involves understanding the historical contributions of cities and other local governments to nation building, and the tug-of-war between local governments' weakness in the intergovernmental system and the historical relevance of local power.

When examining the vertical dimensions of city administration, most texts emphasize that local governments are, legally and technically, municipal corporations established by an act of the state legislature. Known as *Dillon's rule*, the state-created status of local governments means they draw their powers or discretion from above. Local governments "owe their origins to, and derive their powers and rights wholly, from the legislature" (Miller and Cox 2014, p. 16). Cities, municipalities, and towns have autonomy within the wiggle room the state grants them, or what courts interpret those powers to be.

Variation in state-local relations across the U.S. landscape is the rule rather than the exception. According to the U.S. Advisory Commission on Intergovernmental Relations (ACIR), this variation occurs on four dimensions of local discretion:

1. Structural, such as the local government's form of government (mayor-council, council-manager, blended form) or internal organization;
2. Functional, or the array of responsibilities to be delivered at the local level;
3. Fiscal, the revenue raising (e.g., taxing), borrowing, and spending powers of the local government, a constant source of strife for existing cities and those trying to incorporate as the state legislature controls tax rates and their allocation among local governments; and
4. Staffing, or the size of the local government bureaucracy and its type, and conditions of employment.

Discussions of these four dimensions are found across this book (see Chapter 1 for forms of local government and organization; Chapter 6 and Chapter 7, respectively, for fiscal and human resource administration; and the rest of the book for an examination of service responsibilities, performance, and civic participation in local governance).

Beyond their status as creatures of the state, local governments were, and are, creatures of the people. The humble place of local government in the federal set-up may be balanced by recalling the significance of local action in the life of a young nation. While the states were the fundamental polities, possessing residual powers from the constitutional battle with Washington, D.C., local governments were the governments that mattered to an immigrant nation, providing programs in poverty relief, law enforcement, and education, among other areas of responsibility. City charters and taxing powers from above gave local democracy a dynamism that the states lacked. At that time, municipal expenditures in those areas were bigger compared to what the federal and state governments spent. For a long time, "the bedrock of American domestic government was local" (Derthick 1999, p. 130).

The states assumed dominance later, and historic localism gradually waned with the nationalizing reforms of the 20th century. Reapportionment and other voting rights decisions by the higher courts activated controls from the upper levels and reduced the place of the local polity in American life (Derthick 1999). Nonetheless, as modern-day attitude polling shows, local government commands greater trust among governmental levels, reflecting its historical position and its unique role as an aggregator of people's values.

Local governments are creatures of the people, as well. Local government structures and processes embody the values of their citizen-constituents. Their hopes and wishes are heard by and represented in this institution that is closest to them. Today, extreme sensitivity characterizes many municipalities, in that they would rather go it alone than wait for, or allow, the states or federal agencies to act on matters deemed by the community to be disproportionally urgent at the local level (see the immigration-law enforcement battles in Arizona, Texas, and California).

FRAGMENTATION AND SPECIAL DISTRICTS

In today's metropolitan America, fragmentation, too many overlapping governmental units, is the chief feature of government organizations (Neiman 2000, p. 186). Often, fragmentation exists as a response to local desires. However, it can impede the search for meaningful solutions to wicked problems.

One effect of this tendency is the dizzying array of local special-purpose entities (Katz and Bradley 2013, p. 174): school districts, fire districts, library districts, sewer districts, mosquito control districts, public benefit corporations, industrial development authorities, transportation authorities, port authorities, workforce investment boards, redevelopment authorities, control boards, and emergency financial managers.

Not all rise to the definition of a special district or represent separate governments. According to the Census Bureau, the term "special district" excludes school districts. Special districts are separate governments, which in 2012 totaled 38,266 nationwide, providing specific services that are not being supplied by existing general-purpose governments.

> Many entities that carry the designation "district" or "authority" are, by law, so closely related to county, municipal, town or township, or state governments that they are classified as subordinate agencies of those governments . . . and are not counted as separate special district governments.
>
> (United States Bureau of the Census 2015)

California's Senate defines special districts as "any agency of the state for the local performance of governmental or proprietary functions within limited boundaries" (California Senate Local Government Committee 2010, p. 2). In California, local governments can also create a particular kind of special district, called joint-purpose authorities (JPAs), engaged in the financing and construction of public facilities, such as libraries, City Hall and other buildings, or the purchase of big-ticket, capital items. These JPAs then ease the facilities back to the local government that created them, according to the *Special Districts' Annual Report* of California (2013).

The territories of special districts may be contiguous, or non-contiguous. Special districts may be *single-function* entities, providing only one service, such as fire protection, cemetery, or waste management, unlike cities. Alternatively, like cities, they may be *multifunction*, providing two or more areas of service. A special district created to serve one area of service may grow to cover more functions over time. Hence, special districts also serve some sort of regionalized purpose, leading Miller and Cox (2014, p. 166) to dub them as "the 'other' regional governments." (Please see the discussion of administrative regionalism later in this chapter.)

Like cities and counties, many special districts have corporate powers of eminent domain, entering into contracts, suing and being sued, imposing fees and levies, and engaging in debt (e.g., issuing bonds) to perform their state-designated services. However, districts do not possess police powers, unlike cities.

Special districts may or may not have governing boards or financing mechanisms, depending on their statutory authority. In California, more than a third have independently elected or appointed boards serving fixed terms. The voters in the area elect the board of these independent districts, or, in the case of some water districts, the landowners in the district. The sizes of the board vary. The larger districts mirror the council-manager city, in that they may have large councils and hire a manager to manage day-to-day operations. Other special districts are governed by city councils or county boards (e.g., Board of Supervisors in California counties). For example, the San Bernardino County Board of Supervisors is also the ex-officio governing board for the Yucca Valley Recreation and Park District (State of California Senate Local Government Committee 2010). At the end of fiscal year (FY) 2012, California's 4,711 special districts operated under these three types of governing bodies (State of California State Controller's Office 2013, p. v.).

To finance their services, *enterprise* districts impose user fees like a business. In these areas, it is possible to see the correspondence between the charges and the benefits received. During times of fiscal stress, enterprise districts with their fee-generating capacity have better chances of weathering a crisis, as California's enterprise districts demonstrated in the 1990s (California Senate Local Government Committee 2010). Other districts rely more on general taxes or property taxes collected by the state and allocated among different local governments, school districts, and special districts. Examples of these districts that are non-enterprise are mosquito abatement districts and fire protection districts with "public-goods" types of services. Some districts that are non-enterprise districts may still charge a certain fee, but these are minimal.

When special districts go into debt financing to carry out new capital projects or to improve existing infrastructure, such as issuing general obligation bonds that will be paid for by property taxes, they need to seek voter approval (two-thirds of voters in California). They can also enter into debt by borrowing from banks or other local governments, the state, and federal government.

Special districts are distinct from tax increment financing districts (TIFs) or benefit assessment districts, which are designations used for particular *financing* mechanisms of area economic development projects, not for *providing* services. The funds from the benefit assessment, however, may be used by the state, local government, or special district to provide public services.

If local governments are, historically, the level of government the public has trusted the most, some special district advocates claim that special districts are "the best examples of small-town democracy" (California Senate Local Government Committee 2010, p. 1). The allure of special districts arises from their ability to respond to problems that might not be handled well by individual local governments or as flexibly as local governments do their other functions.

However, as expressions of governance and adaptation within system constraints, special districts exemplify the labyrinthine nature of the American governmental system. Special districts were created as solutions to new problems that old structures had difficulty addressing, but like any policy response, over time they have also posed new problems. Calls abound to explain and justify their creation. Some critics call them "the worst form of fragmented government," complicating local government (California Senate Local Government Committee 2010, p. 1). They duplicate some of the functions of cities and counties, creating conflict at the local level, straining resources with an abundance of bureaucracy, and reducing accountability when citizens are confused about where tax dollars go and which local entity provides a particular service. "[G]overnment fragmentation . . . obscures responsibility for services, and . . . prevents public agencies from efficiencies that can be achieved by larger, regional units of government" (Neiman 2000, p. 186). Finally, critics charge that special districts can hinder regional planning:

> Having numerous special districts can hamper planning efforts. For example, it can be difficult to organize the various water, sewer, and fire services in one region to deliver services to property owners and residents. Because about 2/3 of the districts have independent governing boards, no single agency coordinates their efforts.
>
> (California Senate Local Government Committee 2010, p. 12).

In California, state law allows special districts to override county and city general plans and zoning ordinance, so that "land use conflicts are possible" (California Senate Local Government Committee 2010, p. 6).

How do regions interject themselves, then, in the theory and practice of intergovernmental relations? The *intergovernmental governing system* is defined by Miller and Cox (2014, p. 5) as that "structure [that] is made up of expectations, administrative networks, financial flows, and authority relationships such as state and federal mandates." This broader definition does not exclude Pelissero's definition quoted earlier in this chapter; rather, it opens up the possibility of a broader set of expectations, networks, financial flows, and authority relationships, in which local governments participate.

REGIONALISM AND LOCAL GOVERNMENTS

The vulnerability of local economies to costly and unpredictable disasters is reflected by the fact that up to 40 percent of businesses never reopen in the wake of natural or man-made disasters. Communities are exposed to serious impacts when this happens, and communities are coming together to develop regionalized response plans for rebuilding, and to develop resilience to future events.

Regional collaboration enables local governments to accomplish more for their constituents. In 2008, only three counties escaped disaster declarations in Arkansas. The Southwest Arkansas Planning and Development District (SWAPDD), one of the eight planning regions in the state, recognized the need to develop a database of infrastructure and economic information in the region that could be used for future recovery efforts.

> For businesses, staff collected data on location, number of employees, and contact information when owners wished to provide it. For infrastructure, they gathered information on the locations of critical facilities and transportation infrastructure as well as the service areas and customer base numbers of all public water and wastewater systems. All data was collected in a format that could be mapped using ArcGIS.
>
> (NADO 2014, p. 5)

Economic Development Administration (EDA) grants were leveraged by the SWAPPD and the City of Stamps to secure additional funding from the Arkansas Economic Development Commission and the Delta Regional Authority. The database has been providing the region with baseline information for its economy, which can be overlaid with data on disasters' impacts to quickly assess the damage and to mobilize recovery efforts. Also, the database allows the communities to prefill applications for post-disaster assistance; develop hazard mitigation plans for member counties; help local partners identify funding opportunities; and submit application information, letters of support, and environmental review forms "with the touch of a button" (NADO 2014, p. 6). Information on flooding and other hazards is also to be added to the database. Updating the database is supported by local governments' small monthly fees to keep their water and wastewater information current. The project is said to strengthen understanding among the staff in the region of their local planning and district-wide activities. Replication of the project was underway, as SWAPPD shared it with other regions that recognize the critical role of better data in regional disaster planning and recovery.

DEFINING THE REGION

Coming from the Latin word *regere*, the word *region* originally referred to tracts of land under a regent that commanded singular rule over it (Foster 2011, p. 55). *Regional planning* is "the management of issues or action on behalf of goals that cross boundaries in regions" (see Seltzer and Carbonell 2011 for a complete discussion of regionalism's history). The strategies include, but are not limited to, resource planning, protection, and controls; smart growth or sustainable design policies; tax revenue sharing; land and development rights acquisition programs; and innovative regional strategic investments (Montgomery 2011a).

Regions today consist of both mandated or externally imposed areas drawn from above, and organic areas that emerge from bottom-up collaboration among many levels of government, including their nongovernmental or private sector partners. We have come a long way since the time of regents; we now have an assortment of regions, some with more substantial policy and administrative roles than others. Foster (2011, p. 55) notes that regions may also be defined by:

1. Natural features, such as watersheds, special resource areas, or climatic zones (e.g., the Chesapeake Bay Watershed, which encompasses 64,000 square miles of urbanized and undeveloped territory across parts of six states and the District of Columbia);
2. Human-drawn, political-administrative boundaries crafted from municipal, county, or state building blocks (Omaha Metropolitan Area, defined by the U.S. Office of Management and Budget as eight counties in Nebraska and Iowa); or
3. Territories of cultural or linguistic characteristics ('Ecotopia,' the politically progressive, environmentally conscious coastal region between Alaska and Northern California).

On this list, the most common definition of regions is the second one—regions weave local and state political and administrative forces for planning and implementing programs. This definition is closest to the statistical definition of *metropolitan* regions: the Office of Management and Budget (OMB) defines MSAs by defining their boundaries "solely for the preparation, presentation, and comparison of data . . . to help government agencies, researchers, and others achieve uniform use and comparability of data on a national scale" (OMB Bulletin 1999).

A "metro" region, per OMB definition, contains an urban core population of at least 50,000 or more, while a "micro" region at least 10,000 but less than 50,000. In 2009, there were 942 metro and micro-regions. An urban nation, the United States has more than 90 percent of its inhabitants living in a metro region. Most of the medium-to-large regions, with at least one million people, are geographically concentrated in the South and West (Miller and Cox 2014, pp. 96–99). According to the foremost scholars in the field, the metropolitan region is the "conceptual and organizing framework around which future governance will occur" (Miller 2008, p. 3, 21).

REGIONAL DEVELOPMENT AND PLANNING BODIES

Perhaps the public might recognize regional mechanisms better with their area-wide, planning-oriented label: *regional development organizations* (RDOs). The term "RDOs" is commonly used to refer to regional bodies that may be known locally as:

- Councils of government (COGs);
- Area development districts;
- Economic development districts;
- Planning and development districts;
- Planning and development commissions;
- Regional development commissions;
- Regional planning commissions; and
- Regional councils.

These RDOs possess varying mixtures of planning powers, autonomy, and memberships. RDOs serve as U.S. Economic Development Administration-designated economic development districts and are responsible for preparing comprehensive economic development strategies. Often, RDOs administer the metropolitan planning organizations and their rural counterparts, the Rural Transportation Planning Organizations. The policy boards of these RDOs are controlled by a majority of local government officials. According to the National Association of Regional Development Organizations (NADO), a network of 540 multi-jurisdictional regional planning and development organizations aims to strengthen the economic competitiveness and quality of life across America's local communities.

▶ BOX 3.1   REGIONAL FOOD SYSTEMS

One way to integrate rural and urban regions and promote economic development, public health, and sustainability goals is by fostering local and regional food systems. An example of a regional initiative in this area is provided by the Sacramento, California region, which has the fourth largest agricultural economy in the world; with 70 percent of its land in rural agriculture, only about 2 percent of 1.9 million tons of regional food consumption is locally grown (NADO 2015, p. 6). To address this issue, the Sacramento Area Council of Governments (SACOG) launched the Rural-Urban Connections Strategy to link locally grown food to local markets. Stakeholders adopt a rural perspective on land use, agriculture infrastructure, economic opportunities, forest management, and government regulations to drive the effort. Their work produced the Sacramento Regional Food Hub Feasibility Analysis, which revealed that a four-stage, seven-year "for-profit hub model was the most financially sustainable approach for the region, with an emphasis on direct market channels between producers and local institutions" (NADO 2015, p. 6). Plans include acquiring a 22,000-square-foot facility that would house aggregation, sorting, packing, packaging, processing, and distribution services, providing smallholder farmers opportunities to tap into the local market, and further conducting case studies for counties interested in the food hub business model.

Approaches to Studying Regional Governance

David Miller catalogs the major ways regional governance is studied (2008, pp. 10–14) by the number of local governments involved; the way local governments coordinate between each other and the region as a whole; and the primary ways governments can interact.

Conceptions of regional governance (based on the *number* of local governments involved) fall on a continuum of centralization, according to Miller (2008, p. 11): on the centralized end are regions that may be called "consolidationist," with a structure imposed externally, often by an action of the state government. Consolidationist regions are characterized by a relatively small number of independent local governments with authority concentrated in a small number of public institutions, such as the consolidated governments (cities with counties) in Jacksonville, Indianapolis, and Nashville. More decentralized regional approaches employ the interlocal agreements or the "linked function" strategy. The goal is increasing efficiency and enhancing consumer choice by utilizing economies of scale in delivering local government services. In California, counties operate on the Lakewood Plan, wherein they act as service providers. Municipalities in this region also purchase services from the private sector. The most decentralized, "complex network" regions have large numbers of local governments participating in cooperative and competitive relationships. Citizen participation and citizen preferences in service delivery are supposed to be maximized in this kind of arrangement.

Based on the way local governments coordinate between each other and the region as a whole, Miller (2008) cites the work of Hitchings (1998): at one end are "ad hoc" regions wherein local governments voluntarily come together to a discussion forum on issues such as land use. They may form councils of government, but they do not have a written physical development plan at the regional level. It is said that most metropolitan regions in the United States fall into this category. In the middle of the continuum are "advisory" regions that become "supervisory" if a regional body is delegated the responsibility of administering the plan and overseeing its compliance, but the actual implementation is done at the local level. San Diego and Denver are two examples of supervisory regions. At the other end of the continuum are "authoritative" regions that possess a regional body, a plan, and the statutory authority to force compliance upon local governments. The Twin Cities Metropolitan Council of Minneapolis and St. Paul in Minnesota and the Metro in Portland, Oregon are examples of these regions, which are unique (Stephens and Wikstrom 1999, p. 101).

Miller's (2008) own approach consists of classifying regions based on the primary ways governments can interact regarding planning and development coordination, service delivery cooperation, fiscal sharing, and jurisdictional boundary realignment. The first form is called coordinating regionalism, which deals with the integrated planning of the region as a whole.

The second form, administrative regionalism, is one of the most pervasive arrangements, and this is related to Miller and Cox's (2014, p. 166) dubbing of special districts as the "other regional governments." Under this regionalism fall

> [t]he functional transfer of services from municipal governments to either special districts or county governments, and the day-to-day negotiations between all types of local governments that lead to a myriad of cooperation agreements at an operational level between those governments.
>
> (Miller 2008, p. 13)

An increasing percentage of these districts are "regional" special districts (about 23 percent of all special districts in 2002) whose jurisdictional boundaries were "either coterminous with one or more counties or had a service area that was larger than a single county" (Miller 2008, p. 13). Counties have had a strong role in this development: urban counties served to regionalize metropolitan America when they began taking on new responsibilities cutting across some municipalities. Note that OMB draws the metropolitan area from a core population nucleus—the county is the building block going outward to the localities connected to it in social and economic terms (Miller and Cox 2014). Interlocal agreements, in Miller's classification, are the most common form of administrative regionalism.

The third form, a recent innovation, is called fiscal regionalism. Here the local governments create a metropolitan, regional funding mechanism for a variety of needs. Examples of this type are cultural asset districts, tax and revenue sharing programs, and peaceful co-existence plans (Miller 2008, p. 14).

Finally, structural regionalism is the most radical form in that the annexation, mergers, and consolidations may be applied to city and county boundaries. In the first three forms, the governments retain boundaries; with this structure the boundaries are adjusted and the powers and responsibilities altered.

As political bodies, individual local governments may attempt to modify their boundaries in response to changing demands on services, citizen values, or governmental capacity to address public needs. Counties and municipalities may unify or *merge* their jurisdictions: counties with other counties, municipalities with other municipalities, or municipalities consolidated into city-counties, often through a referendum in the localities involved. In a city-county consolidation, the new entity assumes the powers and responsibilities of a county and a municipality. County-city consolidation, in particular, is "a reform idea that does not die" (Leland and Johnson 2004, p. 27). The idea hinges on promises of efficiency or economic development often targeted to narrow interest groups whose support is crucial to the merger (Durning and Sanford 2010). However, studies have found that about 80 percent of referenda to unify a county and a municipality failed (Leland and Thurmaier 2006), and the promised outcomes of consolidation often do not materialize (Feiock 2004).

Waves of Regionalism throughout History

To Wallis (2008, pp. 95–98), regionalism may be conceived as waves, with each wave distinguished by a different focus. For the first wave, emerging during the last quarter of the 19th century, the focus was on territorial expansion through annexation and incorporation of smaller municipalities. The second wave, from the 1920s, confronted conflicts between different levels and forms of government at a time of economic depression. Regional authorities and districts focused on planning capacity and the use of zoning. The third wave, during the 1960s and 1970s, was marked by federal efforts to impose regionalism to meet goals in infrastructure development, environmental protection, and social equity. The fourth wave is said to overlap with the third wave, in which states over time became interested in infrastructure and social equity issues, such as affordable housing. Today's blend of regionalism is the fifth wave of locally based, coalition-based regionalism.

Perhaps the numerous approaches themselves reflect the underlying tensions between authority and legitimacy, between the legal and socio-political natures of local governments, as Miller (2008) and Wallis (2008) have observed.

▶ BOX 3.2 COALITION-BASED REGIONALISM

Coalition-based regionalism could be seen in the activities of San Francisco Bay Area coalitions, the New Jersey Highlands Coalition, Treasure Valley Partnership in Idaho, Denver's Mile High Compact, Southern Massachusetts Vision 2020, Cape Cod Commission, and Envision Utah (Wallis 2008). As an example, in San Francisco, Bay Vision 2020 aimed to strengthen regional planning capacity "by combining several key regional planning and service authorities" (Wallis 2008, p. 109). This vision was a product of years of coalition-building efforts, led by the Bay Area Council and its partners. The Council is an organization founded in 1945 by key businesses like Wells Fargo, Bank of America, and Pacific Gas and Electric to advocate policy for the nine-county Bay Area. The Council currently boasts of more than 275 of the largest employers in the region as supporting its work, and its mission is to make the Bay Area the "most innovative, globally competitive, and sustainable region in the world" (Bay Area Council 2015).

The Council's concern during its early years was infrastructure improvement to connect the communities of the Bay Area into a single region, worried that its fragmented governance was making Los Angeles leave the Bay Area behind. The Council's focus was distinctly "metropolitanist," with the business district taking the lead in policy advocacy (Wallis 2008, p. 108; Hartman 1986). Around the same time the Council was working to advance its goals, two other groups with a greater focus on environmental and housing issues—People for Open Space (POS) and the San Francisco Urban Planning and Renewal Association (SPUR)—emerged in 1958. One of their first

campaigns was to save the Bay Area from landfill and development. They were a key force in establishing special districts to preserve open space in the 1970s (Wallis 2008, p. 109).

These groups later coalesced with the Greenbelt Congress to form the Greenbelt Alliance, developing a more coherent strategy to advocate for permanently protected greenbelt. The Alliance later partnered with the Bay Area Council in 1990, leading to the production of the Bay Vision 2020. Since then they have established urban growth boundaries in the region, typically through incorporation in municipal or county comprehensive plans. The Bay Vision 2020's principal goal of combining key regional planning and service authorities failed to pass the legislature (Wallis 2008, p. 109), but later, there were other successes in coalition-based regionalism. For example, Plan Bay Area 2013 was adopted by the Association of Bay Area Governments (ABAG) and the Metropolitan Transportation Committee. Because the preservation of open space is often seen as conflicting with the goal of affordable urban housing, Plan Bay Area 2013—recently redrafted as Plan Bay Area 2040—unifies these interests by directing growth to occur within the existing urban footprint (e.g., near urban boundaries, near public transit), and to distribute funds from the One Bay Area Grant program to the production, acquisition, and rehabilitation of affordable homes in places that are doing the most sustainable and equitable development. The 2040 draft maintains this focus, with Priority Development Areas—infill areas near transportation corridors—targeted for 77 percent of new housing development and 55 percent of new jobs (Sluis 2017).

The Quest for Adaptive Forms of Regionalism

"Negotiated agreements and understandings" (Wallis 2008, p. 107) may be key to balancing the problem of legitimacy versus authority, especially as the pool of players widens beyond governmental entities. Two forms may be relevant in this respect. Metropolitan regionalism is the "new kid on the block" and a form of regionalism in which cities, not just states, could play a prominent role. According to Miller (2002), metropolitan areas are moving toward regional resolutions that are "homegrown" and "evolutionary."

> As systems, metropolitan regions are adapting to the changing environment . . . paradoxically. At the same time that these systems of local government are becoming more diffused or decentralized, they are becoming more coordinated . . . because most lasting regional approaches emerge as negotiated agreements and understandings between players over time. Externally imposed solutions . . . seldom work. . . . Outside influences and the local response are interpreted locally.
>
> (p. 4)

Cities are the nerve center of metropolitan regionalism. At a Forbes Reinventing America Summit, pathways to maximizing cities' core strengths were focused on innovations arising from the horizontal dimension that cities must navigate. In the words of Mayor Rahm Emmanuel of Chicago, "One of the nuttiest things going on is this battle between the public and private sector. We are partners. The model we should have is creating a partnership for the best results for the people we serve" (Vander Veen 2014).

Metropolitan regions may be similar to what Wallis (2008, p. 107) called coalition-based regionalism, a type of regional governance that started in the mid-1980s due to devolution, economic globalization, growing concern for equity, and the emergence of sustainable, integrated approaches to growth management. More organic than the state- or federal government-mandated entities, the homegrown characteristics of such coalitions:

- Arise from a recognition that their individual efforts are inadequate, in response to a threat to the economic, environmental, or social well-being of the region;
- Derive their legitimacy from greater engagement of local governments;
- Use participatory visioning and voluntary compacts;
- Have wider interest-group involvement and strong nonprofit and business ties, some of which are already partners on previous efforts; and
- Focus less on building government capacity to plan and more on developing multi-sector, regional governance focused on strategic growth issues and shared values (e.g., sustainability, equity).

Wallis (2008, pp. 96, 107–119)

BOX 3.3 REGIONALISM STRATEGIES IN CITY SUSTAINABILITY PLANS

- "Work with our regional partners to enhance the transportation linkages between the Peninsula and Southside areas of Hampton Roads and provide transit options." Virginia Beach, Virginia, p. 143.
- "Coordinate our transportation systems with our regional partners and provide linkages to key destinations including regional military institutions, airports, ports, educational institutions, and employment centers." Virginia Beach, Virginia, p. 143.

- "Work with our regional partners to promote Hampton Roads as a center of excellence in healthcare, technology, marine science, maritime industry, and agriculture/aquaculture." Virginia Beach, Virginia, p. 143.
- "Work with neighboring cities to minimize and/or reduce regional pollutant sources upward of the city." Virginia Beach, Virginia, p. 149.
- "Maintain high air and water quality to ensure a healthy regional population and

BOX 3.3 (CONTINUED)

quality of life." Virginia Beach, Virginia, p. 149.

- "Partner with our neighboring cities to centralize access to services, where appropriate, across the region." Virginia Beach, Virginia, p. 151.
- "Work together between the City government and the community to

optimize natural disaster preparedness." Virginia Beach, Virginia, p. 151.

Source: City of Virginia Beach, Virginia. 2013. A Community Plan for a Sustainable Future. City of VA Beach Environment and Sustainability Office. March 12, 2013. Accessed on February 22, 2017 from www. vbgov.com/government/offices/eso/sustainability-plan/Documents/vb-sustainability-plan-web.pdf.

METROPOLITAN COLLABORATION AND NETWORK BUILDING

Recently, cities' engagement on a global scale has been promoted by programs like the Brookings Institution's Metropolitan Policy Program and its collaborators, the Global Cities Initiative with JP Morgan Chase, and the Brookings-Rockefeller Project on State and Metropolitan Innovation. According to Brookings, "metro areas are unsure of how to harness emerging forms of global capital," and global competition is compelling metro areas to intensify their efforts (McDearman and Donahue 2015). For these, the archaic intergovernmental responses no longer suffice, and, in fact, inhibit "revolution."

Describing the urban city-anchored *metropolitan revolution* in their book of the same name—which avoids mentioning the word "regionalism," instead using "collaboration" and "network building"—Katz and Bradley (2013, pp. 7–8) described the traditional intergovernmental context with today's dynamics of cities and metros (see Table 3.1).

TABLE 3.1

Characteristics of the Federal Government, States, and Cities

The Federal Government and the States	Cities and Metro Areas
Legacy institutions: hyper-political and partisan	Integrated, action-oriented, rewarding innovation, imagination, and pushing boundaries
Hopelessly fragmented and compartmentalized	Using cultural norms rather than regulatory mandates to inspire best practice
Frustratingly bureaucratic, prescriptive	Focused on "getting the future right"
Present-oriented	Organic communities naturally connecting the dots between issues, blending the ecosystem and the enterprise
Confining the reach of solutions to the powers and resources at hand	
Focused on atomistic firms and workers and silver-bullet tax and regulatory solutions	Constituting active, participatory democracy, collectively stewarding their places, guiding their regions, and coproducing their economies
Constituting passive, representative democracy	
Think of constituencies as competing for scarce resources	Think of networks and teamwork, owning and experiencing challenges rather than studying them
Leaders dominated by legislatures, rewarding partisan calculus	Tangible in ways that abstract national actions cannot be

Their programs, according to Brookings, are powered by ideas of innovation, export promotion, and low-carbon footprint in engaging the states and local governments and their partners in corporate and civic communities.

Barrier to Regionalism: The Lack of a Regional Ethic

According to Beverly Cigler (2008), the "key forces that constrain or spur development are regional in nature" (p. 301). The absence of strong regional structures can hinder the sustainability goals of local communities. "When everyone is in charge, no one is in charge, leading to lost opportunities for collaboration, leveraging resources, and coordinating information that could lead to a clearer understanding of industries and workers and his or her respective needs" (Cigler 2008, p. 301). So, why is regionalism "institutionally weak" (Visser 2004), or not as popular as the business-minded, intersectoral, or metro-based networks?

Scholars have continuously grappled with the nation's lack of a "regional ethic." Miller and Cox (2014) believe that much of this can be attributed to the isolation that the federal system allows communities. This isolation is a major hurdle for the integration of resources, efforts, and authorities in advancing solutions beyond local borders. "If it were just a question of facts and data, regional planning would win the day. . . . [H]owever . . . Local control and the aspiration to maintain local institutions . . . are desires that are not easily replaced" (Seltzer and Carbonell 2011, p. 3). Wallis echoed the legitimacy-authority ambivalence at the local level:

> A consistent problem faced by efforts to develop the capacity to manage growth and associated land development at the regional scale is the lack of perceived legitimacy. Regional power is seen as diluting local authority, which is the level of government at which most citizens believe land use decisions should be made.
>
> (2008, p. 106)

Local governments' confidence to define and resolve issues by themselves is bolstered by the fact that they are more positively regarded than are the states and the federal government. ICMA Director Robert O'Neill, Jr. (2012) noted in "The Coming Decade of Local Government" the vitality of local governments versus the paralysis-plagued Washington, D.C. and deficit-ridden states. Arguing for the greater meaningfulness of local action, he pointed to some characteristics that remained unique to local governments. First, public trust in local governments continued its historically higher trend, compared to trust in the states and the national government. Second, showcasing no paralysis, many cities were ably passing policy initiatives reflecting their constituents' service preferences during a budget crunch. Finally, the proximity of citizens to their local government, in combination with the favorable regard, was allowing for increased governmental engagement of community segments to define what citizens deemed essential. The convergence of these developments, after a recession in which local governments braved significant dumping of responsibilities from above, was palpable. This preference for smaller, rather than larger, governmental units to promote action is entrenched in practice and theory (see Ostrom, Tiebout and Warren 1961). In Box 3.4, a veteran city manager of California cities, Bryan Montgomery, reflects on the challenges of regionalism.

BOX 3.4   REGIONALIZATION AND LOCALISM FROM A CITY MANAGER'S PERSPECTIVE

According to Bryan Montgomery, city manager of Oakley, California, decisions and actions by one city can impact adjacent cities. In today's suburban cities, it is often hard to tell that you are leaving one city and entering another. In these instances, it is critical to plan major roadways; coordinate law enforcement and other public safety services; consider land use impacts outside your borders; form transit system, water, sewer, and stormwater utility systems; and even jointly address matters such as code enforcement and other health, safety, and welfare issues—particularly with adjacent cities.

Bryan is a strong believer in the "regionalization" of services. Collaboration almost always leads to more efficient services or services that otherwise would not have been provided. An example of regionalization in East Contra Costa County is Tri-Delta Transit (Eastern Contra Costa Transit Authority), which operates bus routes through Pittsburg, Antioch, Oakley, Brentwood, and the surrounding unincorporated areas. None of these cities on its own could operate such an efficient and effective service. By collaborating, these cities can provide access to jobs and schools, provide service to county clinics and local hospitals, reduce road congestion, and help senior citizens and people with disabilities remain independent, among others. Regionalization in East Contra Costa County also built the State Highway 4 Bypass. The County and the cities of Pittsburg, Antioch, Oakley, and Brentwood formed a joint powers authority, developed a plan, imposed a fee, and

built a large segment of State Highway that would have never been built otherwise.

A key impediment to regionalizing services is the desire for city officials to "have their own." A city may have a long-standing history of having a fire department, and with that history comes a community bond and a sense of pride that keeps the fire department in place, even if consolidation with other nearby departments would be much cheaper and more efficient. Technology such as the Automatic Vehicle Locator (AVL) uses GPS to dispatch the nearest available fire response vehicle to an incident without regard to what public agency that vehicle belongs to. If used, this type of technology lends itself to consolidating services, if the political will exists to do so.

With intergovernmental relations, the principle is the same—one entity should plan, coordinate, cooperate, communicate, and collaborate for the benefit of the whole. A county, a special district, the state, and the federal government can make decisions and take actions that very much adversely affect (or benefit) a city. This increasing interdependence calls upon public administrators to hone the specific skills and acquire the "new governance" tools of which Lester Salamon (2002) wrote. It gets back to being more of a leader than a manager; recognizing that government is more and more a task of "arranging" rather than just "doing"; finding ways to collaborate instead of competing; and exercising skills of negotiation and persuasion, rather than command and control.

TECHNOLOGY AND PERFORMANCE MEASUREMENT IN COLLABORATIVE ACTIVITIES

Besides the use of alternative service agreements among themselves and with the private sector, local government investments in technology and performance measurements can go a long way in enhancing their intergovernmental and intersectoral relationships. Planning and implementation over multiple, layered, or expanding jurisdictions in response to various interests require technological support. Information technologies, such as geographic information technology (GIS), cloud computing, and next-generation 911 systems, are some of today's indispensable tools for urban administration. GIS, in particular, is a staple of urban and regional planning, from assessment and forecasting of problems and scenarios to the development, execution, and monitoring of areawide plans. Prominent in land use regulation and infrastructure support, GIS provides analysts fast, reliable data on trends that might be important to decision-makers, such as housing, diseases, or crime. These data may be shared among partner organizations, allowing different entities to understand where their data, systems, and interests converge, and to use GIS for better guidance, coordination, or implementation of plans and services.

An example of a metro region harnessing GIS is Miami-Dade, one of the most disaster-prone urban regions in the country. Miami-Dade's system was installed to aid planning and productivity analysis for its 35 municipalities. However, it was also largely a response to the region's vulnerability to natural disasters (hurricanes, floods, earthquakes). Thus, emergency management is the focus of its Florida Interoperable Picture Processing for Emergency Response (FLIPPER), a set of programs integrated with a Web-enabled crisis information management system using secure, real-time information.

> Miami-Dade's GIS has approximately 400 layers of data that are shared by the various agencies. FLIPPER allows users to view more than 6,000 critical facilities, such as schools, fire and police departments, hazardous materials sites and hospitals within a specific vicinity. The system uses a long list of tools—Twitter, Bing Maps, hazardous plume modeling, live traffic, the U.S. National Grid and population estimates—all tied to FLIPPER and viewable via a unified map interface.
>
> (Flynn 2011)

County and municipal agencies also benefit from using the technology for predictive analysis regarding population, housing, and law enforcement, to name a few. The City of Miami maintains its GIS, but by agreement, the county and city share GIS data, and the county supplies and updates the vast majority of the data that the city uses (Flynn 2011).

Another technology facilitating intergovernmental and inter-organizational collaboration can be found in *Collaborate.org*, a central geospatial platform that can be used to share data and resources and to collaborate on projects. Developed by Stanford and NASA engineers, the platform provides the backbone of the Exemplary State Initiative of the State of Hawaii. Users are able to view live sensor data (e.g., aerial photography, satellite imagery, air traffic, live television feeds, social media feeds, and air quality) and use collaboration tools like calendars, video conferencing, task lists, and document sharing capability. Organizations can collaborate on projects regarding water supply, power, education, and infrastructure by sharing, accessing, and leveraging each other's data and resources (Wood 2013a).

Participatory Technology

Citizen activism appears to be increasing at the same time as technologies are being designed with public input in mind. Planning technologies combined with e-government tools are enabling agencies to offer services such as online mapping, fee processing, and submission of applications relating to land and economic development. It is essential for real-time monitoring and decision support for services that the public needs daily, such as traffic regulation and trash pickup. Other tools to bring people's views to the table, promote transparency, and ultimately create stronger plans include the Internet and social media (Fregonese and Gabbe 2011, p. 227). They can "visualize facts, data, and sound arguments to capture the public mind" (ibid., p. 229). GIS can also facilitate participatory governance, regarding bringing in citizen inputs to the planning process.

> Planning support systems can measure and compare performances of different planning scenarios according to planner- or citizen-defined indicators for land use, transportation, natural resources, and employment, to name a few. The ultimate goal is to bring together all potential players . . . on a common vision for their community.
>
> (ESRI 2006)

Beyond planning, citizen engagement continues to the execution of plans and monitoring of developments. In the Miami-Dade region, the GIS team asks residents to contribute more data: for example, in the event of an emergency, residents are encouraged to email or text message information about damage to their homes and neighborhoods (Flynn 2011).

Technology in intergovernmental relations and regional efforts also makes interactive monitoring an avenue for public participation. One example of a project that openly monitors trends and indicators of regional growth is *The Metro Monitor*—available at www.brookings.edu/research/interactives/metromonitor#/M10420. User interactive, this is hosted by the Brookings Institution and tracks the performance of the 100 largest U.S. metropolitan areas in terms of jobs, unemployment, output, and housing prices. The analysis of these indicators is focused on change during three time periods: the recession, the recovery, and the combination of the two (recession + recovery). The determination of each period is place- and indicator-specific—1 indicates the best performance, 100 the worst.

Barriers to Maximizing Technology's Role

The major barriers to harnessing GIS and other technologies in intergovernmental or regional efforts are budgets, organizational culture, and inter-organizational trust. For example, a huge challenge to using GIS and other technologies is the cost. The most expensive and challenging part of maintaining a GIS is "getting the data and existing maps into a digital, usable format—a stumbling block for many governments" (Flynn 2011). Governments and private agencies are known to be spending twice as much on GIS data as on applications and services. With the recession having hit local governments hard beginning in 2007, technology budgets suffered cuts like other items, and might just be recovering. According to Pasadena City's Information Officer, "it is necessary for leaders to invest in GIS efforts to prepare for the future" to find new capabilities from shared data (Wood 2013a).

The dollar costs are just the more visible obstacle. The deeper barriers are political, organizational, and inter-organizational. Politically, some departments might want to keep proprietary data if they provide a source of income (Wood 2013a). Culturally,

> [t]he barriers to using GIS to inform city and municipal governance . . . in many cases . . . can't be worked out by engineers and eliminated with a software upgrade. Rather, they run deeper . . . like those concerning governmental organizational culture, budgeting logic, and inadequate or difficult-to-use original data sets.
>
> (Groshgal 2013)

Apprehensions with collaborative technology due to culture may be overcome, as shown in the experiences of Oakland County, Michigan, and Livermore in California. According to Rob White, Chief Information Officer of Davis, California,

It takes people a little bit of time to recognize that you're not going to be gaming them. . . . But after a few meetings, people begin to realize that the story remains the same and it continues to be, "Here's my open-source." And, then people start to do the same thing. It just takes the first step of allowing yourself to be vulnerable.

(Wood 2013b)

In running its G2G Cloud Solutions, a technology sharing service that allows governments to piggyback on Oakland County's existing services, Oakland County focused on long-term partnerships and collaboration and thereby overcame some of the apprehensions of its partners.

Performance Measurement

The performance movement took a stronghold in government agencies under the Clinton Administration, and it has not let up since. Especially for initiatives that involve multiple stakeholders and jurisdictions, regional planning bodies must strive to measure outcomes and processes for greater transparency and accountability. Outside of government, research-led consortia, such as the Brookings Institution's *Metro Monitor*, also track some of the vital signs of metro regions, providing up-to-date indices that may be of use to local and regional leaders.

Another example is in the field of transportation, where federal legislation in 2012 ("Moving Ahead for Progress in the 21st Century") established goals for performance-based approaches within statewide, metropolitan, and non-metropolitan transportation planning. A performance-based transportation system would include the creation of baseline information, identification of goals and objectives, performance measures, preferred trends and targets, system performance report, the forecast of future conditions and needs, strategies and investments, and a financial plan (U.S. Department of Transportation 2014). In California, Plan Bay Area 2013 is held by the federal transportation agency as a model of the performance-based metropolitan transportation plan, adopted by the Metropolitan Transportation Commission (MTC—the planning office for the region) and the Association of Bay Area Governments (like a council of governments). Plan Bay Area includes ten key targets, including addressing greenhouse gas emissions and adequate housing, to adhere to state laws, as well as equity concerns, economic vitality, and transportation system effectiveness.

With the targets clearly identified, MTC and ABAG formulated possible scenarios— combinations of land use patterns and transportation investments—that could be evaluated together to see if (and by how much) they achieved (or fell short of) the performance targets.

(U.S. Department of Transportation 2014, p. 16)

Transportation is replete with multi-faceted concepts like "livability" and "economic vitality," and so regional leaders must ensure that performance measures are specific, measurable, and clearly defined for all stakeholders to understand what is being measured, and to recognize if those indicators are of the greatest value to the community. For example, "mobility" could be measured by "average transit travel time to work" and "average travel speeds on highways" to gauge if goals are being met (U.S. Department of Transportation 2014, p. 61).

To conclude, Carleton Montgomery's (2011b, p. 346) thoughts may be relevant here in assessing how far the performance movement has seeped into intergovernmental and regional initiatives. Montgomery notes that, first, regionalism is not pervasive enough. Second, he thought most regional efforts are using simple metrics, and there is no common approach to measuring success. Third, rigorous studies evaluating regional programs are still few. Lastly, given the long-range plans of most regional programs, evaluating their performance is difficult. Nonetheless, across multiple domains, the author believes that "real, if incomplete success" can be found in regional initiatives in the United States, most especially in shaping land use (ibid.).

CONCLUSIONS

This chapter explored how cities navigate the horizontal and vertical dimensions of the intergovernmental system, as the democratic gravity from below and the multiple authorities from above constrain and propel them to consider alternative routes to accomplishing their service objectives. One way that local governments have done this is by reproducing themselves in the form of special districts, to find some way of targeting their services and to find wiggle room for revenues that the federal system does not always provide them. However, districts have promoted more duplication and complexity than clarity and efficiency.

On the one hand, the short distance between local administrators and their constituents—compared to the case with the state and federal government—allows for a better facilitation of interests and consensus to emerge regarding service demands. On the other hand, speed for action does not always entail capacity for action; other governments with more resources and powers may be needed. Creating more local units may not solve service problems but merely fragment them.

Consequently, intergovernmental (including inter-municipal service sharing), intersectoral (including contracting), and regional arrangements (in their various configurations) are viable alternatives to atomized action on wicked dilemmas. A historical preference for anything local and the political culture often draw communities away from more integrated or centralized solutions. Among those localities that do try, coalition-led regionalism and metropolitan regionalism are fast drawing adherents in response to a perception of governmental rigidity vis-à-vis the vitality that the non-traditional partnerships could offer, especially when aided by technology, capital, and well-designed performance measures.

This chapter has shown regions are not the natural environs of cities, and to understand local governments is to grasp their civic and historical significance in the public's consciousness. The intergovernmental system is inhabited by cities; however, the complex still allows them a measure of adaptivity. These are points that are critical for students to understand, as outlined in two of NASPAA's Urban Administration student learning outcomes covered here.

SELECTED WEB RESOURCES

- Brookings Metro Monitor www.brookings.edu/research/interactives/metromonitor#/M10420
- National Association of Development Organizations www.nado.org
- National Conference of State Legislatures www.ncsl.org
- National Governors Association www.nga.org/cms/home.html
- United States Conference of Mayors www.usmayors.org
- White House Office of Intergovernmental Affairs (it also ran a blog during the Obama Administration) www.whitehouse.gov/administration/eop/iga

EXERCISES AND DISCUSSION QUESTIONS

1. **Know Your City:** Intergovernmental Networks
   - In what county is your city?
   - If there are regional bodies, what are they? Look for regional transportation organizations, Councils of Governments (COGs), etc.
   - What kind of special districts exist in your area?
   - How does the state government appear to get along with cities in your area?
2. What are the pros and cons of one city working with another to provide services?
3. A regional mosquito control board operates in your area. It provides spraying around the

region, not just for your city. However, your city thinks the services are too expensive. Moreover, citizens do not like the idea that they have to pay taxes to a regional body. However, others are worried that the mosquito spreading the Zika virus (an infected *Aedes* species mosquito) is going to spread in your area. On its own, your city cannot afford to spray against the mosquito. If you were the city manager, what do you do?
4. What are the forces that keep citizens and city governments from working together as a group on regional issues? On what issues would working together be a positive thing?

REFERENCES

Andrew, Simon. 2009. "Regional Integration through Contracting Networks: An Empirical Analysis of Institutional Collective Action Framework." *Urban Affairs Review* 44 (3): pp. 378–402.

Atkins, Patricia S. 2008. "Metropolitan Forms, Fiscal Efficiency, and Other Bottom Lines." pp. 53–91 in *Urban and Regional Policies for Metropolitan Livability*. Edited by David K. Hamilton and Patricia S. Atkins. New York: M. E. Sharpe.

Bay Area Council. 2015. "About Us." Accessed on November 15, 2015 from www.bayareacouncil.org/about-us/

Brown, Trevor, and Potoski, Matthew. 2003. "Contract Management Capacity in Municipal and County Governments." *Public Administration Review* 63 (2): pp. 153–164.

Carr, J. 2004. "Whose Game Do We Play? Local Government Boundary Change and Metropolitan Governance." pp. 212–239 in *Metropolitan Governance: Conflict, Competition, and Cooperation*. Edited by R. Feiock. Washington, D.C.: Georgetown University Press.

Cigler, Beverly A. 2008. "Economic Development in Metropolitan Areas." pp. 296–323 in *Urban and Regional Policies for Metropolitan Livability*. Edited by David K. Hamilton and Patricia S. Atkins. New York: M. E. Sharpe.

Derthick, M. 1999. *Dilemmas of Scale in America's Federal Democracy*. Washington, D.C.: Woodrow Wilson Center Press.

Durning, D., and Sanford, P. 2010. "Unification Promises and Outcomes. The Case of Athens and Clarke County, Georgia." pp. 215–244 in *City-County Consolidation: Promises Made, Promises Kept?* Edited by Suzanne M. Leland and Kurt Thurmaier. Washington, D.C.: Georgetown University Press.

ESRI. 2006. Accessed on November 5, 2015 from www.esri.com/library/brochures/pdfs/gis-sols-for-urban-planning.pdf

Feiock, Richard C. 2004. "Do Consolidation Entrepreneurs Make a Deal With the Devil?" In *City-County Consolidation and Its Alternatives: Reshaping the Local Government Landscape*. Edited by Jered B. Carr and Richard C. Feiock. Armonk, NY: Routledge.

Feiock, Richard C. 2007. "Rational Choice and Regional Governance." *Journal of Urban Affairs* 29: pp. 47–63.

Flynn, Laurie J. April 1, 2011. "Miami-Dade County Harnesses GIS Data." *Government Technology* 24 (4): pp. 15–18.

Foster, Kathryn, A. 2011. "A Region of One's Own." pp. 55–82 in *Regional Planning in America: Practice and Prospect*. Edited by Ethan Seltzer and Armando Carbonell. Cambridge, MA: Lincoln Institute of Land Policy.

Fregonese, John, and Gabbe, C. J. 2011. "Engaging the Public and Communicating Successfully in Regional Planning." pp. 222–242 in *Regional Planning in America: Practice and Prospects*. Edited by E. Seltzer and

A. Carbonell. Hollis, NH: Lincoln Institute of Land Policy.

Grodzins, Morton. (2013). "The Federal System." pp. 37–36 in *American Intergovernmental Relations: Foundations, Perspectives, and Issues*. Edited by Laurence J. O'Toole, Jr. and Robert K. Christensen. Washington, D.C.: Sage/CQ Press.

Groshgal, Benjamin Weinreb. 2013. "The Rocky Road to GIS." Data-Smart City Solutions. Harvard Kennedy School Ash Center. Cambridge, MA. Accessed on December 5, 2015 from http://datasmart.ash.harvard.edu/news/article/the-rocky-road-to-gis-276

Hartman, Chester. 1986. *City for Sale*. Philadelphia: Temple University Press.

Hefetz, Amir, and Warner, Mildred. 2004. "Privatization and Its Reverse: Explaining the Dynamics of the Government Contracting Process." *Journal of Public Administration Research and Theory* 14 (2): pp. 171–190.

Hitchings, Benjamin B. 1998. "A Typology of Regional Growth Management Systems." *Regionalist* 3 (1 and 2): pp. 1–14.

Hodge, Graeme A. 2000. *Privatization: An International Review of Performance*. Boulder, CO: Westview.

Joaquin, M. E., and Greitens, T. J. (2012). "Contract Management Capacity Breakdown? An Analysis of Local Governments From 1997 to 2007." *Public Administration Review* 72 (6): pp. 807–816.

Katz, B., and Bradley, J. 2013. *The Metropolitan Revolution: How Cities and Metros Are Fixing Our Broken Politics and Fragile Economy*. Washington, D.C.: Brookings Institution Press.

Leland, Suzanne M., and Johnson, Gary A. 2004. "Consolidation as a Local Reform: Why City-County Consolidation Is an Enduring Issue." In *City-County Consolidation and Its Alternatives: Reshaping the Local Government Landscape*. Edited by Jered B. Carr and Richard C. Feiock. Armonk, NY: Routledge.

Leland, Suzanne M., and Thurmaier, K. 2006. "Lessons From 35 Years of City-County Consolidation Attempts." In *Municipal Yearbook*. Washington, D.C.: ICMA.

McDearman, Brad, and Donahue, Ryan. 2015, May 27. *The 10 Lessons From Global Trade and Investment Planning in U.S. Metro Areas*. Washington, D.C. Brookings.

Miller, David Y. 2002. *The Regional Governing of Metropolitan America*. Cambridge, MA: Westview Press.

Miller, David Y. 2008. "Exploring the Structure of Regional Governance in the United States." pp. 1–23 in *Urban and Regional Policies for Metropolitan Livability*. Edited by David K. Hamilton and Patricia S. Atkins. New York: M. E. Sharpe.

Miller, David Y., and Cox, Raymond W. III. 2014. *Governing the Metropolitan Region: America's New Frontier*. Armonk, NY: M. E. Sharpe.

Montgomery, Carleton K. 2011a. "Introduction." pp. 1–31 in *Regional Planning for a Sustainable America*. Edited by Carleton K. Montgomery. Brunswick, NJ: Rutgers University Press.

Montgomery, Carleton K. 2011b. "Fulfilling the Promise of Regional Planning." pp. 346–361 in *Regional Planning for a Sustainable America*. Edited by Carleton K. Montgomery. Brunswick, NJ: Rutgers University Press.

NADO. National Association of Development Organizations. 2014. *Lessons From the Storm: Case Studies on Economic Recovery and Resilience*. Accessed on February 3, 2016 from www.nado.org/about/

NADO. National Association of Development Organizations. May 2015. *Creating Opportunity and Prosperity Through Strengthening Rural-Urban Connections*. Accessed on February 3, 2016 from https://www.nado.org/wp-content/uploads/2015/06/RuralUrbanConnections_FINAL_.pdf. Accessed on October 10, 2015

Nathan, Richard P. 2008. "Updating Theories of American Federalism." pp. 1–25 in *Intergovernmental Management for the 21st Century*. Edited by Timothy J. Conlan and Paul L. Posner. Washington, D.C.: Brookings Institution Press.

Neiman, Max. 2000. *Defending Government: Why Big Government Works*. Upper Saddle River, NJ: Prentice-Hall, Inc.

O'Neill, Robert Jr. June 27, 2012. "The Coming Decade of Local Government." *Governing*. Accessed on November 5, 2016 from http://www.governing.com/columns/mgmt-insights/col-coming-decade-local-government-citizen-trust.html

Ostrom, V., Tiebout, C., and Warren, R. 1961. "The Organization of Government in Metropolitan Areas: A Theoretical Inquiry." *American Political Science Review* 55 (4): pp. 831–842.

Pelissero, J. P. 2003. "The Political Environment of Cities in the Twenty-first Century." pp. 1–24 in *Cities, Politics, and Policy: A Comparative Analysis*. Edited by John P. Pelissero. Washington, D.C.: CQ Press.

Rittel, H. W., and Webber, M. (1973). "Dilemmas in a General Theory of Planning." *Policy Sciences* 4: pp. 155–169.

Salamon, Lester M. 2002. *The Tools of Government: A Guide to the New Governance*. New York: Oxford University Press.

Schattschneider, Elmer Eric. 1960. *The Semi-Sovereign People: A Realist View of Democracy in America*. New York: Holt, Rhinehart and Winston.

Seltzer, Ethan, and Carbonell, Armando. 2011. "Planning Regions." pp. 17–52 in *Regional Planning in America: Practice and Prospects*. Edited by E. Seltzer and A. Carbonell. Hollis, NH: Lincoln Institute of Land Policy.

Sluis, Matt Vander. April 11, 2017. "Draft of New 'Plan Bay Area' Calls for More Sustainable, Inclusive Future." Greenbelt Alliance. Accessed on June 23, 2017 from http://www.greenbelt.org/blog/draft-new-plan-bay-area-calls-sustainable-inclusive-future/

State of California, Senate Local Government Committee. 2010. *What's So Special about Special Districts?* 4th ed. Sacramento, CA. Accessed on October 10, 2015 from http://www.sco.ca.gov/ard_locarep_districts.html

State of California, State Controller's Office. 2013. *Special Districts' Annual Report*.

Stephens, G. Ross, and Wiskstrom, Nelson. 1999. *Metropolitan Government and Governments: Theoretical Perspectives, Empirical Analysis, and the Future*. New York: Oxford University Press.

Stephens, G. Ross, and Wikstrom, Nelson. 2007. *American Intergovernmental Relations: A Fragmented Federal Polity*. New York, NY: Oxford University Press.

Thurmaier, Kurt, and Wood, Curtis. 2002. "Interlocal Agreements as Overlapping Social Network: Picket-fence Regionalism in Metropolitan Kansas City." *Public Administration Review* 62 (5): pp. 585–598.

United States Bureau of the Census. 2015. *Local Governments by Type and State, 2012*. Washington, D.C. Accessed on March 2, 2016 from http://factfinder.census.gov/faces/tableservices/jsf/pages/productview.xhtml?src=bkmk

U.S. Department of Transportation. 2014. *Model Long-Range Transportation Plans: A Guide for Incorporating Performance-Based Planning*. Washington, D.C.: Federal Highway Administration.

Vander Veen, Chad. March 31, 2014. "Reinventing America City by City." *Government Technology: Solutions for State and Local Government*. Accessed on September 3, 2015 from www.govtech.com/local/Reinventing-America.html

Visser, James A. 2004. "Voluntary Regional Councils and the New Regionalism: Effective Governance in the Smaller Metropolis." *Journal of Planning Education and Research* 24: pp. 55–63.

Wallis, Allan. 2008. "Developing Regional Capacity to Plan Land Use and Infrastructure." pp. 92–125 in *Urban and Regional Policies for Metropolitan Livability*. Edited by David K. Hamilton and Patricia S. Atkins. New York: M. E. Sharpe.

Warner, Mildred, and Hefetz, Amir. 2010. *Privatization and Reverse Privatization in US Local Government Service Delivery*. Paper prepared for Public Service International and the Council of Global Unions Conference, Geneva, Switzerland. October.

Wood, Colin. June 3, 2013a. "Hawaii Uses Collaborate.org as Its Data Sharing Backbone." *Government Technology*. Accessed on November 5, 2015 from www.govtech.com/geospatial/Hawaii-Uses-Collaborate-org-as-its-Data-Sharing-Backbone.html

Wood, Colin. April 5, 2013b. "Overcoming Hindrances to Public-Sector Collaboration." *Government Technology*. Accessed on December 6, 2015 from www.govtech.com/policy-management/Overcoming-Hindrances-to-Public-Sector-Collaboration.html

Wright, Deil. 1988. *Understanding Intergovernmental Relations*, 3rd ed. Pacific Grove, CA: Brooks-Cole.

Zeemering, Eric, and Delabbio, Daryl. 2013. *A County Manager's Guide to Shared Services in Local Government*. Washington, D.C.: IBM Center for the Business of Government.

Engaging
Urban Residents

Thomas highlights the role of citizens in communities today as citizens, customers, and partners (Thomas 2012). Public administrators often believe that more citizen input into the public policy process will improve government, because citizen engagement improves government transparency and, thus, residents' trust in government (Kim and Lee 2012). Moreover, citizen engagement has become more and more important for city government, as seen in two NASPAA Urban Administration student learning standards:

- 3. Articulate the purposes of and processes for communicating with citizens in local governance.

(Commission of Peer Review and Accreditation (COPRA), 2009)

The current chapter describes the different types of communication with citizens and citizen engagement and the many different types of citizen engagement strategies available to city governments; in today's environment, many of these strategies involve social media strategies and technology.

Lukensmeyer and Torres (2006) define citizen engagement as "part of a family of democratic reform ideas that includes public participation, public involvement, participatory democracy, deliberative democracy, and collaborative governance" (p. 9) and "a commitment from government to cultivate deeper levels of knowledge among citizens generally about the issue at hand and potential solutions, and to provide opportunities for citizens to exercise that knowledge in service of policy and program development on a regular and ongoing basis" (p. 8). They argue that government managers need to shift from just exchanging information (communicating) with citizens to allowing citizens to process information about policies and to engage actively. They also argue that managers need to move from seeing residents as merely passive consumers of government processes to being active shapers of policies and programs. Lukensmeyer and Torres (2006, p. 7) suggest a spectrum of citizen involvement with citizens becoming more and more active, ranging from just informing, consulting, engaging, and collaborating with citizens, to empowering them.

A pyramid of civic engagement (Figure 4.1) provides a more descriptive idea of the scope of engagement with each stage of involvement.

Today, many cities recognize the importance of civic engagement and have appointed Citizen or Civic Engagement Officers for various departments or delegated these activities

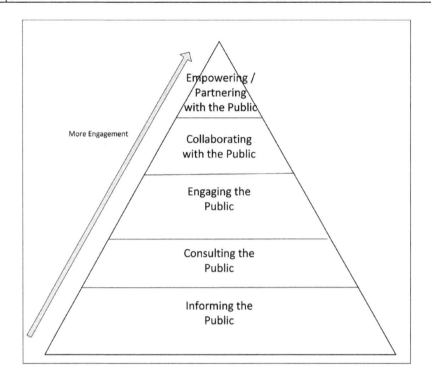

FIGURE 4.1
Pyramid of Civic Engagement

Source: Developed from Lukensmeyer and Torres, 2006, Table 1, p. 7.

to staff with other responsibilities. As with budgeting and human resources, these functions can be treated as staff functions and exist across the city structure.

In today's cities, there are numerous reasons to try to engage citizens (Bryson, Quick, Slotterback and Crosby 2012, pp. 25–26: Table 2; Lukensmeyer and Torres 2006). These include:

- In some cases, the fact that citizen participation is required by law;
- Educating and informing the public about issues and the consequences of potential solutions;
- Enhancing government's capacity for decision-making by improving information;
- Legitimately providing citizens a chance to impact government and its policies, as expressed by democratic theory;
- Enhancing citizen support for government policies;
- Increasing the trust citizens have in government by providing opportunities for input and transparency about public processes; and
- Thereby, increasing government legitimacy.

Whatever the reason, many governments, including cities, are incorporating ways to more effectively engage their citizens in the policy-making and implementation processes and are actively experimenting with new techniques and technologies for doing so. Many engagement processes in the past have not been effective, achieving only cynical citizens and forgotten input. Experts in the field now believe the quality of civic engagement is influenced by how the processes themselves are designed.

CIVIC ENGAGEMENT TOOLS

Using the five levels of involvement suggested by Lukensmeyer and Torres (2006), Table 4.1 suggests a categorization of various civic engagement tools across the five levels of civic engagement. Each of the tools is then described.

TABLE 4.1

Civic Engagement Tools and Techniques

Goals	Techniques/Tools
Informing the public	• Poster and media campaigns • Social media • Websites • Study circles
Consulting the public	• Aggregate opinions from social media • Citizen advisory groups • Citizens juries • Conversation cafés • Crowdsourcing • E-consultation: discussion forums, online chats • Online simulation games to help the public understand policy issues • Opinion polls/surveys • Public comment periods • Public meetings
Engaging the public	• Town hall meetings • 21st Century Town Meetings • Charrettes • Public deliberations: a wide variety of techniques • Online deliberations using a variety of tools • Deliberative polls • ChoiceWork Dialogues
Collaborating with the public	• Idea generation and priority ranking (group decision-making tools) • Online collaborative document development • Multi-stakeholder negotiations • Policy consensus processes • Public deliberations • Using shared online work spaces for policy development • Wikis
Empowering/partnering with the public	• Budget/policy simulations • Coproduction of services • Participatory budgeting

Source: Adapted from Lukensmeyer and Torres (2006, p. 17: Table 3: Four Levels of Public Involvement) and Thomas (2012) with many added tools.

Informing the Public, or One-Way Communication

A public affairs office or staff person in any local government department will have the responsibility for informing the public, the most basic form of civic engagement—and also, the most passive and one-directional of all means. Informing the public involves one-way communication from the city to the residents.

Poster and media campaigns. Public Affairs staff can release information to the public on any topic through press releases or signs posted throughout the community or in city buildings.

Social media. Social media like Facebook, Twitter, or blogs can be used to provide information to the public, while social media sites like Flickr, Instagram, or Pinterest can be used to release images. Social media will be discussed in depth later in this chapter.

Websites. One of the most important functions of e-government, through cities' websites, is to inform the public on demand, 24–7–365.

Consulting the Public

Consulting the public also entails one-way information; in this case, information comes from residents to the city.

Aggregate opinions from social media. Cities can use surveys to query the public about different topics and then use the aggregated totals to draw conclusions about what the public thinks.

Crowdsourcing. Over the Internet's various means of communicating, organizers propose a call for help, information, or input on a particular issue and a means for submitting participants' ideas. Participants self-select whether or not they join in, and the organizers then draw conclusions from the results.

E-consultation, discussion forums, online chats. These are more formal means of seeking engagement; the city can open up a discussion on an online forum or have online chat sessions about particular topics.

Online simulation games. Used to help the public understand policy issues, online simulations are often used to gain public input into their priorities on budgets. The online component then allows the users to choose the amounts they would give to each budget category, with the online system determining whether the result was a balanced budget or not.

Opinion polls/surveys. Cities can survey their residents to discern their views on any topic. Using computer-aided telephone interviewing (CATI), survey firms can ask complex questions with the different kinds of options that are likely to be involved in many difficult public policy issues.

Public comment periods. A public comment period can be held at any point during any public meeting to accept input from residents on any topic. Residents wishing to speak sign in, and, once the item is on the agenda, the individual chairing the meeting calls on the residents and hears their comments.

Public hearings. A public hearing is a widely used means of trying to understand resident views on an issue or a project; statutes or local regulations often require public hearings. A topic for the hearing is announced along with place, date, and time. Residents attend the hearing and take turns providing their opinions on the topic to officials at the meeting.

(Participipedia.net 2015)

Engaging the Public

Engaging the public involves a two-way exchange of information or actual dialogue on some public policy issue. There are many deliberative engagement techniques and tools. Face-to-face deliberative techniques include small groups and face-to-face discussions; the differences among them are in the number of participants engaged, how the participants receive information about the issue, and how they decide upon their conclusions.

Charrettes. Charrettes are deliberative engagement and consultative processes often used in urban planning processes. Charrettes can involve anywhere from 50 to 1,000 participants, are representative of the community, and can last for days or weeks (recommended four to seven days [Lennertz, Lutzenhiser and Failor 2008]). There are three stages: the planning or pre-charrette stage, the workshop stage, and the post-charrette stage. During the workshop stage, participants meet in small groups to discuss the issues, develop priorities, and then work out strategies and designs for specific projects. The post-charrette involves a final report on the project. While charrettes are used for a wide variety of policy issues, they have been adopted by a range of planning communities for use in development processes. (Participedia 2015; National Charrette Institute 2015). Between participant meetings, planners provide a design to provide a vision for a project or community, which is then taken back to the participants and stakeholders for more input, in a very iterative process. Often, the design team involves a project sponsor and a multidisciplinary group including architects, planners, engineers, and others (Lennertz et al. 2008). The final report then encapsulates the ideas and priorities captured over a period of some meetings from a wide variety of participants.

BOX 4.1 CAREER PATHWAYS OF A CIVIC ENGAGEMENT PROFESSIONAL

Current Position

Hua is an Online Engagement Manager for a large city; she has been in that position since 2014. Officially, her classification is "City Administrator Analyst," and she reports to a Deputy City Administrator. She works on broader digital strategies that leverage technology to engage community members in Oakland.

Education

B.A. in Sociology

Other Training

Coursework at General Assembly training group in User Acquisition Marketing and Digital Marketing

Career Pathway

Hua began her career at a service organization working with homeless veterans. As the agency's first Policy Analyst, she worked in the heart of a large city to identify and communicate the struggles of the more than 2,000 at-risk and chronically homeless military veterans. In that position, she presented to the State Senate, the U.S. Veterans Administration, and other key decision-makers to speak on enhancing government process. Later, she joined the U.S. Department of Labor to implement and manage performance measures for hundreds of nonprofit employment programs, including more than 100 community partners in eight U.S. states.

▶ BOX 4.1 (CONTINUED)

Then, she got the position as an Online Engagement Manager to innovate and untangle complex government processes and support the City in presenting community issues and services in a digestible way. One specific project is to oversee a key City initiative, the "Digital Front Door," which is reinventing the way American cities provide digital services to their constituencies, in partnership with Code for America.

Learning about the Job

Hua learned what she needed to do the job via on the job training at start-up companies, policy organizations, government agencies, and nonprofits.

A Typical Day

Here's a typical schedule for Hua:

8 am: Review priority emails.

8:45 am: Head to the office; likely take a phone call on the way to the office.

9:30 am: First check-in with partners on City website redesign project.

9:45 am: Glance at the City's social media accounts for anything urgent that needs to be pushed out and responded to — she oversees the City's main Twitter and Facebook presences).

10 am: Check-in with worker from Fellowship program and contractors that she is managing (she oversees a content writer, a web coder, and a few other contracts).

10:30 am: Meet with volunteers and staff working in the City Civic Design Lab (she is working to develop a design lab and engagement center inside City Hall).

11:30 am: Short break, long enough to grab lunch and bring it back to her desk.

11:45 am: Return phone calls requesting tech support around the public records request system (which she also oversees); check for any public records request in her inbox or other urgent issues.

12:30 pm: Review the City homepage, social media, etc. in preparation for a 1 pm Communications meeting.

1 pm: Communications meeting — She meets with the City Public Information Officer, Media Relations Coordinator, and Communications Director to identify any Citywide issues.

2:30 pm: Review City contracts for renewal or negotiation. (In many cases, she reviews potential City digital products or digital solutions and offers advisement and executes City contracts with vendors.)

3:00 pm: Attend meeting around some Citywide issue (e.g., housing, City emergencies, shootings, etc).

4:00 pm: Review outbound messaging and content to be published on the City website.

5:00 pm: Work on drafting City "administrative instruction" (e.g., internal policies, procedures).

6:30 pm: Go home. Eat. Exercise.

9:00 pm: Respond to emails. Review documents at the request of various City partners and entities.

Professional Associations and Networking

Hua belongs to and is active with the International Association for Public Participation (IAP2, www.iap2.org/). She also attends events in the tech community and community events for the City. Additionally, she attends a few events with early career professionals around her age and stage of career. Mostly, her networking strategy is to identify leaders in her industry and reach out to them personally for coffee or informational phone calls and mentoring.

Most Rewarding Part of the Job

The most rewarding aspect of Hua's job has been to be able to introduce new ideas and concepts into government.

▶ BOX 4.1 (CONTINUED)

Most Helpful to Her Career

Understanding internal politics and issues have been key in getting anything done in City government. The expertise and knowledge that she has adopted have helped her work effectively in an extremely lean but innovative organization.

Challenges

The biggest challenge for her has been being a young female professional of color. She is constantly asked for her credentials and has colleagues that cite "decades" of expertise, research, and knowledge to negate her insights. Furthermore, she finds she has to repeat herself through several meetings to have a point heard, minimally acknowledged, and sometimes adopted.

To address this challenge, she tries to present ideas in a variety of formats: in person, in writing, and through presentations. Typically, that requires communication in all three formats for an acknowledgment from colleagues.

Recommendations for Students

Hua would say: just do it. There is no perfect degree, and most of the jobs in technology and the "civic engagement and technology" space have yet to be invented. Her job did not even exist when she graduated college eight years ago.

ChoiceWork Dialogues. ChoiceWork Dialogue is a face-to-face deliberation technique including between 30 and 45 representative participants, selected randomly. The first part of the session is the "Opinion Formation" process, where participants review workbook materials prepared about the policy issue. Next, they meet in small groups in a "Working Through" session, where they first take a survey on the topic and discuss the policy options, possible trade-offs between various solutions and scenarios, as well as funding. At the end of the session, they take another survey; the results of this survey comprise the citizen input on this topic. The whole session lasts approximately eight hours. This process is used for a variety of policy issues in the United States and Canada, including health care, education, and environmental issues.

(Participedia.net 2015)

Citizen advisory boards. In many communities, volunteer citizen advisory boards are legally required means of accessing citizen input. Board members are selected to represent the community, often by fulfilling certain proscribed roles (e.g., neighborhood member, architect, planner, realtor, etc. on a planning board). When important decisions have to be made by cities, these citizen advisory boards are then consulted after being presented with information about an issue.

(Participedia.net 2015)

Citizen conferences. Citizen conferences are typically one-day events for small (recommended 6 to 18) groups of citizens selected randomly from a community. Participating in discussion, dialogue, and deliberation, conference participants ("citizen advisors") usually receive a nominal fee for attending. Participants listen to presentations from a panel of experts on the policy issue of concern then break into small groups to discuss options and solutions. They can consult with the experts during their deliberation. The goal of the participant-citizen advisors is to arrive at a set of recommendations that are then presented to the public.

(Participedia.net 2015)

Citizens juries. Like a jury in a judicial setting, a citizens jury is made up of randomly selected individuals from the community (from 18 to 24). Created by the Jefferson Center in Minneapolis, the process brings selected participants together, who hear expert witnesses providing information about an issue (just as in a trial), and then deliberate on a "verdict." A final report is also written. This process has been used on health policy issues as well as to compare candidates for office.

(Participedia.net 2015; Lukensmeyer and Torres 2006)

Conversation cafés. Conversation cafés are more informal means of seeking public input. Tables are set up in local coffee shops, and hosts assemble small groups of people and arrange a dialogue on a particular issue, based on a set agenda. A "talking object," an object that is held by the person who has the floor to speak, is then passed around to others so that they may speak. Begun in Seattle, conversation cafés also offer subdivisions of the method (Café Lite, or short conversations; Instant Café, or spontaneous discussions; and Super Café, or large events).

(Participedia.net 2015)

Deliberative polling. Deliberative polling combines citizen deliberation with polling before and after educational sessions on an issue, to inform citizens and then learn how their views changed. Begun by Stanford faculty member James Fishkin in 1988, the method has now been used in a variety of countries across the world.

(Participedia.net 2015; Lukensmeyer and Torres 2006)

e-Deliberation. e-Deliberation was an online tool that allowed collaborative decisions among participants. In the system, ideas or other contributions were awarded points. The final result was a strategy on the issue of interest. However, this platform was shut down in February 2015 since it "failed to reach escape velocity."

(Participedia.net 2015; retrieved from
http://participedia.net/en/methods/e-deliberation)

Study circles. Participants learn about and discuss issues in a series of small groups (8 to 12 individuals); participants then come together to develop recommendations, based on what they have learned. First developed in Sweden, this method is also called Dialogue-to-Change, Dialogue-to-Action, or dialogue circles.

(Participedia.net 2015; Lukensmeyer and Torres 2006)

21st Century Town Meetings. A 21st Century Town Meeting is a process developed by America Speaks; it can include anywhere from 500 to 5,000 participants who should be representative of the entire community. Members sit in small groups with a facilitator and discuss the policy issue of interest. During the session, a moderator uses wireless handheld devices to call periodically for straw votes on the issue or solutions. Ultimately, each group's scribe captures the discussion, and themes in the discussion are input into group decision-making software or groupware. A final report contains recommendations, the themes, and the results of the final polls.

(Participedia.net 2015; Lukensmeyer and Torres 2006)

Collaborating with the Public

Collaborating with the public involves much more active, two-directional strategies of civic engagement.

> *Idea generation and priority ranking.* Many tools are available to help groups generate ideas while working together. Basic brainstorming techniques are frequently used in lots of group interactions, and, now, online tools and software are available that help individuals visualize their generated ideas. Beyond that, group decision-making software allows groups to generate ideas and then prioritize and vote for items while group members remain anonymous, allowing for much easier discussion among members.
>
> *Online collaborative document development.* Online document development tools like Google Docs could be used by city officials to seek input on proposals. Under this process, a draft proposal would be posted online, open to all, and citizens could then comment on and edit the draft.
>
> *Shared online work spaces for policy development.* Similar to online collaborative document development, shared online work spaces can be used. An online room designated for proposed policy discussion can be set up for discussions between participants. The policy discussion can be shared with city officials so they can learn about views on policies.
>
> *Wikis.* Wikis are online sites that enable registered individuals to add text or edit existing text of a document. They can be used as brainstorming tools and as ways to solicit input and discussion on ideas already generated. San Jose, California used a wiki-like tool called Wikiplanning to seek input from its residents during a futures project called 2040 Envision San Jose. Citizens began by going online, viewing a video, and reading online materials. The city ended up with more than 4,500 online participants and 240 pages of comments.

(Leighninger 2011)

Empowering/Partnering with the Public

Empowering or working with the public is the most participative type of civic engagement. Citizens not only provide their input; they actively work with city officials on projects.

> *Budget/policy simulations.* These can be important tools for empowering the public. Cities such as Alameda, California and others have partnered with nonprofit vendors and other organizations to present their citizens with these interactive tools, particularly when faced with difficult budgetary situations. These tools have allowed citizens to act as budget decision-makers; they work with policy choices in an interactive online environment until their budget is "balanced." A California nonprofit, Next 10 (next10.org), licenses its interactive web-based app to cities interested in using the tool in their community. Several cities across the country have utilized this application, including the City of Long Beach, California (Figure 4.2).

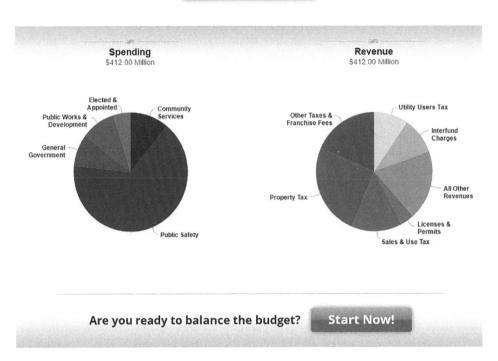

FIGURE 4.2
City of Long Beach, California Budget Challenge Opening Page

Source: Next 10. 2017. Long Beach Budget Challenge. Accessed on February 19, 2017 from http://longbeach.budgetchallenge.org/pages/overview.

Participatory budgeting. Participatory budgeting will be discussed in depth in the next chapter. The process involving a great deal of planning and citizen involvement has now been used extensively in many cities and jurisdictions around the world and has a great deal of potential.

ENGAGING WITH TECHNOLOGY

Technology is everywhere today, and so, of course, it needs to be part of any city's civic engagement strategy. However, it is important to remember that not everyone has access to computers or knows how to use them. Using the Internet requires the basic skills necessary to operate a web browser, to effectively utilize search engines and features like online forms and drop-down menus, and to navigate using hyperlinks while still being able to situate oneself in an online location. Then the user must also know how to access information and features by searching and reaching a particular feature (van Deursen and van Dijk 2009). Finally, to use social media or discussion forums, the user must also know how to sign up for accounts and effectively utilize other kinds of software.

Leighninger (2011) categorizes online tools into those that help users collaborate, those that survey attitudes, and those that help users prioritize options. To those should be added tools that allow discussion and questioning.

Social Media Engagement

The universe of social media today includes a wide variety of tools (Table 4.2), spread far beyond the social networking that dominates the field. The most dominant of these are Facebook and other social networking tools, including LinkedIn, a professional networking tool; governments often use these tools to make announcements or to post job notices. Twitter, a microblogging tool with only 140 characters per message or tweet, is another widely used tool for making announcements. Some governments have blogs (weB LOGS) by elected or appointed officials, which can be used to talk about policy issues or upcoming events. Videos of the mayor, the council, or special events are posted by many cities on video sites like YouTube, as are pictures (on photo sites like Flickr, Pinterest, Instagram, or even Snapchat).

Crowdsourcing is a way of gathering input in a relatively rapid manner; tools like Mindmixer or UserVoice are used for those purposes. Online policy discussions can be handled by any discussion forum technology; one example is Peak Democracy.

Social media management tools become more useful the more focused an agency's social media strategy is. Given Twitter's current demand for only 140 characters, sites like Bitly or TinyURL can be used to produce a short URL that can be placed in a tweet and sent out, rather than having to use a long URL.

TABLE 4.2

Social Media Tools for Local Government

Type of Social Media Tool	Examples
Social networking	Facebook, LinkedIn, Google+
Microblog	Twitter
Blog	WordPress, Tumblr
Video	YouTube, Vimeo
Photo or image sharing	Flickr, Pinterest, Instagram, Snapchat
Crowdsourcing	Mindmixer, UserVoice
Online discussion tool	Peak Democracy
Utility to reduce size of web links	TinyURL, Bitly
Organizing tool for social media	Hootsuite

Source: Based upon Schulz 2013. Figure 2: The Electronic Communication Toolbox.

> ► **TABLE 4.3**
>
> **Pew Internet Foundation Survey Results on Use of Social Media Tools, 2015**
>
> | | All Adults | Online Adults | Online Urban Adults | Online Suburban Adults |
> |---|---|---|---|---|
> | Facebook | 58% | 71% | 71% | 72% |
> | LinkedIn | 23 | 28 | 32 | 29 |
> | Pinterest | 22 | 28 | 25 | 29 |
> | Instagram | 21 | 26 | 28 | 26 |
> | Twitter | 19 | 23 | 25 | 23 |
>
> *Source:* Duggan, Maeve, Ellison, Nicole B., Lampe, Cliff, Lenhart, Amanda, and Madden, Mary. 2015. "Social Media Update 2014." Accessed on October 19, 2015 from www.pewinternet.org/2015/01/09/social-media-update-2014/ (p. 2, 5, 6, 7, 8).

The use of social media tools by city governments for civic engagement becomes more important as more Americans use these tools. Table 4.3 shows that 58 percent of all American adults (71 percent of all online adults) use Facebook, the most heavily used social media tool. The data also indicate there is little difference in the usage of these social media tools between online urban and suburban adults and all online adults (Duggan, Ellison, Lampe, Lenhart and Madden 2015).

There has been a strong movement of local governments onto social media. In a 2015 survey of ICMA membership, 88.2 percent reported their local government had some social media presence. Facebook was the most widely used (80 percent), followed by Twitter (60 percent), YouTube (39 percent), and LinkedIn (28 percent). Respondents reported far less usage of any other tools (ICMA 2015, p. 5).

Using Twitter in Cities

The development of Twitter skills is very easy. Twitter users' addresses are preceded by the @ symbol. Tweets from other users can be re-sent with or without comments. With the use of the # symbol (hashtag) before a term or phrase, users interested in the same issue may track tweets on the same topic. Using this feature, users can track the quickly moving Twitter universe to see what issues, people, or events are "trending." Users follow one another and gain more and more followers to see tweets; they form networks or subnetworks based upon whom they know or their interests. Once users start to follow other users, their Twitter "feed" becomes a series of automatic updates from all they follow.

The potential for Twitter as a civic engagement tool is enormous. As of June 30, 2015 (according to the company), Twitter had 316 million users, 80 percent of whom were active users on their mobile devices; 500 million tweets were sent every day (Twitter 2015). The reach of important events or individuals is now routinely measured by how many tweets are sent; in fact, the interest in them is often tracked by a graph showing the number of tweets per minute over time.

Government agencies like cities will often use Twitter to follow up on press releases by sending the release out via all social media venues as well as to traditional media; they may also highlight the release of a report, or call attention to an important trend or

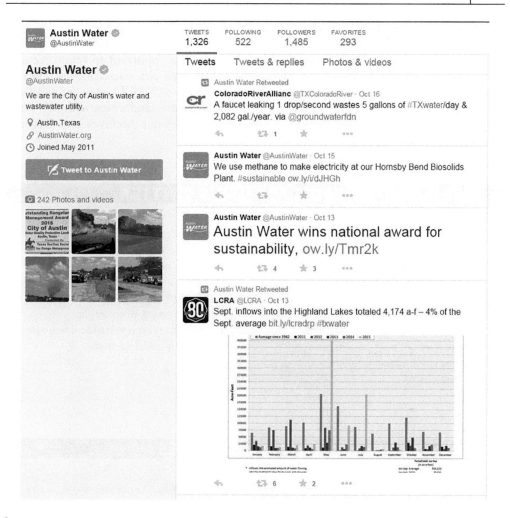

FIGURE 4.3
Use of Twitter by Austin, Texas Water Department

Source: Austin Water. 2015. Twitter Fee. Accessed on October 19, 2015, from https://twitter.com/AustinWater.

event. Individual city agencies may do the same but, of course, would focus on their issues and news. Because a tweet can include links to photos, URLs, videos, or other media, it has a great deal of utility, and can vastly increase how far the information goes (Mergel 2012). Twitter posts can also automatically go to Facebook and other social media outlets. Figure 4.3 illustrates the use of Twitter by the Austin, Texas Water Department (@AustinWater).

Further, city agencies should not just use Twitter to post events but could also use it to have conversations over policy and other issues with their citizens, as another channel of communication. Lee Rainie, the director of the Pew Research Center's Internet and American Life Project, states, "The common reputation of Twitter is that it is frivolous, which isn't the case. If it's set up right, it is a rich environment of lots of learning and sharing of important material. It is not just 'what I had for breakfast'" (Mergel 2012, p. 13).

A critical point about Twitter and some other types of social media is that, for government agencies with official records-keeping policies or laws, Twitter feeds, like emails, are considered official records. As such, it will be important to retain records of the official Twitter feeds and to incorporate them into city social media policies. The federal National Archives and Records Administration (NARA) provides excellent guidance on ways federal agencies can retain social media, and cities with the same type of policies can find their information helpful (National Archives and Records Administration 2013).

BOX 4.2 STRATEGIES FOR USING TWITTER

Strategies for using Twitter include:

1. Push, or "informational broadcasting" to push out information from the city;
2. Pull, which is educational in nature, as city officials comment on events or policies or "pull" citizens back to the city's website for more information;

3. Networking, a transactional and empowering strategy, as staff interact with community members on issues through "responsible exchanges" (Mergel 2012, p. 16); and
4. Customer Service, when service representatives provide standard responses to frequently asked questions.

(Mergel 2012)

BOX 4.3 USES OF TWITTER BY CITIES

Some of the ways cities can use Twitter include:

• Highlighting events;
• Starting a conversation about a policy issue;

• "Live tweeting," or commenting on, a city conference;
• Showing off an award received by a city department; and
• Sending out the link to an important new report.

Social media managers will need to utilize advanced tools to be able to handle the volume of messages with which they might be interacting. There are several tools, like Tweet-Deck and Hootsuite, available today to help users manage multiple Twitter accounts, and more are emerging all the time.

Wikis

Wikis are shared online documents on which users can work together to write and edit a document. Wiki software (MediaWiki, DokuWiki, FlexWiki, and others) can track edits made in a document. Wikis can be used by government agencies to allow open, collaborative project work sites, to gather comments on a policy, report, or document.

The U.S. Environmental Protection Agency has a wiki called Watershed Central Wiki (https://wiki.epa.gov/watershed2/index.php/Main_Page) that offers those interested in watershed management the opportunity to identify the watershed of their interest on a map and then write an article on the watershed. Users are invited to provide best practices or case studies, talk about management tools, or add any other watershed-oriented information. Articles are included about everything from decision support tools to managing volunteers.

Melbourne, Australia's wiki was used for planning for the city's future in the Future Melbourne Wiki (Figure 4.4). The wiki is one of many participatory tools, including blogs and public forums, that the Melbourne community was invited to use to comment on the plan, discuss it, or even edit the city plan. The project began with six public forums to introduce issues before the City. Transcripts of these and a variety of other public meetings were posted in the wiki, and citizens were asked to comment. An editorial team worked quickly with comments as they were posted, moving or incorporating them into the plan so that users would realize they had been incorporated (Mergel 2011).

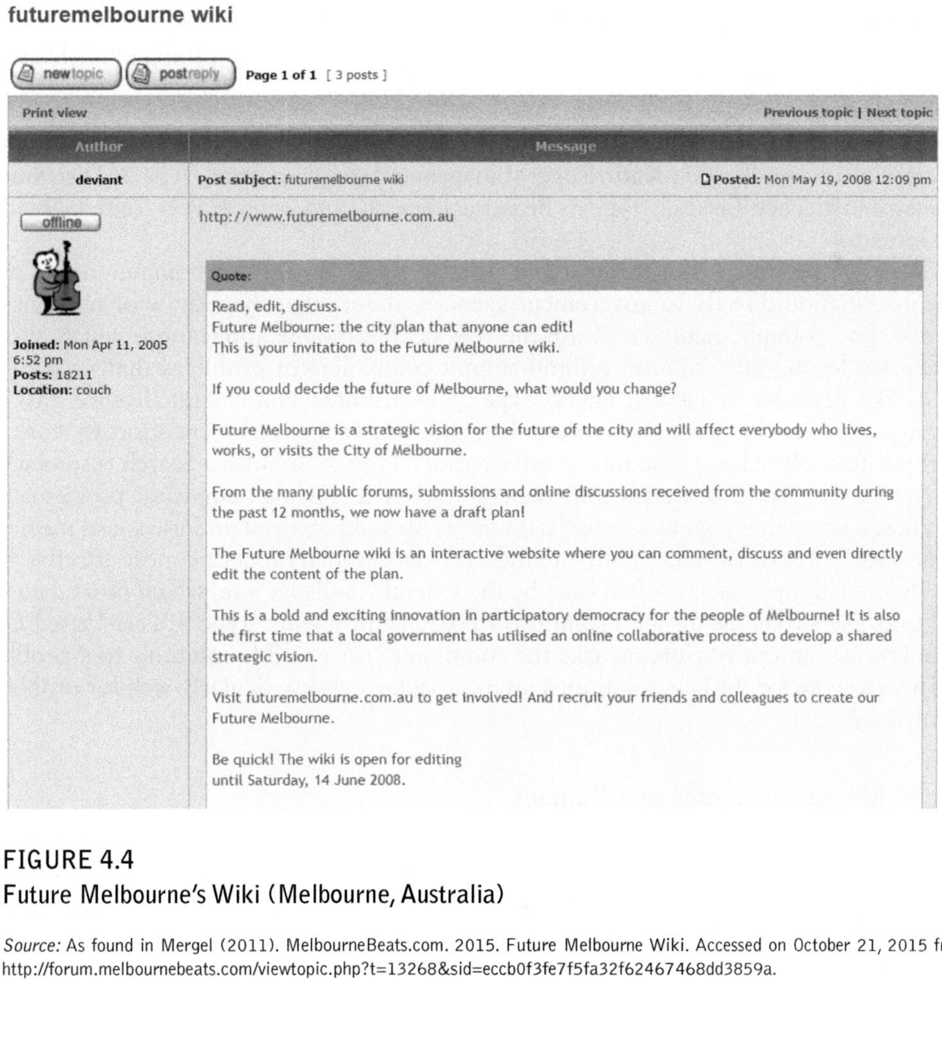

futuremelbourne wiki

(newtopic) (postreply)   **Page 1 of 1** [3 posts]

Print view		Previous topic | Next topic
Author	Message	
deviant	**Post subject:** futuremelbourne wiki	Posted: Mon May 19, 2008 12:09 pm

offline

Joined: Mon Apr 11, 2005 6:52 pm
Posts: 18211
Location: couch

http://www.futuremelbourne.com.au

> **Quote:**
> Read, edit, discuss.
> Future Melbourne: the city plan that anyone can edit!
> This is your invitation to the Future Melbourne wiki.
>
> If you could decide the future of Melbourne, what would you change?
>
> Future Melbourne is a strategic vision for the future of the city and will affect everybody who lives, works, or visits the City of Melbourne.
>
> From the many public forums, submissions and online discussions received from the community during the past 12 months, we now have a draft plan!
>
> The Future Melbourne wiki is an interactive website where you can comment, discuss and even directly edit the content of the plan.
>
> This is a bold and exciting innovation in participatory democracy for the people of Melbourne! It is also the first time that a local government has utilised an online collaborative process to develop a shared strategic vision.
>
> Visit futuremelbourne.com.au to get involved! And recruit your friends and colleagues to create our Future Melbourne.
>
> Be quick! The wiki is open for editing until Saturday, 14 June 2008.

FIGURE 4.4
Future Melbourne's Wiki (Melbourne, Australia)

Source: As found in Mergel (2011). MelbourneBeats.com. 2015. Future Melbourne Wiki. Accessed on October 21, 2015 from http://forum.melbournebeats.com/viewtopic.php?t=13268&sid=eccb0f3fe7f5fa32f62467468dd3859a.

Mergel also provides several best practices for agencies using wikis. She suggests:

- Having managers participate in the wikis themselves to lead the way and model the importance of using the wiki;
- Setting a time limit for contributions;
- Having users sign in before using to try to reduce negative comments;
- Using moderators to monitor comments and work to build a coherent document from comments, if that is the goal; and
- Making sure to thank those who contribute to the wiki.

(Mergel 2011, p. 31)

Crowdsourcing

Unlike most other social media, crowdsourcing is not reliant upon one type of software. Instead, it is a phenomenon that can occur with or without technology, although, mostly, it does include a technology angle. Crowdsourcing is when:

- "An organization has a task it needs to be performed
- An online community voluntarily performs the task
- The result is mutual benefit for the organization and the online community."

(Brabham 2013, p. 1)

It also involves a combination of top-down and bottom-up processes.

Brabham (2013) identifies four kinds of government problems that can be addressed by crowdsourcing: Type 1: Knowledge Management and Discovery, Type 2: Distributed Human Intelligence Tasking, Type 3: Broadcast Search, and Type 4: Peer-Vetted Creative Production.

Type 1: Knowledge Management and Discovery asks residents in communities to provide information directly to government agencies about what they know or find out on a topic. For example, many cities use the SeeClickFix mobile application, which allows citizens to locate, take pictures of, and submit complaints of problems that need to be fixed, like potholes or broken lights. Type 2: Distributed Human Intelligence Tasking recruits people in the community to use their time to join a government effort to work on a project to analyze large amounts of information. Type 3: Broadcast Search is somewhat different from Type 2 in that it asks the community to solve an empirical problem. For instance, a city could post bus transit data on its open data portal and use social media to request members of the community analyze the data to determine the most effective bus schedules. This approach is often used by the federal Challenge site, which posts datasets and asks users to come up with solutions to specific problems. Type 4: Peer-Vetted Creative Production crowdsourcing asks the community for possible solutions to a problem and also to vote for the best solution. This approach works particularly well for problems involving design.

Social Media Strategies and Policies

Social media should not be fragmented contributions or ad hoc means of civic engagement. Cities need to develop a strategy for effectively using social media. This strategy needs to include the goals for the use of social media by the city, the ways in which various social media will be utilized, and the staff to be employed.

It is also crucial that cities develop sound policies for social media, both for official accounts and also to address employees' usage of their social media at work. Policies for official accounts will be addressed here. Important elements to address in a city's social media policy include discussions about:

BOX 4.4 CITIZEN ENGAGEMENT STRATEGIES FROM CITY SUSTAINABILITY PLANS

Some cities have citizen engagement strategies, like these, as part of their sustainability plans.

- "Provide regular, meaningful, and equitable opportunities for citizens to shape the future of their communities." Dover, New Hampshire, p. 2.
- "Require that local decision-making processes are transparent and evident to the public through the provision of information, participatory tools, education, and an open process." Dover, New Hampshire, p. 5.

- "Empower community development corporations, neighborhood advisory committees, and sustainability advocacy groups." St. Louis, Missouri, p. 116.

Sources: City of Dover, New Hampshire. Not Dated. City of Dover Sustainability Goals with Purpose Statements. Accessed on February 22, 2017 from www.dover.nh.gov/Assets/government/city-operations/2document/planning/outreach/sustainabilitygoals.pdf.
   City of St. Louis, Missouri. 2013. City of St. Louis Sustainability Plan. Accessed on February 22, 2017 from www.stlouis-mo.gov/government/departments/planning/documents/city-of-st-louis-sustainability-plan.cfm.

Public records laws. Technology is moving faster than most states are in updating their public records laws. Traditionally, public records were papers generated by the executive, legislative, judicial, or public agencies. Public records laws included requirements and standards for dealing with these records, including how long they have to be stored and how they can be accessed. Law-makers took some time to figure out how to deal with email, but, eventually, most laws now indicate that agency emails are also public records and must be treated accordingly. With the development of social media like Twitter, public records laws at the federal level indicate tweets are public records, but states and their laws are lagging behind, and the legal situation is not clear. To be safe, city agency tweets should not be deleted but must be kept in an archive just like other public records.

Official social media account management. Cities need to decide how many accounts to allow and who maintains those accounts. Should there be one overall account for the city, or should all departments also have accounts? In either of these cases, who is responsible for the account?

Social media message content and approval. Most importantly, who is responsible for creating and approving content from the city that goes out over social media? A long, involved vetting process would defeat the purpose of fast-paced social media. However, some coordination and approval process needs to be developed to ensure messages stick to the city's overall social media strategy, are appropriate, and are timely. References should also be made to the city's overall Acceptable Use Policy

(AUP), indicating the approved AUP of the city also applies to its usage of social media. Further, how often should content be pushed out via the various types of social media?

Acceptable uses. For social media that involves back and forth exchanges with citizens, like Facebook, policies need to include what is appropriate citizen conduct on city-sponsored sites, in responding to or addressing the city. Further, the policy needs to state the steps the city would take if users engaged in inappropriate conduct on city-sponsored sites; i.e., would the city take down the offending message, or would they remove the user's account altogether?

Freedom of information. Policies should address the need to abide by any freedom of information or e-discovery laws existing in their state, most likely by incorporating plans to store and manage appropriately social media from the city.

Disclaimers. Some cities incorporate disclaimers stating the city does not endorse outside entities, as well as references to the city's privacy and copyright policies.

(Hrdinova, Helbig and Peters 2010)

GUIDELINES FOR CIVIC ENGAGEMENT PROJECTS

Cities can also make use of guidelines for specific civic engagement projects. These guidelines can include some of the following:

- Determine the purpose and desired outcomes of the civic engagement exercise. Potential outcomes from the process should be not just substantive (i.e., polling data showing public responses) but also procedural (a process was set up that could continue in the future).
- Involve all stakeholders in the design and implementation of the exercise, including policy-makers.
- Based upon the desired purpose, determine the means for civic engagement; i.e., which of the many tools available will be used to engage? There are many tools and techniques of civic engagement. Choosing the right tool or technique depends on the complexity of the question being asked and the resources and time available for the process, as well as the expertise in civic engagement and group process available in the community.
- Set up guidelines and rules for the process, incorporating feedback from stakeholders as well as experts in the civic engagement tool selected.
- Determine the level of resources needed and seek to find them. Critical resources include time, substantive expertise, group process skills, and funds for copies, rooms, training, and similar items required for group meetings.
- Decide who needs to be involved in the actual civic engagement. ICMA (2014, p. 28) quotes Woodrow Wilson as saying, "I not only use the brains I have but all I can borrow." This provides some interesting direction to the question of who needs to be involved in any civic engagement process. Again, it is important to think of the potential project regarding both substance and process, when considering who needs to be invited. It is crucial to ensure opinions and residents from all groups of the city are included in the project to ensure diversity.
- Organize the engagement itself, reach out to potential participants, and begin to educate them on the process selected. Consider using both face-to-face and online

methods to engage. Work to ensure all issues discussed are framed in a neutral manner.

- Host your engagement yourself, ensuring you can evaluate both process and outcomes.
- Publicize the outcomes of the process and its successes.
- Afterward, make plans for improving the process for the future.
- Work to keep communication going with participants and sustain their involvement in the process.

(International City/County Management Association 2014a, pp. 17–18; Bryson et al. 2012: Table 1: Design Guidelines for Public Participation, p. 24; Lukensmeyer and Torres 2006, pp. 9–10)

BOX 4.5   MEASURING PERFORMANCE IN CIVIC ENGAGEMENT

Traditional performance measures for civic engagement are output measures that track interactions between city staff and the public:

- Number of people attending meetings;
- Number of people calling with comments; and
- Number of meetings held.

Since the birth of social media, a whole new group of metrics must be incorporated into an effective performance measurement scheme for citizen engagement. These are categorized into several areas:

1. Reach. Reach includes the number of followers (like in Twitter or Facebook) and the growth of those followers.
2. Engagement. On a website, engagement could involve the number of visits, the number of unique visits (eliminates the same person returning to the site), the number of page views, audience size, referrers (sites from which users came to your site), popular content, and search engine queries. On Twitter, engagement can be measured by number of impressions (number of times users saw the tweet), engagements (number of times users interacted with a tweet),

and the engagement rate (number of engagements divided by the number of impressions). The number of retweets and likes are critical Twitters measures, as are replies or clicks on any links in the tweet. For Facebook, important measures are the number of likes (or other interactions) and the number of shares.

3. Acquisition. Measures in this category are mostly for websites and involve the amount of time on the site and on individual pages, plus the percent of users who return to the website.

4. Conversion. This category is mostly for private sector efforts, where companies want to know if interacting with a tweet or a website will convert into users going to a site and buying something from the company. For the public sector, if tweets are being sent out for events, for instance, the city might want to know how many residents converted that action into actually coming to the event.

5. Activity. This category is also mostly for the private sector, which wants to know if the cost of running its social media is bringing in enough business to justify the money being spent.

(Chitwood 2013)

CONCLUSIONS

City managers working in civic engagement will always need to keep themselves updated on new strategies, new technologies, and the fast-moving best practices of what works and what does not. This chapter reviewed strategies and some best practices in the field, including the kinds of policies that are needed—to cover acceptable use, official account management, freedom of information, and disclaimers. In today's world, being able to engage the public is a crucial part of city management. Learning how to do that effectively is an ongoing process, and is an important component of what NASPAA believes urban administration students need to learn.

SELECTED WEB RESOURCES

- Sites that will convert web addresses (URLs) into short addresses so that they can be used on Twitter Bitly http://bitly.com or Tiny URL http://tinyurl.com/
- Center for Civic Education www.civiced.org/home
- Facebook https://facebook.com/
- International Association for Public Participation (IAP2) www.iap2.org/
- Instagram www.instagram.com
- LinkedIn www.linkedin.com/
- Twitter https://twitter.com/

EXERCISES AND DISCUSSION QUESTIONS

1. **Know Your City:** How Does Your City Try to Engage Citizens?
   - Are there newsletters about city activities?
   - Do city departments hold town halls?
   - Does the mayor or city manager hold open office hours?
   - Are there satellite offices for the city?
   - What does the city's social media look like? How does it use Facebook, Twitter, and other types of social media?
   - How many people go to city council meetings? Are they televised to the public? Are televised meetings archived for later viewing?
   - Are there other kinds of engagement strategies used by the city or by individual departments, such as the planning department?
2. Do you think cities should televise their city council meetings? Why or why not?
3. What kind of strategy would you devise to make sure that your city reaches out to citizens of all races, ethnicities, ages, and lifestyles? How realistic is your strategy?
4. Justify a new social media outreach campaign to engage the residents in your community, even when the budget is tight.

REFERENCES

Brabham, Daren C. 2013. *Using Crowdsourcing in Government.* Alexandria, VA: IBM Center for the Business of Government.

Bryson, John M., Quick, Kathryn S., Slotterback, Carissa Schively, and Crosby, Barbara C. 2012. "Designing Public Participation Processes." *Public Administration Review* 73 (1): pp. 23–34.

Chitwood, Luke. 2013. "5 Social Media Metrics That Your Business Should Be Tracking." *The Next Web.* Accessed on January 15, 2017 from https://thenextweb.com/socialmedia/2013/10/29/5-social-media-metrics-business—tracking/

Commission of Peer Review and Accreditation (COPRA). 2009. Recommended Mission-Specific Elective Competencies: Local Government Management. Accessed August 18 2017 from https://naspaaaccreditation.files.wordpress.com/2014/04/naspaa-icma-local-govt-competencies.pdf

Duggan, Maeve, Ellison, Nicole B., Lampe, Cliff, Lenhart, Amanda, and Madden, Mary. 2015. *Social Media Update 2014.* Pew Internet Research.

Hrdinova, Jana, Helbig, Natalie, and Peters, Catherine Stollar. 2010. *Designing Social Media Policy for Government: Eight Essential*

Elements. Albany, NY: Center for Technology in Government, University at Albany, SUNY.

International City/County Management Association. 2014a. *Civic Engagement: 10 Questions to Shape an Effective Plan*. Washington, D.C.: International City/County Management Association.

International City/County Management Association. 2014b. *2014 ICMA Digital Use Survey Results*. Accessed on October 2, 2015 from http://icma.org/en/icma/knowledge_network/documents/kn/Document/ 071.53/ICMA_Digital_Use_Survey_2014

Kim, Soonhee and Lee, Jooho. 2012. "E-Participation, Transparency, and Trust in Local Government." *Public Administration Review* 72 (6): pp. 819–828.

Leighninger, Matt. 2011. *Using Online Tools to Engage—And Be Engaged by—The Public*. Alexandria, VA: IBM Center for the Business of Government.

Lennertz, Bill, Lutzenhiser, Aarin, and Failor, Tamara. 2008. "An Introduction to Charrettes." *Planning Commissioners Journal* 71 (Summer 2008): pp. 1–3.

Lukensmeyer, Carolyn J., and Torres, Lars Hasselblad. 2006. *Public Deliberation: A Manager's Guide to Citizen Engagement*. Alexandria, VA: IBM Center for The Business of Government.

Mergel, Ines. 2011. *Using Wikis in Government: A Guide for Public Managers*. Alexandria, VA: IBM Center for the Business of Government.

Mergel, Ines. 2012. *Working the Network: A Manager's Guide for Using Twitter in Government*. Alexandria, VA: IBM Center for the Business of Government.

National Archives and Records Administration. 2013. *NARA Bulletin 2014–02: Guidance on Managing Social Media Records*. Accessed on October 19, 2015 from www.archives.gov/records-mgmt/bulletins/2014/2014-02.html

National Charrette Institute. 2015. *NCI Charrette System*. Accessed on September 18, 2015 from www.charretteinstitute.org/

Participedia.net. 2015. Accessed on September 17, 2015 from http://participedia.net/en

Schulz, Jerry. 2013. "Engaging Your Citizens Using Social Media." *In Focus Strategies and Solutions for Local Government Managers* 43 (4): 2013. Washington, D.C.: International City/County Management Association.

Thomas, John Clayton. 2012. *Citizen, Customer, Partner: Engaging the Public in Public Management*. Armonk, NY: M. E. Sharpe.

Twitter. 2015. "Twitter Usage/Company Facts." Accessed on October 19, 2015 from https://about.twitter.com/company

Van Deursen, A. J. A. M., and van Dijk, J. A. G. M. 2009. "Improving Digital Skills for the Use of Online Public Information and Services." *Government Information Quarterly* 26 (2009): pp. 333–340.

City Budget and Financial Management

THE BUDGETING AND FISCAL AFFAIRS PROCESS

The budgeting and fiscal affairs functions are among the most basic functions for any city. Services cannot be provided, and city employees cannot be paid if something goes seriously wrong in the fiscal area. The material in this chapter corresponds to the NAS-PAA Urban Administration student learning outcome, "6. Apply the management of local government financial resources," in that it provides an overview of the various types of budgets and the budgeting process, a discussion of some critical issues in fiscal affairs today, like pension obligations, and an overview of the various areas of effective financial management.

The budgeting and financial management process (Figure 5.1) incorporates the planning document for the city's revenues and expenditures (the city budget) as well as accounting for how much is spent and how much revenue is raised (the accounting process). The budgeting process involves a set of instructions going to city agencies, which then develop their budget request for the next year. These requests are reviewed by the city's fiscal agency and then are weighed against city priorities and other agency requests by the city's chief administrative officer (like the city manager). The mayor makes the final decision of what to present to the city's policy board (the city council or commission) and typically presents the budget together with a message about its priorities and important initiatives. The council then reviews the budget and passes it after discussion, public input, and, often, making changes.

The financial management functions occur during the budget execution stage after the budget is approved and the funds are being spent and raised. Financial management includes policies and processes for purchasing (procurement), cash management, internal policies and procedures to regulate the control of funds, processes, and policies for investing funds.

The next stage is the audit of all fiscal processes. The results of the financial audit, as well as the performance measurement of city services and functions, are then used to evaluate the results of the budgeting and financial management process. Those results, in turn, are used to prepare the next year's budget in what becomes a continuing cycle.

Typically, these functions are organized in an office of fiscal affairs; in a budget and finance office; or, in a much smaller city, perhaps in an administrative office (along with human resources, perhaps). In bigger cities, the budget and the finance functions might be organized separately.

FIGURE 5.1
The Budget and Finance Process in Cities

Source: Developed by author.

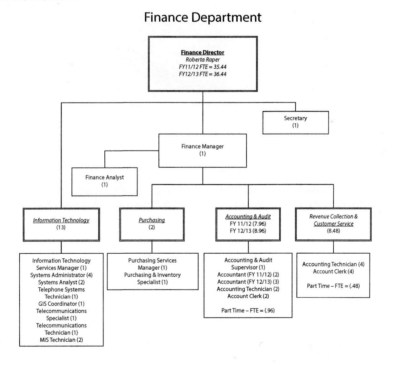

FIGURE 5.2
Organization Chart of Napa, California Finance Department

Source: City of Napa, CA. 2016. Department of Finance Organization. Accessed December 8, 2016, from http://www.cityofnapa. org/images/finance/financeorg.pdf.

In Napa, California, the function of developing the budget plan for the City is operated from the City Manager's Office. However, there is also a Finance Department (Figure 5.2), which includes the purchasing, accounting and auditing, and revenue collection functions of financial management—but also includes the information technology function, which is unusual.

LOCAL GOVERNMENT REVENUES AND EXPENDITURES

Local government spending varies enormously by state and size of local government, but certain types of functions are considered to be local functions, and this is reflected in spending patterns (Figure 5.3). While in some states, education spending is the sole province of school districts, in others, education is directed by local jurisdictions. Public safety, housing, and local transportation dominate local spending, as do utilities.

Across all local governments, aid from state government is the largest source of revenue (Figure 5.4); property taxes, a source of revenue organized by local governments themselves, is the second largest revenue source, providing 26 percent of all local governments' revenues, followed by the Other category, then sales and other taxes.

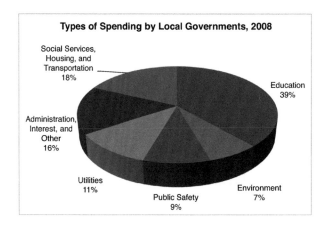

FIGURE 5.3
Categories of Local Government Spending, 2008

Source: Figure 1: Types of Spending By Local Governments, 2008. In Congressional Budget Office. 2010. Fiscal Stress Faced By Local Governments: Economic and Budget Issue Brief. Available at http://www.cbo.gov/sites/default/files/12-09-municipalities_brief.pdf, March 25, 2015.

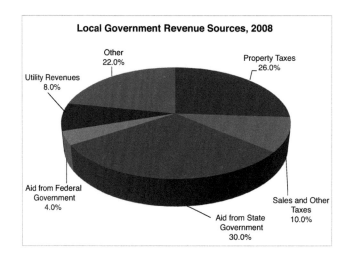

FIGURE 5.4
Local Government Revenue Sources, 2008

Source: Figure 2: Sources of Revenues for Local Governments, 2008. In Congressional Budget Office. 2010. Fiscal Stress Faced By Local Governments: Economic and Budget Issue Brief. Available at http://www.cbo.gov/sites/default/files/12-09-municipalities_brief.pdf, March 25, 2015.

TYPES OF BUDGETS

Overall, there are two kinds of budgets—the operating budget and the capital budget. The operating budget is typically for one year only and expresses what funds will be raised and spent during one year. The capital budget usually covers five to seven years and only includes the funds for buildings, roads, and other large capital expenditures.

Operating Budgets

There are three basic formats of operating budgets, although there are many variations on each; the different formats nudge decision-makers into asking different kinds of questions about priorities, services delivered, and costs of services.

The first, and most basic, is the line item budget, or object of expenditure budget. This type of budget is simply a list of the types of revenues and, then, the types of expenditures that the city has. The list of revenues and expenditures begins with the most fixed (least-changing) type of revenue or experience and ends with the revenue and expenditures that change the most. Therefore, the list of expenditures usually begins with Salaries and the related Benefits line.

Typically, there is a column of numbers for the preceding year's actual revenues and expenditures, a column for this year's estimated figures (because the year is not complete, so the final figures are not known), and then the column that represents the point of the budget, the budgeted figures for the next year (Figure 5.5). Once the budget is approved

	FY 2014 AMENDED BUDGET	FY 2015 RECOMMENDED BUDGET	$ Variance	% Variance
Revenues:				
Property Taxes:				
Current Year	$ 17,550,000	$ 18,100,000	$ 550,000	3.1%
Motor Vehicle	750,000	650,000	(100,000)	-13.3%
Prior Year/Delinquent	205,000	245,000	40,000	19.5%
Local Option Sales Tax	12,850,000	13,900,000	1,050,000	8.2%
Other Taxes:				
Franchise Fees	6,340,000	6,400,000	60,000	0.9%
Insurance Premium Tax	2,900,000	3,025,000	125,000	4.3%
Alcohol Beverage Excise Tax	1,750,000	1,800,000	50,000	2.9%
Motor Vehicle Title Tax Fee	85,000	865,000	780,000	917.6%
Other Taxes	1,697,000	1,714,500	17,500	1.0%
Licenses & Permits	1,747,500	1,985,100	237,600	13.6%
Intergovernmental	426,252	380,000	(46,252)	-10.9%
Charges for Services	2,316,200	2,567,150	250,950	10.8%
Fines & Forfeitures	2,850,000	2,302,100	(547,900)	-19.2%
Interest	50,000	50,000	-	0.0%
Other Revenues	278,173	292,842	14,669	5.3%
Other Financing Sources:				
Interfund Transfer (Hotel/Motel Fund)	1,480,000	1,662,000	182,000	12.3%
Total Operating Revenues	$ 53,275,125	$ 55,938,692	$ 2,663,567	5.0%
Fund Balance Carryforward	5,684,667	4,086,612		
Total Revenues	$ 58,959,792	$ 60,025,304		

FIGURE 5.5

City of Alpharetta, Georgia Line Item Budget—Revenues

Source: City of Alpharetta, Georgia. Accessed November 29, 2014, from http://www.alpharetta.ga.us/index.php?m=publications&id=40.

	FY 2014 AMENDED BUDGET	FY 2015 RECOMMENDED BUDGET	$ Variance	% Variance
Expenditures (by Category):				
Personnel Services:				
Salaries	$ 24,246,646	$ 24,818,821	$ 572,175	2.4%
Group Insurance	6,280,137	6,909,563	629,426	10.0%
Pension (Defined Benefit)	2,352,726	2,176,655	(176,071)	-7.5%
Pension (401A)	1,278,570	1,262,388	(16,182)	-1.3%
Miscellaneous Benefits	2,370,352	2,584,005	213,653	9.0%
subtotal	$ 36,528,431	$ 37,751,432	$ 1,223,001	3.3%
Maintenance and Operations:				
Professional Fees	$ 2,008,698	$ 1,980,125	$ (28,573)	-1.4%
Repair/Maintenance	1,122,900	1,128,050	5,150	0.5%
Maintenance Contracts	1,721,345	2,133,632	412,287	24.0%
Professional Services (IT)	1,272,218	1,270,501	(1,717)	-0.1%
General Supplies	929,198	940,020	10,822	1.2%
Utilities	2,392,034	2,504,445	112,411	4.7%
Fuel	856,886	790,100	(66,786)	-7.8%
Miscellaneous	2,124,605	2,144,638	20,033	0.9%
subtotal	$ 12,427,884	$ 12,891,511	$ 463,627	3.7%
Capital/Lease:				
Fire Truck Leases	$ 275,215	$ 295,930	$ 20,715	7.5%
Tyler ERP Lease	101,431	106,187	4,756	4.7%
Work Order Software Lease	71,728	75,692	3,964	5.5%
Miscellaneous	26,000	27,000	1,000	3.8%
subtotal	$ 474,374	$ 504,809	$ 30,435	6.4%
Other Uses:				
Contingency	$ 434,800	$ 531,800	$ 97,000	22.3%
Insurance Premiums (Risk Fund)	690,800	545,000	(145,800)	-21.1%
Gwinnett Tech Contribution (Debt Svc)	265,000	288,640	23,640	8.9%
Donations/Contributions	45,000	45,000	-	0.0%
subtotal	$ 1,435,600	$ 1,410,440	$ (25,160)	-1.8%
Total Operating Expenditures	**$ 50,866,289**	**$ 52,558,192**	**$ 1,691,903**	**3.3%**
Interfund Transfer:				
Capital Project Fund	8,093,503	7,467,112		
Total Expenditures	**$ 58,959,792**	**$ 60,025,304**		

FIGURE 5.6
City of Alpharetta, Georgia Line Item Budget—Expenditures

Source: City of Alpharetta, Georgia. Accessed November 29, 2014 from http://www.alpharetta.ga.us/index.php?m=publications&id=40.

by the city council, it is a legal document, and managers (within certain parameters) must spend what is in the plan.

As can be seen in Figures 5.5 and 5.6, Alpharetta, Georgia includes data for only two years but then incorporates other useful information—the percent and dollar change recommended for next year's budget. This budget illustrates the principle that it is important to include both the percent change and the dollar change since using only one can lead to misleading conclusions.

Conclusions drawn from this portion of Alpharetta's budget (Figure 5.5) are that property taxes are the largest source of revenue and that the recommendation from the city manager is for a 5 percent increase in revenues from the previous year.

As stated earlier, salaries are typically the first expenditure listed in a line item budget, then other Personnel Services (like benefits). Expenditures are budgeted to increase by 3.3 percent, so the intention is to have a slight surplus at the end of the fiscal year (since when revenues are greater than expenditures, there is a surplus). Many jurisdictions use surplus funds as a reserve or emergency fund, which is a financial management best practice.

Another way of organizing and formatting the proposed budget is the program budget. This format does not present information as types of revenues or expenditures but by the program. This format allows decision-makers to focus not on what is being purchased (as with the line item budget) but on what programs should receive priority spending. Table 5.1 illustrates the format of a program budget. With this type of a budget, expenditures can be more easily tracked by program area, and decision-makers can more readily make budget choices according to their policy preferences.

A third type, a performance budget, typically pairs program- or department-level expenditure proposals with performance measure proposals for that department. Figure 5.7 presents a portion of the department-level performance budget for the City of Alexandria, Virginia Department of Community and Human Services' proposed budget for 2015.

TABLE 5.1

Example of a Program Budget, Ames, Iowa—Expenses Section

Program	2010/11 Actuals	2011/12 Adopted	2011/12 Adjusted	2012/13 Adopted	%Change from Adopted
Public Safety	$15,432,960	$16,072,685	$16,529,355	$16,958,227	5.5%
Utilities	$56,459,893	$62,870,799	$64,860,655	$64,577,847	2.7%
Transportation	$11,442,931	$11,748,820	$12,064,204	$12,346,114	5.1%
Community Enrichment	$11,840,010	$10,220,055	$11,614,506	$10,188,853	−0.3%
General Government	$6,410,810	$6,982,711	$7,186,947	$7,227,370	3.5%
Total Operations	$101,586,604	$107,895,070	$112,255,667	$111,298,411	3.2%

Source: City of Ames, Iowa. *Your City of Ames 12/13 Program Budget.* Accessed on December 11, 2014 from www.cityofames.org/modules/showdocument.aspx?documentid=8235.

CITY OF ALEXANDRIA, VIRGINIA

Department of Community and Human Services

ALEXANDRIA FUND FOR HUMAN SERVICES

To ensure **healthy & thriving residents,** this program provides Alexandria fund for human services (AFHS) children and youth priorities, and Alexandria fund for human services community partnership priorities in order to ensure all children and youth thrive and succeed, and increase self-sufficiency and meaningful quality of life for the city's most vulnerable adults. Based on the recommendations in the November 2013, "Report of the Alexandria Fund for Human Services Review Committee," the current Fund for Human Services awardees will continue to receive funding in FY 2015, pending implementation of the staff recommendations for FY 2016 and beyond. A link to that report can be found here, 14-2340 AFHS Review Committee Report (18 Nov 2013).

Program Totals	FY 2013 Actual	FY 2014 Approved	FY 2015 Approved
% Total All Funds Budget	1.6%	1.6%	1.6%
Total Expenditures	$2,012,585	$2,033,259	$1,996,430
Non-Personnel	$2,012,585	$2,033,259	$1,996,430
Full Time Equivalents (FTEs)	0.00	0.00	0.00
Performance Measures			
# of children and youth served	4,013	3,000	3,000
# of residents served	10,472	10,000	10,000
% of Community Partnership priorities funded that achieve 70% of outcomes	99%	90%	90%
% of youth showing improvement in life functioning and/or life circumstances	N/A	70%	70%

FIGURE 5.7
Example of Performance Budget for City Department

Source: City of Alexandria, VA. FY 2015 Approved Operating Budget. Accessed on December 11, 2014. Available at https://www.alexandriava.gov/uploadedFiles/budget/info/budget2015/FY%202015%20Approved%20Section%2012%20-%20Healthy%20and%20Thriving%20Residents.pdf.

CIVIC ENGAGEMENT OVER THE BUDGET

Because the city budget is the clearest statement of what the city values and because it states "who gets what," city officials often try to get residents involved in some way with budget considerations, and citizens often want to be involved. So there are many variations to the basic budget process that work to involve citizens more actively and to seek out citizen input (Ebdon and Franklin 2006).

As discussed earlier, some cities have partnered with Next10 to use its online simulation to outline the budget choices for the city. Then citizens see if they can balance the city's budget by working through these budget choices. For Los Angeles, citizens are asked to identify budget priorities and make budget choices to eliminate the $216 million shortfalls for the 2013–2014 Fiscal Year (City of Los Angeles 2014). Next10 also presents this opportunity for the California state budget and policy areas such as California's water policy options.

Participatory budgeting is another effort at engaging citizens in at least a segment of the budgeting process. Organized by the Participatory Budgeting Project, it involves citizens gathering in public discussion groups to brainstorm ideas for improving their communities. Members of the group then organize these ideas into projects, which are voted upon by the citizens. The government then funds and implements these ideas. The idea began in Brazil in 1989 and now has expanded to more than a thousand cities across the globe. Chicago and New York City were early American cities involved. Chicago is now in its fifth cycle; this last cycle involved 2,956 people across four wards, who allocated $10.3 million. In New York City, 17,000 participated in allocating $29.4 million in its third cycle. A smaller city, Vallejo, California, just emerging from bankruptcy, is also partici-pating with 3,917 citizens participating in allocating $5.8 million citywide. Throughout, the Project provides technical assistance, guidance, and training for the cities and citizens involved (Participatory Budgeting Project 2014).

PENSION OBLIGATIONS

Since cities, like all government agencies, provide services, most of the expenditures in their budgets go to pay their employees' salaries and benefits. A critical issue for govern-ments today is the growth in employee health care costs, the costs of paying pensions to government retirees, and the costs of paying Other Post-Employment Benefits (OPEB)—these are the health care costs for government retirees (currently 63 percent of all OPEB costs). These recently became even more important because accounting rules changed (in Government Accounting Standards Board [GASB] Rules 45 and 68). Governments now have to account for the money they need to pay their retiree health care costs and more effectively take into account what they owe for employees' pensions; in the past, they often used a "pay as you go" method and could pay current retirees' health care costs out of each year's operating budget. Getting past the "pay as you go" system to one where enough funds are saved to pay for future retirees' health care and pensions is necessary to have a fully sustainable pension system.

To do that, governments need to set aside money each year into a trust fund specifi-cally for pensions to retired employees and for any health care costs. That money is then invested, and any money gained from investments can be used to reduce the amount that the governments need to pay themselves.

But not all governments pay enough each year to cover those obligations. A study by the Pew Charitable Trusts in 2013 of the 61 most populous cities plus any others with more than 500,000 in population found that these cities had only enough assets on hand to cover 74 percent of the estimated $385 billion of what they owed to retired employees. Even more troubling is that these cities had only enough funds on hand to cover 6 percent of the OPEB—mostly health care costs for retirees. Findings like these and others have led to numerous efforts around the country to reform government pension systems by chang-ing their structure, funding, or promised benefits (Pew Charitable Trusts 2013).

There are three sources of funds cities use to pay pensions; first are contributions by employees, second are any contributions from the city itself (to match those of employees) and third are the funds gained from investing employee and city contributions. One reason many governments are not paying enough to cover their full pension obligations each year is that they are overly confident about how much they will earn from investing pension contributions.

Aside from the usual risks involved with investing, some pension fund managers in Canada are beginning to be concerned about the possible effects of climate change on their investments. They requested a study, realizing that climate change was coming but that they needed more information before knowing how the impacts would affect their investments of their pension funds. Their consultants indicated that some indus-tries (like infrastructure, real estate, and agriculture) could benefit from a two-degree Celsius increase in temperature. However, others, like energy and mining, could suffer. Conclusions drawn by others are that climate change is "one of the biggest risks faced by Canadian pension plans, and managers may be forced into taking public stands to fulfill their legal duties" (Bickis 2017: http://m.thespec.com/news-story/7103713-how-will-climate-change-affect-pensions-). When the same consulting firm began work in the United States in the fall of 2016, it stated that even under the two-degree scenario, pension funds could lose billions of dollars in assets. Further, it suggested that part of pension fund managers' fiduciary duties is to acknowledge these risks and act accord-ingly (Bickis 2017).

BOX 5.1   CAREER PATHWAYS IN BUDGETING AND FINANCE

Current Position

Director of Finance

Education

B.A. in Political Science and Economics
Master of Public Administration

Other:

- Advanced writing class
- Course in business communications
- Accounting class
- Continuing education courses through the California Society for Municipal Finance Officers (CSMFO) and the Governmental Finance Officers Association (GFOA)

Career Pathway

Teresa began her career as an Analyst in the Budget Analyst's Office for a large city after seeing a job ad while in her M.P.A. program's budgeting class. After four years as a Budget Analyst, she moved to a department in the same city and became a Senior Administrative Analyst for the large city's Department of Public Works. There, she was responsible for transportation grants and its financial management. After two years in that position, she was promoted to the Manager, Finance and Budget position for that large department.

At that point, she left the large city and went to work for a special district as its Deputy Director, Finance and Administration. Living in an area with lots of suburban cities, Teresa's next step was to move to a smaller city as its Director of Finance and Administration. Beginning in 2015, she became Finance Director for a larger suburban city.

She learned her job from her formal education as well as from each job and each project on which she has worked.

A Typical Day

Most days, Teresa interacts with the staff in her department, asking and answering questions on projects or other financial issues, brainstorming solutions to problems. She also researches and answers questions posed by members of other City departments as well as the City Manager, members of the public, and City Council. She works on her own analytical projects; for example, right now she is managing a development impact fee study, a project on debt financing for a recycled water project, the mid-year budget, and presentation materials for meetings she attended this week, and she just wrote a debt policy and staff report for City Council review. Depending on the time of year, Teresa may also be engrossed in budget preparation or the Consolidated Annual Financial Report (CAFR).

Teresa attends meetings with outside agencies with which her city has a business relationship, like the water and sewer treatment agencies or nearby cities. She also attends meetings with the City Manager and department head staff on higher profile projects and activities. And, she attends City Council meetings twice a month.

Professional Associations and Networking

Teresa is a member of the CSMFO and GFOA. Teresa attends their conferences and trainings. She also develops relationships with finance directors in neighboring cities and jurisdictions and networks at the CSMFO and GFOA events and trainings.

Most Help to Her Career

Teresa believes that understanding policy, politics, and public services in addition to finance and budget has been most helpful to her career; this allows her to help city

BOX 5.1 (CONTINUED)

management and policy-makers make decisions within the City's policies and services context.

Most Challenging

The most challenging aspects of Teresa's job include addressing unprincipled behavior by staff or people in leadership roles such as awarding sole source contracts to friends, lying about financial information, or protecting someone who has done something illegal.

Overcoming These Challenges

"First, it is really important that a finance professional always seek to ensure integrity in the organization's financial data and processes even if doing so feels like a personal risk. That said, some of the actions I've taken to address unprincipled behavior include: adopting financial policies that clearly define how we are going to conduct business and providing correct financial information with appropriate documentation and analysis to counter false information provided by someone else. I have also worked to ensure

that I am in accord with the City Manager and City Council."

Most Rewarding

Teresa enjoys finding solutions to problems, whether it is identifying the appropriate way to address an accounting system glitch or figuring out how to fund an important capital project. She finds it gratifying that there is always a solution in the world of budget and finance.

Recommendations for Students

"Get a master's degree in public administration or public policy to obtain a better understanding of policy and government services. I would also recommend taking business writing classes and presentation classes since communication skills are more important than technical skills in leadership positions.

"Finally, I would highly recommend learning to let go of the details. Trust staff to do their jobs. This is not only empowering to staff but it frees up the finance director to focus on bigger, more strategic projects, initiatives, and build relationships."

CAPITAL BUDGET

The other major type of budget is the capital budget, which includes only major projects and typically incorporates a five- to seven-year time horizon. A list of major projects is presented, usually along with the priorities for their completion. Often, the system through which the projects are ranked is discussed. This can be based upon a benefit-cost analysis or some other system developed by the city.

The most critical part of the budget is the proposal for how these projects are being financed. Since expenditures and programs within operational budgets last only one year, the means by which they are financed also should last only one year—the financing should match the life of the expenditure. Since capital projects can last anywhere from three years (computers) to up to 50 (buildings), the financing for these projects also should match the life of the project. Managers do not want to have to pay for a building that will last 50 years from their one-year operating budget. Therefore, capital projects are typically paid for through municipal bond financing.

Municipal bonds are a financing instrument bought and sold to raise money for city projects. When a city wants to raise money for a capital project, it does it by working with

▶ **TABLE 5.2**

Bond Rating Agencies' Bond Ratings

	Moody's	Standard and Poor's	Fitch's
Highest quality, lowest credit risk	Aaa	AAA (Investment grade—extremely strong)	AAA
	Aa	AA (Investment grade)	AA
	A	A (Investment grade)	A
	Baa	BBB (Investment grade)	BBB
	Ba	BBB- (Investment grade)	BB
	B	BB+ (speculative grade)	B
	Caa	BB	CCC
	Ca	B	CC
Lowest rating, typically in default	C	CCC	C
		CC	RD
		C	D
		D	

Source: Developed from www.fitchratings.com/web_content/ratings/fitch_ratings_definitions_and_scales.pdf, https://media.ratings.standardandpoors.com/documents/SPRS_Understanding-Ratings_GRE.pdf, and www.moodys.com/researchdocumentcontentpage.aspx?docid=PBC_79004 (December 12, 2014).

bankers and attorneys to create a bond issue, a legal agreement for the city to raise money by borrowing it. The bond issue creates bonds (debt instruments) to be sold to investors. The city sells the bonds to an investment bank, which in turn sells them to investors. From these transactions, the city gets the money for its project and then pays back the bonds by paying interest every year (and eventually, the principal itself) to the investors who purchased their bonds. Particularly since municipal bonds are tax-free, they can provide a good return for those investors who prefer more stable investments. Every year, cities with outstanding bonds should put aside funds in a separate fund so that they are able to pay their obligations.

The degree of risk that investors undertake when they purchase municipal bonds is determined by the bond rating of the jurisdiction issuing the bonds. These bond ratings are mostly conducted by three large companies—Moody's, Standard and Poor's, and Fitch's. Each of these agencies has a set of criteria that they use to evaluate government agencies of all kinds—as well as private companies. Then, when these government agencies seek to borrow money through issuing bonds, potential investors know how risky it might be to purchase those bonds. The higher the rating, the less risk for the investors—so the less agencies have to pay in interest to get those investors to take a risk by purchasing bonds. The lower the rating, the more governments have to pay to borrow money because investors are taking on more risk.

FISCAL STRESS

Just as individuals have fiscal stress in their lives, so do governments like cities. Fiscal stress in cities can be a result of many factors. These can include (Goldberg and Neiman 2014; Coe 2008):

- Federal then state reductions in revenues to cities;
- Federal government or states requiring cities to implement programs but without funding them (unfunded mandates);
- Recessions or other economic difficulties;
- People moving out of the city or having to foreclose on their homes, resulting in a reduction of city revenues like property taxes;
- State requirements to limit revenues or expenditures;
- Demographic changes either requiring new programs or resulting in reductions in revenues;
- Mismanagement; and
- Decision-making focused on the present without taking future repercussions into account (like signing union contracts for salary increases or pension benefits whose future costs are beyond the capacity of the government to pay).

BOX 5.2 SALINAS, KANSAS FINANCIAL TREND MONITORING INDICATORS

Salinas, Kansas developed a Financial Trend Monitoring System (FTMS) based on Cash Solvency (ability to pay bills in the short-term), Budgetary Solvency (ability to cover expenses over the next budget period), Long-Run Solvency (ability to cover expenditures in the long-run), and Service Level Solvency (ability to provide services to citizens). These are performance measures for fiscal affairs.

They are based upon a series of financial indicators that are monitored.

Community

Population
Real Property Value
Personal Income Per Capita
Residential Development Employment Base

Revenue Indicators

Revenue Per Capita
Sales Tax Revenue
Property Tax Revenue

Intergovernmental Operating Revenue
Uncollected Property Taxes

Expenditures

Expenditures Per Capita
Fringe Benefits
Employees Per Capita
Capital Outlay

Operating Position

Growth in Revenue vs. Growth in Expenditures
Current Liabilities
Fund Balance for All Funds
Liquidity (amount of cash easily available)

Debt Structure

Long-Term Debt
Debt Service
Debt Margin

Source: City of Salinas, Kansas. 2011. *Financial Trends Monitoring System.* Accessed on January 18, 2017 from www.salina-ks.gov/filestorage/18184/18549/18560/18562/Financial_Trends_Monitoring_System.pdf.

Fiscal stress has increased to the point that there are many more cities close to bankruptcies since the Great Depression during the 1930s. Recent history shows New York City in crisis in 1975, while, in 1978, Cleveland was the first city since the Depression to not be able to pay off its bonds. In 1991, Bridgeport, Connecticut had to be taken over by the state when it could not pay its bills, and several cities were taken over by New York State during the 1970s and 1980s. Orange County, California was a county-level government that declared bankruptcy after the County Treasurer bet on highly risky investments and lost not just the County's funds but that of many other jurisdictions. In 1996, Florida took over Miami; in 2003, Pennsylvania had to increase oversight of Pittsburgh (U.S. Congressional Budget Office 2010; Coe 2008).

Even more recently, numerous cities in Michigan, including Detroit, were put under receivership and had emergency managers appointed for them. In California, Stockton, Vallejo, and San Bernardino all filed for bankruptcy post-2010.

Stockton, California

Stockton is an agricultural and very diverse city that had grown rapidly during the late 20th century. The city was a distant, but still doable, location to buy housing for people making the commute to and from San Francisco and the Bay Area—people who could not afford to live in the Bay Area itself. From 2001 to 2006, housing prices grew in Stockton with the demand from the Bay Area, and the area grew and its economy prospered, driven by the real estate market. Optimistic about further growth, the City worked on redeveloping its downtown marina and waterfront and several hotels and historic buildings. By also adding employees to the City's rosters, the main portion of any city's budget, the General Fund, grew. To raise money to fund these projects, it sold bonds (which it would subsequently need to repay).

During the "up" times in the mid-2000s, the City agreed to very generous contracts with its employees, which locked in salary increases and pension obligations for city employees.

As the Great Recession hit beginning in 2007, housing prices collapsed (declining in Stockton by as much as 70 percent) and the foreclosures began. As residents lost their jobs due to the recession and then lost their houses, those houses went empty. In Stockton, there were whole streets, practically whole neighborhoods, that were empty. Once residents started losing their homes, they also stopped paying property taxes to the City, so City revenue declined sharply. The City stopped hiring new employees but still went into a deficit (i.e., spent more than it received in revenues) of $5 million in 2008, $1 million in 2009, and $7.5 million in 2010. By 2010, any reserves the City had were almost gone. The City searched for ways to make up the deficit, but a city government provides services, so most of its budget is spent on salaries and benefits for its employees. This was, of course, true for Stockton, which spent 76 percent of its General Fund budget on salaries and benefits. The importance of this distinction is that, when a city needs to cut its budget, it does not have very many ways it can cut its budget without having to cut employees' salaries, benefits, or jobs.

By 2012, it had made cuts and declared fiscal emergencies for two years in a row, which allowed the City not to have to pay the salary increases to which it had earlier agreed (increases of 2.5 to 7 percent, depending on how revenues were growing). At the same time, other portions of the budget, like health care for both employees and City retirees, kept increasing.

When this happened to Stockton, it doubled what the City had to pay in OPEB costs— and Stockton did not have the money to pay this. Stockton had already tried to borrow money by selling bonds, but it had done that right before the economy went sharply into deficit and it was already having a hard time making payments on those bonds. As a result of this and the City's other financial problems, Moody's reduced its rating to "junk" level (the lower of the bond ratings).

So, in 2012 Stockton entered bankruptcy mediation (a new California law required cities to go into mediation for 60 days with its creditors before going into full bankruptcy) (Evans, Kosenko, and Polyakov 2012). After mediation, it went into full bankruptcy and worked to try to turn around the situation by negotiating with creditors, amid other strategies.

By February 25, 2015, Stockton had done enough work to have an approved plan to exit bankruptcy (City of Stockton 2015). As part of that plan, Stockton upheld its pension obligations but significantly reduced what it owed to other creditors and developed plans for "living within its means." It renegotiated contracts with its labor unions, altered health care arrangements with its retirees, and raised the sales tax to provide additional police officers. Bankruptcy did not erase its debt, but it did allow the City time to restructure and renegotiate so that it can better manage it and start the recovery (Wilson 2015).

Detroit

The causes of Detroit's bankruptcy come from a variety of very different factors from those in Stockton. Detroit's peak in population (1.85 million) came in the late 1940s as car manufacturing was growing and people moved from the South to Detroit to work. However, in the 1960s, those jobs were already disappearing, as the auto industry began to automate, union and labor tensions increased, and the industry began to decentralize its plants outside of Detroit. The 1960s also saw many whites moving to the suburbs around Detroit in the beginnings of a massive "white flight" after an increase in racial tensions, largely brought about by declining jobs. Those who remained were increasingly elderly and in need of even more services (New York Times 2013).

Detroit had not diversified its economic base and so remained largely an auto manufacturing town with few other industry jobs to replace the auto manufacturing jobs. After more decades of decline, by 2013, Detroit had only 688,701 population remaining in what was the largest population decline of any city (except for New Orleans after Hurricane Katrina, although more residents left Detroit than left New Orleans) (Sugrue 2007; Seelye 2011; U.S. Census 2015). Crime increased. Citizens already considered City services to be inadequate, and so even more left. The white flight of the 1970s was followed by black flight to the suburbs after 2000.

As with Stockton, the disappearance of jobs and then people, leaving more than 20 percent of the lots in the City vacant (Seelye 2011), had a wrenching effect upon the city government, and revenues (property taxes) plummeted. Analysts cited a lack of leadership by a series of mayors as not doing enough to solve Detroit's problems, contributing to the City's decline and high deficits. Several recent mayors either were jailed for a variety of misdeeds (Kwame Kilpatrick) or did not run for re-election after the Governor appointed an emergency manager under Michigan law so that the mayor essentially had little remaining authority (Dave Bing). The current mayor is Mike Duggan, who is working to bring the City out of bankruptcy (New York Times 2013).

The State's emergency manager, Kevyn Orr, prepared a comprehensive report detailing the City's fiscal situation (Helms and Guillen 2013). The report included:

- Costs for retiree benefits that were up to one-third of the City's budget ($5.7 billion unfunded retiree health care costs);
- Cash on hand at time of report—(negative) $162 million;
- Accumulated deficit that would be greater than $600 million except for City borrowing to cover it;

- City no longer able to borrow any money (with $9.4 billion in bonds and other debt) because it could not repay the loans after years of deferring loan payments;
- Average monthly decline in population from 1950 to 2010—1,575 per month; and
- 78,000 vacant structures and 60,000 vacant parcels of land—so no property taxes from these.

(Helms and Guillen 2013)

Almost worse for residents was Orr's report on City services (Guillen 2013):

- After five chiefs over five years and with outdated equipment, Orr highlighted a situation in the police department of "slow response times, an inefficient deployment of officers, poor case-closure rates, and extremely low employee morale."
- Safety hazards were faced by the fire department due to so many vacant properties plus equipment problems.
- A City-owned lighting system was often down for repairs.
- The water and sewerage system was behind on maintenance and needed $1.5 billion in improvements.

Finally, labor costs and pension and health care costs for retirees were an important part of the problem, $7.5 billion of the total $15 billion in long-term debt; Orr believed that the pension systems were vastly underfunded. Current employees had 48 different collective bargaining agreements with their unions, all of different provisions. Under bankruptcy, obligations made to employees and retirees would be potentially open to change—particularly given their large share of the budget (Groden 2014; Guillen 2013).

Detroit went under Chapter 9 bankruptcy protection in July 2013. The City developed a plan to reduce its debt by $7 billion, spend $1.7 billion to update its services, and reduce its obligations to its retirees, and went into bankruptcy. It was under the protection of the court in bankruptcy for 17 months, emerging from bankruptcy in December 2014. The City was then turned back over to its elected officials, including the City Council and is proceeding to implement its plan. It remains to be seen how successful the City will be, considering that, among other factors, some analysts believed that the City needed to develop a new middle class to become a functioning city once again. Since then, business leaders have led the way in moving businesses back to downtown Detroit, and others have followed, in an unexpected resurgence of the city. So things are moving in the right direction, but there are still difficult fiscal issues to address (Saunder 2016).

FINANCIAL MANAGEMENT

After budgets have been developed by staff and city managers or mayors then approved by cities' legislative bodies, the budget is then a legal document. It must then be implemented by those same managers, by keeping track of expenditures through the accounting process, carefully managing the cash flow through the city, and utilizing other financial management processes.

The accounting process carefully keeps track of every expenditure and revenue transaction, showing where funds come from and what they are used for and then compiling all of those accounting transactions into financial statements that report on the overall fiscal health of the city. There are three main financial statements: a balance sheet showing assets (what the government owns) and liabilities (what it owes); an income statement (how much expenses and revenues it has); and the statement of changes in fund balance, or equity. This last statement provides an overall view of how well the government is doing. The financial statements also include information on how much debt the city has taken on and how much the city pays each year to reduce that debt. Moreover, the auditors who prepare the city's financial statements also make some statement about the kinds of policies and procedures that the city has in place to ensure accountability and good stewardship of its financial resources. The content of these financial statements is presented to decision-makers as aids to deciding the fiscal future of the city.

After the budget is approved, the monies are distributed and are spent according to the plan set out in the budget. At this stage, the financial management of the revenues and spending is implemented. The accounting system keeps track of what has been spent and what has been received. However, there are many other elements of a financial management system.

BOX 5.3 BUDGET AND FINANCIAL MANAGEMENT STRATEGIES FROM CITY SUSTAINABILITY PLANS

The budget and financial management function can also be important in a city sustainability plan.

- "Ensure that public revenue sources are economically sustainable, promote equity and redress existing inequities, and foster health ecosystems now and into the future." Dover, New Hampshire, p. 5.
- "Ensure that local government procurement, expenditures, and financial investments support best practices in social responsibility related to employment, environment, and community development." Dover, New Hampshire, p. 5.

Procurement and Purchasing

- "Create sustainable standards and guidelines for City purchases." Avondale, Arizona, p. 44.
- "Adopt an internal City sustainable purchasing policy by 2018." Longmont, Colorado, p. 6.
- "All applicable purchases meet Energy Star or equivalent by 2016." Avondale, Arizona, p. 53.
- "All City departments are using life cycle cost and sustainability evaluations for

public projects by 2018." Longmont, Colorado, p. 6.
- "Act as a responsible steward of public funds and take a long-term life-cycle approach to new construction, upgrades, and maintenance of infrastructure." Virginia Beach, Virginia, p. 75.
- "Reduce paper towel orders 5% by 2016, 10% by 2018, 20% by 2020." Avondale, Arizona, p. 44.
- "Reduce bottled water orders 2% by 2015, 5% by 2018, 20% by 2020." Avondale, Arizona, p. 44.

Sources: City of Avondale, Arizona 2014. Municipal Sustainability Plan. June 16, 2014. Accessed on February 22, 2017 from www.avondale.org/DocumentCenter/View/34278 Arizona.

City of Dover, New Hampshire. Not Dated. City of Dover Sustainability Goals with Purpose Statements. Accessed on February 22, 2017 from www.dover.nh.gov/Assets/government/city-operations/2document/planning/outreach/sustainabilitygoals.pdf.

City of Longmont, Colorado. 2016. Sustainability Plan. November 2016. Accessed on February 22, 2017 from www.longmontcolorado.gov/home/showdocument?id=16700.

City of Virginia Beach, Virginia. 2013. A Community Plan for a Sustainable Future. City of VA Beach Environment and Sustainability Office. March 12, 2013. Accessed on February 22, 2017 from www.vbgov.com/government/offices/eso/sustainability-plan/Documents/vb-sustainability-plan-web.pdf.

Financial management is part of the Budget Execution stage of budgeting. After the budget is approved and money is being spent, a series of financial management systems are necessary to ensure prudent and accurate stewardship of the funds.

- Accounting system. The accounting system keeps track of what is spent by the city and what funds are received. These transactions are monitored and then aggregated into a series of financial statements.
- Financial statements. A series of three or more financial statements are used to summarize and present the city's overall fiscal condition, based on the results of the accounting system's report on spending and receiving revenues.
- Internal controls. Internal controls are a series of policies and procedures that ensure good stewardship of the city's funds and that funds cannot be misspent, wasted, or stolen.
- Risk management system. Risk management systems are about insurance and ensuring that the city is not exposed to unnecessary risks that could cost unnecessary money. So, city managers ensure that city property is safe, try to reduce the safety risks for those who use city property, and ensure that the city is properly covered by insurance for risks that are unpredictable.
- Purchasing. City purchasing is an area of potentially high-risk for misuse of funds. Policies and procedures need to be set up to ensure that goods and services that are purchased are what the city needs, and no more, that an unbiased process has been used to decide from whom those goods and services are purchased, and that the city actually receives the goods and services it believes it has purchased. Ethical bidding and contracting processes should be set up to ensure that all who are interested have an equal opportunity of doing business with the city.
- Pension assets management. If the city has a pension system, the city's retirees have paid their money into that system, frequently matched by their employer, the city. Most governments today have defined contribution, rather than defined benefit, plans. This means that the amounts retirees receive are based on what they contributed into the plan. Once these contributions are paid into the plan and matched by the city, they are invested to try to increase the amount available to pay out to retirees. The management of those pension funds is a very controversial and expensive item in any city's budget today.
- Assets management. Keeping track of the city's assets, or inventory, is important so items like computers, printers, and furniture are retained and managers know where they are located and their condition.
- Cash management. Revenues do not flow equally into city coffers throughout the year; some months there will be more than others. To ensure the city has adequate cash on hand, fiscal managers must sometimes save or invest excess cash at one period and access that saved or invested cash at low-cash periods to pay the bills throughout the year.
- Investment management. Fiscal managers invest pension funds and excess cash found during the year in conservative, relatively stable investments; while funds are waiting to be used, the funds can be earning the city more money through investing (and more than just sitting in a checking or savings account). However, managers need to have strong investment policies behind them stating the city's attitude toward risk and giving investment managers guidance as to how the funds should be invested. It is critical that they are invested according to how a "prudent person" would invest. There have been several significant scandals (Orange County, California) where the Treasurer there has invested not just his own government's funds but those of other governments—and lost them all due to risky investments.

CONCLUSIONS

This chapter has reviewed basic concepts and processes in public sector budgeting as well as discussed important city fiscal issues like pension obligations and the effects of the mortgage housing crisis on several cities. Performance measures have long been used in city budgeting as warning signs of impending fiscal stress; a number of these measures were also reviewed here. City budgets and finance are part of NASPAA's student learning outcomes for Urban Administration and are considered to be part of the first overall goal, Leading and Managing, as well as the specific SLO for fiscal management under the Urban Administration emphasis.

SELECTED WEB RESOURCES

- The Bond Buyer www.bondbuyer.com/
- Fitch's www.fitchratings.com
- Government Finance Officers Association www.gfoa.org/
- Government Accounting Standards Board www.gasb.org/
- Moody's www.moodys.com/
- Standard and Poor's www. standardandpoors.com/

EXERCISES AND DISCUSSION QUESTIONS

1. **Know Your City**: What Is Your City's Fiscal Situation?
   - How much does your city spend each year?
   - What is the main revenue source for the city?
   - How much debt does your city carry?
   - Did your city's budget increase or decrease for this coming year?
   - Does your city have its financial statements available on its website?
   - Is your city's proposed and approved budget located on its website? Is it presented in a user-friendly manner?
   - Does your city have budget hearings where the public is able to provide input into how the city spends its money?
2. Does your city have a local property tax or a local income tax? Do you think your city requires residents to pay too many taxes?
3. If your city had to cut its budget by 10 percent, what do you think should be cut?
4. If your city had 10 percent extra revenue, what should the city do with that money?
5. How should the city decide how to spend its money? Do citizens have enough say in how those decisions are made? What could you do to change that?
6. How can cities make their budgeting process more transparent to their citizens?

REFERENCES

Bickis, Ian. 2017. "How Will Climate Change Affect Pensions?" *The Hamilton Spectator*. Accessed on February 10, 2017 from http://m.thespec.com/news-story/7103713-how-will-climate-change-affect-pensions-/

City of Stockton. *Chapter 9 Bankruptcy*. Accessed on March 25, 2015 from www.stocktongov.com/government/departments/manager/bankruptcy/

Coe, Charles K. July–August 2008. "Preventing Local Government Fiscal Crises: Emerging Best Practices." *Public Administration Review* 68 (4): pp. 759–767.

Ebdon, Carol, and Franklin, Aimee L. May–June 2006. "Citizen Participation in Budget Theory." *Public Administration Review* 66 (3): pp. 437–447.

Evans, S., Kosenko, B., and Polyakov, M. 2012. *How Stockton Went Bust: A California City's Decade of Policies and the Financial Crisis that Followed. California Common Sense.* Accessed on March 26, 2015 from http://

cacs.org/research/how-stockton-went-bust-a-california-citys-decade-of-policies-and-the-financial-crisis-that-followed/

Goldberg, Jeffrey, and Neiman, Max. 2014. *Managing Budgets during Fiscal Stress: Lessons for Local Government Officials.* Alexandria, VA: IBM Center for the Business of Government.

Groden, Claire. 2014. "Detroit and Stockton Are Just the Beginning of an Attack on Public Pensions." *New Republic,* December 22, 2014. Accessed on March 27, 2015 from www.newrepublic.com/article/120630/stockton-detroit-bankruptcies-gut-budgets-and-imperil-pensions

Guillen, Joe. 2013. "Status Report on Services, More in Detroit's Fiscal Crisis." *Detroit Free Press.* Accessed on June 10, 2013 from www.freep.com/article/20130610/NEWS01/306100102/Status-report-services-more-Detroit-s-fiscal-crisis

Helms, Matt, and Guillen, Joe. 2013. "Detroit's 45-day Report: Orr Calls City 'Dysfunctional and Wasteful After Years of Mismanagement, Corruption'." *Detroit Free Press.* Accessed on March 27, 2015 from www.freep.com/article/20130512/NEWS01/305120163/detroit-financial-crisis-kevyn-orr-report

New York Times. 2013. "Anatomy of Detroit's Decline: Interactive Feature." *New York Times.* Accessed on March 30, 2015 from www.nytimes.com/interactive/2013/08/17/us/detroit-decline.html

Participatory Budgeting Project. 2014. *Real Money, Real Power: A Report on the First Five Years of the Participatory Budgeting Project.* Accessed on December 10, 2014 from www.participatorybudgeting.org/wp-content/uploads/2014/04/PBP-5-Year-Report.pdf

Pew Charitable Trusts. 2013. *A Widening Gap in Cities: Shortfalls in Funding for Pensions and Retiree Health Care.* Accessed on March 27, 2015 from www.pewtrusts.org/en/research-and-analysis/reports/0001/01/01/a-widening-gap-in-cities

Saunder, Pete. 2016. "Detroit After Bankruptcy." *Forbes,* April 24, 2016. Accessed on March 30, 2015 from www.forbes.com/sites/petesaunders1/2016/04/24/detroit-after-bankruptcy/#250574f838e4

Seelye, Katharine Q. 2011. "Detroit Census Confirms a Desertion Like No Other." *New York Times,* March 22, 2011. Accessed on March 30, 2015 from www.nytimes.com/2011/03/23/us/23detroit.html

Sugrue, Thomas J. 2007. "Motor City: The Story of Detroit." Gilder Lehrman Institute of American History. Accessed on March 30, 2015 from https://www.gilderlehrman.org/history-by-era/politics-reform/essays/motor-city-story-detroit

U.S. Congressional Budget Office. December 2010. *Fiscal Stress Faced by Local Governments.* Washington, D.C.

Wilson, Kurt O. 2015. "An Open Letter to the Community Stockton Exits Bankruptcy." *City of Stockton,* February 25, 2015. Accessed on January 17, 2017 from www.stocktongov.com/files/OpenLetterCommunity_CM_ExitBK_2015_2_25.pdf

CHAPTER

6

Employees as Human Resources

Albert C. Hyde

AN INTRODUCTION TO THE URBAN
PUBLIC SECTOR WORKFORCE

It is no accident that human resources management plays such an important role in contemporary urban public management. Look at any city or urban county government's
budget, and in general more than two-thirds of the operating costs are for personnel.
While many sectors of the economy have been subject to huge shifts in employment because
of the forces of technology, marketization, and globalization, urban governments with their
emphases on education, public safety, and health and human services have retained their
workforces (so far). This is not to say that there have not been some major changes, especially due to contracting (or marketization as it is better termed) and technology, but urban
governments still have large professional workforces. The fact that human resource management is especially called out in the NASPAA standards for Urban Administration lends
weight to the importance of being able to effectively manage the personnel in cities, as city
managers work to effectively provide urban services.

This chapter examines the workforce that is presently employed by urban governments and sifts through where this workforce is regarding the larger population of state
and local government, what kinds of governmental units does it work for, and what functions or professions are involved. It also provides a brief history of civil service reform—
which can rightly claim to have had its core origins in the good government efforts of the
19th century first advanced in U.S. cities. How that reform effort has affected the structure, legal framework, and functions of modern public personnel administration is also
examined. A structural example is used—taking the City of New Orleans—to illustrate
how a civil service commission and a central personnel management agency are related,
where they are found in the larger city organizational structure, and how the modern functions of personnel management operate.

Two major environmental dimensions of modern urban human resources management are then examined. First is the advance of collective bargaining and the changing
role of unions and negotiating strategies. The changing role of unions is critical to consider because urban human resources management operates, more than any other level of
governments in the United States, in a public union environment. The second contextual
dimension is pension and benefits and the looming struggle for many cities to get their

103

pension systems under control and ensure that they have the resources to fund their obligations for the future.

By way of a conclusion, there is a review of functional (internal) and organizational environment (external) metrics and how urban public human resources management (HRM) can and should be assessed for productivity, performance, and impact. However, to understand the objectives and effectiveness of urban HRM strategies and processes, some context is needed. Who are the employers and the employees that make up the nearly 14 million members of the local government workforce in the United States and that comprise the "talent pool" of urban public human resources management? As a result of learning this material, students will have progressed in their knowledge required under the NASPAA Urban Administration goal for human resources management.

MUNICIPAL MANAGEMENT AND CIVIL SERVICE REFORM: A SHORT HISTORY

Urban public human resources management has its definitive history. Early government textbooks in the first quarter of the 20th century that focused on municipal management touted civil service reform as a core principle in the progressive effort to modernize management. Equating civil service reform and modernization was not an exaggeration. The *American City Magazine*, a leading voice in urban development, noted in 1911 that any city in the present state of municipal advancement and progress that had no provision for civil service was as much behind the times as a city without electric lights, telephones, and streetcars (Hyde and Shafritz 2016).

While space permits only a brief historical note, it is important to see the transition of civil service reform to personnel administration to modern human resources management for context. The first period (1890s–1950s) was indeed simply converting workforce hiring and selection from the spoils systems and city machine politics that relied on city hiring or patronage to remain in power. The early reformers assumed as one early textbook noted, "Personnel is largely a matter of standards, and standards are the result of education" (Munro 1919, p. 204). As city government hiring and selection moved to ensuring that the most qualified were selected, the reformers insisted that the civil service is administered by a neutral, non-partisan Civil Service Commission. A Commission served as both executive overseer and judicial reviewer of disputes and policy issues. This civil service commission model assumed that the classic model of politics-administration dichotomy was in effect. This model is nicely summarized in the following description of the two-part effective urban administration: "Of course they need able leadership . . . the mayor-city manager and the department heads furnish such leadership, but no amount of vision or ambition on the part of these major officials can fully compensate for untrained, indifferent and unintelligent employees" (Zink 1939, p. 360).

However, there were always tensions about the Civil Service Commission administrative model. As city and county governments became larger, the workforces more specialized and professional, personnel practices more sophisticated and complex, and the executive political leadership more demanding and assertive about its agendas, the seeds of the second period of civil service as personnel management (1960s–1990s) were sown. The central issue of this period was structural, the role of the Civil Service Commission. As Mosher and Kingsley (1941, p. 48) warned in their personnel textbook: "Civil service tradition" is "greatly complicated by the existence of this semi-external and so-called nonpartisan employment agency. The assignment of extensive power to the civil service commission has caused a division of control in the personnel field that has proved to be harmful . . . the attitude of 'operating heads' is at best one of toleration and at worst one of outspoken intolerance."

So civil service reform in U.S. governments at all levels began separating the executive and judicial powers within the civil service system. The primary task was to establish a central personnel management office to handle the workforce management functions and implement policies, but one that was clearly working for the executive. Some cities retained their Civil Service Commission as an appeals board, while others created other avenues to handle disputes and increasingly legal suits filed by employees. By the 1970s, as public unions came into prominence in local government, unions would represent employees and raise the stakes of how employee disputes would be handled.

In summary, during this period of civil service, reform in the United States was caught up in public management reform, meaning it was more important to have human resources responsible to the political executive or appointed executives and helping shape the government's management agenda. This coincided with the growing strength of unions in government, which meant that the central HR function had to handle collective bargaining responsibilities (something a Civil Service Commission was not designed to do). Added to this, by the 1980s, a second factor was growing—that of contracting out services, which added additional complexity to the workforce management role and was even more difficult to reconcile with the ideals of having a Civil Service Commission as the executive manager.

To allow this division to be seen a little more clearly, the stated roles and responsibilities of the City of New Orleans' central personnel agency, still called the Civil Service Department (www.nola.gov/civil-service/), are contrasted to those of the City's Civil Service Commission. The City Civil Service is divided into two parts:

- The Civil Service Department (typically called Department of Human Resources or Personnel, elsewhere) is a constitutionally created entity. The department is responsible for the overall administration of the personnel function in City government.
- The Civil Service Commission, likewise a constitutionally created entity, is the policy-making body that exercises oversight of activities of the Civil Service Department. The five members of the Civil Service Commission are appointed by the New Orleans City Council to overlapping six-year terms. Four of the members are nominated by the Presidents of designated local universities, and one member is a City employee nominated by fellow employees. The commission is a quasi-judicial body with the power to make rules that have the force and effect of law. In its judicial capacity, the Commission serves as the court of the first instance for all employee appeals resulting from disciplinary actions. In its legislative capacity, it adopts rules and establishes policies that regulate the conduct of labor and management in the merit system.

(New Orleans Civil Service Commission 2016)

A final perspective is offered by looking into the Civil Service Department, not so much to see how it is structured but to get a sense of what the "functions" of a modern human resources management office are. There are six such functions:

- Staffing (workforce planning and staffing allotments);
- Classification and Compensation;

- Hiring and Selection;
- Performance Appraisal and Promotion;
- Training and Development; and
- Employee Relations (Assistance Programs and Dispute Resolution).

Here is how they are covered in the division responsibilities for the City of New Orleans Department of Civil Service (City of New Orleans, Civil Service Department, 2016):

Director's Office

Personnel Director
Deputy-Personnel Director

Divisions

Recruitment and Selection Division   This division responds to the personnel staffing needs of City agencies. The Testing Section recruits applicants, screens all applications, administers and scores the examinations, and prepares lists of eligible candidates. The Certification Section maintains registers of eligible candidates and certifies them to appointing authorities to fill vacancies or to promote existing employees.

Classification and Compensation Division   Classification and Compensation is responsible for the maintenance of a uniform and equitable system of job classification of employee positions and the compensation for each. The staff of this division conducts job audits of positions, performs salary and fringe benefit surveys, and investigates complaints regarding inappropriate assignment or compensation. This division also receives, processes, updates, and maintains personnel forms and records for City employees.

Test Development and Validation Division   This division formulates, develops, and validates examination procedures and determines the best measures to use in assessing the knowledge, skills, and abilities of prospective candidates for employment and promotion.

Management Services Division   Management Services is responsible for coordinating the employee appeal process before the Civil Service Commission. This division is also responsible for the review of personal and professional services contracts for compliance with Civil Service Rules.

Public and Employee Relations Division   Public and Employee Relations provides information to employees, departments, and the public concerning the functions and activities of the Civil Service Commission and Department. This division is involved in the development of programs to address specific problems and grievances of City employees. This division provides information to departments to keep employees informed of current policies and programs that affect their employment. Coordination of public records requests, employee elections, and substance abuse testing are also a part of this division.

Employee Growth and Development Division   Employee Growth and Development coordinates and develops programs for employee personal and professional growth and development. These programs include training modules that are specifically job-related and are designed as vehicles for promotion and advancement. This division also administers the employee performance appraisal process.

A third period of development (2000–present) is now emerging. It reflects the major challenges that confront large and small cities and most local governments. Contracting or outsourcing is now an ever-present force as governments continue to examine what functions and services they will provide and how and what workforce they will require. Contracting in the 1980s and 1990s was first aimed at direct services and utilities that could be priced (garbage collection, custodial and security services, utilities, and ambulance services are good examples). A second wave involved social services as nonprofit organizations were rewarded contracts to handle a range of housing assistance, employment training, welfare, and health care services. A third wave now involves both administrative functions and essential city services such as police and fire and charter schools. It will be instructive to see how urban human resources managers handle potential contracting of IT services and even their core personnel functions. Many of these decisions are driven by personnel costs and technology factors. In addressing these challenges, it is important to examine the effect of collective bargaining and public unions that are a major aspect of managing human resources in cities.

BOX 6.1   CAREER PATHWAYS IN PERSONNEL MANAGEMENT

Current Position

Catherine is currently a Personnel Analyst for a major city.

Education

B.A., Sociology
M.P.A.

Career Pathway

Catherine started as a Personnel Analyst Trainee in a major city and is now a Personnel Analyst. This position is a permanent Civil Service position.

Learning about the Job

Catherine participated in an HR training program that was offered by her current agency. The program provided both classroom-style workshops and hands-on training in various aspects of human resources, such as Recruitment, Employee Relations, Equal Employment Opportunity, Operations, Workforce Development, and Workers' Compensation.

Finding Her Way to Public Works

Catherine initially interned and worked for elected officials during and after

BOX 6.1 (CONTINUED)

undergraduate school. She became more interested in city management and ended up pursuing a Master's in Public Administration. During the M.P.A. program, she interned in a city manager's office, and it was there that she learned about governmental human resources management. That internship eventually led her to apply for the HR training program.

A Typical Day

Catherine provides HR services to a specific division in the agency, so her day consists of answering questions for staff in that division and processing requests. She also works on special projects, which entails compiling/analyzing data, as well as training and consulting hiring managers and other HR analysts on a new hiring process that she helped develop.

Professional Associations and Networking

Catherine is a member of Pi Alpha Alpha, the national honor society for students of public administration. She likes to network through LinkedIn and human resource management conferences.

Most Helpful to Her Career

Catherine has found that it is important to have supervisors/managers who are willing to

coach and mentor her and provide her with new opportunities to learn.

Challenges

Other divisions within Catherine's agency often have a negative perception of human resources because HR processes are not always transparent and can take a long time.

Overcoming These Challenges

Catherine tries to be as transparent and proactive as possible to overcome other divisions' negative perception of her division. Also, she is working on projects that aim to make various HR processes more efficient and effective.

Most Rewarding Part of the Job

Catherine says, "In government, our employees are our most important resources. It is rewarding to hire employees who are motivated to deliver services to our community as well as work on a variety of projects that address process inefficiencies and employee engagement."

Recommendations for Students

Catherine recommends taking advantage of the many paid and unpaid internships that are available, stating that internships provided her with invaluable knowledge and experiences.

WHAT IS THE URBAN PUBLIC WORKFORCE AND FOR WHOM DO THEY WORK?

The urban public workforce is public sector employees and contractors who work for governments in urban areas. If one uses the U.S. Census definitions of urban areas, 80.7 percent of the U.S. population live in either an "urban area" of more than 50,000 people or in an "urban cluster," an area with 2,500 to 50,000 people. These definitions are important because a baseline metric often used in modern human resources management is the ratio of employees per citizens served. If the same Census data is used (state and local governments are surveyed every five years), one might make the calculation that 80 percent of the nearly 14 million local government employees, both full-time and part-time, constitute the urban public workforce.

Table 6.1 and Figure 6.1 provide a historical comparison of the growth of the government workforces since 1962. Essentially, the size of the federal workforce peaked in the early 1990s

TABLE 6.1

The Growth of the Government Workforce and the U.S. Population, 1962–2012

	1962	1972	1982	1992	2002	2012
Government Employment	(000s)	(000s)	(000s)	(000s)	(000s)	(000s)
Full-Time & Part-Time Employment	9,388	13,759	15,841	18,165	21,039	22,044
Local Government	5,169	8,007	9,249	10,531	13,277	13,954
State Government	1,680	2,957	3,744	4,587	5,072	5,290
Federal Government	2,539	2,795	2,848	3,047	2,690	2,800
Local Per Capita	36	26	25	24	22	23
State Per Capita	111	71	62	56	57	59
Federal Per Capita	73	75	81	84	107	112
U.S. Population (000s)	186,538	209,896	231,664	254,995	287,804	314,100

Source: U.S. Census Bureau 2014. *"2012 Census of Governments"* Employment Summary. C12-CG EMP: p. 7.

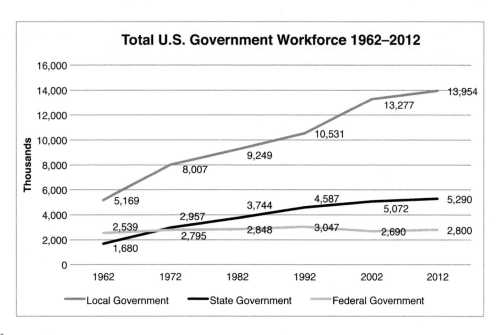

FIGURE 6.1
The Growth of the Government Workforce

Source: U.S. Census Bureau 2002. *Government Organization* 1 (1): pp. 4–7.

and had been declining ever since (regarding the numbers of workers per capita). State government workforce growth has continued to increase marginally, but the workers per capita ratio has stabilized. Only in local government has there been a modest increase in the overall size of the workforce and a per capita ratio that has kept pace with the population growth.

However, it is more complicated than that, and this section uses several tables and graphs to explain some of the key differences among cities and the forms of government that have public employees. While the concept of "urban area" is useful for showing the extent to which Americans are becoming urbanized, the U.S. Census Bureau also provides a better measurement by reporting on the number of Americans who live in "incorporated places, or cities" (U.S. Census Bureau 2013, p. 1). Accordingly, the U.S. Census notes that 62.7 percent of the U.S. population lived in 19,508 "cities" in 2013. The size of these 19,508 cities varies considerably, however, as Table 6.2 illustrates. One tends to think of cities in a global context as the primary driving force for population change, but even the top 200 U.S. cities with a population exceeding 200,000 account for only 15 percent of the U.S. population. As Table 6.2 illustrates, each of the eight size categories of U.S. cities from the smallest (less than 10,000) to more than a million has about 10 percent share of the U.S. population.

However, what makes the urban government workforce difficult to analyze as a whole is the fragmentation of the types of government entities. Table 6.3 shows a 50-year time spread of forms of government units. There is little change in the total number; the more than 91,000 units of governments in 1962 are now at 89,000. Counties are the same (there are exceptions such as Massachusetts, which in the late 1990s had the state government take over the functions of all of its counties). There are slightly more municipalities and fewer townships. However, the number of school districts has decreased by nearly two-thirds, while the number of special districts has doubled. The real point is that when

TABLE 6.2

U.S. "Cities" (Incorporated Places) by Population Size, 2000–2013

Category by Size	Number of Cities	Number of Cities	Population "Census" (in Millions)	Population "Estimate" (in Millions)	Pct. of U.S. Population	Pct. of U.S. Population
	2000	2013	(281.4 U.S.) 2000	(316.7 U.S.) 2013	2000	2013
Number of Cities	19,454	19,508	174.1	198.2	61.9%	62.7%
>1 mil.	9	9	22.9	24.3	8.2%	7.7%
500–999	20	25	12.9	17.3	4.6%	5.5%
250–499	38	41	13.7	15.0	4.9%	4.8%
100–249	173	216	25.7	32.4	9.1%	10.2%
50–99	363	450	24.9	31.1	8.8%	9.9%
25–49	644	718	22.6	24.9	8.0%	7.9%
10–24	1,435	1,553	22.6	24.5	8.0%	7.7%
<10,000	16,772	16,949	28.7	28.6	10.2%	9.1%

Source: U.S Census Bureau 2015. *Current Population Reports.* March 2015: p. 2.

TABLE 6.3

Number of Local Governments by Type in U.S., 1962–2012

Local Governments	1962	1972	1982	1992	2002	2012
Totals	91,185	78,218	81,780	84,975	87,525	89,004
Counties	3,043	3,044	3,041	3,043	3,034	3,031
Municipalities	17,997	18,517	19,076	19,279	19,429	19,522
Townships	17,144	16,991	16,734	16,656	16,504	16,364
School Districts	34,678	15,781	14,851	14,442	13,506	12,884
Special Districts	18,323	23,885	28,078	31,555	35,052	37,203

Source: U.S. Census Bureau 2002. *Government Organization* 1 (1): pp. 4–7.

one points to the public workforce in an urban area, one is pointing to at least four different types of public entities that employ that workforce. Most teachers work for the school districts, transit and utility workers may work for a special district, police and firefighters work for a city government, and parks and corrections workers work for a county.

WHO IS THE URBAN PUBLIC WORKFORCE AND WHAT DO THEY DO?

Table 6.4 and Table 6.5 provide a more in-depth view of the modern American urban workforce. As it happens, the 2002 and 2012 Censuses have conducted what they call a snapshot analysis of the local government workforce. Since the numbers of local government workers have held fairly steady, the two reports can show two different dimensions;

TABLE 6.4

U.S. Local Government Employees by Employer, 2002

Type of Government 2002	Total (thousands)	Full-Time (thousands)	Part-Time (thousands)	FTE* (thousands)	Percentage Total FTEs
Counties	2,729	2,257	472	2,662	23.4%
Municipalities	2,972	2,376	596	2,594	22.8%
Townships	488	273	215	323	2.8%
School Districts	6,367	4,706	1,661	5,390	47.4%
Special Districts	721	537	184	611	5.4%
Total Governments	13,277	10,150	3,127	11,379	100.0%

*Full-time equivalent

Source: U.S. Census Bureau 2014. Jessie, Lisa, and Tarleton, Mary. "2012 Census of Governments." Employment Summary Report. C12-CG EMP: p. 7; and U.S. Census Bureau 2004. *Compendium of Public Employment 2002* Volume 3 Public employment GCO 2(3) 2.

in 2002, the snapshot report shows how large the workforces are across different types of governments (for both full-time and part-time, though sadly no numbers are provided for contract employees), and, in 2012, the snapshot reports on what functions they work in.

It will come as no surprise that school districts employ the largest number of local government workers (47.5 percent), just as education is the largest function (also 47.5 percent). Municipalities and counties each have about 23 percent of the local government workforce. While special districts have only 5 percent of the workforce, this number is a misnomer since it does not include a count of how many contract employees are part of their budgets. Other large functions should not come as a surprise either with health care, police, utilities, and fire in the top rankings. Their percentage shares are diminished because of the inclusion of education in the table.

However, the question this section began with concerned the conventional metric for ascertaining the number of public workers needed to serve citizens. This question does come up in the media and is even used by some governments in their budget documents to justify their workforce levels. When the 2012 Census data were released, one media source (*The Washington Examiner*) took the 100 plus U.S. cities with a population more

TABLE 6.5

U.S. Local Government Employees by Function, 2012

Function 2012	State Employees	Pct. of State	Local Govt. Employees	Pct. of Local
	Full-Time & Part-Time	*Workforce*	*Full-Time & Part-Time*	*Workforce*
Education (Elem. & Secondary)	1,909,288	27.0%	5,781,754	47.5%
Health & Hospitals	629,083	8.9%	898,073	7.4%
Police	107,718	1.5%	883,053	7.3%
General Govt. & Finance	219,458	3.1%	755,169	6.2%
Education (Higher)	2,598,785	36.7%	603,630	5.0%
Transportation & Transit	266,691	3.8%	546,357	4.5%
Public Utilities & Waste Mgt.	9,109	0.1%	435,004	3.6%
Fire	0	0.0%	426,663	3.5%
Social Services & Housing	321,535	4.5%	406,698	3.3%
Parks & Natural Resources	185,578	2.6%	391,980	3.2%
All Others	203,557	2.9%	351,633	2.9%
Corrections	444,534	6.3%	263,289	2.2%
Judicial & Legal	175,056	2.5%	254,224	2.1%
Libraries	7,352	0.1%	179,217	1.5%
All Functions	7,077,744	100.0%	12,176,743	100.0%

Source: U.S. Census Bureau 2014. Jessie, Lisa, and Tarleton, Mary. "2012 Census of Governments." Employment Summary Report. C12-CG EMP: p. 7; and U.S. Census Bureau 2004. *Compendium of Public Employment 2002* Volume 3 Public employment GC0 2(3) 2.

than 200,000 took out the school and special districts' workforce and compared the difference. It then asked the question: Why does San Francisco (the highest city) have one employee per 28 citizens while San Diego has one per 137 citizens (Rosiak 2013)?

Table 6.6 is an attempt to explain the variance found with the use of the workforce per capita metric as well as to update it by cross-referencing the city's current budget.

TABLE 6.6

Decile Sample of U.S. Cities by Employees Per Capita (2012 Census)

City/Ranking	Employees Per Capita	2012 Population	City Workforce Total	City Payroll (000s)	Mean Salary
San Francisco[1]	28	805,235	28,660	$2,564,000	$90,702
Atlanta	51	420,003	8,091	$371,573	$45,931
Boston	65	617,594	9,390	$687,646	$74,347
Minneapolis	74	382,578	5,111	$310,851	$62,309
Orlando	85	238,300	2,799	$169,484	$60,697
Pittsburgh	94	305,704	3,251	$183,233	$57,387
Phoenix	103	1,445,632	13,924	$941,073	$68,685
Fort Worth	116	741,206	6,386	$384,495	$61,492
Boise	127	205,671	1,616	$88,901	$57,760
San Diego	137	1,307,402	9,501	$733,740	$78,759
Las Vegas	225	583,756	2,594	$214,500	$88,113

2015 Appendix	2016 Workforce	City Budget— General Fund	Budgeted Wages & Salaries	Budgeted Benefits	Percent for Personnel Costs for Public Safety
San Francisco	30,111	$8,959,830,801	$3,246,650	$1,371,426	52%
Atlanta	9,378	$605,388,585	$255,100	$118,632	62%
Boston	8,219	$1,201,656,000	$743,825	$181,450	77%
Minneapolis	4,875	$1,300,000,000	$336,800	$139,600	37%
Orlando	3,186	$401,607,332	$144,544	$124,766	67%
Pittsburgh	3,250	$524,882,112	$223,894	$149,521	71%
Phoenix	14,421	$3,307,788,000	$1,424,377	N.A.[2]	43%
Fort Worth	6,407	$610,902,639	$312,216	$131,523	73%
Boise	1,646	$190,751,135	$86,341	$43,940	68%
San Diego	7,299	$1,288,000,000	$522,400	$356,300	68%
Las Vegas	3,272	$469,484,282	$156,686	$124,030	60%

Source: Compiled by author referencing city budgets and Census data.

1 City-County consolidated
2 Not available—Not broken out in either the City Budget or Comprehensive Annual Finance Report (CAFR)

The 100 plus cities were ranked by number of employees per citizen (EPC), and one city was chosen at random from each of the 11 deciles. As mentioned, all school district and special district workforces were removed to show the municipal workforce, although there were still several exceptions noted in the table. Using the 2012 Census data, the table shows the EPC calculation, city population, annual city payroll, and mean salary. An additional variable is introduced addressing the question of how much of the city workforce is dedicated to public safety, i.e., police and fire. Table 6.6 updates the sample showing the cities' current workforce and how much is budgeted out of their general fund for wages and benefits.

A few observations can be allowed with the caveat that this is not analysis, merely an exploration of conventional metrics and the range of variance. The two most conventional metrics from personnel textbooks are that personnel costs are 60 to 70 percent of the operating budget and that public safety is 40 to 50 percent or almost half of a city's workforce. Table 6.6 shows that the conventional metrics do hold for the most part for the sample. Nine of the 11 cities have 40 percent of their workforce in public safety. Moreover, eight of the sample cities have personnel costs more than 60 percent. A third conventional metric is that benefits will be about 30 percent of salary costs. That convention does not hold, as ten of the 11 cities have benefits to salary ratios of more than 40 percent, and the sample, albeit small, average was more than 50 percent.

This discussion of the numbers of employers and employees provides some context for the subsequent assessment of HRM processes and challenges. Human resource management is vital because human resources are where city governments spend the largest percentage of their budgets. However, that would be missing the larger point that the variation among cities and other units of government makes human resource management decisions both complex and competitive.

The public urban workforce (or local government), like its state and federal counterparts, is older than the private sector workforce, as well as more highly educated. The average age of a local government employee is 44 (the private sector mean age is 40), but more than 35 percent of local government workers are more than 50 (the private sector more than 50 component is 26 percent). Given the numbers of local government employees in education, having 26 percent of local government workers with a four-year degree, and another 23 percent with a graduate degree (compared to 19 percent and 8 percent for the private sector), is to be expected. While having an older, more educated (and, as will be seen, unionized) workforce has its advantages; it also presents challenges regarding succession planning (finding the next generation), salary comparability (wage and benefits), and retirement security (pension liability).

DIVERSITY AND REPRESENTATIVE BUREAUCRACY

One other dimension to understanding workforce demographics and dynamics in urban public human resources management should be considered: how representative of the urban population is the public workforce. The importance of this factor has been reinforced by the riots in Ferguson, Missouri after Michael Brown was killed by the City Police there in early August 2014. Underneath the widespread and heavily publicized protest activity directed at alleged police misconduct, which has spread to Baltimore, Chicago, and other cities, special attention was given to the characteristics of the police force in Ferguson. While Ferguson is a small city where African-Americans were 67 percent of the population, a large percentage of the police force was white (50 out of 53 officers). This lack of diversity greatly diminished the department's credibility and made it even more difficult to explain why 85 percent of traffic stops, 90 percent of citations, and 93 percent of all arrests were for African-Americans.

Moreover, Ferguson is hardly unique. A 2007 national survey of police departments showed hundreds of police departments in the United States where the percentage of whites in the police force exceeds by more than 30 percentage points the populations in the communities they serve (Askenas and Park 2015). Minorities today make up just a third of police forces nationally, as Table 6.7 illustrates.

Recently, the U.S. Census Bureau conducted a 50-year review of the diversity of local government employment in large metro areas in the United States. The purpose of the study was threefold. First, it is the large metro areas where the U.S. population has become

TABLE 6.7

Diversity of State and Local Governments, 2013—Full-Time Employment by Race for Levels of Government with Special Reference to Police

		TOTAL		White	Black	Hispanic	Asian	Native American
		Number	Percent	Percent	Percent	Percent	Percent	Percent
All State & Local Governments	TOTAL	5,622,923	100%	65.3%	18.8%	11.3%	4.0%	0.7%
	Male	3,055,022	54.3	37.8	8.3	5.9	2.0	0.4
	Female	2,567,901	45.7	27.5	10.5	5.4	1.9	0.3
County Governments	TOTAL	1,354,810	100%	68.7%	14.2%	12.4%	3.9%	0.7%
	Male	661,168	48.8	35.5	5.9	5.4	1.6	0.3
	Female	693,642	51.2	33.3	8.3	6.9	2.3	0.4
City Governments	TOTAL	1,397,114	100%	63.4%	19.2%	13.1%	3.7%	0.6%
	Male	987,730	70.7	47.8	11.1	9	2.4	0.4
	Female	409,384	29.3	15.6	8.1	4.1	1.4	0.2
Special Districts	TOTAL	653,288	100%	54.2%	26.2%	12.7%	6.3%	0.5%
	Male	319,047	48.8	26.5	12.4	6.4	3.3	0.3
	Female	334,241	51.2	27.7	13.9	6.3	3.1	0.2
School Districts	TOTAL	4,621,748	100.0%	74.0%	12.4%	10.8%	2.2%	0.6%
	Male	1,161,980	25.1	18.1	3.4	2.9	0.6	0.2
	Female	3,459,768	74.9	55.9	9.0	7.9	1.6	0.5
Police	TOTAL	591,734	100%	66.2%	16.1%	13.9%	3.2%	0.6%
	Male	420,879	71.1	49.9	8.9	9.6	2.3	0.4
	Female	170,855	28.9	16.3	7.1	4.3	0.9	0.2

Source: U.S. Equal Employment Opportunity Commission. 2013. "Job Patterns for Minorities and Women in State and Local Government."

most diverse, tracking the change in the percentage of whites in central cities from 76.3 percent in 1960 to 41 percent in 2008. Therefore, it is important that local governments keep pace. Second, the U.S. Census Bureau points to the long practice of local governments being a primary job source and a major pathway toward upward social mobility. Finally, the Census Bureau emphasizes the importance of mobility within local government—that minorities make progress in advancing to the upper ranks and higher salaried positions in local government. This Census Bureau study has detailed information for the largest 100 metro areas. With it, any city human resource manager can see their metro area's demographics (White, African-American, Hispanic, and Asian) and compare both their overall representation in diversity and their level of social equity in promotion advancement by measuring low-income versus high-income rates versus the rate of population diversification (Gardner 2013; U.S. Census Bureau).

That the results indicate unequal progress is to be expected. African-Americans have made the most progress—first in overall representation (especially in the South) and now nationally, being more proportionately represented in the higher ranks. Now, it is Hispanics and other minority groups that are lagging (especially in the West where their representation in the population has risen markedly). The study concludes that mobility rates, as shown in the higher ranks, have progressed for minorities, but local governments in urban areas are still pressed to keep up with greater rates of population diversification.

Table 6.7 also shows another dimension that must be accorded attention—the gender gap. The national averages are distorted by occupational segregation rates that still exist. Since teachers are more than half of the workforce of local government and more than 75 percent of teachers are female, this pushes the gender diversity rate of school districts to a largely female workforce. Likewise, police and fire are still largely male-dominated work domains (more than 70 percent), meaning municipal governments are largely a male workforce. Counties and special districts are more at parity.

As comparable worth, the term for concerns that employees receive comparable pay, no matter their gender, re-emerges in the national economy, urban governments may have to address the long-standing problem of gender occupational segregation. Completing this reexamination will bring new attention to discrimination and occupational policies and practices for the LGBT community. Metrics will be put in place in the future to assess how governments—as the front runners for advancing equal opportunity in our society—are doing and what needs to be done. All of this takes time; it was only 50 years ago that the Civil Rights Act of 1964 passed, making discrimination by race, sex, color, religion, and national origin illegal. Further, it was only in 1980 that the Census inserted formal questions on Hispanic origin so that Hispanic ethnicity could be measured.

COLLECTIVE BARGAINING AND LABOR RELATIONS

One key area in which urban human resources management is different from other forms of public and certainly private sector management is the extent to which labor relations and collective bargaining are major dimensions. As of 2015, public sector employees were five times more likely to be union members (32.5 percent to 6.7 percent) than private sector workers. Moreover, among public sector employees, the local government had the highest membership rate. In 2015, local government membership was at 41.3 percent compared to state government at 30.2 percent and federal employees at 27.3 percent. The usual explanation is that the public sector's public safety workers (police, corrections, and firefighters) are much more unionized. However, it is education that is the driving force, as a recent U.S. Bureau of Labor Statistics report notes; it is the high percentage of women working as public-school teachers that also counts for the 60 percent presence of women as union members. This also means that women constitute the majority of public sector union members (Dunn and Walker 2016).

However, the significant presence of unions in urban government is not universal. Indeed, five states still do not allow public workers the right to collective bargaining. More recently, the collective bargaining rights of public sector employees were severely curtailed in two states, Wisconsin (2010) and Indiana (2011). In a third state, Ohio, restrictions were later overturned by voter referendum.

Among the 40 plus states that allow collective bargaining, only 12 allow teachers the right to strike. More limited still, only two states, Hawaii and Ohio, allow firefighters and police the right to strike. While the right to strike is seen as significant, recent practices show that public sector strikes, or work stoppages, are rare. This does not mean, as the Chicago teachers' strike or the BART transit workers' strikes in San Francisco in 2013 revealed, that there will not be bitter and difficult union confrontations. It does mean that strikes (and work lockouts) have been on the decline for a decade now. Work stoppages where more than 1,000 employees are involved have declined from an average of 83 per year from 1980 to 1989 to 35 from 1990 to 1999, down to 20 in the 2000–2009 decade. Since 2009, the average is down to 14 per year with only four per year being public sector strikes (U.S. Bureau of Labor Statistics 2010–2014). From 2009 to 2015, there were only 25 public sector major work stoppages involving 112,000 total urban government workers or less than .05 percent of the total local government workforce. While the strike is passé, public sector unions have learned to adapt, replacing confrontation and conflict with negotiation and other forms of dispute resolution or pursuing challenges in the courts.

The modern urban human resources manager now works with a range of methods for impasse resolution. Impasse itself is a transitory term; it is usually seen as a call for outside assistance when negotiations break down. The most common techniques used to break the impasse are mediation and arbitration. Mediation or conciliation is any attempt by an impartial third party to help settle disputes. A mediator has only the power of persuasion; their "suggestions" are advisory and may be rejected by both parties.

Arbitration is the more powerful tool. Here, an impartial third party (the arbitrator) will conduct a hearing, listen to both sides, and render a decision that may or may not be binding on both sides. (Arbitrators are usually selected jointly by labor and management, recommended by the Federal Mediation and Conciliation Service, by a state or local agency offering similar referrals, or by the private American Arbitration Association.) Compulsory arbitration is a negotiating process whereby the parties are required by law to arbitrate their dispute. Some state statutes concerning collective bargaining impasses in the public sector mandate that parties who have exhausted all other means must submit their dispute to an arbitrator. The problem with arbitration is that it undermines bargaining itself. Neither side is likely to make a serious attempt at compromise or even honest negotiation if it sees arbitration as the likely outcome.

The other means that unions rely on in current labor relations practice are court challenges. This is especially apparent regarding cuts in compensation, pension, and other benefits. Unions have challenged furloughs, pay freezes, and almost any of the attempts by governments for pension and benefit retrenchment (to be discussed in the next section) with a great deal of success. Often the objective of a court challenge is simply to force management to come to the bargaining table and negotiate some form of settlement.

However, the future success of unions in the public sector is far from certain. A recent decision by the State Supreme Court in Wisconsin attests to this. Unions challenged Act 10, Governor Scott Walker's signature law curtailing collective bargaining for public workers. In a 5-to-2 decision, justices rejected arguments that the restrictions on collective bargaining violated freedom of association and equal protection rights, among others. Justice Michael J. Gableman wrote the majority opinion, "No matter the limitations or 'burdens' a legislative enactment places on the collective bargaining process, collective bargaining remains a creation of legislative grace and not constitutional obligation" (*Madison Teachers et al. v Scott Walker* 2014). This decision was a highly significant case for local government unions because of the substantial reductions in union membership in Wisconsin that have followed. A recent media report found 132,000 fewer union members, mostly teachers and other public workers, putting "Wisconsin, the birthplace of public-employee unions, near the bottom third of states for unionized workforce" (Umhoefer 2016).

Public sector unions have confronted a larger challenge regarding preserving their ability to represent the public workforce. In a 1977 case (*Abood v. Detroit Board of Education*), the U.S. Supreme Court upheld public unions' right (in those states that permit collective bargaining) to charge nonmember workers a "fair share" of union dues or fees. Requiring nonmembers to pay that fair share prevents nonmembers from benefiting from a union's collective bargaining gains without paying for them, referred to as the free rider problem.

However, in 2012, a group of nonunion members filed a class action suit alleging that their First Amendment rights were violated when a union imposed an additional fee to cover advocacy expenses on nonunion members from whom it was collecting agency fees. In *Knox v. Service Employees International Union (SEIU)* (2012), the U.S. Supreme Court ruled that, although California law allowed for agency fees, the SEIU violated its nonunion members' free speech rights by not notifying them of the additional special assessment it had imposed for "political advocacy" purposes. The Court switched the burden to SEIU to give nonunion members the opportunity to opt in as opposed to having to file to opt out.

Finally, a 2014 case is also a potential harbinger of new times for labor unions. In *Harris v. Quinn* (2014), a minority of home care workers who did not want to join the union sued, saying that state law (Illinois) required them to pay an "agency fee" to cover the cost of representation. In this case, the U.S. Supreme Court ruled (5–4), stating that requiring home care workers to pay an agency fee constituted a violation of freedom of speech and association. This case is likely to be revisited. In 2016, following the death of one of its conservative core justices (Justice Antonin Scalia), the U.S. Supreme Court deadlocked 4-to-4 in a case that threatened the ability of public sector unions to collect fees from workers who chose not to join and did not want to pay for unions' collective bargaining activities. The deadlocked court affirmed the lower court ruling allowing unions to collect fees. However, the ruling provides no precedent and leaves the door open for further challenges.

The point of these cases is to show the two sides of the current legal dimension of public sector labor relations in city management. On the one hand, labor unions are pursuing every adverse change in compensation, pensions, and benefits to protect their members (current and retired). On the other hand, they are being challenged in some states regarding limits to bargaining and the ability to collect dues and retain members.

▶ BOX 6.2   UNDERSTANDING PENSIONS

Understanding public pensions can be quite challenging; here are some basic concepts involved in the public pension process.

1. When governments have pension programs, employees pay every month into the pension system. Those contributions are often, but not always, matched by their government employer itself. As explained in Chapter 5, those combined funds are then invested (hopefully, in very conservative investments) so that the amount of funds increases every year. As employees retire, their pensions are paid out of these funds.

2. Pension plans can be either defined contributions plans or defined benefits plans. For governments, the most expensive pension systems are those that have defined benefits, as these pension plans pay retirees a set amount of benefits, no matter how much they paid into the system. These are the gold standard of pension plans, and governments who have them are rapidly trying to get rid of them because they are so expensive. For defined contribution plans, the only thing that is constant is how much employees pay into the plans.

3. Governments have to have enough funds on hand to pay both their current expenses and the pension payments to retirees. If they have 100 percent of what they need to pay not just current retirees but what they agree to pay current employees when they retire, they have a fully funded retirement system. The big challenge for many cities today is they have only partially funded retirement systems.

4. With only partially funded retirement systems, governments tend to "pay-as-you-go," or use this year's money in the budget to pay this year's retirees, and just hope they will have enough employees to pay retirees what they are owed, in the future.

5. Then, the GASB stepped in to say that governments must fully state what they owe for their pensioners' health care plans and their pensions—i.e., their full liabilities. This decision was to ensure governments fully account for what they really owe to current employees and to retirees.

6. Therefore, cities and other governments are now having to find ways to reform their pension systems so that they can adhere to the GASB standards, balance their current budgets, and make good on what was promised to their retirees.

PUBLIC PENSIONS—REFORM VS. RETRENCHMENT FOR CITIES

It is hard to comprehend that just 15 years ago, the majority of public pension systems in the United States were at funding levels near 100 percent, meaning that state and local government had pension fund assets adequate to cover the required payments for their system beneficiaries (Mitchell, McCarthy, Wisniewski, and Zorn 2001). Now, financial headlines all over the country feature stories about cities facing dire financial straits because of lack of funds to cover required payments, the increasing percentage of the city budget that is the annual required contribution to cover pension funding, and what is increasingly viewed by many as excessive payments to retirees. City bankruptcies in Vallejo, California (2008), Central Falls, Rhode Island (2011), Detroit, Michigan (2014), and Stockton, California (2015), have also changed the perception of the perils of the pension situation (Slavin 2016).

A recent headline article about the City of Los Angeles nicely illustrates the dimensions of the current pension dilemma. Los Angeles passed pension reform in 2011. It struck down pension spiking (the practice of raising a salary in an employee's last year of employment before retiring, to increase the pension base and thus their pension). It also lowered the cap on what total pensions could be and increased the worker contribution rate for pensions and health care benefits. However, the reform has slowed pension cost growth only slightly. Retirement costs alone account for almost 20 percent of the operating budget. Los Angeles's average annual pension payments are among the highest in the country—for its police and fire—nearly $63,000 (Jamison 2016). Efforts to cut pension payments only apply to new employees.

The true picture among American cities is more mixed. Munnell and Aubrey, the leading researchers on public pensions, find that about 20 percent of U.S. cities, led by the City of Chicago, have pension problems that constitute an enormous challenge (Munnell and Aubrey 2016a). However, many cities and states have their costs under control and are only spending about 10 percent of their source revenues on pension payments. The issue of health care costs further complicates the picture, but a better picture of that will emerge as more cities comply with new financial reporting requirements that specify how these costs and future liabilities are shown in budgets. These new standards, part of the GASB 45 and 68 (2015) standards, dictate that the annual management costs and future financial liability for pensions and benefits must be fully disclosed. These standards now extend to pension plans that are shared plans, as is the case with many teacher plans that are managed by the state with contributions from the city and the school district (Munnell and Aubrey 2016b).

Reforms or retrenchment efforts are following a three-track model. The first track is to raise contribution levels by employees for both pensions and other post-employment benefits (OPEB, i.e., health care). A second track involves raising eligibility years of service and retirement age along with eliminating pension spiking, to have employees paying contributions into the system for a longer period. The third (and hardest track to get approved) is to cut benefit levels—first by limiting Cost of Living Adjustments (COLAs) and, then, by lowering benefit levels to reflect the fund's financial state. There is one path that can be pursued—that of declaring bankruptcy and then negotiating with the pension funds for lower or deferred payments, just like any bondholder.

These retrenchment tracks are all subject to legal challenges, and given the space limitations here, it is best to concentrate on the legal dimensions to better understand the space to maneuver that cities have. Public pensions were once considered a "gratuity" that could be modified or withdrawn by the state at any time. Monahan's (2010) analysis of state pension cases notes that, presently, in nearly all states and localities, pensions are protected by law. (In Indiana, involuntary plans are still considered a gratuity.) Thus, nearly all states' courts consider pensions to be either a contract between employees and retirees and the state or local jurisdiction or as "property," protected by the Fifth and Fourteenth Amendments to the Constitution. Some states have an explicit constitutional provision protecting public pensions, while others have clear statutory language. Where this is not the case, courts have still found a contractual obligation implicitly in the legislative history or through other circumstances (e.g., inclusion in collective bargaining agreements). When the public entity attempts to modify pension benefits by, for example, changing the benefit formula, beneficiaries frequently challenge that action. The courts then must decide if a contract existed when it took effect and whether that revision is consistent with the explicit or implicit contract. A substantial "impairment" usually may be justified if it is considered "reasonable and necessary to achieve an important public purpose" (Monahan

2010, p. 18). However, this can be a high standard to meet, and even jurisdictions facing dire financial straits have failed this test. Beyond that, the extent to which benefits can be altered varies from state to state. In most, retirees can consider their benefits safe, but the rights of current employees are unclear. In some states, only benefits for past retirees are protected, while in others, future benefits are as well; in others, it remains unclear.

In some states, where courts have been unable to find the existence of a contract, they instead consider them property. Under the Fifth and Fourteenth Amendments, this means they cannot be reduced without due process of law. Moreover, in theory, if that property is "taken," the employee must be provided with just compensation under the Fifth Amendment. However, this theory provides less protection for employees than the contract theory, because as long as the state can provide a rational reason for a change in benefits (such as a financial crisis), those changes may be justified. Challenges under the takings clause seeking just compensation are rarely successful.

Unfunded pension liabilities can be a significant factor in driving a locality to declare bankruptcy, in which case U.S. bankruptcy law comes into play. Vallejo, California was among the first to declare its union contracts, including their pension provisions, null and void as part of the bankruptcy process. Most unions were able to renegotiate their contracts with the city. However, in an unprecedented decision that caught nationwide attention, U.S. Bankruptcy Judge Michael McManus issued a decision on March 13, 2009, voiding the contract of the holdout union in Vallejo.

The bankruptcy statute includes a section (1113) that requires entities filing bankruptcy under Chapter 11 to follow certain requirements before rejecting collective bargaining agreements. However, Judge McManus ruled Congress did not extend this provision to Chapter 9 bankruptcies, which apply to municipalities, and so they were free to jettison collective bargaining agreements (*In re City of Vallejo* 2009). This ruling was subsequently affirmed by a U.S. District Court judge in 2010. Faced with the threat of losing their pension contracts, the city and unions went to negotiations to find a settlement that would avoid nullifying the contracts in 2010. A final settlement resulted in cuts in workers' pay, reductions in health care and other benefits, and increased workers' and retirees' contributions, but left pensions intact. That was still a better outcome than what Vallejo bondholders ended up with—being paid only five cents for every dollar owed.

Public sector unions will undoubtedly continue pursuing legal channels to reverse any blocking or rolling back of pension and benefit "claw back" efforts, a term describing efforts to get corporate executives and board members to return pay raises and bonuses paid for short-term financial gains. Over the last decade, numerous states have passed legislation to reduce pension benefits for future employees, or taken other budget steps to lower pension-related costs for current employees. In a similar vein, voter propositions have been passed to reduce pension benefits or obligations. Unions had challenged all such efforts as violations of promised contracts made to employees when they were hired.

An example shows the range and extent of these challenges. The City of San Jose, California passed by a solid margin (69 percent) a voters' proposition requiring city employees to pay more into their pensions and retiree health care plans. This plan also gave city workers an option to either transfer to a lower pension or remain in the current plan with higher annual contribution increases. In a mixed judgment, a Superior Court judge ruled that the city cannot force workers to pay more for their pensions, but that the city could reduce pay to cover unfunded liabilities (*San Jose Police Officer's Association vs. City of San Jose* 2013). Both the city and unions appealed this, but, ultimately, the reform proposal was repealed entirely through a court ruling in tandem with a resolution approved by the San Jose City Council in May 2016. In short, public employees and retirees enjoy at least some legal protection from having their benefits reduced or modified in some other way that adversely affects them, though the amount of protection varies from state to state.

What is to be learned at this time about the legal status of public pensions and benefits for urban human resource managers? The more obvious point is that pension reform or "retrenchment" through budget decisions, legislation, or the ballot box is going to be challenged. The three main threads of retrenchment—raising funding, changing benefits and rules, and changing systems—are going to be contested at every step by employee groups, especially if any of the reforms affect any mix of current employees and retirees. Whether the legal underpinning is as solid as a constitutional guarantee or is considered a contract or a promise, the courts are most likely to rule that reform cannot change the rules or benefit levels for those in the system. There is more leeway, of course, when the reforms affect only future employees—under the premise that the rules as they are when an employee is hired (and what they base job and career decisions on) are what applies. Of course, there is a bankruptcy option, should it lead to a point where the government is fiscally insolvent—meaning that it does not have the financial means or capability to raise future funding to cover its obligations. In this extreme case of bankruptcy, the remaining question then will be where in the queue of bondholders, unpaid contractors and suppliers, other unpaid beneficiaries, and litigants will pension holders be?

In August 2016, the Court of Appeals in California issued a ruling that takes direct aim at the absolute contract concept (what is often referred to as the California Contract Model after a 1977 court decision). However, this very recent decision states that a state legislative act in 2013, primarily aimed at reducing pension spiking, was permissible. Specifically, the court states, "A public employee does not have a vested right to a pension; they have only a right to a 'reasonable' pension—not an immutable entitlement to the most optimal formula for calculating the pension" (*Marin Association v Marin County* 2016, p. 2). The difference between a reasonable pension and a maximum allowable pension remains to be seen, as well as whether the California State Supreme Court will uphold the Appellate Court's decision.

PERFORMANCE MEASURES FOR MODERN URBAN HUMAN RESOURCES MANAGEMENT

To add a final perspective to the emerging third era of civil service development regarding the definition of objectives, a discussion of evaluating performance will be used. Recalling the six core functions of human resources, one focus would be to explain what human resources management does as a summation of the technical objectives for each division and to match an appropriate metric. Staffing would be about designing an optimum organization structure, classification would be about arranging for competitive pay and benefit levels for each job category, and hiring would be about filling vacancies in a timely fashion. These objectives all have compliance and productivity measurements; in short, determining whether each function is being performed correctly, in compliance with civil service policies, and efficiently regarding cost and time to complete. The following examples of possible performance measures provide further illustration:

- Staffing (workforce planning and staffing allotments)
  - Metric: Ratio of Management/Staff/Line Workers, Overtime Levels
- Classification and Compensation
  - Metric: Pay Comparability (Benchmark Surveys)

- Hiring and Selection
  - Metric: Ratio of Top Candidates Hired, Average Time to Fill Vacancy
- Performance Appraisal and Promotion
  - Metric: Ratio of Satisfactory Performance Ratings, Promotions by Race and Gender
- Training and Development
  - Metric: Training Hours Completed by Work Levels, Online Training Hours
- Employee Relations (Assistance Programs and Dispute Resolution)
  - Metric: Number of Grievances Filed and Time-Resolved, Employee Morale Surveys

These performance goals are important, but as internal functions, they can cause managers to become obsessed with the means and mechanics of the hiring or training, etc., and lose sight of the larger organizational performance goals of the government and the service needs of its citizens. Such a vision would lead human resources managers to create two tiers of performance metrics. In addition to ensuring functions are well executed, larger goals such as having a succession plan to ensure workforce continuity and having a representative workforce reflecting the diversity of the city's population illustrate this second higher tier. After all, this is what modern urban human resources management is most about—having a workforce that embodies the highest ideals of public service and performs at the highest levels of competence that the workforce embodies.

CONCLUSIONS

This chapter has reviewed the relative number of staff in the public and private sectors and at different levels of the public sector. It has provided an overview of the functions of human resources management staff in cities, reviewed relevant court cases, and presented performance measures for personnel management. Along with city budget and finance, personnel management is one of the areas specifically highlighted by NASPAA in the student learning outcome goals for the field of Urban Administration, and this chapter has provided an overview of those functions and processes.

SELECTED WEB RESOURCES

- American Society for Training and Development (ASTD), now Association for Talent Development (ATD) www.td.org/
- International Public Management Association for Human Resources http://ipma-hr.org/
- Society for Human Resource Management (SHRM) www.shrm.org/

EXERCISES AND DISCUSSION QUESTIONS

1. **Know Your City**: Employees as Human Resources
   - What percentage of your city's total budget is spent on salaries and benefits for its workers?
   - Are your city's workers represented by a labor union(s)? Which one(s)?
   - When are their next contracts due to be renegotiated?
   - When was the last time your city's workers got a raise?
   - Do you ever see advertisements for jobs within the city government? How are those jobs advertised?
   - How diverse is your city's workforce?

2. Do you believe that public sector employees should be allowed to strike? Why or why not?

3. Why would it be important that a city bureaucracy is as diverse as the city itself?

4. What steps should a city take to ensure the diversity of its workers?

REFERENCES

Askenas, Jeremy, and Park, Haeyoun. 2015. "The Race Gap in America's Police Departments." *New York Times*, April 8, 2015.

Burton, Paul. 2016. "Why Pension Funding Crises Hits Schools the Hardest." *The Bond Buyer*, October 18, 2016.

Couturier, John J. May–June 1976. "The Quiet Revolution: Public Personnel Laws." *Public Personnel Management* 5 (3): pp. 151–167.

Dunn, Megan, and Walker, James. 2016. "Union Membership in the United States." *U.S. Bureau Of Labor Statistics*. Accessed on December 2, 2016 from www.bls.gov/spotlight/2016/union-membership-in-the-united-states/pdf/union-membership-in-the-united-states.pdf

Gardner, Todd. 2013. *The Racial and Ethnic Composition of Local Government Employees in Large Metro Areas 1960–2010*. Center for Economic Studies, U.S. Census Bureau CES, 13–38.

Hyde, Albert C., and Shafritz, Jay M. (Eds.). 2016. "Introduction." p. 16 in *Classics of Public Administration*. New York: Cengage Publishing.

Jamison, Peter. 2016. "Paying for Public Retirees Has Never Cost LA Taxpayers More: And That's After Pension Reform." *Los Angeles Times*, November 18, 2016.

Mitchell, Olivia S., McCarthy, David, Wisniewski, Stanley C., and Zorn, Paul. 2001. "Development in State and Local Pension Plans." pp. 11–37 in *Pensions in the Public Sector*. Edited by Olivia S. Mitchell and Edwin C. Hustead. Philadelphia: University of Pennsylvania Press.

Monahan, Amy. 2010. "Public Pension Plan Reform: The Legal Framework." *Education, Finance & Policy* 5; Minnesota Legal Studies Research No. 10–13 (SSRN, Accessed January 1, 2017 from http://ssrn.com/abstract=1573864).

Mosher, William E., and Kingsley, J. Donald. 1941. *Public Personnel Administration*. New York: Harper and Brothers.

Munnell, Alicia, and Aubrey, Jean Pierre. 2016a. "An Overview of the Pension/OPEB Landscape." *Conference on Municipal Finance*. Brookings Institution, Washington, DC.

Munnell, Alicia, Jean Pierre Aubrey 2016b. "How will State Unfunded Pension Liabilities Affect Big Cities" Issue Brief Center for State and Local Government Excellence. Accessed on December 6, 2016 from http://slge.org/publications/how-will-unfunded-pension-liabilities-affect-big-cities.

Munro, William B. 1919. *Principles and Methods of Municipal Administration*. New York: The McMillan Company.

New Orleans, Civil Service Commission Webpage. 2016. Accessed on December 5, 2016 from www.nola.gov/civil-service/commission/

New Orleans, Civil Service Department Webpage. 2016. Accessed on December 5, 2016 from www.nola.gov/civil-service/

Rosiak, Luke. 2013. "Exography: 19 U.S. Cities Have Proportionally Bigger Workforces Than Bankrupted Detroit." *Washington Examiner*, July 30.

Slavin, Robert. 2016. "Why the Municipal Pension Crises Will Worsen." *The Bond Buyer*, August 2016.

Umhoefer, David. 2016. "For Unions in Wisconsin, a Fast and Hard Fall since Act 10." *The Milwaukee Journal Sentinel*, November 29, 2016.

U.S. Bureau of Labor Statistics. 2010–2014. *Work Stoppages Reports*. Accessed on December 6, 2016 from www.bls.gov/wsp/

U.S. Census Bureau. 2002. *Government Organization*. Volume 1, Number 1, pg. 4–7 GC02 (1) 1.

U.S. Census Bureau. 2004. *Compendium of Public Employment*. 2002 Volume 3 Public employment GC0 #2(3).

U.S. Census Bureau. 2014. Jessie, Lisa and Tarleton, Mary. "2012 Census of Governments" *Employment Summary Report* (C12–CG EMP).

U.S. Census Bureau. March 2015. Cohen, Darryl T. "Population Trends in Incorporated Places: 2000-2013". *Current Population Reports* (P 25–1142).

U.S. Equal Employment Opportunity Commission. 2013. *Job Patterns for Minorities and Women in State and Local Government* (EEO-4)- 2013. Accessed on December 6, 2016 from www.eeoc.gov/eeoc/statistics/employment/jobpat-eeo4/index.cfm

Zink, Harold. 1939. *Government of Cities in the United States*. New York: The McMillan Company.

COURT CASES REFERENCED [COURT JURISDICTION IN BRACKETS]

[U.S. Supreme Court]

Abood v. Detroit Board of Education, 431 U.S. 209 (1977)
Harris v. Quinn, 573 U.S. ___ (2014)*
Knox v. SEIU, 567 U.S. 310 (2012)

[State Courts]

In re City of Vallejo, Case No. 08–26813 -A-9 (2009) [Eastern District, State of California]

Marin Association of Public Employees v. Marin County Employees Retirement Association and State of California, A139610 (August 8, 2016) [Court of Appeals, First District, State of California]

Madison Teachers, Inc. et al. v. Scott Walker et al., Case 2012AP2067 (July 31, 2014) [Supreme Court of Wisconsin]

San Jose Retried Employees' Association v. City of San Jose, Case 1–12-CV 233660 (January 17, 2013) [Superior Court, Santa Clara County, State of California]

---

* For U.S. Supreme Court—newer cases from subsequent future volumes do not yet have official page numbers and typically use three underscores in place of the page number. As of December 2016, *Harris v. Quinn* had not been recorded.

Data, Information, and Communications

Today's urban manager needs to understand more than the traditional public administration skills—she also needs to understand data, information, knowledge, and their communication. In this chapter, the open data and government movement, civic technology, telecommunications, smart cities, and data visualization will be discussed. These movements are growing quickly, and it is hard to keep up with the exciting things happening in this field, but this chapter will provide an overview. Also, the official role that communications with the media and the public plays in governments, that of public information, will be reviewed. Currently, there are no NASPAA standards about data and technology except for the data-oriented student learning goal, "To analyze, synthesize, think critically, solve problems and make decisions" (Commission on Peer Review and Accreditation, 2009) standard. For communications, we have the Urban Administration emphasis standard, to articulate the purposes of and processes for communicating with citizens in local governance. In today's highly technological world, data, information, and communication (through technology) are critical components of providing government service.

To begin, a datum is a fact about some item; data are more than one fact. Information also incorporates description or perspective about an item, while knowledge is a full range of understanding about an area. Communications is the transfer of data, information, or knowledge of any of this to others. With technology, it is frequently done with telecommunications, but it also is conducted by skilled communicators.

DATA

As technology and our knowledge of the world have advanced, we have moved into a data-driven environment. Data, and our ability to measure, store, and use them, are constantly growing. In 2012, IBM estimated 2.5 exabytes were being created every day (see Table 7.1 for measurements of data); that amount doubles every 40 months. Walmart receives more than 2.5 petabytes every hour from transactions with customers (McAfee and Brynjolfsson 2012).

The concept of "big data" has also recently emerged into the public arena. "Big data" are datasets so large that they cannot be analyzed and used with traditional database and analytic tools. As McAfee and Brynjolfsson (2012) state, the term "big data" incorporates

TABLE 7.1

How Amounts of Data Are Measured

1 bit (b)	One piece of data (0 or 1)
1 byte (B)	8 bits of data
1 kilobyte (KB)	$1,000^1$ or 1,000 bytes (1 thousand)
1 megabyte (MB)	$1,000^2$ or 1,000,000 bytes (1 million)
1 gigabyte (GB)	$1,000^3$ or 1,000,000,000 bytes (1 billion)
1 terabyte (TB)	$1,000^4$ or 1,000,000,000,000 bytes (1 trillion)
1 petabyte (PB)	$1,000^5$ or 1,000,000,000,000,000 bytes (1 quadrillion)
1 exabyte (EB)	$1,000^6$ or 1,000,000,000,000,000,000 bytes (1 quintillion)
1 zettabyte (ZB)	$1,000^7$ or 1,000,000,000,000,000,000,000 bytes (1 sextillion)
1 yottabyte (YB)	$1,000^8$ or 1,000,000,000,000,000,000,000,000 bytes (1 septillion)

the sheer volume, velocity, and variety of data today. The potential of big data is in the patterns that could be detected within the datasets, patterns that could be applied to solving problems within institutions like cities. Just two examples of big data in cities that could be important are the number of riders and their travel patterns within municipal transportation systems and the energy usage data of homes and businesses for cities with municipal utilities. Finding patterns within that data could help solve transit and energy conservation problems.

In the business world, tracking, storing, and analyzing data is now called business analytics, but the same processes and tools exist in the public sector. Analysts often speak of "data mining" as a method of investigating these big datasets; data mining includes traditional methods of statistical analysis, particularly exploratory data analysis, but also pattern and visual analysis found in data visualization tools and databases, and tools from newer fields like artificial intelligence.

Storing these ever-larger amounts of data has also presented challenges. In 1965, Gordon Moore suggested Moore's Law: every year, the amount of memory that could fit on a computer circuit will double. In practice, this means that computers and computer devices get smaller and smaller. Moore's Law has, to date, proven accurate, and memory in devices has increased exponentially; as it has, the size of devices has declined, but their power has increased. The ability to store more and more data, in smaller and smaller media, has grown in similar ways. The need for new ways of storing such volumes of data has also changed enormously. Storage ability grew and grew, from storing data on magnetic tape to hard drives to 5.25" floppy disks, to CDs and DVDs, to 3.5" floppy disks, to today's flash drives. The very first computers could store only kilobytes of data, but today's phones routinely have 32 GB (gigabytes) of capacity. Mainframe and computer servers have also grown in storage and analytic capacity. Large institutions today with lots of data build "data warehouses" for all of their data, organized so that the data can be easily accessed by enrolled users, and set up with tools to allow users to analyze and understand the data. "Data farms" have been created with many, many servers together to accommodate the big data storage needs of institutions. Enormous "data centers" are also being built, like the one supposedly being built in Utah ("Bumblehive") that would accommodate one yottabyte of data (Wall 2014). Moreover, data are now being stored in the "cloud," or in online data centers, rather than in a user's or organization's hardware.

Even new types of jobs and careers are emerging—the newly developed job title of data scientist has become txvery popular today and is growing fast, with universities trying to keep up with the demand for the training required to work with, understand, and communicate the meaning of all these data. Governments today often have Chief Data Officers (CDOs) in addition to Chief Information Officers (CIOs).

With increasingly enhanced communications technologies, data and information are moving faster and faster across more devices and more geographies. Inevitably, these rapid changes are altering our world and our cities. As in the private sector, public sector managers have a growing need to be able to store their data in a secure fashion, analyze the data for important patterns and conclusions, provide access to the data to the public and businesses, and be able to communicate results in an understandable fashion. As data and information grow, the desire for more public accountability has also increased. Together, they have become calls for an emphasis on data-driven decisions and accountability in the public sector.

Open Data

Open data are defined as data that are freely available and accessible to all, that can be reused and redistributed, and in which there can be universal participation (Gurstein 2013). Further, an Open Government Working Group laid out eight principles for the use of public data. They proposed data are open when they are: 1) complete; 2) primary; 3) timely; 4) accessible; 5) machine-processable; 6) non-discriminatory; 7) non-proprietary; and 8) license-free (Dawes 2010). Together, this means that data should be in a format that can be easily accessed by users, with software that does not belong to any one company, nor should it require a license to be able to utilize.

On his first full day of his first term in office in 2009, President Obama signed an executive order obligating federal agencies to provide their data to the public. President Obama's Memorandum on Transparency and Open Government defined three foundational principles: transparency, participation, and collaboration, all important values for the public sector. That Memorandum was followed by another executive order requiring data to be machine-readable—in other words, to require creators of data to submit data in a format that is easily utilized by users and already available to be read by computers. The U.S. government created its open data portal (data.gov) soon after, which now contains more than 180,000 datasets. Thus began a worldwide open government and open data movement.

Cities were among the first to take advantage of the new open data movement. In 2009, the CIOs of Chicago, Los Angeles, Boston, New York, Seattle, Washington, D.C., and San Francisco worked together to create a common interface for applications like 311 data (Douglas 2010). By doing this, they hoped to make their data freely available to citizens and businesses. Cities like London, Palo Alto, Boston, and others also started developing portals, pages on their websites to offer their city's data to citizens and the business community, often with the help and support of nonprofits. States also began to build their data portals, as did other countries.

Open Data Portals   Open data are provided through web portals that allow users to use applications to access and download data and to analyze or put data into charts. Citizens can download datasets like city employees' salaries, recent crimes, and 311 service call data. Businesses can download restaurant public health inspection data, bus schedule data, and other data to allow them to create interactive maps with geographic information systems software or building permit data.

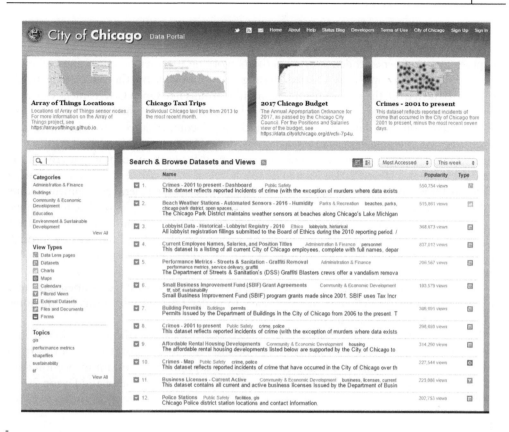

FIGURE 7.1
City of Chicago Open Data Portal

Source: City of Chicago Data Portal. 2016. Accessed on January 23, 2017 from https://data.cityofchicago.org/.

Figure 7.1 provides an illustration of one of the earliest and most successful city open data portals, the City of Chicago Open Data Portal. The four tiles at the top highlight data available on the site: Array of Things Locations (sensors), Chicago Taxi Trips, 2017 Chicago Budget, and Crimes—2001 to present. The middle portion of the site is a searchable list of datasets available on this site, along with the number of views (popularity) and the type of data. For instance, the second listed is Beach Weather Stations—Automated Sensors—2016—Humidity; it has been viewed 515,861 times and is a chart of humidity from sensors. The site includes datasets, maps, charts, calendars, and other data types. The datasets can be downloaded and used by businesses or citizens.

Chicago's Open Data Project   In Chicago, open data became a priority when a candidate for mayor, Rahm Emanuel, sponsored an event focusing on the issue. Once elected, he then appointed the nation's first CDO. Brett Goldstein was appointed to that office by Chicago's new administration in 2011. Like many other cities, Chicago worked with national organizations like Code for America (with their Fellows program, many of whom went to cities and worked on these projects) and with local community organizations that assisted on projects developed from local data.

Civic Technology

In the early 2010s, a new era of civic technology activism began to emerge, with city staff, computer programmers, academics, and activists working together on managing city data. New technology startups were created, basing their products on the data made newly available to them from the government. Community groups like Open Government Chicago, Smart Chicago Collaborative, and OpenOakland formed and worked with cities (to various extents) on their data. "Hackathon" and "apps" competitions were held where data "nerds" created computer applications from city data. Hacking, in this context, refers to a sustained effort working with data to either create new applications or find patterns in the data (Goldstein and Dyson 2013; Kassen 2013). Some of these efforts have been channeled into competitions for the best app; groups like Kaggle or even the federal government and its Challenges.gov site host these competitions on a regular basis. Examples of civic tech mobile applications that have been developed include Chicago's Sweep Around Us (showing street sweeping days), ParkBoston (allowing users to pay for parking throughout the city through the app), Where's My School Bus (another Boston app allowing parents to track their children's school bus), and PDX FoodSpy (providing information on restaurant inspections).

The new field of data journalism developed, also taking advantage of open data and the new software tools available to create easy to understand visualizations for the journalists' publications (Goldstein and Dyson 2013).

Many cities were already familiar with success stories like Baltimore's CitiStat and CompStat in local police departments. Cities became further invigorated by stories from cities like New York, which showed great success with popular restaurant inspection data and used city data to solve problems in forecasting house fires (Goldstein and Dyson 2013; Helbig, Cresswell, Burke and Luna-Reyes 2012). To date, the movement continues to grow.

Data Visualizations

With a timely confluence of online data provision and new technologies that allow much easier data analysis and chart-making, the field of data visualization (using charts and graphics to understand better and communicate the meaning of data) has expanded enormously in the past several years. However, effective data visualizations, or graphic displays, have been used to help users understand patterns since the 1750s. One of the very first visualizations, and one of the most influential, ever, illustrates how data visualizations help users understand underlying patterns in data (Bachand 2012). This visualization is based on a map showing cholera cases in the London of 1854. John Snow, now considered one of the founders of the public health and epidemiology field, was trying to understand how residents were getting cholera. So he mapped out the 500 cases of individuals who had died over a ten-day period and their home locations on this map, then noted the clusters, and realized victims mostly lived around one particular water pump. The city realized that pump was contaminated, shut it down, and was soon able to control the epidemic (see Figure 7.2).

Data visualizations can be most helpful to city managers today, as it has repeatedly been shown that most users understand information and patterns from visual cues far better than information provided just in a numeric format. To illustrate this point, observe Figure 7.3, illustrating the various types of expenditures proposed by the mayor of Seattle in 2015. While some visualization designers do not believe in using pie charts, arguing the relative size of the circles can obscure perceptions, within the same pie, the slices can be useful for comparing agencies' relative shares of a city's budget.

Deciding upon the most appropriate graph type is one of the most important steps to effective data visualization development. Beyond that, there are numerous features that aid the developer in emphasizing patterns in a dataset. This is particularly true of online,

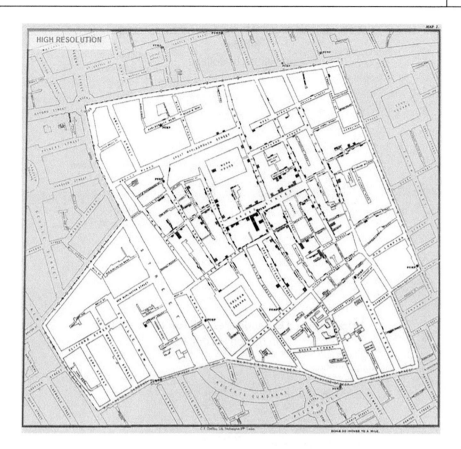

FIGURE 7.2
John Snow Cholera Map of London, 1854

Source: Kelley, Peter. 2012. Documents that Changed the World Podcasts: John Snow's Cholera Map, 1854. Available at: HYPERLINK "http://www.washington.edu/news/2012/08/28/documents-that-changed-the-world-john-snows-cholera-map-1854/" www.washington.edu/news/2012/08/28/documents-that-changed-the-world-john-snows-cholera-map-1854/.

interactive data visualizations, or vizzes, as they are commonly referred to in this field. Some of the most common features are:

- The size of a data point, which can be set to vary with the value of a variable;
- The color of a data point, which can be used to distinguish between different categories of a variable;
- The shape of a data point, which may also be used to indicate a category of variable;
- Labels on each data point, which can provide additional information about the data;
- Drop-down menus or check lists, which allow the user options, such as year or different organization, from the dataset;
- Filters on the data, which allow the user to choose a particular subset of the dataset to examine; and
- Sliders, which can allow the user to select a continuous variable (year) so that the progression of a variable over time is illustrated.

There are a growing number of tools, including those for mapping, available to develop effective data visualizations. Excel is one such tool, which can be used for basic

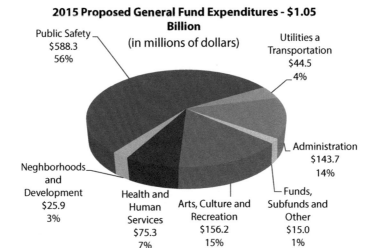

2015 Proposed General Fund Expenditures - $1.05 Billion
(in millions of dollars)

Public Safety $588.3 56%

Utilities a Transportation $44.5 4%

Administration $143.7 14%

Neghborhoods and Development $25.9 3%

Health and Human Services $75.3 7%

Arts, Culture and Recreation $156.2 15%

Funds, Subfunds and Other $15.0 1%

2015 Proposed Expenditures - All Funds, $4.8 Billion*
(in millions of dollars)

Utilities and Transportation $2,832.2 59%

Administration $680.4 14%

Public Safety $591.2 12%

Funds, Subfunds and Other $62.4 1%

Neighborhoods and Development $146.2 3%

Health and Human Services $208.4 5%

Arts, Culture and Recreation $ 294.8 6%

FIGURE 7.3
Pie Charts—Seattle, Washington Budget Expenditures

Source: City of Seattle, Washington. 2015. "Mayor's Office Budget, City of Seattle." Accessed on January 27, 2017 from http://murray.seattle.gov/wp-content/uploads/2014/09/budget-highlights-9-22-final-v4.pdf.

visualizations. However, there are also dedicated data visualization tools, such as Tableau, Google Charts, d3, Infogr.am, Canva, and PowerBI. The software package R is a statistical analysis tool that has powerful data visualization capabilities, while QGIS and Carto are both mapping applications.

As noted previously, in Chicago, several nonprofit groups and many citizens join together on a weekly basis with city workers to work on data and data applications. One of the groups that emerged from the open data was 2nd City Zoning, which used the open data from the City of Chicago to make interactive mapping applications (or data visualizations) that allow citizens to explore zoning in their neighborhoods (Figure 7.4). This application includes information about city zoning rules as well as music from the game Sim City.

BOX 7.1 TUFTE'S CONSIDERATIONS FOR DATA VISUALIZATIONS

Edward Tufte, a political scientist who is widely acknowledged as an influential figure in understanding data and data visualization, provided several considerations he believes are important when working with data. The user should:

- Show the data
- Induce the viewer to think about the substance rather than about methodology, graphic design, the technology or graphic production, or something else
- Avoid distorting what the data have to say
- Present many numbers in a small space

- Make large data sets coherent
- Encourage the eye to compare different pieces of data
- Reveal the data at several levels of detail, from a broad overview to the fine structure
- Serve a reasonably clear purpose: description, exploration, tabulation, or decoration
- Be closely integrated with the statistical and verbal descriptions of a data set.

Source: Tufte, Edward R. 2001. The Visual Display of Quantitative Information (2nd Edition). Cheshire, Connecticut: Graphics Press: p. 15.

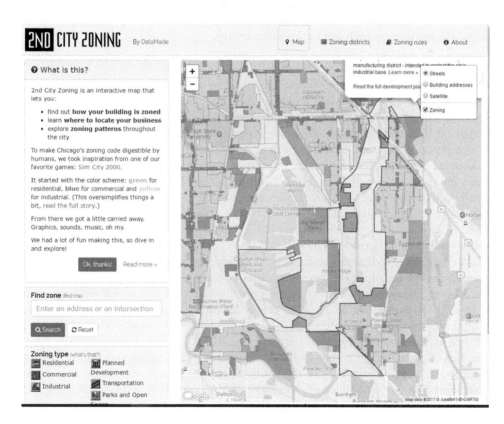

FIGURE 7.4
2nd City Zoning Web Application Made with Chicago Open Data

Source: 2nd City Zoning. Accessed on December 20, 2016 from https://secondcityzoning.org/#/?id=11287.

TELECOMMUNICATIONS AND WIFI NETWORKS IN CITIES TODAY

Telecommunications is the transmission and reception of information using electrical means over networks. There have been enormous changes in the telecommunications fields in the recent past, moving from separate television, radio, cable TV, telephone, and Internet companies and technologies to the convergence of these technologies together with the same companies providing data, information, communications, and entertainment, or Internet Communications Technologies (ICT).

Since the Internet was developed, the speed at which data can be transmitted over networks has increased enormously—from slow dial-up connections to hard-wired early generation networks to very fast fiber optic cable networks to wireless communications and satellite networks. Considering Internet connections to be a public good important for their citizens and businesses to access, many cities have tried to create citywide wireless networks through broadband telecommunications technologies. Further, many cities have tried to provide or subsidize Internet service as a measure to encourage equity in their communities and to help reduce the digital divide, the inequitable different rates of access to the Internet by income or race/ethnicity.

Some of these efforts have failed (Philadelphia), sometimes due to private sector firms shutting them down because they represented unwanted competition for their businesses. Some cities tried public-private partnerships (3Ps) in their effort to develop these networks, and these have failed (San Francisco). Many cities have had to settle for providing free WiFi in their downtown areas, providing only paid WiFi, or providing only WiFi "hotspots" (small areas with available connectivity).

SMART CITIES

Another relatively new movement has been the smart cities movement. The actual definition of a smart city, however, is difficult to achieve. For many, it is incorporating the "Internet of Things" (IoT), with technology integrated into much of the city's infrastructure, automating many city tasks. For example, a new city in South Korea, Songdo, has been built as a completely networked, prototype smart city. In Songdo, buildings incorporate a great deal of automation (lights come on automatically, heat and air adjust automatically). Sensors are placed throughout city streets, electrical grids, water and waste systems, and roads to track activity. These sensors allow systems to track and respond to demand. Radio Frequency Identification (RFID) chips in cars create maps and allow the system to track traffic demands (Townsend 2014).

Few cities aspire to that extent of technology incorporation, however. Some cities, like Rio de Janeiro in Brazil, are using smart cities concepts by incorporating technology to aid in disaster management. This system eventually had a control center with representatives from 30 departments, all tracking real-time information from their units' systems. Singapore, Barcelona, Spain, and Oslo, Norway are also pioneers in worldwide smart city development, along with New York City (Adams 2017).

In New York City, the emphasis is first on creating the largest and fastest municipal WiFi network by providing WiFi to the entire city by 2025. Innovators are also working on the country's first "quantified community" in Hudson Yards, a 14-acre square public space with technology to monitor air quality, traffic, and energy consumption. Another project, the Midtown in Motion, will incorporate sensors and cameras into the road grid to help manage traffic (Adams 2017).

BOX 7.2 DATA AND INFORMATION TECHNOLOGY STRATEGIES IN CITY SUSTAINABILITY PLANS

Cities incorporate the need for data and technology infrastructure into their sustainability plans, particularly to address equity.

Data

- "Collect and share data on local climate conditions and place drivers." St. Louis, Missouri, p. 188.

Infrastructure

- "Make computers and internet access broadly available." St. Louis, Missouri, p. 195.
- "Maximize Wi-Fi availability throughout the city." Virginia Beach, Virginia, p. 81.
- "Provide and market a smart grid, Wi-Fi hot spots and technological infrastructure." St. Louis, Missouri, p. 36.

- "Partner with communications providers to ensure all citizens have optimum communications access as technology changes." Virginia Beach, Virginia, p. 81.
- "Develop a virtual meeting network." St. Louis, Missouri, p. 193.
- "Encourage innovative and useful app and website development." St. Louis, Missouri, p. 194.

Sources:
City of St. Louis, Missouri. 2013. City of St. Louis Sustainability Plan. Accessed on February 22, 2017 from www.stlouis-mo.gov/government/departments/planning/documents/city-of-st-louis-sustainability-plan.cfm.
City of Virginia Beach, Virginia. 2013. A Community Plan for a Sustainable Future. City of VA Beach Environment and Sustainability Office. March 12, 2013. Accessed on February 22, 2017 from www.vbgov.com/government/offices/eso/sustainability-plan/Documents/vb-sustainability-plan-web.pdf.

In 2015, the Obama Administration began a funding initiative to help cities incorporate technology and networks with this smart city definition: "communities that are building an infrastructure to continuously improve the collection, aggregation, and use of data to improve the life of their residents—by harnessing the growing data revolution, low-cost sensors, and research collaborations, and doing so securely to protect safety and privacy" (Obama White House 2015).

The Administration was providing new funds to use technology in fields like "safety, energy, climate preparedness, transportation, health, and more" (Obama White House 2015) through four main strategies:

- Creating test beds for 'Internet of Things' applications and developing new multi-sector collaborative models;
- Collaborating with the civic tech movement and forging intercity collaborations;
- Leveraging existing Federal activity; and
- Pursuing international collaboration.

(Obama White House 2015)

A key project in smart cities is to develop increased broadband access and speeds that can support the kind of networking and control needed when trying to connect city systems together to make them stronger and more responsive. Other projects are smart building technologies and improved technology for the national electrical grid. In Chicago, the

University of Chicago is already helping to create the Array of Things so researchers can test their system of sensors, computing, and communications systems to be used in the future (Obama White House 2015).

COMMUNICATIONS AND WORKING WITH THE MEDIA

Another important task in cities is to work with the local, and sometimes regional or national, news media. Cities often need to have news go out to the public, and social media is not yet widely available to accomplish this task. City government might have to tell citizens about streets closed for repairs, to talk about a new program, to explain a mistake made by a city employee, to provide updates during a disaster, or to talk about the accomplishments of city employees. To do this, city managers will rely upon their public affairs or media staffs.

In most cities, the public information office is located close to or in the mayor's or city manager's office (see Figure 7.5). Looking at Figure 7.5 with the organizational chart from Irvine, California, we can see its Department of Public Communication reports to the City Manager. Within that department (Figure 7.6) are Public Information, News Media, and Social Media, so the office combines both new and old media.

Box 7.3 illustrates the wide variety of tasks that public information professionals in government can be expected to perform: liaising with the media, developing printed materials, supervising press and social media releases, and setting up civic engagement with the public. Public information officers need to know about their agency history and responsibilities; have excellent writing, oral communications, and media relations skills; be good at networking; and know how to interact with the public. They become, in many cases, the public face of their agency and so must be professional and open in a variety of situations, including crises and emergencies.

Otis Taylor, an opinion columnist for the *San Francisco Chronicle* talking about the number of women elected and appointed officials in office in Oakland, California, commented on the importance of the city's police department spokesperson. Taylor stated, "Moreover when Oakland was reeling in the days after the Dec. 2 Ghost Ship fire that killed 36 people, it was Officer Johnna Watson, the city's police spokeswoman, who provided a stalwart voice while providing details to the media and the public" (Taylor 2017) (Figure 7.7). Note the police and fire department officials are standing behind the Public Information Officer reporting on the tragedy; they had their job, and her job was to report on the tragedy and the actions of the police department (and in this case, also the fire department).

Agencies that are interested in marketing their work more effectively to the public, or thinking more strategically about communicating what they do, think about their goals strategically and first recognize they are not in a commercial setting but are engaged in social marketing or communication to the public. Social marketing is the use of sound marketing principles and techniques to influence an intended audience to "voluntarily accept, reject, modify, or abandon a behavior for the benefit of individuals, groups, or society as a whole" (Synodinos, Bockh, Cook and DuPont n.d., p. 5). Such efforts are typically audience-focused and research-based but approach communication not from an expert, but instead from the audience, and what/how they are ready to hear. Audiences typically want to know what is in it for them, not information from the agency, so agencies must boil it down to how the information affects the audience and why would they care.

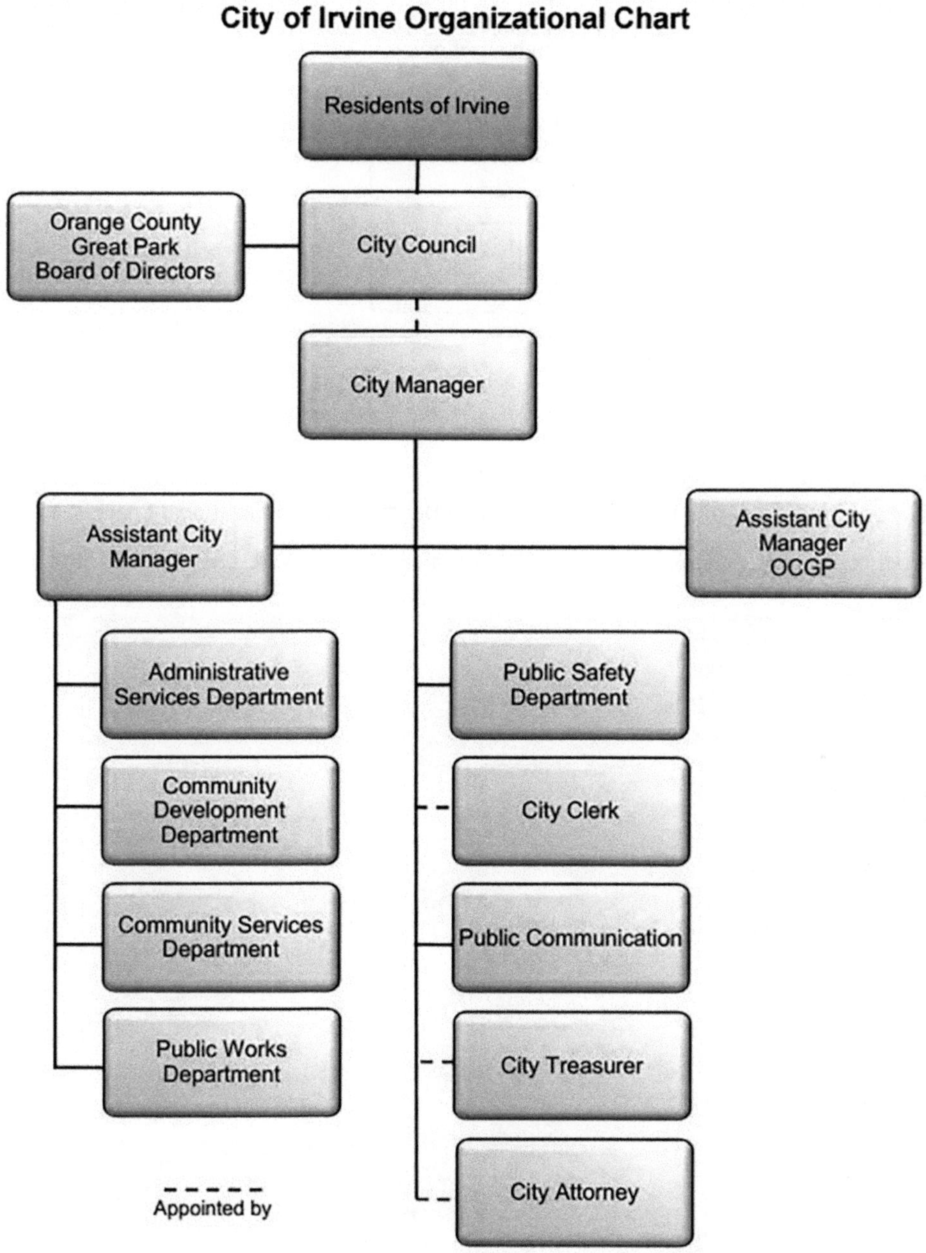

City of Irvine Organizational Chart

FIGURE 7.5
City of Irvine, California Organizational Chart

Source: City of Irvine. 2017. Accessed on January 30, 2017, from http://legacy.cityofirvine.org/civica/filebank/blobdload.asp?
BlobID=14311.

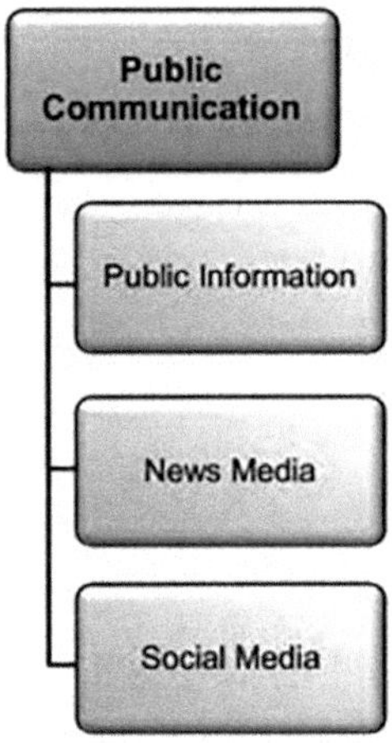

FIGURE 7.6
City of Irvine, California Public Communication Department Organizational Chart

Source: City of Irvine. 2017. Accessed on January 30, 2017, from http://legacy.cityofirvine.org/civica/filebank/blobdload.asp?BlobID=14311.

FIGURE 7.7
Oakland Police Department Public Information Officer Speaks to Public about Fire in Community

Source: Taylor, Jr., Otis R. 2017. "Oakland Police Department's public information office Johnna Watson speaks about the Ghost Ship tragedy" San Francisco Chronicle. January 30, 2017 Photo by Michael Short, Special to the Chronicle. Accessed on January 30, 2017, from http://www.sfchronicle.com/news/article/Oakland-s-women-firmly-in-charge-as-U-S-leader-10892566.php?cmpid=gsa-sfgate-result).

BOX 7.3 · PUBLIC INFORMATION OFFICER JOB—POSITION DESCRIPTION, NASHVILLE, TENNESSEE

Full-Time Civil Service Metro Water Services, City of Nashville

Position Description

This position within Metro Water Services will provide support to link our internal and external customers, stakeholders, and community partners with our services, programs and initiatives. *May require flexible work hours including evening or weekend work.*

Typical Duties

- Handles personal and phone contact with Metro and other city officials, regulators, media representatives, intradepartmental personnel, customers and the general public.
- Collects data and prepares presentations and various documents/correspondence such as press releases, reports, award submittals, speeches/speaking points, and newsletter articles.
- Conducts media interviews as needed.
- Contributes to strategic thinking and implementation of public engagement and outreach efforts.
- Assists in research, gathering and documenting data which may be of confidential nature.
- Monitors and analyzes media/community issues to identify items of relevance to Metro Water Services; advises

management of issues that could affect operations or public perception.
- May represent the department in various committees and community forums or serve as a liaison.
- Assists in incident response and crisis management strategies.
- Identifies and coordinates opportunities for Metro Water Services to partner and coordinate with stakeholders, other Metro Departments, organizations, and the community to improve customer understanding of Metro Water Services and the value of water.
- May provide consultation on complex programs or projects.
- May develop additional methods, techniques and processes for evaluating and obtaining program results related to outreach activities.

Minimum Qualifications

Bachelor's Degree from an accredited college or university and two (2) years experience disseminating information and planning public relations activities. Valid driver license. *No substitution.*

Source: Government Jobs. 2017. Public Information Officer Position. Accessed on January 30, 2017 from www.governmentjobs.com/jobs/1634788/public-information-representative?page=2&keyword=Public%20Relations&pagetype=searchPage.

One tool used by many public information officers is an eight-step communications planning process developed by the National Cancer Institute. These steps are:

1. Determining where the agency is now, with its communication situation.
2. Setting reasonable goals for communication.
3. Deciding on the intended audiences.
4. Developing the message and then trying it out.

5. Figuring out how to deliver the message—on television, social media, press conference, or press releases? Develop or select messages to use and distribute. Develop partnerships and collaborations.
6. Create an action plan for how the communication will be distributed.
7. Develop and pre-test materials to be used in delivering the message.
8. Implement, evaluate, and then change the plan.

(Synodinos et al. n.d., p. 13)

Workers in the public information area have to know the laws affecting public information quite well, and government agencies have to operate within the constraints of their state and federal laws. Many states have laws patterned on the federal Freedom of Information Act, which provides a way for the public (including the press) to request certain public documents. Officials have to know and understand their state law if they have one, as well as their own city's policies on providing public documents. Some cities have policies stating their intention to be open and transparent with the public; employees need to know what the practices are that fall under these policies (Politano 2009).

Also, officials need to understand the definition of public records under their state's laws. If a document request is for public records, that request could include emails or social media postings, depending on the state law in that area.

Birr (1999) provides some general tips for those in government agencies dealing with the press:

- Honesty is the best policy;
- Speed is second only to accuracy;
- Always assume you are on the record with a reporter, meaning that anything you say could be used in an article as an official statement from the city;
- Don't assume any knowledge on the reporter's part;
- Stick to confirmed, verifiable facts;
- Deal only with your area of involvement and experience;
- If you cannot comment on something, explain why;
- It is okay to say, 'I do not know';
- Speak simply and avoid jargon;
- Be open and cooperative as possible; and
- Project calmness and control.

(Birr 1999, pp. 108–110)

CONCLUSIONS

This chapter has discussed some of the exciting issues currently emerging in American cities around data, information, and communications. The open data movement is now worldwide, making more and more data available from public sector agencies to citizens and businesses. This has allowed the use of data for civic tech activists creating mobile apps from city data and allowed citizens to explore public sector issues themselves. More and more people are working with data visualizations to help residents understand trends in government and public policy issues. More and more cities are also getting involved in the smart city movement and using technology to monitor and improve city services. Finally, an overview of the public affairs/communications function and its importance in cities was presented. Understanding the issues and needs of data, information, and communications is critical today to fulfilling NASPAA expectations on being able to effectively communicate with the public.

RESOURCES

- FlowingData, the website by Nathan Yau, the author of one of the best books on visualization (*Visualize This: The FlowingData Guide to Design, Visualization, and Statistics*) flowingdata.com/
- Information design is a resource for design professionals with a focus on information design www.informationdesign.org/
- International Society of Chief Data Officers www.iscdo.org/
- National Association of State Chief Information Officers www.nascio.org/
- National Information Officers Association: www.nioa.org/site/
- Public Technology Institute www.pti.org/
- Vizworld.com is a news site for visualization—one that appears to be very out of date at this point www.vizworld.com/

EXERCISES AND DISCUSSION QUESTIONS

1. **Know Your City**: Data and Information Technology
   - Does your city have an open data portal? How many datasets are available there, and what kind?
   - What kind of projects does the information technology department conduct? Is the department responsible for the televising of city council meetings? Does it work with the cable TV contracts for the community?
   - Where is the information technology department located in your city's organizational chart?
   - Is there a public affairs officer in the city manager or mayor's office in your city?
   - Does your city regulate cable television for its citizens?
2. What ideas do you have for helping others understand the data in a presentation?
3. What are the pros and cons of allowing businesses to use a city's data (through its open data portal) to make money? Should part of their profit go back to the city?
4. Should it be up to a city to provide free wireless connection to its citizens, throughout the city? Why or why not?
5. How should a city help make sure Internet access is provided to all its citizens?

REFERENCES

Adams, Dallon. 2017. "These Smart Cities Are Building Infrastructures for the 23rd Century." *Digital Trends*, January 1, 2017. Accessed on January 30, 2017 from www.digitaltrends.com/home/smartest-cities-in-the-world/

Bachand, Jen. 2012. *What Are the Top 5 Visualizations of All Time? Tableau Software Blog.* Accessed on December 10, 2016 from www.tableausoftware.com/about/blog/2012/11/top-5-visualizations-all-time-19810

Birr, Tim. 1999. *Public and Media Relations for the Fire Service.* Tulsa, OK: PennWell Fire Engineering.

Commission on Peer Review and Accreditation. 2009. NASPAA Standards. Accessed on August 18 2017 from https://naspaaaccreditation.files.wordpress.com/2015/02/naspaa-accreditation-standards.pdf

Dawes, S. S. 2010. "Stewardship and Usefulness: Policy Principles for Information-based Transparency." *Government Information Quarterly* 27 (2010): pp. 377–383.

Douglas, Merrill. October 18, 2010. "G7: CIOs from Seven Big-Cities Work Together to Develop Open-Source IT Solutions." *Government Technology.* Available at http://www.govtech.com/e-government/G7-Big-City-CIOs-Work-to-Develop-Open-Source-IT-Solutions.html

Goldstein, Brett with L. Dyson. 2013. *Beyond Transparency: Open Data and the Future of Civic Innovation.* San Francisco: Code for American Press.

Gurstein, M. (2013). "Should 'Open Government Data' Be a Product or a Service (and Why Does It Matter?)" *Gurstein's Community Informatics.* Accessed on May 11, 2015 from https://gurstein.wordpress.com/2013/02/03/

is-open-government-data-a-product-or-a-service-and-why-does-it-matter/

Helbig, Natalie, Cresswell, Anthony M., Burke, G. Brian, and Luna-Reyes, Luis. 2012. *The Dynamics of Opening Government Data Center for Technology in Government*. University at Albany, SUNY.

Kassen, M. (2013). "A Promising Phenomenon of Open Data: A Case Study of the Chicago Open Data Project." *Government Information Quarterly* 30 (4): pp. 508–513.

McAfee, Andrew, and Brynjolfsson, Erik. 2012. "Big Data: The Management Revolution." *Harvard Business Review*, October 2012.

Obama White House. 2015. *FACT SHEET: Administration Announces New 'Smart Cities' Initiative to Help Communities Tackle Local Challenges and Improve City Services*. Accessed on January 29, 2017 from https://obamawhitehouse.archives.gov/the-press-office/2015/09/14/fact-sheet-administration-announces-new-smart-cities-initiative-help

Politano, Phil. 2009. *Public Information Officer*. Upper Saddle River, NJ: Pearson Prentice Hall.

Synodinos, Jean, Bockh, Emily, Cook, Patrick, and DuPont, Courtney. Not dated. *Welcome to Strategic Communication Planning*. Accessed on January 30, 2017 from www.healthysafechildren.org/sites/default/files/Screen-Reader-Friendly-Version-of-Introduction-to-Strategic-Communication-Planning.pdf

Taylor, Otis. 2017. "Oakland's Women Firmly in Charge as U.S. Leader Flail." *San Francisco Chronicle*, January 30, 2017. Accessed on January 30, 2017 from www.sfchronicle.com/news/article/Oakland-s-women-firmly-in-charge-as-U-S-leader-10892566.php?cmpid=gsa-sfgate-result

Townsend, Anthony M. 2014. *Smart Cities: Big Data, Civic Hackers, and the Quest for a New Utopia*. New York: W.W. Norton and Company.

Wall, Matthew. 2014. "Big Data: Are You Ready for Blast-Off?" *BBC News*, March 4, 2014. Accessed on November 6, 2015 from www.bbc.com/news/business-26383058

Urban Service Delivery

With M. Ernita Joaquin

Chapter 8 discusses how cities provide services to their citizens. Urban service delivery has changed a great deal over the past 40 years, incorporating technology into e-government and m-government (mobile), and providing most services through contracting and collaborating with the nonprofit or private sector. These methods are discussed, along with the more recent 311 service call system used by many cities today. Learning about urban service delivery in this chapter is in direct response to NASPAA's Urban Administration student learning outcome to lead, manage and serve the management of local government core services and functions. Discussions of public goods also allow us "To articulate and apply a public service perspective," which is the fourth overall NASPAA standard.

PUBLIC GOODS AND URBAN SERVICE DELIVERY

The government provides public goods and services that would otherwise be under-provided by the private sector. In exchange, citizens pay taxes to governments so governments can afford to provide the public goods. Public goods are those items that benefit the entire public; if one person receives the public good, then no one may be excluded from receiving it. One person receiving the good does not reduce its supply for others. On the other hand, a private good is the exact opposite; the good is mutually exclusive, for if one person has it, no one else can have it, and once used by one person, another cannot use it since the supply will be exhausted. One example of a pure public good would be the light coming from a lighthouse, which spreads over the water and aids everyone in its reach. It cannot be diminished just because one ship is using it, and if one ship can use it, so can others.

Public education and public health are examples of public goods, but not pure public goods; the private sector under-supplies private education, but the public as a whole does benefit from public education, and, so, the public pays taxes to support public schools. An example of a private good is an apple—if one person is using it, no one else can use it, and once it is used, there is none left for others.

Public sector service delivery has changed a great deal since the Reagan Administration in the 1980s. At one point, government agencies themselves provided public services, but the devolution that started in that era shifted services and funds from the federal level to the states and then to local governments. To save money, many governments looked to alternative means of providing services, including contracting out to nonprofit and private sector companies. So government became less and less a service provider and more and more a purchaser and a contract manager, so much so that government was then termed the "hollow state" (Milward and Provan 2000) because there was little there. Milward and Provan (2000, p. 362) define the hollow state as, "any joint production situation where a government agency relies on others (firms, nonprofits, or other government agencies) to jointly deliver public services." They state, "At the same time, the central government has become *hollowed out* as power is devolved to state and local governments. Thus, a variety of government agencies have chosen to share their authority for collective action with nonprofit agencies and private firms in a network of mutual dependence" (Milward and Provan 2000, p. 36). These trends have led to the increased "fuzziness" of the boundaries between the public, nonprofit, and private sectors today, as service providers to citizens can come from organizations from any sector, or in fact a combination of them (Kettl 2015). This chapter will explore many of those means of service delivery existing in cities today.

THE CONTEXT OF SERVICE DELIVERY BY CITIES

Citizens contact government for services for a variety of reasons (U.S. General Services Administration 2010):

- Informational. Citizens seek information or provide it to government agencies. An example would be a citizen providing information to a government agency so that they can apply for unemployment benefits.
- Beneficial. The citizen contacts an agency to obtain some benefit, whether it be financial, diplomatic, or administrative; for example, a citizen wants to take some recreation classes, so they contact their city's park and recreation department.
- Dutiful. Citizens contact government because they are required to do so, as in the requirement to pay property taxes when they receive their property tax bill.
- Commercial. Citizens sometimes need to purchase a good or service from government, such as buying a dog license or a map of local hiking trails.
- Intergovernmental. Citizens also might seek information from one level of government about another level of government. For instance, someone might go to a city to find out about federal home loan programs.

Public sector services are delivered via only a limited number of channels, or modes: face-to-face, telephone, postal mail service, e-delivery through the Internet (web or email), and m-government, or mobile devices.

Service delivery is categorized according to the complexity of delivering the service. The service delivery could be uncomplicated (such as providing a dog license), of limited complexity (providing recreation classes), or highly complex (like the services provided by child protection agencies) (Buckley 2003).

To further explain, Table 8.1 combines these factors into a two-dimensional scheme incorporating complexity of tasks and delivery mode, with examples. E-government and m-government service delivery modes can handle several different types of services but are more appropriate for those services that are uncomplicated (relatively routine) or of limited complexity. The complexity of providing government services is such that Thomas

---

TABLE 8.1

Public Sector Service Delivery—Channels of Delivery and Complexity

	Face-to-Face	Telephone	Postal Mail	E-Government (Internet)	M-Government (Mobile)
Uncomplicated	Car registration Complaint submission Service request	Complaint submission Service request	Complaint submission Service request	Complaint submission Service request	Complaint submission Service request
Limited Complexity			Revenue collection	Revenue collection	
Highly Complex	Child protection services				

Source: Based upon Buckley (2003) and Stowers (2010).

(2012) refers to the public as fulfilling three entirely different roles: citizen, customer, and partner.

The types of services also differ by level of government. Those provided by cities are different from those provided by other levels of government since cities are where most residents live. So cities provide the public safety services like police and fire protection but also planning and building services, community development and housing, libraries, parks, and streets that people use in their daily lives. Some larger cities also provide health and human services, but in general, these are county-level services.

Table 8.2 provides even more differentiation of which kinds of services do best in which kinds of situations. Ebbers, Pieterson and Noordman (2008)'s table has two axes—Interactivity and Initiator. Either the Organization or User (i.e., citizen) can initiate service, and interactivity can be either single- or two-sided. In this table, when the Organization initiates, the result is either Allocution or Registration. When the User initiates, there is either Consultation or Conversation, either one- or two-way discussion. When money rather than information exchanges hands, the result is a transaction.

TABLE 8.2

Modes of Interaction in Service Delivery

		Interactivity	
		Single Sided	*Two Sided*
Initiator	Organization	Allocution	Registration
	User	Consultation	Conversation

Source: Based on Table 1 in Ebbers, W. E. P., Pieterson, W. J., and Noordman, H. N. (2008). "Electronic Government: Rethinking Channel Management Strategies." *Government Information Quarterly* 25 (2008): p. 185.

Many government services are provided by people on the streets dealing directly with citizens—like police officers or social workers; these types of workers are considered "street-level bureaucrats" (Lipsky 1983). Because street-level bureaucrats work in the field, they are away from direct supervisors and have more discretion in how they apply the rules and practices of their job. Typically, they develop rules of thumb for making decisions to make their jobs easier, since they make hundreds of decisions every day. For instance, police officers rarely give out a ticket for every person who speeds one or two miles per hour over the speed limit, even though the law would suggest that would be their duty. Instead, officers often use their discretion to ticket those who are driving five to ten miles per hour over the limit or who have a record of previous speeding. If they ticketed every person who is just over the limit, they would be doing nothing but writing speeding tickets—so they might let drivers off with a warning after stopping them for a violation.

MEANS OF URBAN SERVICE DELIVERY

Within the context of today's hollowed-out government, other options have developed to achieve local government governance and service goals. Cities may enter into market-like arrangements with other local or state governments, private business, and nonprofits in producing and delivering goods and services within their territories. The most notable of these arrangements are contracting out, public-private partnerships, and interlocal cooperation or shared services agreements. Many cities today have also developed 311 service request systems to provide direct access to citizens and their requests.

Public-Private Partnerships

Public-private partnerships are also known as P3s, PPP, or 3Ps. P3s are when public sector agencies work together on projects with private sector companies. Government agencies have worked for years with private sector firms, and P3s are just more formal ways of identifying those means of providing public services. The National Council for Public-Private Partnerships identifies seven key steps for successful partnerships. They are:

1. Use identifiable public sector figures as spokespersons and advocates.
2. Make sure the partnership is backed by sound laws and agreements developed through a transparent process.
3. The public sector agency should have a group working on just the P3s who can go through the considerable public sector processes like contracting out, bidding, and writing Requests for Proposals (RFPs).
4. A business plan outlining the relationship between the partners should be developed to serve as a map to the project.
5. Revenues necessary to fund the project should be identified.
6. Important stakeholders should be identified and kept informed and involved.
7. Partners should be carefully selected.

(National Council for Public-Private Partnerships 2017)

Contracting

The practice of government agencies contracting with the private or nonprofit sector to provide services has been around for some time. However, that practice started increasing in the 1980s, when the federal government began its devolution efforts, mostly without any accompanying funding. As one strategy for dealing with the new responsibilities, cities and states began increasing their efforts at contracting out the actual responsibilities to provide services to private and nonprofit sector agencies, in exchange for a fee from the government agency. This purchase of service contracting has now become a major pathway for the provision of government services. It has also led some to the "fuzzy boundaries" (Kettl 2015) between the public, private, and nonprofit sectors as they are all providing public services to the "hollow state," since government agencies are so rarely providing anything of their own (Milward and Provan 2000).

Many types of services are now contracted out from the government; at the city level, these can include trash collection, child support enforcement, ambulance services, managing jails, or providing health services within jails.

There are a variety of kinds of service contracting—competitive, negotiated, or cooperative. However, for a city agency, the process of contracting out services to be delivered by another entity involves many of the same basic steps.

1. The agency plans the services required.
2. The agency prepares an RFP, which defines the scope of the services and any other requirements that a private or nonprofit agency needs to fulfill to bid for the city contract to provide the service. The RFP lays out the parameters of service delivery that would be acceptable to the agency, and the organization bidding on the contract tries to write a plan that lays within those parameters and requirements. Writing an RFP is a learned skill; it is important to write the requirements broadly enough that the RFP will draw in multiple bids from organizations wanting to provide the service, but not so broadly that potential contractors do not know what is required. Criteria for selection of a contractor should also be incorporated into the RFP. Related to RFPs are Requests for Information (RFIs); these are used by government agencies when they do not know enough about the service or product to write the RFP and are seeking general information.
3. The agency distributes the RFP widely enough that a wide variety of potential contractors can see and consider it. Often, for large contracts, government agencies will hold bidders' conferences so that organizations considering a bid may ask questions. The bidding process is one that needs to be conducted fairly, without favoritism to any one potential contractor. Typically, the city's policies will include strict guidelines on how the bidding and contracting process works, and these must be followed.
4. After proposals have been written by potential contractors and submitted on time, the city agency must review all proposals and judge them according to objective criteria. Typically, an agency has a panel of judges (who could be staff) who assign points for each element of the criteria based on their review of the proposal. Criteria can include things like the specificity of the plan for providing service, the experience of the potential contractor in providing this service, the level of innovation and detail, and the reasonableness of the proposed budget.
5. Based on the results of the review, the contractor is selected. Once the contractor has been selected, and the contract signed, the city agency enters another crucial stage—monitoring the contract as the contractor does the required work. This is the stage at which, all too often, agencies fail to ensure that the contractor fulfills all requirements and ensures the city services are provided effectively to citizens. Contract analysts must engage in site visits, develop effective performance management systems, and then ensure that there is follow-up; reports must be reviewed, and details scrutinized.

BOX 8.1 EXAMPLE OF RFP—OVERVIEW OF REQUEST FOR PROPOSALS FOR PUBLIC OUTREACH AND CONCEPTUAL DESIGN OF THE KAINS AND ADAMS STREETS BICYCLE FACILITY STUDY

Title of RFP

Request for Proposals for Public Outreach and Conceptual Design of the Kains and Adams Streets Bicycle Facility Study
Issue Date: January 27, 2017
Proposal Due Date: February 27, 2017

Introduction

The City of Albany, CA (City) Community Development Department invites qualified professional firms or teams of firms (hereafter Consultant (s)) to submit a response to this Request for Proposals (RFP) to provide professional transportation planning and engineering services for public outreach and development of the conceptual design for the Kains and Adams Streets Bicycle Facility Study (the Project).

The selection of a Consultant will be based upon qualifications to perform the requested services. The Consultant's response to this RFP and subsequent interview will be utilized to select the firm or firms most qualified for this project. General information about the project scope, RFP requirements, deliverables, and the schedule for completing the work are presented below.

Scope of Consultant Services

The City anticipates that the design process will take 10 months from the time of grant award. Once plans are adopted, and depending on the type of improvements and their costs, the City will include the Kains and Adams Bicycle facility projects in the next Capital Improvement Plan (CIP) update. The CIP is updated every two years and provides many opportunities for staff to identify available sources of funding for project implementation. Depending on the cost, the projects could be implemented using non-competitive local funds or through competitive grants. The City

has an extensive record of securing funding for project implementation once plans or projects are approved. It is expected that the project resulting from this request, will be implemented within the next three years after project adoption.

Tasks Included under Scope of Consultant Services

1. Project Kick Off and Community Outreach
2. Research suitable bicycle facility options for Kains and Adams Streets (Deliverable will be a memorandum with highlights from this research along with pros and cons for each type of facility)
3. Alternative Recommendations (Deliverables include schematics of alternatives and presentation to City Council Committee for feedback)
4. Refine Preferred Alternative and Develop Cost Estimates (Deliverable is conceptual plans and estimates and two public meetings).

Project Schedule

- March 2017—consultant selection
- October 2017—City Council approval of conceptual plans and cost estimate

Selection Process and Criteria

Selection Process Staff will review the responses to this RFP and will base selection on the following aspects.

- Responsiveness to the RFP
- Qualifications of individuals to be assigned to this project
- Experience and demonstrated success of the Consultant in preparing similar evaluations

- Evidence that the Consultant understands the project purpose and requirements
- Consultant's approach to the project
- Evidence of the Consultant's ability to prepare a well-written document and accompanying technical drawings/ Schematics
- Demonstration of commitment to project and ability to deliver the finished product on time.

The consultants, which the City in its sole discretion, has determined to be the most qualified to perform this work will be identified as the top-rated consultants. The top-rated consultants will be asked to make a presentation of their proposal to the selection committee. The Consultant's key person or Project Manager will be required to attend the interview. Based on the results of the interview, a contract will be negotiated with the highest scored proposer. If agreement cannot be reached, negotiations with other proposers, in order of their respective final scoring will be conducted until tentative agreements can be reached.

Source: City of Albany, California. 2017. RFP Kains Final. Accessed on February 5, 2017 from www. albanyca.org/index.aspx?recordid=3642&page=1217.

Most agencies are contracting out to provide services today, but not even one-half believe it is reducing their costs (Brudney, Fernandez, Ryu and Wright 2005). In today's hollowed-out government, however, contracting is frequently necessary because many cities do not have the staff on board to provide all important services.

While clearly generating some benefits in narrow areas (garbage collection, ambulance services, and printing, for example), contracting worldwide has had mixed results (Hodge 2000). With limited markets for some services, contracting has inadvertently increased the risk of program failure (Brown and Potoski 2003; Cooper 2003; Hefetz and Warner 2004). Recent trends of bringing services back, or "reverse privatization," indicate a lack of savings and quality of some contracted services. In metropolitan areas with heterogeneous environments, such reversals were found to be more likely (Warner and Hefetz 2010).

A key issue is local governments' capacity to manage burgeoning contracts, from the cycle that begins with the feasibility study to the selection and award of contracts, to the implementation and evaluation of the contract. In Joaquin and Greitens's (2012) study of 537 local governments' contracting decisions and management for a decade (1997–2007), a statistically significant decline showed in some aspects of contract management capacity across all local governments; this was especially true for municipalities and local governments with professionalized administration (i.e., city manager or county administrator). They also discovered that the number of less complex contracted services declined, while the number of more complex services climbed. The overall downward trend in local contract management capacity raised questions, yet the results could also indicate increased capacity of local governments to perform contracting with less study and oversight, as their experience is increased with time. This may be true in contracting that involves wicked problems, where the local government might not easily manage hazards at the early phases of the contract. Perhaps contracting was being used by some municipalities to help address intractable problems, and that organizational learning about contract mechanisms was occurring among local managers.

▶ BOX 8.2   CAREER PATHWAYS IN CONTRACTING

Current Position

University Professor, formerly Contracting Manager

Education

B.A., Economics
M.A., Economics; M.P.A.
Ph.D., Public Administration

Career Pathway

Bill's degrees in Economics were important to helping him think analytically. The specifics of contracting, service delivery, and contract management were all skills he learned on the job.

Bill started his career in the budgeting field for part of the Human Resources Administration of a large city. He became a middle manager in that office, the Deputy Director. When it created a new contracting program, he was asked to be the director of that program because his managers believed he had the necessary skills and knowledge to do the job.

Part of his contracting position involved overseeing budgeting for the contract program, developing initiatives for cost savings, and financially monitoring the performance of contractors with accounting staff and having independent CPA firms audit the contracting organizations.

A Typical Day in Contracting

A typical day in Bill's contracting office would include meeting with his staff over current issues, meeting with people above him and with other parts of the organization about issues crossing the borders of different areas, meeting with other government agencies, and meeting with contract organizations.

Overall, the typical day is quite varied and could include issues about budgeting, technology, service delivery, negotiating, and others. That is one of the reasons he particularly enjoyed his contracting position.

Most Helpful to Him in His Career

To Bill, having good analytical skills is the basis for approaching and solving problems in whatever area he works. Good interpersonal skills are also very important, particularly in contracting. Everyone needs these skills in communicating with contractors and clients receiving the service, which in some cases are delicate issues. Also, interpersonal skills are also important in dealing with other agencies in city government and representing one's agency at public meetings.

Most Challenging

To Bill, the biggest challenges were working within the confines of the laws of the state and city in which he worked. This was due to issues and circumstances in which he could see that government could more effectively serve clients if his office were not limited in what they could do. He found this difficult as he was forced to deny permission for contractors to do certain things. The personnel system in his city government also presented challenges in hiring the people believed to be the most effective in a job.

To overcome these challenges, he used whatever discretion he had, which was usually on the margins, to overcome these challenges.

Most Rewarding

Among many, Bill thought these tasks were most rewarding: overseeing the provision of a contracted essential service (home health care, primarily for elderly adults); negotiating contracts; solving technical issues related to billing systems and others; finding ways to reduce costs while having as little effect on service delivery as possible; working with contractors to improve their performance; working with other city agencies; and being the voice of New York City government to clients and the public for home health care.

Also, Bill liked the fact that he got to work with a great variety of issues.

Recommendations

"Learn through your formal education and on the job, so that you develop the analytical and interpersonal skills you will need to be effective in contracting and service delivery. These skills do not have to be directly related to the particular area of contracting and service delivery (e.g. home health care) you end up in."

"Join professional organizations in contracting, and network with people directly involved in contracting or other related fields you feel will be useful to you. Go to career fairs to learn more about different fields and positions. Talk to faculty members whom you feel will be helpful and the career office in your school."

Interlocal Agreements

Interlocal agreements take advantage of multiple cities within the region all trying to provide the same services to their citizens; rather than duplicate their efforts, governments collaborate and work together to provide a particular service across their jurisdictions. An early study of interlocal agreements in the Kansas metropolitan area showed widespread use of interlocal cooperative agreements, creating a sort of "picket-fence regionalism" among a network of local public service providers in the areas of law enforcement, recreation, roads, and utilities, for example (Thurmaier and Wood 2002). Promoting this platform of action today, the *County Manager's Guide to Shared Services in Local Government* (Zeemering and Delabbio 2013) describes how budget stress after the Great Recession has pushed local governments to explore cooperative service agreements with neighboring jurisdictions, in search of savings and new revenue streams. As the authors define the term, shared services among local governments involve the buying or selling of services, at no cost or on a fee-for-service basis. They may develop an informal understanding, a contract, or an interlocal agreement to jointly produce or consolidate a service.

While Zeemering and Delabbio (2013)'s report is focused on *county* experiences, their findings may well suit cities and other local governments. Synthesizing advice from practitioners and results of their survey of county government officials, the authors identified five steps to establish strong service relationships. These were: 1) create a shared services assessment team; 2) define the strengths in each participating government; 3) consider pilot projects; 4) discuss and document responsibilities with all partners; and 5) make appropriate changes as needed.

E-Service Delivery

There are four stages of digital interaction between government and citizens. These are information provision or communication; secure interaction or transaction; secure contraction; and complete transaction process (Jansen and Olnes 2016). Online service delivery can be through any one of these stages.

There are some critical elements for successful online services. These are:

- A "smooth adaptation of traditional processes to modern technology" (Wimmer 2002);
- Adequate security, authenticity, and privacy (Wimmer 2002);

- The ability to re-organize internal and back-room information and processes into an external and Internet approach (Wimmer 2002);
- Easily navigated sites to help citizens and businesses unfamiliar with government structures (Stowers 2006);
- Ability to help the citizen in completing the service (Wimmer 2002);
- The demand for the service (Wimmer 2002);
- User trust (Beynon-Davies 2005); and
- Marketing the service.

Beynon-Davies (2005) and Stowers (2010) also assert that these factors are not enough to create successful services—that marketing campaigns by the agency are necessary to alert citizens to the available service and to bring them to the site.

Jansen and Olnes (2016) have created a framework for e-government service quality that includes efficiency, effectiveness, and democracy (involvement and participation). Also part of quality is the content and appearance of the information, the ease of use, the reliability and functionality of the interaction environment, trust in government and the site, and citizen support.

In general, e-government saves time and money for citizens and can save time and money for the government agencies themselves. Numerous studies have now found that e-government saves time and money (Texas Online Authority 2003; Beynon-Davies 2005). Ebbers et al. (2008) report that the Canadian Customs and Revenue Agency's traditional services are 20 times more expensive than their online services. An early study of the Texas case also indicates that not only are services conducted much faster but that agencies can provide those services far cheaper through reduced need for additional personnel (Texas Online Authority 2003).

Services that are highly repetitive and uncomplicated are those that are best to place online. Online permitting involves anything from providing copies of permit applications and enhancing a permit by fax process, to allowing the online completion of the permit application, access to permit application status, and searching for permits across the community. This area has some of the most potential for saving city departments and staff money since simple permitting actions (like permits for installation of hot water heaters or roofs) can be done online. This allows staff members to spend their time on serving citizens with more complicated tasks or problems.

BOX 8.3 TYPES OF E-GOVERNMENT SERVICE FEATURES PROVIDED BY GOVERNMENTS

These technological features of websites today provide for endless kinds of services provided to citizens by their governments. For instance, live streaming video is used to provide live city council meetings as well as video of creeks to indicate possible flood dangers. Features include:

- Basic information about the jurisdiction;
- Document provision;
- Communication with officials;
- Downloadable forms;
- Interactive forms;
- Interactive databases;
- Multi-media applications;
- E-commerce applications;
- Facility location services;
- Mapping applications;
- GIS applications;
- Videos; and
- Streaming, live video.

GIS and other mapping applications, while not large efficiency producers, have allowed the creation of exceptional value-added applications for today's cities, applications that would not have been possible without the technology involved in the Internet today. The provision of pdf-formatted maps of cities and downloadable maps, and the ability to interact with map overlays of various aspects of cities (zoning, earthquake faults, utility provision), are an enormous benefit to developers, citizens, and policy-makers alike.

311 Service Call Systems

Basic city services include tasks like filling potholes in roads, removing graffiti, picking up trash, and towing abandoned vehicles. Many cities now handle those types of communications through a 311 system or some other type of call system (Mayor's Action Center, etc.). The 311 system is very much like the emergency 911 call system but set aside for just service calls. By calling or contacting a central office of their city government, citizens initiate those services to report problems and ask for resolution; their complaints or requests for services are then routed by the 311 office to the appropriate city agency for resolution and service. The 311 systems came about when the Federal Communications Commission approved the 311 number for non-emergency police calls, initially in Baltimore, Maryland in 1996, and then approved them for wider use across the nation in 1997. According to Dispatch Magazine On-Line, in 2008 18 percent of the U.S. population had access to the 311 system (Association of Government Contact Center Professionals (AGCCP) 2014; Dispatch Magazine On-Line 2013).

Indianapolis reports that its Mayor's Action Center handled 213,990 calls in 2012 (an average of 17,833 calls per month). The most requested services were to fix potholes, report stray animals, or report excessive weeds in a yard (Dispatch Magazine On-Line 2013).

BOX 8.4   PROFILE OF A CITY'S 311 CALLS— SAN FRANCISCO'S CALLS FROM 2015

Number of Calls in 2015: 349,614
Top Ten Types of Calls in 2015 and Their
Percent of Total Calls:

Percent Resolved at the end of Year: 95.1
Source of Calls: 43.5 percent came from
phone calls

Type of Call	Percent
Graffiti	16.4
Bulky Items Pickup	13.7
General Cleaning	11.3
Hazardous Materials	5.7
Abandoned Vehicle	5.7
Damaged Parking Meter	2.1
Sewage Backup	2.0
Illegal Postings	2.0
Illegal Encampment	1.9
Pavement Defect	1.6

Top Three Departments Receiving Requests:

Department	Percent
Department of Public Works	44.5
Recology (Recycling and Trash)	16.2
Department of Parking and Traffic	13.8

> ### BOX 8.5 SERVICE DELIVERY STRATEGIES FROM CITY SUSTAINABILITY PLANS
>
> - "Increase timeliness and effectiveness of response to customer request calls to 311 by June 30, 2021." Grand Rapids, Michigan, p. 7.
> - "Ensure that 100% of sidewalk snow removal complaints will be abated within 72 hours of the non-compliance notice expiration annually." Grand Rapids, Michigan, p. 7.
> - "Establish a food storage and processing facility by 2018." Longmont, Colorado, p. 7.
>
> - "Increase access to healthy foods through a variety of initiatives." Longmont, Colorado, p. 7.
>
> *Sources:* City of Grand Rapids, Michigan. 2016. Sustainability Plan FY 2017–2021. Accessed on February 22, 2017 from http://grcity.us/ Documents/2016-07-22%20Sustainability%20Plan. pdf.
>
> City of Longmont, Colorado. 2016. Sustainability Plan. November 2016. Accessed on February 22, 2017 from www.longmontcolorado.gov/home/ showdocument?id=16700.

To date, there has been little research conducted on 311 services, not even the most basic descriptive information. However, in some cities, the open data movement has resulted in 311 data being made freely available to citizens and businesses wanting to learn more about government policy and services.

CONCLUSIONS

This chapter has reviewed how many urban services are delivered today, including contracting out, e-government, interlocal agreements, and 311 service call systems. Service delivery is very sensitive to new technologies, and cities need to keep up with citizen demand for up-to-date solutions. Cities also need to monitor the effectiveness of service delivery through performance monitoring systems. Performance measures for service delivery can include service quality and quantity as well as responsiveness. These can be the number of residents served, citizen perception of service quality, and percent of service requests that are resolved within a certain time period. Understanding urban service delivery systems is crucial to fulfilling NASPAA's Urban Administration student learning goals.

SELECTED WEB RESOURCES

- Center for Technology in Government (University at Albany [State University of New York]) www.ctg.albany. edu/
- Government Technology Magazine www. govtech.com/
- National Council for Public-Private Partnerships www.ncppp.org/

EXERCISES AND DISCUSSION QUESTIONS

1. **Know Your City**: Understanding Your City by Knowing How It Provides Services to Its Citizens
   - Does your city provide online services to its citizens via its e-government website?

- Does your city have a 311 service request system? Can residents call in or can they also use a 311 website, or a mobile app?
- Does your city have mobile apps to help provide citizens with information or easy ways to use city services? If so, what are they?
- Does your city engage in any public-private partnerships through its economic development office? What are these projects?
- Does your city share services with other cities in your area?

2. How equitable is it for a city to provide services on its website, or through mobile apps, when not everyone in the community can afford access to the Internet or have a smart phone? How could you make it more equitable?

3. What do you think about street-level bureaucrats and the amount of discretion they have to make decisions in the field? How could you reduce the discretion of street-level bureaucrats?

4. How can citizens help make their city governments accountable to them in providing urban services?

5. How can governments make their service delivery efforts more transparent to their citizens?

6. If cities are participating in public-private partnerships, how can they maintain their public service perspective?

REFERENCES

Association of Government Contact Center Professionals (AGCCP). 2014. *AGCCP Website.* Accessed on July 29, 2014 from www.agccp.org/

Beynon-Davies, Paul. 2005. "Constructing Electronic Government: The Case of the UK Inland Revenue." *International Journal of Information Management* 25: pp. 3–20.

Brown, Trevor, and Potoski, Matthew. 2003. "Contract Management Capacity in Municipal and County Governments." *Public Administration Review* 63 (2): pp. 153–164.

Brudney, Jeffrey L., Fernandez, Sergio, Ryu, Jay Eungha, and Wright, Deil S. 2004. "Exploring and Explaining Contracting Out: Patterns among the American States." *Journal of Public Administration Research and Theory* 15 (3): pp. 393–419.

Brudney, Jeffrey L., Fernandez, Sergio, Ryu, Jay Eungha, and Wright, Deil S. 2005. "Exploring and Explaining Contracting Out: Patterns among the American States." *Journal of Public Administration Research and Theory* 15 (3): pp. 393–419.

Buckley, Joan. 2003. "E-service Quality and the Public Sector." *Managing Service Quality: An International Journal* 13 (6): pp. 453–462.

Cooper, Phillip. 2003. *Governing by Contract: Challenges and Opportunities for Public Managers.* Washington, D.C.: Congressional Quarterly.

Dispatch Magazine On-Line. 2013. "3-1-1 Systems." *Dispatch Magazine On-Line,* September 23, 2013.

Ebbers, W. E. P., Pieterson, W. J., and Noordman, H. N. (2008). "Electronic Government: Rethinking Channel Management Strategies." *Government Information Quarterly* 25 (2008): p. 185.

Hefetz, Amir, and Warner, Mildred. 2004. "Privatization and Its Reverse: Explaining the Dynamics of the Government Contracting Process." *Journal of Public Administration Research and Theory* 14 (2): pp. 171–190.

Hodge, Graeme. 2000. *Privatization: An International View of Performance.* Boulder, CO: Westview Press.

Jansen, Arild, and Olnes, Svein. 2016. "The Nature of Public E-Services and Their Quality Dimensions." *Government Information Quarterly* 33: pp. 647–657.

Joaquin, M. E., and Greitens, T. J. (2012). "Contract Management Capacity Breakdown? An Analysis of Local Governments From 1997 to 2007." *Public Administration Review* 72 (6): pp. 807–816.

Kettl, Donald. 2015. *The Transformation of Governance: Public Administration for the 21st Century,* Updated ed. Baltimore: Johns Hopkins Press.

Lipsky, Michael. 1983. *Street Level Bureaucrats: Dilemmas of the Individual in Public Service.* New York: Russell Sage.

Milward, Brint H., and Provan, Keith G. 2000. "Governing the Hollow State." *Journal of Public Administration Research and Theory* 10 (2): pp. 359–379.

National Council for Public-Private Partnerships. 2017. "7 Keys to Success." *NCPPP.* Accessed on January 30, 2017 from www.ncppp.org/ppp-basics/7-keys/

Stowers, Genie N. L. 2003. "Issues in E-Commerce, E-Procurement, and E-Government Service Delivery." In *Digital Government: Principles and Best Practices.* Edited by Alexei Pavlichev and David Garson. Hershey, PA: Idea Group.

Stowers, Genie N. L. 2006. "User Help Features." *International Journal of E-Government Research* 2 (4): pp. 24–39. Reprinted in Norris, Donald (Ed.). 2008. *E-Government Research: Policy and Management.* Hershey, Pennsylvania: Idea Press, as Chapter 6.

Stowers, Genie N. L. 2010. *City Hall on the Desktop: Transforming the Delivery of Urban Services.* Paper presented at the American Society for Public Administration Conference, San Jose, April 2010.

Texas Online Authority. 2003. *Cost-Benefit Study of Online Services.* Accessed on January 2008 from www.nascio.org/awards/nominations/2003Texas9.doc

Thomas, John Clayton. 2012. *Citizen, Customer, Partner: Engaging the Public in Public Management.* Armonk, NY: M. E. Sharpe.

Thurmaier, Kurt, and Wood, Curtis. 2002. "Interlocal Agreements as Overlapping Social Network: Picket-fence Regionalism in Metropolitan Kansas City." *Public Administration Review* 62 (5): pp. 585–598.

U.S. General Services Administration USA Services. 2010. *Segmentation of Government Customers.* Accessed on March 3, 2010 from www.usaservices.gov/aboutus/CustomerSegmentation.doc

Warner, Mildred, and Hefetz, Amir. 2010. *Privatization and Reverse Privatization in US Local Government Service Delivery.* Paper prepared for Public Service International and the Council of Global Unions Conference, Geneva, Switzerland. October.

Wimmer, M. A. (2002). "Integrated Service Modelling for Online One-stop Government." *Electronic Markets* 12 (3): p. 150.

Public Safety and Emergency Management

This chapter discusses the critical areas of public safety (police and fire protection) and emergency management in cities. As will be seen, much of cities' funds are spent on providing public safety; it is a crucial area in cities and needs to be provided effectively. This is an important area, and learning about it also (like data, information, and communication) falls under the NASPAA Urban Administration standard on learning about managing the core functions of a city.

POLICE

Whatever the popular perception, the reality is that from 2004 to 2013, violent and property crime victimization steadily declined in American cities, as well as in suburbs and rural areas. Serious violent crimes decreased from 14.6 per 1,000 residents aged 12 and over to only 8.8 per 1,000 residents, while overall violent crimes went from 37.3 to 25.9 per 1,000 residents. Likewise, property crimes in cities declined from 220.1 per 1,000 households in 2004 to 165.3 in 2013 (Truman and Langton 2014).

Within the widely cited "protect and serve" role of the police, police officers have four main roles in society:

- Law enforcement. These tasks include arresting people officers think have broken the law, investigating potential crimes, and serving warrants for arrests.
- Order maintenance. Police officers have a role to play in establishing and maintaining social order, which can include responding to disturbances of any type.
- Convenience norms. Police enforce certain norms in our society, such as directing traffic and enforcing driving and parking laws.
- Miscellaneous services. The police also provide a wide variety of other kinds of services for citizens, like providing information, helping people who are lost or hurt, or looking for lost children or the elderly.

(Gaines 2015)

A wide variety of studies have examined how police officers spend their days. One-third of their days is spent patrolling, while practically 40 percent is spent responding to calls

(18 percent of crime-related calls, another 20 percent of non-crime-related calls). Another 7 percent of officers' time is spent providing general services to citizens, 13 percent on administrative tasks, and the final 9 percent on personal time (Gaines 2015).

Often, when we think of police departments, we think of those similar to the ones seen on television—the large departments in New York City and Los Angeles. However, most city and township departments are small—approximately one-half have fewer than ten sworn officers. More than 12 thousand (12,501) police departments at the local level have, at least, one full-time police officer; in 2008, local police departments had an average of 2.3 full-time officers per every 1,000 residents.

We also think of police departments as often being full of white, male officers. However, many police departments have made strides in diversifying their ranks; of course, that does not mean that all departments are diverse. About 25 percent of all officers were from a racial or ethnic minority in 2007, compared to 1987, when only about 16 percent of officers were minorities; 10 percent of 2007 officers were Hispanic. Moreover, 12.5 percent of all officers were women in 2007, compared to only around 7 percent in 1987 (Reaves 2015).

Models of Policing

The first models of policing focused on maintaining order in society, which later shifted more toward crime fighting. However, in the 1980s, many police departments began using a new approach to policing, "community policing," that focused more on relationships with community groups and residents and involved officers in problem-solving and preventing crime rather than arresting criminals. Under this model, neighborhood meetings and crime prevention workshops were set up with a focus on preventing "disorder" in communities. Trying to reduce disorder was often signified by the "broken window" theory, whereby if the neighborhood had an appearance that was positive (i.e., no broken windows), then fewer crimes would occur. Also under the community policing model were additional types of patrolling beyond the regular police officers riding in their cars; officers walked their "beats" as in the distant past, rode their patrol areas on bicycles and horses, and worked out of neighborhood police substations (Gaines 2015). In fact, by 2007, 55 percent of local police departments utilized foot patrols and 32 percent used bicycle patrols (Reaves 2011).

One example of community policing strategy is in Chicago's police department. "Unlike many other community-policing programs limited to a single unit in the department, the Chicago Alternative Policing Strategy (CAPS) is department-wide. The strategic plan for reinventing CPD (Chicago Police Department) describes CAPS as a 'wholesale transformation of the department, from a largely centralized, incident-driven, crime suppression agency to a more decentralized, customer-driven organization dedicated to solving problems, preventing crime, and improving the quality of life in each of Chicago's neighborhoods. In fact, CAPS is a city program with strong support from the Mayor's office and close involvement of city agencies, which had been directed to give top priority to 'CAPS service requests' that affect crime and neighborhood safety" (O'Neil 2013, p. 28). So instead of community policing just occurring in the police department, Chicago's strategy also includes actions by other city departments to reduce factors that could influence crime.

The terrorist attacks on September 11, 2001 produced changes as citizens' fears of terrorism brought police to more aggressive tactics. Soon, technology and increased intelligence gathering and even increased usage of military equipment were added to the mix, but community-based policing once again became the most desired model in the mid-part of the 2000s, after integrating intelligence gathering and technology into the model. Ironically, community-based policing focuses on relationship building, and those relationships also help police departments gather intelligence on potential problems in the community.

Structure of Police Departments

Within a city's organizational structure, police departments typically either sit alone or in a department of public safety, along with the fire department. Within police departments, there are usually patrol, investigation, and traffic units.

Police departments are different from other city agencies in that they are organized and run according to a quasi-military hierarchical model, in which officers wear uniforms, have military-like ranks, and are expected to have military-like discipline within their ranks. Those ranks typically include:

- Entry-level police officers;
- Sometimes, a rank of Corporal;
- Sergeants (line supervisors in the field), usually responsible for supervising a group of police officers in the field;
- Lieutenants, who are middle managers, supervising a group of sergeants, typically in function-oriented groups like Patrol, Homicide, or Traffic;
- Captains, who might have command of a precinct or a functional group such as a division, depending upon the size of a city;
- Majors;
- Assistant, or deputy, chiefs; and
- Police chiefs.

Police departments are usually organized across functions (like patrol, detectives bureau), and then geography (divisions and then "beats" across the city) and time (shifts in the day). A mid-sized city like Gainesville, Florida (Gainesville Police Department 2015) has one chief, one major, four captains, 15 lieutenants, 35 sergeants, 32 corporals, and 206 officers. These leaders then run the Investigations Bureau, Operations (District 1) and Operations (District 2), and the Professional Standards and Support Service Bureau. The Investigations Bureau has 13 divisions (Table 9.1).

TABLE 9.1

Units in the Investigations Bureau, Gainesville, Florida Police Department

- Criminal Investigation
- Crimes Against Persons
- Crimes Against Property
- Domestic Violence
- Juvenile Resource
- Internet Crimes Against Children
- U.S. Marshall Liaison
- Forensics
- Special Investigations
- Narcotics
- High-Intensity Drug Trafficking Areas (HIDTA)
- Drug Enforcement (DEA)
- Interdiction

Source: Gainesville, Florida Police Department. 2015. Organizational Chart. Downloaded on June 15, 2015 from www.gainesvillepd.org/Portals/2/Organization%20Chart/GPDOrgChart10.pdf.

The Operations Bureau has the most officers, including those in patrol cars. This bureau also includes Mounted/K-9 units, the Traffic Safety Team, School Crossing Guards, School Resource Officers, the Airport Unit, a unit for the major mall in town, and one for downtown. All units are cross-organized into shifts of the day and geographical areas of the city. The Professional Standards and Support Services Bureau includes Facilities/Vehicles, the Cadet Explorer program, the Training Unit, Records and Information Technology, and Fiscal and Personnel services. Directly under the Police Chief and Major are Internal Affairs (the unit responsible for investigating possible misdeeds by the police, themselves), Crime Analysts, and Community Relations. Other units or programs often found in police departments are crime prevention, neighborhood watches, bicycle patrols, and drug awareness programs.

Personnel Services

In police departments, human resources and personnel bureaus are crucial because of the importance of recruiting diverse applicants for police positions, screening applicants to ensure eventual candidates are appropriate for police work, and then providing the needed training to do their job effectively. This job begins with recruiting, as police departments go into areas of their communities that are underrepresented in the current make-up of their departments. Today that includes recruiting in African-American, Latino, and Asian communities, recruiting for additional women officers, and, often, recruiting in LGBTQ communities.

Screening potential candidates by departments includes multiple types of standards. These standards differ across departments but typically involve vision, education, physical fitness, and agility standards. Also, candidates must pass health examinations, background checks incorporating criminal and driving record checks, and psychological screening—some departments also include credit checks (Gaines 2015). Educational standards required by departments have increased over time, but still, only 1 percent of all departments require a four-year college degree, and only 16 percent require any college (Gaines 2015: location 2970). Requirements in job ads are often written regarding numbers of credit hours post-high school.

Once "screened in," rather than "screened out," candidates must go through a rigorous application process including both written tests and oral interviews. After being hired, candidates must attend a police academy, where they learn about the legal system and federal/state/local laws, patrol procedures, use of firearms, and physical defense, among other topics. Training is crucial for police officers to ensure that they know and will follow the laws and procedures of their jurisdictions. Typically, states have created minimum training standards for all their police departments, often monitored by something like a Peace Officer Standards and Training (POST) Commission (Gaines 2015, location 3211). If they succeed in graduating from the academy, officers typically begin working with a field training officer (FTO) or mentor for their first months in the field. Throughout their careers, there will also be continued professional development and training.

Training is critical to the development of the police officer in today's society since officers operate with a great deal of discretion in their everyday work. Lipsky (1983) coined the phrase "street-level bureaucrats" to describe those frontline workers, like police officers, social workers, and teachers, who work with a minimum of immediate supervision yet have to make decisions many times a day. Lipsky argued that these workers develop "rules of thumb," to help reduce the uncertainty in making these decisions. Maynard-Moody and Musheno (2000, p. 356) further explored this reality and found that for frontline workers like police officers, "decisions are based on their judgments of the individual citizen client, tempered by pragmatism. Street-level judgments are grounded in what is possible to achieve, given the nature of the individual citizen client and the constraints imposed by the state." Managers believe the more training an officer has, the more likely they will be to rely on their training and the less likely they will be to rely on their views of the citizen client or rules of thumb.

Use of Force

One of the most important areas of training and policy for any police force is on the use of force, to reduce the number of cases of citizen and officer injury and death. The International Association of Chiefs of Police defined the use of force as, "The amount of effort required by police to compel compliance by an unwilling subject" (International Association of Chiefs of Police 2001). The use of force is viewed by at least 80 percent of police departments as a continuum, typically including the following range:

- No force used—an officer is present, and that is enough to resolve the situation.
- Verbalization—officers issue calm commands for identification.
- Empty-hand control—officers use physical force only to gain control, through either soft technique (grabs, holds) or hard techniques (punches, kicks).
- Less-lethal methods—officers use blunt impact (batons) to immobilize or chemicals (sprays or projectiles) or Conducted Energy Devices (CEDs, or tasers) to gain control.
- Lethal force—officers use firearms to stop a suspect's actions.

(National Institute of Justice 2015)

Some departments break this continuum down into even more levels. Actions by alleged offenders dictate the level of use of force found on the continuum. An officer has to evaluate offender behavior on an offender behavior continuum, which includes the following:

- Offender is compliant.
- Offender is verbal and passive.
- Offender is physical and defensive.
- Offender is physical and active.
- Offender is deadly.

These continua are usually laid out in law enforcement policies to guide officers on the conditions under which force is to be allowed. Terrill, Paoline and Ingram (2011) found, however, a wide variety of views on how effective those policies were to police officers.

A 2011 study attempted to identify the types of force that were associated with the most beneficial outcomes (i.e., fewer citizen and officer injuries or deaths) but was not able to do so. The study was able, however, to determine that roughly 80 percent of the departments surveyed utilized some continuum.

These issues became critical in American cities with the increasing number of deaths of numerous African-Americans at the hands of police officers, particularly the peak of deaths during the summer of 2014—many of them videotaped by other citizens. It is hard to get nationwide data on killings by police, so organizations like the *Washington Post* (www.washingtonpost.com/graphics/national/police-shootings/) and the privately run Fatal Encounters website (www.fatalencounters.org/) organized by D. Brian Burghart, editor of the *Reno News and Review*, have been undertaking the task of gathering data from communities across the country and posting them. According to the Fatal Encounters site, there were 1,490 police killings across the country during 2016. This issue became white-hot during the summer months of 2014, when a series of high-profile police killings occurred. Killed during that summer were Michael Brown (Ferguson, Missouri), Eric Garner (Staten Island, New York on July 17 as he was allegedly selling untaxed cigarettes), John Crawford III (Beavercreek, Ohio in a Walmart on August 5), and Ezell Ford (Los Angeles on August 11). They have been joined by others since, but that summer brought the issue into the public eye. Many would say the difference in these killings now compared to those in the past is the widespread availability of cell phones so that they are now videotaped, unlike in the past.

BOX 9.1 CAREER PATHWAYS IN POLICE AND LAW ENFORCEMENT

Current Position

Police Management Analyst for Police Department in mid-sized city

Education

B.A., Psychology
M.P.A.
Certificate, Administration of Justice
Police Officer Standards and Training (POST)
Certificate in Records Management

Career Pathway

1. Police Records Clerk (seven years)
2. Senior Police Records Clerk (five years)
3. Police Information and Analysis Supervisor (or Records Supervisor) (six years)
4. False Alarm Program Manager (six years)
5. Police Management Analyst (almost eight years and currently). This position is not civil service; it is "at-will," which means Dana can be fired at any moment.

Learning about the Job

Most of it was on the job training from her early years in the public safety field, but for her current position, she needed to know other fundamentals; she learned about those by completing the M.P.A. program.

Finding Her Way to Public Safety

When she was working on her degree in Psychology, she took the only course the Psychology department had on criminal justice at the time and found it interesting. She had to do an internship for one of her Psychology classes, so she volunteered to be a "Probation Aide" with the county juvenile probation department. She assisted a Probation Officer and met with a couple of clients on a weekly basis. She did that for a year and then graduated. At the time she was going to undergraduate school, she was working as a file clerk in an auto repair shop.

After that, she thought she was going to become a probation officer but then saw an ad in the newspaper for a "Police Records Clerk" job in a small city police department. She took the civil service test for it, along with hundreds of other people, and was one of three hired. Originally, she told the recruitment sergeant that she would stay for one year.

Dana found she enjoyed the field but never wanted to become a police officer. She was promoted to Senior Police Records Clerk and then subsequently looked for more advancement, so she became the Records Supervisor at another, nearby small city police department.

There, Dana was its first civilian supervisor, so it brought a whole new set of challenges for her and those she supervised. She was there just a few years when she was encouraged by one of her police officer friends who was getting his Master's degree in Criminal Justice to go for her Master's degree.

In 2002 after graduating with the M.P.A. degree, she was looking online at the jobs available for a large city nearby when she found a listing for a "False Alarm Program Manager" for the then Emergency Communications Department (the 911 department). This was a brand new position—and it was to roll out a program that billed residents and businesses every time an officer responded to a false burglar alarm call. Dana applied, interviewed, and was hired almost immediately. She felt bad about leaving her old city, so she offered to work at her old job part-time, and for six years, she typed police reports on the weekends.

Six years later, Dana learned that there was going to be an opening for her current position (Police Management Analyst), and she asked the Police Chief if he would consider her. She got the job but notes that if she did not have the education she received while obtaining her M.P.A. (budgeting, public speaking, policy, etc.), she would not have been qualified for her current position.

A Typical Day

For Dana, a typical day is spent monitoring program budgets (the Police Department has six separate program budgets) with accountability for revenue and expenditure performance. She is also responsible for maintaining all of the department's social media accounts—Facebook, Twitter, Nixle, Instagram, and Nextdoor. She is the only staff person who posts on and monitors these accounts, although she does have a substitute when she is on vacation. The social media job also involves working after hours, since she wants to maintain the integrity of the Police Department's social media profile.

Dana also keeps track of the Police Department's training budget, which is a budget within the overall comprehensive budget, and keeps the command staff aware of the status. She responds to inquiries from the public and others regarding city

law enforcement activities. She writes a weekly crime bulletin that is emailed to subscribers and is also put on the website. When the website needs updating, she is also responsible for that. She is also responsible for monitoring and maintaining the department's asset forfeiture fund account. She is a liaison to other departments in the city—the Finance Department, Human Resources Department, City Manager's Office, and Public Works. She is also the first contact for an app called "Public Stuff" that the citizens use to report various issues—abandoned vehicles, speeding, illegal dumping. She coordinates with the appropriate people to respond to their requests. When new employees are hired, she is responsible for obtaining their biographical information and sending it to the Human Resources Department for an in-house monthly online newsletter for employees of her city. She is also the designated photographer for anything related to the Police Department. She assists the Community Department in various events such as Kops and Kids, National Night Out, and internal social functions. She also coordinates the county's drunk driving enforcement grant from the California Office of Traffic Safety; when there is a designated enforcement period, she coordinates all the checkpoints, warrant details, and saturation patrols with 17 police agencies. She is also responsible for preparing all fiscal reports sent to the Office of Traffic Safety.

As far as meetings, Dana attends a monthly budget meeting with the Captains, the Chief, the Finance Director, the Deputy Finance Director, and the Management Analyst. There, they talk about the status of their budgets. She also attends command staff meetings at the Police Department and a monthly meeting with the Assistant City Manager and the representatives from respective departments within the city to talk about social media. Finally, she attends homeowners' or community meetings and will soon be ramping up more community interests.

Professional Associations and Networking

Dana participates in her city's Police Athletic League, is a member of a law enforcement Social Media Group, and attends Police Department and other functions within her city. She also gives back at her alma mater, recently participating as the only civilian female participant in a Speed Mentoring event.

Most Helpful to Her Career

To Dana, getting positive feedback has been most helpful in her career, along with the freedom to run the social media platforms in the voice she has chosen, and receiving the trust and respect that comes with experience and knowledge.

Challenges and How She Dealt with Them

At the beginning of her career, being a civilian woman in a police department sometimes posed a challenge. Dana worked on her delivery of the job, her knowledge and expertise, and her humor and diplomacy so that now people respect her. She realizes she got this job because she was qualified. At the beginning of her career, when she led meetings on managing the county's drunk driving enforcement grant, she would almost always be the only female in a room of up to 20 male sergeants from police departments throughout the county. However, she was responsible for coordinating the events of the grant and needed cooperation from everyone.

The first meeting was intimidating because the attendees did not know her, and she did not know them. She held four of those meetings every year, and just finished the eighth year of managing the grant. That was a certainly a challenge, but her reputation has made it easy to garner participation for each event.

She believes a more current challenge in public safety is how to keep things positive when the world seems to be so anti-police.

Overall, she deals with challenges by keeping her cool and relying on her intelligence and qualifications so she can take the higher road and let her reputation speak for itself.

Most Rewarding Part of the Job

To Dana, the most rewarding thing about this field is knowing that her work helps to make the public feel safe, informed, and listened to. She also enjoys being able to work as a team with her fellow sworn and civilian co-workers.

Recommendations for Students

Dana recommends doing internships if they are available. She also tells everyone they need to get a college degree before doing anything else. It is not necessarily what they learn that is important, but it is more of the process: the delayed gratification, the critical thinking, the public speaking, the research—all of these skills are tremendously important and beneficial. Lastly, she recommends going on to obtain a Master's degree. For her, it *was* what she learned at the Master's level that made the difference for her in this field.

The number of African-Americans killed by police is far greater than the African-American proportion of American society would suggest was possible; the number of killings in that community is very disproportional. ProPublica, a nonprofit investigative journalism organization, has analyzed federal data from 2010 to 2012 that suggest that "blacks, age 15 to 19, were killed at a rate of 31.17 per million while just 1.47 per million white males in that age range died at the hands of police" (Gabrielson, Grochowski Jones and Sagara 2014). So, young African-American men are 21 times more likely to be killed than young white men. Overall, ProPublica reports that 44 percent of those killed by police were white.

CompStat

One important technological tool in today's policing arena is data analysis, visualization, and mapping. The systematic use of data in policing was begun by New York City in 1994 and called the CompStat process (DeLorenzi, Shane and Amendola 2006). Since then, numerous other jurisdictions have adopted this type of project, although sometimes under other names. CompStat allows departments to "collect, analyze, and map crime data and other essential police performance measures on a regular basis, and hold police managers accountable for their performance as measured by these data" (DeLorenzi, Shane and Amendola 2006). In many jurisdictions today, the original model has moved farther away from an accountability system to the use of crime data as a tool to understand patterns of crime and as a way of focusing resources most directly toward current patterns.

Chicago is one city that has expanded the use of its crime data in several significant ways. One piece of the CAPS strategy mentioned earlier is the Citizen Information Collection for Automated Mapping (ICAM), one of the first digital mapping applications using crime data to understand better the patterns of crime within the City. The Citizen ICAM program led to a privately-run effort called ChicagoCrime.org, now morphed into Chicago.Everyblock. com/crime. This site allows users to search for crime reports for their neighborhoods; the broader site provides discussion opportunities and other information for neighborhoods. The existence of that site and the experience developed by providing public data for it, along with the City of Chicago's early experience with geographic information systems, provided the impetus for much of Chicago's success. Moreover, crime data were one of the earliest areas of demand by Chicago's citizens when Chicago's open data portal began.

Today, the Chicago Police Department offers the Citizen Law Enforcement Analysis and Reporting (CLEAR) System, which provides crime incident data (except for murders, which could identify the victim) to allow citizens to understand better crime patterns within their neighborhoods. Moreover, the City of Chicago's Open Data Portal provides crime data from 2001 to the present, which can also be mapped (Figure 9.1).

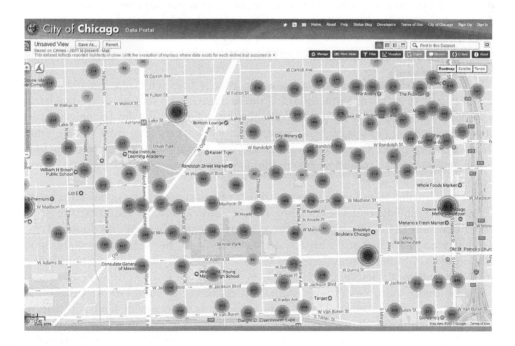

FIGURE 9.1
Map of Crimes from Chicago's Open Data Portal, 2017

Source: City of Chicago Open Data Portal, 2017 Crime Data. Accessed on February 12, 2017 From https://data.cityofchicago.org/ Public-Safety/Crimes-2001-to-present-Map/c4ep-ee5m.

FIRE ADMINISTRATION

Contemporary firefighting began with James Braidwood in Scotland in the 1820s, whose methods then spread to London and other European cities. At that time, American firefighting was a matter of volunteers working as bucket brigades, fire watchers, and fire brigades, which were not very effective. Steam fire engines developed, and the era of professional paid career firefighters began. New York City's Fire Department borrowed the Scottish methods and paramilitary organizational structure in the 1860s to further modernize and become one of the first modern departments in America.

However, the history of the American fire service also follows that of American urban development, in that cities in the 1860s to 1880s grew rapidly with the development of industrialization and increases in immigration. During this time, they also burned on a regular basis due to their density and the building materials used. At that time, fires routinely destroyed whole blocks of homes and businesses. A New York City fire in 1835 lasted days, and, in 1845, one-third of Pittsburgh was destroyed in a matter of hours; both fires destroyed almost 60 acres, and in Portland, Maine (1866) a tremendous fire brought serious losses to the insurance industry (Hensler 2011, pp. 5–6). The so-called 1871 Great Fire of Chicago was followed by other large fires in growing cities across the country, so many that fire departments started to pay their previously unpaid firefighters and purchase more modern equipment.

Elected officials still proved reluctant to limit activities of builders, however, so insurance companies began to play bigger roles in the development of competent fire departments as well as more protective building codes and building materials, to protect their investments. In some early cases, insurance companies themselves paid for fire brigades to protect their investments, and then the industry finally began to organize, gather data, and set up a system for grading fire departments and water supplies in cities. Builders, architects, engineers, and firefighters themselves also played a critical role in developing the new firefighting methods and equipment, more effective building codes and building materials, and improved urban water supply systems that started to protect developing cities (Hensler 2011).

Some of the earliest measures designed to reduce fires were requirements for fire-resistant chimneys and roofing materials. Cities and states also moved to regulate hazardous substances that were fire hazards. After shocking tragedies like the Triangle Shirtwaist Factory Fire of 1911, in which 146 garment factory workers died from flames, smoke, or jumping from upper floors because the doors and windows were blocked or locked by managers, cities also moved to ensure builders and businesses had open exits through which workers could leave.

So, cities learned to reduce the destructibility of fire by providing open space between buildings, by reducing building and population density, and by requiring fire separation walls within buildings and sprinkler systems. Meanwhile, building materials were improved, along with industry rating systems, professional fire departments, and motorized equipment. Gradually, fires destroyed less of cities, usually limited to just one building or even just one floor (Hensler 2011).

The insurance industry's rating system, now called the Revised Fire Suppression Rating Schedule, continues today. This Rating Schedule is a document filed with the state department of insurance that reviews the "fire suppression capabilities of individual communities" according to established Insurance Services Office (ISO) criteria (National Fire Protection Association 2013).

The updated rating system now rates communities on the capacity of the local fire department, the water supply, a community's capacity for emergency communications, and its fire prevention efforts, for a total of 105.5 points. These ratings then translate into a Public Protection Classification (PPC) class, which runs from 1 (the best) to 10 (the worst). Since this rating schedule at least partially determines how much businesses and individuals pay for fire insurance and has been approved by a majority of states, there is an incentive for communities to invest in firefighting and protection capabilities, so their scores improve and premiums decline.

The National Fire Protection Association reports that, in 2013, 1,240,000 fires caused $11.5 billion in property damage, 15,925 injuries, and 3,240 deaths to non-fire personnel. Of these, 39.3 percent were structure fires, 45.5 percent were outdoor fires, and the remainder were vehicle fires (National Fire Protection Association 2015). Fire departments across the country respond to a fire every 25 seconds.

Also in 2013, 97 firefighters lost their lives fighting fires (64 died in 2014), and 65,880 firefighters were injured. Most deaths occurred on site at fire scenes, and most on-duty deaths occurred from cardiac arrest (National Fire Protection Association 2015). Most civilian deaths occur in residential fires (Smeby 2014, p. 37). However, vehicle crashes are also an important cause of death; over one ten-year period up to 1996, 176 firefighters were killed in vehicle-related incidents going to or returning from an alarm (Smeby 2014, p. 132).

Since the development of more effective building codes and fire prevention methods over time, the number of fires in the United States has declined, although their intensity has increased.

Organization

In cities, fire departments are usually stand-alone departments, although sometimes found under an umbrella public safety department along with police departments. Only 31 percent of firefighters nationwide are career firefighters; the other 69 percent are volunteers. Most volunteer firefighters (95 percent) work in departments serving less than 25,000 population (National Fire Protection Association 2015).

Of the 31,644,500 calls to fire departments during 2013, most (67.5 percent) were for medical aid (for those departments that respond to medical emergencies) (Figure 9.2). Fires themselves comprised only 3.9 percent of the calls, while practically twice as many calls (7.4 percent) were for false alarms. Another 4.1 percent were for mutual aid to other jurisdictions, which could involve fire calls.

Through improvements in building codes, building materials, and education, the number of fires occurring in the United States has dropped dramatically over the years. While this is good news, the reality is that the fires that now occur are hotter and spread more rapidly, resulting in earlier structural collapses (Smeby 2014); this is due to the increased use of highly flammable chemicals in buildings. An ironic result is that, because there are fewer fires, firefighters today often get less experience fighting fires.

Fire prevention programs incorporate the adoption of up-to-date building codes that include fire-resistant materials and safety measures; the first among these are sprinkler systems, now required in new commercial buildings but not in residential buildings, even though they are the most valuable tool to quickly put out a fire. Some building codes require complete sprinkler systems if buildings are more than a certain distance from a fire station. Fire inspections can help ensure that builders follow the building code. Poorer areas of communities still suffer more fires due to poorer building materials and lack of some of the basic precautions.

Figure 9.3 illustrates a typical organizational chart for a fire department based upon career firefighter staffing (from Hanover Park, Illinois). Like police departments, fire

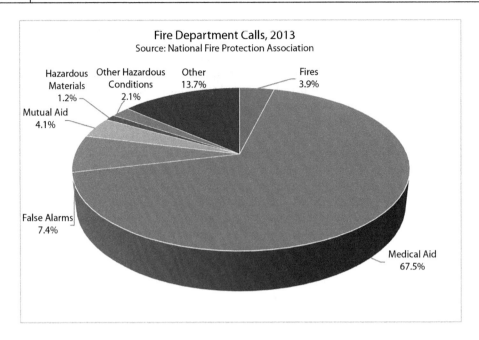

FIGURE 9.2
Fire Department Calls Nationwide, 2013

Source: Developed from National Fire Protection Association, 2013. Retrieved from http://www.nfpa.org/research/reports-and-statistics/the-fire-service/fire-department-calls/fire-department-calls on July 8, 2015.

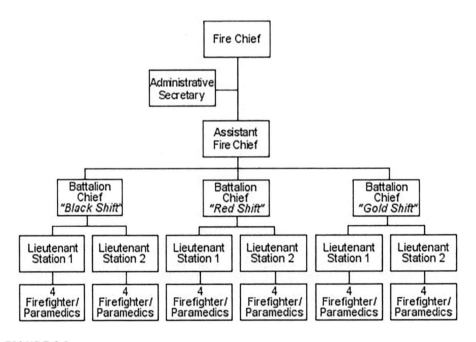

FIGURE 9.3
Hanover Park, Illinois Fire Department Organizational Chart

Source: http://www.hanoverparkillinois.org/Services/Fire-Department/Organizational-Chart-and-Staffing.aspx#Function Retrieved July 10, 2015.

service departments operate in a quasi-military fashion; commanders who take charge of fighting a fire need to be sure that firefighters follow their orders, under an Incident Command or Unified Command system. A fire chief heads the department, and there is usually an assistant fire chief. In small cities like Hanover Park, there are just two stations, both staffing three shifts (black, red, and gold). A battalion chief leads each shift across the city, while a lieutenant leads each shift at a fire station. In addition, departments also have a functional organizational structure, in which the station- and shift-based personnel are simultaneously organized into other battalions: Emergency Services, Training, Operations, and Inspectional Services (EMS).

Firefighters have unusual work schedules. Although these may differ across the country, it is typical for firefighters to be on-duty for two to three days, then off-duty for several more. Another staffing pattern is in the San Diego Fire Department, with three shifts (A, B, or C); each shift works nine to eleven 24-hour shifts per month, beginning at 8 am and finishing the next day at 8 am. On duty, firefighters sleep at the fire station, answer alarms, maintain equipment, and work as a team. Many residents who see fire engines pulled up to supermarkets while firefighters are shopping for food for their shift observe that this ensures the firefighters and their truck are always available in case of an alarm.

Fire department "apparatus," or equipment, begins with the truck company, the first fire engine that goes to the scene of the fire, which is the one with water storage capacity and a hose that can be used to put out small fires. If more support is needed at a fire, the next step would be sending an engine company, whose firefighters ride on the fire engine with the long ladder. National standards come from the National Fire Protection Association (NFPA) and include NFPA 1710, National Standard for the Organization and Deployment of Fire Suppression Operations, Emergency Medical Operations, and Special Operations to the Public by Career Fire Departments. Based upon these standards, there need to be at least four firefighters on each apparatus.

Fighting fires has always involved four basic methods: removing whatever is burning from the fire, reducing the supply of oxygen to the fire, reducing the temperature of whatever is burning or of the flame itself, and using chemicals to alter the course of the fire process (Hensler 2011, p. 3). As houses are built less and less with just wood and brick, the number of fires declines. However, many of the materials inside dwellings today are composed of toxic materials that burn hot and with high toxicity.

Standards from the NFPA (NFPA 1500, Standard on Fire Department Occupational Safety and Health Program) and the U.S. Occupational and Health Administration (OSHA) standard (Fire Brigade and Respiratory Protection) also determine the personal equipment used by each firefighter. Today, each firefighter is required to wear fire Nomex suits, boots, hood, and gloves, and to carry self-contained breathing apparatus (SCBA).

Another standard, NFPA 1001, Standard for Firefighter Professional Qualifications, lays out requirements for training and firefighter competencies. One OSHA regulation (OSHA 29 CFR 1910.134: Respiratory Protection) requires that four firefighters be present before an inside fire can be fought using self-contained breathing apparatus; this regulation is known as "two-in, two-out" (Smedy 2014).

As might be assumed from the emphasis upon written standards, working in a dangerous and volatile environment like an active fire requires all involved to know exactly what they are supposed to be doing. So, in addition to following national standards, having department-level standard operating procedures (SOPs) when going to a fire is crucial. As already stated, the first engine to the fire is the truck engine; the officer on that truck becomes Incident Commander until higher ranking officers arrive. Should the need arise, the Incident Commander calls for more equipment and firefighters; if that is needed, the engine company arrives next, with the ladders. The firefighters on that apparatus are responsible for connecting the hoses to the closest fire hydrant and searching for survivors.

Table 9.2 illustrates the SOPs of one U.S. Fire Department (City of San Diego) for a single-family structure fire. Once the Fire Department gets an alarm, the 1st Engine Company (on the truck carrying a small water supply in a water tank) arrives at the fire first and sets up the Initial Attack Line. The firefighters on that engine investigate to determine if the fire is real and set up the engine's hoses with a water supply. The 1st Truck Company (the engine with the movable ladders) arrives and does search and rescue to ensure all residents are out of the structure. The Truck Company also sets up any ladders needed for aerial use and makes sure the house is ventilated (i.e., windows are open, or the roof has holes in it to vent the fire and smoke from the house). The 2nd Engine Company arrives and ensures the backup hose is connected to the closest fire hydrant. If needed, the 3rd Engine Company comes and stands by as the Rapid Intervention Crew if the firefighters already on-scene need assistance. The Battalion Chief arrives as soon as possible and takes over command, ensuring that the fire attack plan is sound; this senior officer at the scene is also responsible for firefighter safety. The 2nd Truck Company arrives to do subsequent search and rescue and handle utilities. The pump operator on the 1st Engine ensures the pump is running, and the senior officer at the scene ensures accountability. Accountability is crucial—the number of personnel inside and outside the house is tracked at all times so that deaths or injuries can be prevented. On-scene personnel may request air support,

TABLE 9.2

Tasks and Staffing for San Diego Fire Department, Single Family Structural Fires

Task	Staffing Level	Unit Assigned
Initial Attack Line	2	1st Engine
Primary Search and Rescue	2	1st Truck
Ventilation/Ladders, Access	2	1st Truck
Back-up Hoseline	2	2nd Engine
Rapid Intervention Crew	4	3rd Engine
Secondary Search and Rescue	2	2nd Truck
Utilities, Salvage, and Overhaul	2	2nd Truck
Pump Operator	1	1st Engine
Water Supply	1	2nd Engine
Accountability	1	1st Engine
Contingency (optional, non-assigned unit)	4	4th Engine requested)
Air/Light Support	1	Light & Air
Command Officer	1	Battalion Chief
Safety (or other Incident Command System [ICS] position)	1	Battalion Chief
Advanced Life Support (ALS) Ambulance	2	Ambulance/Rehab
Total Personnel:	28	

Source: City of San Diego Fire Department. 2005. Table 4.1: Working First Alarm Single Family Structure Fire. Accessed on June 15, 2015 from www.sdfirefacts.com/items/acreditation%20report.pdf, p. 55.

lights, or even auxiliary engines or an ambulance. Each company operates as a team (City of San Diego 2005).

Screening to be a firefighter and periodic training are crucial to ensure firefighters are ready to endure the stresses of the job. Common stresses include hearing problems from riding on the engines while the sirens are going, sleep deprivation from long on-call periods, extremely high temperatures, vehicle crashes, and exposure to possible toxic agents from fires (Smedy 2014).

A critical performance measure for firefighting is response time to calls. The locations of fire stations are within overlapping circles of services, so no area of the city is farther from what would require the highest acceptable average response time for fire personnel and equipment. The Insurance Service Office (ISO) usually requires, at most, a three-minute response time and response distance of no more than 1.5 miles with a maximum of no more than five-mile response distance. With the inclusion of emergency medical services, however, fire services must work to the four-minute response time for non-breathing or trauma patients (Smeby 2014, pp. 102–103). Adding additional fire stations reduces the response time, while decreasing the number of stations (or closing stations) increases response time. The NFPA 1710 standard requires that the first engine must arrive within four minutes for structural fires (or full first alarm assignment within eight minutes); in both cases, 80 seconds are allowed for fire companies to exit the station and be on their way to the fire. Other performance measures are staffing and ability to deploy effectively.

Fire departments can also utilize risk assessments as a guide for the severity of the fire and for what level of response to call out. Table 9.3 provides such a risk assessment scheme for the San Diego Fire Department. This system allocates points for factors associated with firefighting difficulty to provide much-needed information about what is facing firefighters at a fire. The more points, the higher the risk for firefighters in fighting the fires.

The hiring process for firefighters, as with police officers, begins with an arduous screening process. In this case, potential firefighters are screened for courage, the ability to work and live in teams, the ability to endure high temperatures, and physical strength. Firefighters must be able to carry their personal equipment as well as heavy hoses up numerous flights of stairs (typically, up to 125 pounds), keep calm, remember SOPs in dangerous situations, and learn the complications of fire behavior and fire attack strategies (Smeby 2014).

Following the screening, potential candidates take tests; candidates are then selected based upon test scores and then must attend and pass a fire academy, which is itself quite strenuous. The selection of applicants to be firefighters has been the subject of a great deal of affirmative action and reverse discrimination litigation over the past years. Care must be taken to select candidates based on job-related criteria rather than personal characteristics. Based on the string of legal cases, strategies have been developed to work toward more diversity among firefighters without either discrimination against minorities or reverse discrimination (i.e., disadvantaging those in majority groups).

One popular strategy is banding, where candidates with similar scores and aptitude are put together in a group; candidates are selected from within that band until all are gone, and then the selection moves on to the next band. According to Smeby (2014, p. 81), a common cutoff score for the top band is 85 percent on tests and assessments, so the top band is from 85 to 100 percent. Women, men, and people of different races and ethnicities may all be together in the top band; human resource departments seek diversity from among all of those in that top band and then work to ensure more equity across groups.

TABLE 9.3

San Diego's Point Allocation for Risk Assessment

Risk Factor	Point Allocation
Road Class and Proximity	**0–20 points**
Within 300 feet from an unhindered road	0
Within 300 feet from a limited access road	2
Within 300 feet from an obstructed road	4
Each additional 300 feet from road add:	+4 (maximum +16)
Vegetation/Cover Classification	**0–20 points**
Water, sand	0
Disturbed	2
Urban developed	3
Unspecified riparian, cropland, wetland	5
Grassland	10
Scrub	15
Chaparral	17
Tree cover	20
Slope Severity	**0–20 points**
< 9% slope	2
9–20% slope	8
21–30% slope	14
31–40% slope	16
> 40% slope	20
Fire Hydrant Proximity	**0–5 points**
< 600 feet from hydrant	0
600–1,000 feet from hydrant	2
> 1,000 feet from hydrant	5
Fire Response Time	**0–10 points**
> 90% chance of Fire Response within 5 minutes	0
> 50% and < 90% chance of Fire Response within 5 minutes	5
< 50% change of Fire Response within 5 minutes	10

Source: City of San Diego Fire Department. Accessed on June 15, 2015 from www.sdfirefacts.com/items/acreditation%20report.pdf, p. 127.

Fire and emergency services departments are fortunate, in that some of their services can be used for revenue. Ambulance transport is, of course, the main potential source, and this is one of the main reasons why fire departments are more and more frequently incorporating emergency medical services into their units. However, fire departments could also charge fees for the very problematic false alarms, for reviewing fire prevention plans, and for fire inspections. Charging for false alarms has the added benefit of reducing those alarms. Also, fire district fees could be charged per household or business, according to building square footage or the amount of water that would potentially be needed to fight fires in that building (Smeby 2014).

In times of budget cuts, many fire departments and police departments are being cut along with other city departments. However, some departments are also seeking to share services across jurisdictions or are eliminating their departments altogether then contracting back for those services from other jurisdictions.

Emergency Medical Services

Based on the recommendations of the National EMS Education and Practice Blueprint, there are four levels of emergency service personnel:

1. Emergency Responder (48–60 hours of training), who can carry automatic defibrillators;
2. Emergency Medical Technician (EMT)—Basic (150–190 hours of training), who can provide basic emergency care and transit;
3. EMT—Intermediate, with an additional 150–190 hours of training beyond the EMT; and
4. EMT—Paramedic, the level that provides advanced emergency care, with 1,000 to 1,200 hours of training.

(Smeby 2014)

NFPA standards require that two firefighters arriving in a fire engine company be EMTs and paramedics. Response times for EMS personnel depend upon the nature of the medical emergency. Emergency medical personnel, like firefighters, are also subject to injuries and deaths; 74 percent of their fatalities are due to ambulance crashes (Smeby 2014, p. 131). Factors in these deaths could be vehicle maintenance, training, and safety gear; knowledge of these factors could be used to reduce deaths.

EMERGENCY MANAGEMENT

Disasters fall into three categories—natural, man-made, and intentional. A hazard is a "source of danger that may or may not lead to an emergency or disaster" (Haddow et al. 2013). A disaster is when the requirements of an emergency exceed emergency services' capacities (Haddow et al. 2013, location 1127). When events overcome all elements, then that is a catastrophe.

Natural hazards include the following:

- Floods, the most frequent disaster in the United States;
- Earthquakes;
- Hurricanes;
- Storm surges, or walls of water pushed by the wind, which are typically the primary source of injuries and deaths from hurricanes or other coastal storms;
- Tornadoes;
- Wildfires;
- Mass movements of earth like mudflows, landslides, rockfalls, or avalanches;
- Tsunamis, or tidal waves;
- Volcanic eruptions;
- Severe winter storms;

- Drought;
- Extreme temperatures;
- Coastal erosion;
- Thunderstorms; and
- Hail.

Table 9.4 presents descriptions of how the severity of different types of natural hazards is measured.

Technological hazards are another category of hazards but are man-made. They include structural fires, dam failures, hazardous materials accidents, and nuclear accidents.

Terrorism is an intentional kind of hazard, as are Chemical, Biological, Radiological, and Nuclear (CBRN) incidents, which use any of those weapons of mass destruction.

To manage these disasters, the discipline of emergency management has developed into four areas: 1) Mitigation; 2) Preparedness; 3) Response; and 4) Recovery. Mitigation is a process of identifying possible hazards and then attempting to reduce their impact. Preparedness efforts focus on making arrangements to survive a disaster. The Response stage occurs after a disaster and is run by an Incident Command System (ICS), a system for coordinating all agencies (federal, state, and local) around one command and five systems: command, operations, planning, logistics, and finance. State and local governments also

---

TABLE 9.4

Measures of Severity of Major Types of Disasters

Type of Disaster	Scale of Severity	Measurement of Severity
Floods	Elevation above typical water levels	Feet of water
Earthquakes	Richter and Modified Mercalli Intensity (MMI) Scales	Richter—numbers on a logarithmic scale; MMI measures damages sustained from I (Instrumental) to VI (Strong) to XII (Catastrophic)
Hurricanes	Saffir-Simpson Scale, based on wind speed, storm surge, and damage	Category 1 (winds of 74–95 mph/surge 4–5 feet above normal) to Category 5 (winds of 155 mph/surge more than 18 feet above normal)
Storm Surges	Determined by intensity of the storm, height of tide, and slope of sea floor	Feet of water in surge
Tornadoes	Fujita-Pearson Tornado Scale	F-0 (40–72 mph) to F-5 (261–318 mph)
	Enhanced Fujita-Pearson Tornado Scale	F-0 (65–85 mph) to F-5 (more than 200 mph, complete destruction of structures)
Wildfires	Area of burning/percent contained	Acres
Winter Storms	Northeast Snowfall Impact Scale (NESIS)	Categories 1 to 5 where 1 is Notable, and 5 is Extreme

have emergency operations centers staffed with representatives from all relevant agencies, to make decision-making easier and more immediate. Recovery efforts occur after the disaster ends; it involves picking up the pieces and getting life back to as close to normal as possible as well as dealing with the emotional trauma of a disaster is an important aspect of recovery efforts today.

As identified by Claire Rubin (2012), there are several issues that frequently accompany major disasters:

- Conflict over how centralized decision-making should be, in the aftermath of a disaster;
- How to ensure relief funds and resources get distributed in an equitable manner;
- Ill-defined roles among federal agencies and relief agencies like the American Red Cross;
- "Ad hoc disaster response and assistance plans";

(location 217)

- Conflict between business interests and elected officials over recovery; and
- Unpredictable responses from states and state agencies.

(Rubin 2012, location 216–217)

The history of the development of professional emergency management tracks closely with major disasters hitting the United States; it is also a history of steadily increasing federal government involvement and legal and policy changes resulting from these disasters.

Emergency management has been around for more than a century in some form, but permanent programs only evolved after 1950; before that, Congress would pass relief programs and legislation specific to a particular disaster, or the federal government would provide no relief. Instead, beginning in 1900, the American Red Cross began to offer assistance after being chartered by Congress (as an independent, nonprofit, tax-exempt, and charitable organization and federal "instrumentality"). Only preparations for floods, in the guise of levees and other public works, were provided by the federal government, instead of efforts to mitigate a wide variety of disasters.

BOX 9.2 CAREER PATHWAYS IN EMERGENCY MANAGEMENT

Current Position

Lead Planning and Exercise Coordinator, Department of Emergency Management, large city

Education

B.A., English Literature
M.P.A., Emphasis in Nonprofit Management

Other Training

Harvard University, National Preparedness Leadership Institute (NPLI) Executive

Education Program 2015–2016, Big City Emergency Managers (BCEM)—Target Emerging Leaders Program 2014

Earlier Jobs in Her Career

Jane has served as Exercise Coordinator and other roles in the city's Emergency Operations Center (EOC), deployed to Hurricane Sandy in 2012, and worked in the Westchester County EOC for a week.

She served as Emergency Services Coordinator III for four years and has served as Emergency Services Coordinator IV since 2012.

Learning about the Job

Jane learned from professionals in the field of emergency management (from the Fire Department, Police Department, and Sheriff's Department), took many emergency management courses online and in person, and read emergency plans and studied best practices nationally.

Finding Her Way to Emergency Management

Prior to being in emergency management, she was Executive Assistant to a city department head and, in that role, attended emergency management meetings on behalf of the department. She became interested and moved into the field.

A Typical Day

There is no typical day. She attends and runs multiple meetings during the day. Last week, she evaluated an exercise at a local university, held planning meetings for various exercises for her division, and wrote an After Action Report (AAR) on an exercise during a major community event. As one of the agency directors says, "we are 'responders who plan.'"

Professional Associations and Networking

Jane became a Certified Emergency Manager (CEM) through the International Association of Emergency Managers (IAEM) and networks through going to conferences, meetings, and other events.

Most Helpful to Her Career

What has been most helpful is to simply work hard and lead projects. At times, it is like "herding cats." Often she has zero real authority and needs to get local, state, and federal agencies and nongovernment and private sector entities to work together, which can be the biggest challenge of the job. She needs to lead exercise planning efforts with a planning workgroup who must get through an exercise through consensus building. Each agency has its objective(s), and it is important that they work collaboratively to meet the needs of many departments, agencies, and groups.

Challenges

Not having authority but having to lead is a major challenge. Personalities and egos often get in the way too. Moreover, the field is still predominately white, male, and more than 40 years old. Plus, it is often challenging to "convince" others that she knows what she is doing even though she was never a first responder.

How She Has Dealt with Challenges

Dealing with challenges has been pretty simple—showing others respect, listening, communicating clearly, working to hear all opinions, showing kindness, and supplying meta-leadership. A similar message has been shared in all of the leadership courses she has taken: leaders need to care about people. If you do not, people will not work hard for you. "I care about the work I do, and I work to care about the folks I work with."

Most Rewarding Part of the Job

"If one does this work at the local level you can directly see the fruits of your labor. My team works to exercise disaster and emergency plans. We find gaps and then work with others to make improvements. At the state and federal level you're a bit more removed—all disasters are local, and the planning efforts need to be collaborative and detailed."

Recommendations for Students

- Interning with a government or a nonprofit entity is helpful. It is hard work, and, in many jobs, there is an "on-call" time—she is on call every other month and must do her best to get to the Emergency Operations Center within three hours of getting a call.
- Deploying to a real disaster is helpful too. Plans and exercises only go so far—once you sit and talk to someone who has lost everything, the importance of the work resonates.

During the Cold War years, civil defense laws and measures were developed to prepare and protect the population in case of war with the Soviet Bloc, but after the Soviet Union had fallen apart, much of the civil defense infrastructure moved into emergency preparedness. Emergency management shifted more and more to the federal government, and legislation began to broaden out, rather than be passed just for one specific disaster. The field also focused more on preparedness and mitigation, particularly in the case of floods.

Many reforms have been put into place as a result of disasters, as seen in Table 9.5. Among these reforms are levees and other mitigation efforts against floods, National Flood Insurance, numerous changes to building and zoning codes (including measures to

TABLE 9.5

Major Disasters in American Cities, and Resulting Changes

Year	Disaster	Deaths and Damages	Resulting Changes
1871	Chicago Fire		Modern fire suppression systems
1884	Mississippi and Ohio River Floods		
1888	Great Blizzard, East Coast	400 deaths	
1889	Johnstown, PA Flood	More than 2,000 deaths	Dam safety laws
1900	Hurricane (Galveston, TX)	6,000–12,000 deaths, 3,600 homes destroyed	Local mitigation and awareness of weather forecasting
1906	San Francisco Earthquake and Fire	At least 3,000 deaths, 28,000 buildings destroyed, and 225,000 people homeless. Chinese community and poor particularly hard hit	Some improved construction materials built, improved water supply system. Mostly, denial continued. Study of earthquakes credible
1918–19	Flu Pandemic	500,000–675,000 deaths in the U.S.	
1933	Long Beach, CA Earthquake	120 deaths	First seismic elements to Uniform Building Code, other legislation and policy changes, California passed 1933 Safety of Design and Construction of School Buildings Act (Field Act), California also passed Riley Act requiring all California cities to have building department and inspect new construction

(Continued)

1947	Texas City Explosions	581 deaths (including all of the volunteer fire department) and 3,500 injuries when 2,000 tons of ammonium nitrate exploded	First ever class action lawsuit filed against federal government on behalf of victims, for not having better controlled and managed transit of hazardous materials
1964	Alaska Earthquake (8.4 on the Richter Scale)	130 deaths, thousands of homes lost from tsunami	
1974	Tornadoes in Xenia, OH and Other Tornadoes	300 deaths across 13 states	
Up to 1974	Love Canal	Birth defects and illness due to toxic waste	For the first time, President Carter used authority to move affected families from area
1979	Nuclear Accident at Three Mile Island Plant, Harrisburg, PA		
1980	Mt. St. Helens Eruption		
1989	Loma Prieta Earthquake (San Francisco)		First earthquake to end up with more than $1 billion FEMA funds
1992	Hurricane Andrew, Florida	23 deaths, $26.5 billion in damages in the U.S.	Highlighted poor building practices in South Florida, resulting in best building codes in country for the wind, changes in insurance industry
1993	Great Midwest Flood	48 deaths, $15 billion damages, most damaging flood recorded in the U.S.	For the first time, 14,000–20,000 residents and businesses moved away from flood plains
1993	World Trade Center Truck Bombing	Six deaths, more than 1,000 injuries	
1994	Northridge, CA Earthquake		FEMA spending = $6.97 billion, first earthquake directly under major American city, new changes in building codes
1995	Bombing of Murrah Federal Building, Oklahoma City	168 deaths, more than 800 injuries	

(Continued)

2001	World Trade Center Terrorist Attacks	Deaths of 2,743 at World Trade Center, including 343 New York City firefighters, 37 Port Authority police, 23 New York City police (another 184 killed when plane flew into Pentagon in Washington, D.C.)	The Homeland Security Act of 2002 reorganized the federal government, placing 22 agencies like the U.S. Coast Guard and FEMA under a new agency, the U.S. Department of Homeland Security
2005	Hurricane Katrina	1,856 deaths are attributed to the storm, but there is a great deal of uncertainty about this number	Post-Katrina Emergency Management Reform Act of 2006, Pets Evacuation and Transportation Standards Act of 2006, SAFE Ports Act of 2005
2010	BP Oil Spill, Gulf Coast	11 killed by initial explosion and fire; massive environmental damage ensued	
2011	Joplin, MO Tornadoes	161 deaths from this F-5 tornado; estimated $2.8 billion in damage	
2012	Hurricane Sandy	233 killed across eight countries; none in U.S.; $71.4 billion in damage in U.S.	
2013	Boston Marathon Bombing	Terrorist bombing at finish line of annual marathon; three died	

Sources: Developed from Rubin, Claire, Editor. 2012. *Emergency Management: The American Experience 1900–2010 (2nd Edition)*. Boca Raton: Taylor and Francis Group.

make buildings more capable of surviving hurricanes and earthquakes), and the development of the modern profession of an emergency manager. The Disaster Relief Act of 1966 and the National Flood Insurance Act of 1968 both moved the country forward in recognizing the importance of preparing for disasters, as it became apparent flood plains were increasingly vulnerable, a growing population was moving toward the coast, and the level and kinds of assistance provided post-disaster were increasing. The Disaster Relief Act of 1970 followed, incorporating the first national teams going out to disaster sites to provide first-hand assistance, explicitly adding mitigation and preparedness efforts, providing temporary housing, and assisting local governments with revenues lost from the disaster.

By 1974, after dealing with numerous problems across many disasters, the states took the initiative to develop their policy framework and asked then President Jimmy Carter to create a centralized federal agency to manage federal efforts. By the end of 1978, the level of federal appropriations for disaster relief had grown 70 times (from $16 million in 1953 to $1.1 billion in 1978) (Rubin 2012, location 2432), so it was clear a more coordinated federal effort was needed.

Until this time, federal efforts came from a broad range of federal agencies, but after these requests and study, in 1979 the President created the Federal Emergency Management Agency, incorporating agencies from HUD, Defense, and Commerce into one umbrella agency. FEMA went through growing pains as it provided assistance to disaster after disaster, learning hard lessons and reorganizing throughout the Reagan and George H. W. Bush presidencies. In fact, the agency went through a period of listlessness with little leadership until the presidency of Bill Clinton, who appointed the first emergency preparedness professional to lead it in 1992, even elevating the FEMA head to the President's cabinet and having him report directly to the President.

The 1988 Stafford Act established the importance of FEMA's Hazard Mitigation Grant program, as it became clearer that citizens and businesses moved right back to flood-prone areas after floods (until the Great Midwest Floods of 1993, when large numbers of buildings were moved out of flood plains). The Emergency Management Assistant Compacts (EMAC) laid out a structure for shared authority, which provided a framework for states to provide mutual aid in case of emergencies. The Homeland Security Act of 2002 reorganized the federal government, placing 22 agencies like the U.S. Coast Guard and FEMA under a new agency, the U.S. Department of Homeland Security. Post-Katrina, the Emergency Management Reform Act of 2006 further developed the top-down approach of the federal government, but experts in the field believe more needs to be done.

At the city level for smaller and mid-sized cities, the emergency management function is performed by an emergency coordinator, who is responsible for developing contingency plans for when disaster does strike. In the case of an emergency, other departments are given jobs and roles they must follow. Large cities have emergency management directors with staffs to do training with other agencies and outreach to the community. Many large cities have emergency control centers with computer workstations for those representing agencies throughout the city; the mayor or city manager then operates from that center as the emergency manager. One of the many tragedies of the 9/11 attacks was that the City of New York's emergency command center was in the Twin Towers, so the City and its managers had to quickly regroup and rethink how they were to react, in the absence of a central location and the resources contained within.

Technology is now a widely used and important tool in emergency management. Since much of the local technology can be destroyed in a disaster, managers can save important materials on the "cloud," or the network owned by others but available for lease or rental to the city. Managers on the ground can access those materials via laptop computers or interfaces on mobile devices. Satellite imagery can aid to provide an overview of damaged portions of the city, allowing managers to determine where resources should go (Holdeman 2014). Online or mobile mapping tools like Ushahidi allow users on the ground with mobile devices to "crowdsource," or provide information from damaged areas that are then automatically mapped using the Ushahidi tool. Facebook is now using a tool that allows individuals who live in an area with a current emergency to "sign-in" that they are safe so that their family and friends can readily see their status.

The American Red Cross uses a variety of mobile applications (apps) to provide weather alerts and preparedness information for a wide variety of disasters. Its "I'm Safe" feature operates the same as the Facebook feature. It also monitors social media during a disaster to help identify areas in need of assistance. Also, databases are used to communicate with the many Red Cross volunteers who work during emergencies (American Red Cross 2015).

Hurricane Katrina

Hurricane Katrina began as a mid-strength hurricane that swept through New Orleans and the Gulf Coast states in August 2005. The Bush Administration declared a disaster ahead of time and pre-positioned materials and staff to respond in the aftermath of the hurricane. As current (2015) Mayor Mitch Landrieu stated in the ten-year anniversary commemorations of Katrina, however, "This was not a natural disaster—it was an infrastructure failure" (White 2015). The hurricane hit, there was calm after the storm, and then the levees broke. There was massive flooding in many areas throughout the City, with much damage (Box 9.3). The City was unprepared to take care of its most vulnerable population, as it and the State were unprepared to manage massive flooding from levees that were not adequately built by the federal government's U.S. Army Corps of Engineers. Large numbers of poor people without cars were left stranded in the City without assistance during this disaster.

Ten years after Hurricane Katrina, more white residents than black have returned to the City of New Orleans, as the middle class had more funds available to do so. Many homes in the poorer parts of the City are still not livable, and funding is still unavailable (the Mayor cites $150 billion in damages but only $75 billion in federal aid).

▶ BOX 9.3 IMPACT FROM HURRICANE KATRINA

Deaths	1,856
Missing	705
Impacted	More than 1.5 million people
Displaced	More than 800,000
Rescued by the U.S. Coast Guard	24,273
Rescued by FEMA search and rescue	6,600
Federal disaster relief expenditures	More than $100 billion
Insurance losses	More than $35 billion
National Flood Insurance Program paid	More than $16.1 million on more than 205,000 claims
States with emergency declarations because of refugees from the storm	44 states and District of Columbia

Source: Based upon Haddow, George, Bullock, Jane, and Coppola, Damon P. 2013. *Introduction to Emergency Management (5th Edition).* Atlanta, Georgia: Butterworth-Heineman: location 785–799.

Joplin, Missouri Tornadoes

The year 2011 saw a string of destructive tornadoes in the Midwest and Southeast. On May 22, 2011, residents of Joplin, Missouri had 24 minutes of warning before an EF-5 tornado more than one mile wide came through Joplin with winds of more than 200 mph, for an eventual trail of more than 22 miles. The Joplin tornado became the deadliest tornado in the United States since 1947, with 161 deaths and 1,371 injured. More than 4,300 homes were destroyed, another 3,880 were damaged, and the commercial part of the city was destroyed. Power immediately went out to 18,000 customers due to the large loss of utility poles (Haddow et al. 2013).

BOX 9.4 PUBLIC SAFETY STRATEGIES FROM CITY SUSTAINABILITY PLANS

- "Maintain the lowest crime rate in the nation for a city of this population and market this achievement." Virginia Beach, Virginia, p. 39.
- "Plan, deploy, and maintain physical and social infrastructures such that vulnerability to natural and human hazards and disasters is reduced for all members of community and ensure that communities are adequately prepared to respond to crises, response is effective and

coordinated, and recovery is accelerated." Dover, New Hampshire, p. 4.

Sources: City of Dover, New Hampshire. Not Dated. City of Dover Sustainability Goals with Purpose Statements. Accessed on February 22, 2017 from www.dover.nh.gov/Assets/government/city-operations/2document/planning/outreach/sustainabilitygoals.pdf.
City of Virginia Beach, Virginia. 2013. A Community Plan for a Sustainable Future. City of VA Beach Environment and Sustainability Office. March 12, 2013. Accessed on February 22, 2017 from www.vbgov.com/government/offices/eso/sustainability-plan/Documents/vb-sustainability-plan-web.pdf.

BOX 9.5 SELECTED PERFORMANCE MEASURES FOR POLICE, FIRE, AND EMERGENCY MANAGEMENT

Fire Departments

Some performance measures are provided by the ISO, which evaluates the firefighting readiness of communities as a service for insurance companies.

- The Fire Insurance Ratings from the ISO (Insurance Services Office);
- Number of engine companies;
- Fire incidence rate per 1,000 structures;
- Response time (comprised of dispatch time, turnout time, travel time, access time and set-up time);
- Loss of life and property.

Police Department

- Crime rates for various types of crime;
- Response rate;

- Percent of citizens who feel safe in community;
- Clearance rates (various types of crimes solved);
- Number of complaints about police officers;
- Traffic arrests; and
- DUI (Driving Under the Influence) Arrests.

Emergency Management

- Number of community education events held;
- Number of joint training exercises held with other communities; and
- Number of deaths and loss of property during emergency.

Source: (*Ammons* 2015)

CONCLUSIONS

This chapter has covered the basic concepts in police and fire protection in cities as well as emergency management today. As we learned, most of the cities' budgets are used to cover these areas, and they are also the areas about which most citizens care the most. Careful screening of new personnel and training are critical to developing strong police and fire departments. Like many other services today, emergency management relies upon training and joint, collaborative exercises and work with other jurisdictions. Public safety and emergency management are part of the core areas of urban service delivery emphasized in the NASPAA Urban Administration standards.

SELECTED WEB RESOURCES

- International Association of Emergency Managers www.iaem.com/
- International Association of Police Chiefs www.iacp.org/
- National Emergency Management Association www.nemaweb.org/
- National Fire Protection Association www.nfpa.org/
- U.S. Federal Emergency Management Association www.fema.gov/

EXERCISES AND DISCUSSION QUESTIONS

1. **Know Your City:** Public Safety and Emergency Management
   - Who is the police chief of your city?
   - How many police officers are there for your city? How many are there as a ratio of population to officers?
   - Who is the fire department chief?
   - How many fire engine companies are there in your city?
   - Can you find out the response time for fire emergencies? What is it?
   - How is emergency management organized in your city—is there a coordinator or a full department?
   - Does your city have an Office of Emergency Services control center?
   - Are there neighborhood emergency services trainings available in your city?

2. There have been a large number of unarmed residents killed by police across the country over the past several years, particularly African-American males. How can citizens help increase police departments' accountability in their own community?

3. How can residents work with the police department to develop better relationships in their communities?

4. Does the police department in your community have outreach programs? Does it practice "community policing"? Does it move through the community on bicycles, on horses, by walking, or by just driving through? What difference do you think it could make to have officers use a variety of ways to patrol the city?

5. How can your city make sure that no one is left behind or not provided assistance in case of a crisis, disaster, or emergency?

REFERENCES

American Red Cross. 2015. "Technology Enhances Red Cross Disaster Preparedness and Response." *American Red Cross*, August 12, 2015.

Ammons, David N. 2015. *Municipal Benchmarks: Assessing Local Performance and Establishing Community Standards*, 3rd ed. London: Routledge.

Bureau of Justice Statistics, U.S. Department of Justice. September 2014. *Criminal Victimization, 2013 (NCJ 247648)*. Accessed June 30, 2015 from www.bjs.gov/content/pub/pdf/cv13.pdf

Bureau of Justice Statistics, U.S. Department of Justice. 2015. *Local Police Statistics*, April 8, 2015. Accessed from www.bjs.gov/index.cfm?ty=tp&tid=71

DeLorenzi, Daniel, Shane, Jon M., and Amendola, Karen L. 2006. "The CompStat Process: Managing Performance on the Pathway to Leadership." *The Police Chief: The Professional Voice of Law Enforcement*. Accessed on July 1, 2015 from www.policechiefmagazine.org/magazine/index.cfm?fuseaction=display_arch&article_id=998&issue_id=92006

Gabrielson, Ryan, Grochowski Jones, Ryann, and Sagara, Eric. 2014. "Deadly Force, in Black and White." *ProPublica*, October 24, 2014. Accessed on July 1, 2015 from www.propublica.org/article/deadly-force-in-black-and-white

Gaines, Larry K. 2015. *Policing in America*, 8th ed. New York: Routledge.

Gainesville, Florida Police Department. 2015. *Organizational Chart*. Accessed on June 15, 2015 from www.gainesvillepd.org/Portals/2/Organization%20Chart/GPDOrgChart10.pdf

Haddow, George, Bullock, Jane, and Coppola, Damon P. 2013. *Introduction to Emergency Management (5th Edition)*. Waltham, MA: Butterworth-Heinemann.

Hensler, Bruce. 2011. *Crucible of Fire: Nineteenth-Century Urban Fires and the Making of the Modern Fire Service*. Washington, DC: Potomac Books.

Holdeman, Eric. 2014. "Technology Plays An Increasing Role in Emergency Management." *Emergency Management*, June 26, 2014.

International Association of Chiefs of Police. 2001. *Police Use of Force in America 2001*. International Association of Chiefs of Police.

Lipsky, Michael. 1983. *Street Level Bureaucracy: Dilemmas of the Individual in Public Services*. New York: Russell Sage Foundation.

Maynard-Moody, Steven, and Musheno, Michael. 2000. "State Agent or Citizen Agent: Two Narratives of Discretion." *Journal of Public Administration Research and Theory* 10 (2): pp. 329–358.

National Fire Protection Association. 2013. *ISO Revises Fire Suppression Rating Schedule*. Accessed August 26, 2015 from http://sprinkler.blog.nfpa.org/2013/03/iso-revises-fire-protection-rating-schedule.html

National Fire Protection Association. 2015. *Fires in the U.S.* Accessed on July 8, 2015 from www.nfpa.org/research/reports-and-statistics/fires-in-the-us

National Institute of Justice. 2015. *The Use-of-Force Continuum*. Accessed on June 24, 2015 from www.nij.gov/topics/law-enforcement/officer-safety/use-of-force/pages/continuum.aspx

O'Neil, Daniel X. 2013. "Building a Smarter Chicago." In *Beyond Transparency: Open Data and the Future of Civic Innovation*. Edited by Brett Goldstein and Lauren Dyson. San Francisco, CA: Code for America Press.

Reaves, Brian A. 2011. *Local Police Departments, 2007*. Washington, D.C.: Bureau of Justice Statistics, U.S. Department of Justice.

Reaves, Brian A. 2015. *Local Police Departments, 2013: Personnel, Policies, and Practices* Washington, D.C.: Bureau of Justice Statistics, U.S. Department of Justice.

Rubin, Claire (Ed.). 2012. *Emergency Management: The American Experience 1900–2010*, 2nd ed. Boca Raton: Taylor and Francis Group.

Smeby, L. Charles, Jr. 2014. *Fire and Emergency Services Administration*, 2nd ed. Burlington, MA: Jones and Bartlett Learning.

Terrill, William, Paoline III, Eugene, and Ingram, Jason. 2011. "Final Technical Report Draft: Assessing Police Use of Force Police and Outcomes." *National Institute of Justice*. Accessed on June 24, 2015 from www.ncjrs.gov/pdffiles1/nij/grants/237794.pdf

Truman, Jennifer L., and Langton, Lynn. 2014. *Criminal Victimization, 2013 (Revised)*. Washington, D.C.: Bureau of Justice Statistics, U.S. Department of Justice.

White, Gillian B. 2015. "10 Years After Katrina, New Orleans is Far From Healed." *The Atlantic*. Accessed on September 9, 2015 from www.theatlantic.com/business/archive/2015/08/10-years-after-katrina-new-orleans-is-far-from-healed/402169/

Urban Planning

U rban or city planning is the process of looking ahead to the future of the city and trying to create ways to coordinate all its different components. These different parts include a city's land and its various uses, transportation, housing, economy and jobs, natural resources and parks, community resources and facilities, and cultural components. A comprehensive plan brings together these pieces and a city's people, places, and plans. This chapter will provide an overview of major concepts in the field of planning, beginning with the history and where the planning function is located within city government. The chapter will also include a discussion of zoning, subdivision planning, and current issues in planning, like growth management and transit-oriented developments. Urban planning is yet another topic covered under NASPAA's Urban Administration guidance to students on what they should learn about urban service delivery.

Most urban historians credit the City Beautiful movement of the late 1800s with the initial development of the urban planning profession, along with the Progressive Reform movement of that time, which also led to the creation of the public administration profession. Before then, there was not much going on in the way of organizing American cities. The City Beautiful movement, incorporating urban reforms and landscape designs, was highlighted in the Chicago World's Fair in 1893 when Daniel Burnham and Frederick Law Olmsted (an architect and park designer, respectively) designed the fairgrounds. Many innovations came out of this Fair, which was visited by millions of people. Another important early thinker about cities was Ebenezer Howard, the British creator of the garden city concept. Set out in concentric circles, Howard's cities had gardens and public buildings in the middle, which were then surrounded by homes with other circles of businesses and industrial areas.

From these visionaries came Daniel Burnham's Plan of Chicago, a relatively sophisticated physical plan that laid out streets, highways, and other means of transportation. As part of the planning process, Chicago also created a Planning Commission to implement its plan. Howard also implemented his vision of a garden city in the City of Letchworth, and, later, cities like Radburn in the United States were also influenced by his vision.

ORGANIZATION AND AUTHORITY

Planning departments are usually autonomous but in smaller cities might be combined with the community development, the building, or even the engineering or public works departments. States see the planning function in a variety of different ways and, so, pass enabling legislation (laws that spell out what authority cities have in planning and zoning) that varies from state to state.

Depending on the state and its enabling legislation, each city council has several planning powers: to adopt and amend comprehensive plans, zoning regulations, and subdivision ordinances, to tax and spend, to appoint citizens to commissions, and to delegate some of its authority to these commissions (Duerksen, Dale and Elliott 2009, location 374–378).

PLANNING TOOLS AND STRATEGIES

In the urban planning area, the policy process involves staff developing proposed land use plans, zoning maps, and plans like the comprehensive plan and then presenting the materials to the city council for approval, typically working through the mayor when one is present. In a council-manager form of government, the staff members work with the city manager as their supervisor. Once approved by the council, the ordinances, maps, and plans become legal documents of the city and are implemented.

There are many implementation tools available in the area of urban planning and land use. Duerksen et al. (2009) suggest four categories of implementation tools—those related to the location of development, the scale, quality, and character of development, the impacts of development, and those affecting the equity of development.

One of the most important tasks of any planning department is the development of the comprehensive plan of its city. The comprehensive (or master) plan is the general plan for a city, incorporating not just land use but also housing, transportation, economy, public facilities, environment, parks and recreation, the arts, and the environment. These elements are all coordinated with the centerpiece being the land use plan so that the city has a practical but forward-thinking blueprint for the future. A comprehensive plan includes demographic projections, information on where the building should take place, data about city infrastructure, plans for recreation and parks, and plans for developing the economy.

Zoning

The two most important tools affecting location are zoning and subdivision regulations, which can be either map- or text-based and legally determine where development is going to occur—and whose use has been tested and supported by the courts. Of these, zoning is the most important, and sometimes the only tool used, although planners would say to use zoning alone would be a mistake. Subdivision regulations require that developers get approval before going forward with building and in some sense are an extension of zoning regulations, in that they lay out government requirements in more depth, thereby furthering the implementation of the city's policies.

Zoning is the process through which cities divide the city into geographic areas where different types of functions are allowed to exist, according to the best possible use of the land. Cities are divided by zoning schemes into residential, commercial and industrial, and other areas; these are seen on maps that become the approved zoning ordinance and then guide building and development within the city after that. Residential zones are divided

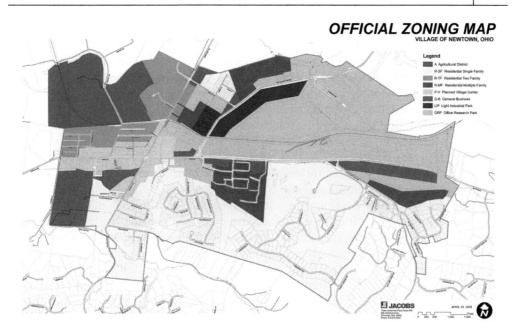

OFFICIAL ZONING MAP
VILLAGE OF NEWTOWN, OHIO

Legend
A   Agricultural District
R-SF Residential Single Family
R-TF Residential Two Family
R-MF Residential Multiple Family
P-V   Planned Village Center
G-B   General Business
LIP   Light Industrial Park
ORP   Office Research Park

FIGURE 10.1
Zoning Map of Newtown, Ohio

Source: Village of Newtown Ohio. 2017. Accessed on August 14 2017 from http://www.newtownohio.gov/webdocs/zoning_map.jpg.

into single family and different densities of multiple family housing (apartments). Different colors displayed on the map indicate different land uses that are approved for development. Figure 10.1 illustrates the zoning scheme for a particular city. The traditional zoning map divides up the space in a city and assigns a particular type of land use to each area. As seen in the Figure, one area might be designated for residential, another for multifamily residential, and another for industrial uses. A city's zoning board and city council approves the map and then only the designated type of usage is allowed in each area.

The approval of this map by the Planning Commission and City Council then formally designates each use for the land, as seen on the map. The ability of cities to designate and enforce such specific uses for specific parts of the city was first upheld by the U.S. Supreme Court in *Village of Euclid v. Ambler Realty Co.* (272 U.S. 365 [1926]), which used a city's police power as the basis for declaring zoning power constitutional.

The patterns in segregated land use seen on this map—homes in one area, retail and offices in another—were heavily influenced by the advent of the automobile in American society. Particularly after World War II, construction and design in the United States followed the development of suburbs away from cities, whose development was itself influenced by better transportation, available land, and easy home loans available from the Department of Veteran Affairs (VA) and Federal Housing Administration (FHA). This use-segregated land use, also termed conventional/high carbon (CHC) because of its sprawled nature and subsequent impact upon resources, has serious consequences (Coyle 2011). These types of communities use up a great deal of land, including agricultural land, and require enormous amounts of gas and energy to maintain as consumers have to get into their cars and drive from their homes to go to work, to shop, and to go to schools. These patterns are automobile-oriented with dispersed growth. Extreme examples of this type of development are strip malls with long lines of stores and their accompanying parking lots and big box stores all accumulated together (often the same set in every city) with enormous parking lots spotted with the same set of chain restaurants. One could easily forget what city they were in, as the effect has also been to homogenize the American landscape.

The alternative to these types of patterns is the resilient/low-carbon (RLC) built environment, which would integrate housing, retail, and work spaces together. Communities and cities built before World War II can be good examples of RLC communities. Housing, shops, restaurants, and schools were all located close to one another in condensed neighborhoods, which encouraged walking, biking, and mass transit rather than transportation only by car. This mixed use development pattern is more compact and bounded, built on a more pedestrian scale, and has transportation patterns that are connected and used by multiple types of transit.

These two models of development are not mutually exclusive, as many cities have mixed use zoning designations in their land use plans. To provide further illustration, Albany, New York's Development Code Article 5 contains definitions for a variety of mixed use zoning districts, indicating different uses allowed depending on the district. For instance, the standard Mixed Use Commercial District is "intended primarily to provide a mix of convenience commercial, personal services, offices and medium density residential uses. The district would typically be anchored by a grocery store and may include a mix of smaller retailers, offices, live-work units, and residences. The MUC district is easily accessible to nearby residences, and commercial uses are compatible in scale and design with adjacent neighborhoods. Uses in the MUC zone will serve area residents and should not draw from the region" (City of Albany 2014, p. 5–1). The Schedule of Permitted Uses table further indicates that Adult Entertainment, Self-Serve Storage, Vehicle Repair, Hospitals, Jails and Detention Facilities, Agriculture, and Kennels are not allowed. Parking requires site plan review, and Religious Institutions require a Conditional Use Permit.

The Village of Ossining, New York has mixed use districts throughout, as illustrated in Figure 10.2, where people are walking among an area of stores and restaurants with residences above.

Subdivision Ordinances

Subdivision ordinances are city ordinances that, working within comprehensive plans, zoning ordinances, and other types of land use and laws, lay out in detail the requirements for development of land into neighborhoods. Starting with the zoning map, subdivision ordinances divide the land into smaller parcels, even individual parcels, and then set out requirements and standards for that development.

The City of Charlotte, North Carolina's subdivision ordinance includes general requirements such as "Residential street design should ensure the creation of a network of low-volume, low-speed roadways. All new development should provide for more than one access for ingress and egress, where feasible. The proposed street system should extend existing streets on their proper projections. Cul-de-sacs and other permanently dead-end streets should be avoided" (City of Charlotte 2010, p. 9). This structure means that new development should have more than one entrance and exit and that developers should work toward low-speed streets. To ensure continuous walkability, no dead-end streets should be allowed.

Other general requirements in the Charlotte ordinance include half streets, mature trees and natural vegetation, and access to parks, schools, and greenways. It is also important to have parallel streets along thoroughfares, public schools, and public park sites, public facilities, street names, proposed water and sewer systems, and easements and restrictions

FIGURE 10.2
Village of Ossining, New York Mixed Use District

Source: Village of Ossining, New York. http://www.villageofossining.org/Cit-e-Access/webpage.cfm?TID=24&TPID=12627.

on land subject to flooding. The goals of all these requirements are to encourage walkable, pleasant streets with all needed resources available to fulfill community needs.

Design standards, stormwater drainage systems, landscaping requirements, and descriptions of the review and approval processes are also typically included in subdivision ordinances. Finally, the ordinance might include the fee schedule for the review of plans and how developers must plan to dedicate land for schools, parks, and roads. Other types of development, like shopping malls, public facilities, and multifamily housing complexes, must also be regulated with their requirements laid out in city ordinances.

Tax, Spend, and Eminent Domain

Cities also have authority to tax and spend and to purchase property. Related to the power to purchase property is the power of eminent domain. The power of eminent domain refers to the power of governments to take property, as long as there is just compensation, for public purposes. While it sounds controversial, this power has been consistently upheld by the U.S. Supreme Court, with cases hinging upon the definition of public purposes and whether or not a transaction is a "taking" (when a property owner does not receive adequate or just compensation for their property). This power has been used by cities to require set-asides for open space, for requiring landowners to give up land to create a right of way (margins of land next to land with other uses), and to redevelop land completely.

Land Acquisition

Land acquisition is another tool that affects how a city will be developed since whether a city can purchase a particular plot of land to serve as a park or conservation area is a function of whether or not the city can purchase or be given the plot in question. Typically, a city will attempt to buy the plot, although sometimes jurisdictions trade one plot of city-owned land for another since they cannot often require a developer to incorporate significant land preservation or parks into their development. Another option, however, is the transfer of development rights (TDR). The TDR tool allows the city to purchase just the development rights of a parcel of land rather than the entire site and, thus, achieve the public purpose.

Citizen Commissions

Cities also have the power to appoint citizen commissions. In the area of planning, these commissions are critical—and powerful. Typically, cities have planning commissions, which approve land use plans and development applications and interpret whether or not a proposed development fits within currently approved land use policies. These are typically appointed by the mayor, city council, or a combination of both, depending on the individual city.

Another type of commission is the zoning board of adjustment, which hear petitions from individuals who apply for waivers from existing land use and other policies. For instance, the Zoning Board of Adjustment in Birmingham, Alabama heard petitions for exceptions to the sign ordinance (businesses wanting signs that were taller than the ordinance stated) or from developers who wanted more density (i.e., more homes) than were laid out in the subdivision ordinance.

Petitioners who want to appeal decisions of these boards would typically have to go to the city council, in some cities, or, in others, directly to local courts. These boards are a crucial way in which citizens participate in their local governments. Often, the ordinances setting up the commissions dictate that certain types of individuals, representing specific groups or stakeholders in the city, are members. For instance, in some cities, individuals representing realtors, builders, local businesses, neighborhood organizations, labor, and ordinary citizens are required to be represented on the boards. Cities also have the power to delegate their authority to commissions like those discussed previously.

Other Tools

Adequate public facilities (APF) regulations in a city also offer the option of being able to focus the location of development, by requiring that development occur where existing public facilities already exist. Not only does this strategy reduce sprawl by focusing development, but it also saves resources by ensuring that development uses up existing public facility capacity before moving on to other areas without facilities. Concurrency regulations are simpler versions of the same idea, keeping developers from getting approvals unless the required public facilities are present.

Many other tools can be used to influence the size, quality, and character of urban developments. These include standards on the size of developments, the size of lots and buildings, how far buildings have to be set back from lot lines or the street, the amount of parking required, how parking is implemented, the size and location of signs, and the architectural style (as in historical areas).

Dimensional standards, or regulations that dictate the size of the development, can be particularly important. These can include the height of buildings, which can be quite controversial since building height is a factor in neighbors' views, and floor to area ratios (FAR), which determine how much of a lot a building can cover. The sheer size of homes can be potentially controversial given recent trends toward "McMansions," large houses taking up much of the space on a lot. These quite large houses frequently negatively impact the character of a neighborhood or create traffic problems.

Form-based standards are a newer tool to influence the scale and quality of local developments. Unlike the more general development regulations, these go further in stating more details of what buildings should look like—not just general size or mass. Originally used for areas like historic districts, they can dictate the style of different parts of a building like a roof, the sides, and windows. To illustrate the nature of the standards, standards can be presented as images indicating the precise nature of desired structures.

More detailed design standards are an additional tool to influence developments. These can address colors of buildings, types of brick or masonry, types of roofs, and other aspects of developments so that quality and the look and feel of particular areas can be influenced.

Finally, additional environmental protection or scenic view protection requirements can be added into regulations as overlays to address how natural areas should be maintained, conserved, or preserved.

Inclusionary and Exclusionary Zoning

One of the big challenges in cities today is to provide adequate housing for all citizens, particularly affordable housing for middle- and working-class citizens. Inclusionary zoning is one way to accomplish this goal, and exclusionary zoning is an effort, intentional or not, that challenges affordable housing and other efforts to integrate housing and other land uses throughout a community.

In a series of cases in the 1970s and 1980s called the Mt. Laurel cases, the U.S. Supreme Court laid out cities' obligations to provide affordable housing and to eliminate existing ordinances that might keep affordable housing from being built (for instance, requirements that all housing be large and on large lots, with no sidewalks). Those restrictive efforts were termed exclusionary zoning.

The kinds of zoning efforts that would provide positive incentives and strategies for affordable housing were termed inclusionary zoning. An inclusionary zoning strategy can include one or more of four basic types of policy features:

1. Either mandated or voluntary programs to include affordable housing in proposed new developments;
2. Programs requiring from 5 percent to as high as 30 percent of a project's total number of new units be affordable units;
3. Various levels of housing cost discounts for the affordable housing; and
4. Various types of incentives or compensation to the builder.

So, an individual city's policy could be a mandate that a set percent of a new housing development's units be affordable housing (10 percent less than market rate) with a density bonus (permission to add units elsewhere to create more units per acre) going to the developer as a result (Bento, Lowe, Knaap and Chakraborty 2009).

Bento et al.'s 2009 study indicated that, of the 65 California cities that participated in inclusionary zoning between 1988 and 2005, 12 percent of their housing units were set aside for affordable housing. Of these, 41 percent were set aside for very low-income residents, 77 percent were set aside for low-income residents, and 61 percent were set aside for moderate-income residents. Developers had to maintain that affordability for an average of 34 years.

The result of this California effort was that more multifamily units were built; in fact, there was a significant, large increase in the ratio of multifamily to single family housing units, for an increase in multifamily units of about 7 percent. At the same time, housing prices also increased 2–3 percent faster than in cities without inclusionary housing; the price increase effect was even higher in high-priced housing markets.

Growth Management and Smart Growth

As Table 10.1 indicates, there are many cities across the country that experience very high rates of growth at one point or another in their history. Much of that growth has been experienced in the West and South, with Riverside-San Bernardino-Ontario, California,

---

▶ TABLE 10.1

MSAs with Most Growth, 1980–1990, 1990–2000, 2000–2010 (Percentage Increase in Parentheses)

1980–1990	1990–2000	2000–2010
Riverside-San Bernardino-Ontario, CA (66.1%)	Las Vegas, NV (83.5%)	Palm Coast, FL (92.0%)
Cape Coral-Fort Myers, FL (63.3)	Naples, FL (65.3)	St. George, UT (52.9)
Las Vegas-Paradise, NV (60.1)	Yuma, AZ (49.7)	Las Vegas-Paradise, NV (41.8)
Orlando-Kissimmee, FL (52.2)	McAllen-Edinburg-Mission, TX (48.5)	Raleigh-Cary, NC (41.8)
Palm Bay-Melbourne-Titusville, FL (46.2)	Austin-San Marcos, TX (47.7)	Cape Coral-Fort Myers, FL (40.3)
Austin-Round Rock, TX (44.6)	Fayetteville-Springdale-Rogers, AR (47.5)	Provo-Oren, UT (39.8)
Phoenix-Mesa-Scottsdale, AZ (39.9)	Boise City, ID (46.1)	Greeley, CO (39.7)
Bradenton-Sarasota-Venice, FL (39.6)	Phoenix-Mesa, AZ (45.3)	Austin-Round Rock-San Marcos, TX (37.3)
Modesto, CA (39.3)	Laredo, TX (44.9)	Myrtle Beach-North Myrtle Beach-Conway, SC (37.0)
Stockton, CA (38.4)	Provo-Orem, UT (39.8)	Bend, OR (36.7)

Source: U.S. Census Bureau. 2011. Population Distribution and Change: 2000 to 2010. Downloaded on June 30, 2014 from www.census.gov/prod/cen2010/briefs/c2010br-01.pdf; U.S. Census Bureau. 2001. Population Change and Distribution: 1990 to 2000. Downloaded on June 30, 2014 from www.census.gov/prod/2001pubs/c2kbr01-2.pdf; Frey, William H. 2012. Population Growth in Metro America since 1980: Putting the Volatile 2000s in Perspective. Brookings Institute. Downloaded on June 30, 2014 from www.brookings.edu/~/media/research/files/papers/2012/3/20%20population%20frey/0320_population_frey.

Las Vegas, Nevada, and Palm Coast, Florida experiencing 66.1, 83.5, and 92.0 percent increases, respectively.

Cities can have a very difficult time managing and planning for growth rates of these dimensions. Moreover, the growth itself can have serious consequences for those cities, including high levels of expenditures for new capital infrastructure, the decline of available farmland, stresses on water quality and water supplies, traffic increases, and generational inequities as current and past residents pay for the amenities used solely by new residents. Difficult political struggles can emerge within the community over whether growth is good because it means new jobs and builds economic growth, whether all growth is bad because it harms the environment, or whether there are options between those two extremes, like adopting growth management strategies for land use development and environmental planning.

Regular zoning strategies and tools can also be used to manage growth, but other tools have been developed specifically for that purpose. One of the first was the urban growth boundary, borders around a city that showed the outer limits of growth – largely until utilities and other infrastructure can catch up with development. Urban growth boundaries provide a designated limit for approved future growth. By designating this boundary, decision-makers can focus the growth within particular areas, can take advantage of existing urban infrastructure, and are able to time the growth to match the planned growth of infrastructure. They still allow developers to build developments—but by infilling (building in vacant areas of existing development rather than moving into completely open land), not by building further out of the city itself.

Other growth management tools include limiting the number of building permits approved per year and the use of development, or impact, fees. Impact fees are fees that are placed directly upon new housing and subsequently used to pay for the new infrastructure required for new housing. Developers can also be required to provide new infrastructure such as schools and utilities themselves, as they are building their homes.

In the mid-1990s, the term growth management seemed to be supplanted by "smart growth," pushed by citizen concerns about urban sprawl (Levy 2013). As stated by the State of Maryland, smart growth goals include saving natural resources, supporting existing communities, and saving tax dollars through reducing sprawl.

▶ BOX 10.1 COMPONENTS OF SMART GROWTH

- Collaboration: community and stakeholder collaboration;
- Predictability: predictable, fair, and cost-effective development decisions;
- Direct growth: direct development toward existing communities;
- Preservation: preserving open space, farmland, natural beauty, and critical environmental areas;
- Distinctive communities: distinctive, attractive communities with a strong sense of place;

- Compact growth: compact building patterns and efficient infrastructure design;
- Mixed uses: reduction of driving for work and shopping;
- Transportation options: a variety of transportation options;
- Housing options: a range of housing opportunities; and
- Walkability: walkable, close-knit neighborhoods.

Source: Duerksen, Dale and Elliott 2009, location 1253 of 3084.

BOX 10.2   COMPONENTS OF A SUSTAINABILITY PLAN

Environment

- Natural Systems (ecosystems and habitat, water and stormwater, air quality, waste, and resource conservation);
- Planning and Design (land use, transportation and mobility, and parks, open space, and recreation); and
- Energy and Climate (energy, greenhouse gas emissions and other air pollutants, renewable energy, and green building).

Economy

- Economic Development (clean technologies and green jobs, local commerce, tourism, and local food system); and

- Employment and Workforce Training (green job training, employment and workforce wages, and youth skills).

Society

- Affordability and Social Equity (affordable and workforce housing, poverty, human services and race and social equity);
- Children, Health and Safety (community health and wellness, access to health care, and public safety);
- Education, Arts, and Community (education excellence, arts and culture, and civic engagement and vitality).

Source: ICLEI Local Governments for Sustainability. 2014. What Is a Sustainability Plan? Accessed on July 15, 2014 from www.icleiusa.org/action-center/planning/ICLEI_What%20Is%20a%20Sustainability%20Plan.pdf.

Sustainable Development

There is much disagreement over the meaning of sustainability and sustainable development. In 1987, the World Commission on Environment and Development defined sustainable development as, "development that meets the needs of the present without compromising the ability of future generations to meet their needs" (Levy 2013, p. 298). In fact, sustainable cities are those where environmental, economic, and social components (Mori and Christodoulou 2012) and sustainable governance (Shen, Ochoa, Shah and Zhang 2011) must all be balanced with one another, in an equitable fashion across generations and among citizens. The importance of sustainable development has increased with the recent awareness of growing climate change, pushing many cities into developing their sustainability plans.

The ICLEI USA provides resources for cities developing sustainability plans, which it carefully distinguishes from climate action plans. It suggests the components in Box 10.2 be included in those plans.

BUILDING CODES AND CODE ENFORCEMENT

Each state has approved building codes in its state laws that set out standards for building construction, including electrical, plumbing, and building mechanics, as well as standards for pools; today, these codes often include regulations for energy conservation and green building. These codes are implemented at the local level through building departments, then monitored and enforced through code enforcement units. In smaller cities, planning and building and code enforcement functions are sometimes organized together.

For example, the mission of the Department of Code Enforcement for the City of Indianapolis and Marion County is to "improve the quality of life in the City of Indianapolis through strategic application of civil code regulation, effective licensing, permitting, inspection, enforcement, and abatement practices; and local government oversight of property use/safety and maintenance, business, event, professional, and construction industries" (City of Indianapolis 2014).

In the life of a building, builders and contractors must abide by the building code as they build, seeking permits and getting plans approved by city officials at each step. This entails city officials reviewing plans for buildings, then inspecting their progress in the field, ensuring that each portion of the building adheres to city and state standards and codes. If not, contractors must fix the construction until it meets the standards.

If substantial changes are desired after a building is completed, permits must also be granted by city officials after they have reviewed the plans and conducted inspections. In some jurisdictions, even something as relatively simple as installing a new water heater requires a city permit. For example, the City of Aurora, New York (City of Aurora New York 2014) requires citizens to obtain permits from the City for all of the following:

- All new construction;
- Decks/patios;
- Additions;
- Gazebos;
- Gas piping;
- Structural alterations;
- Garages;
- Pools (above- and in-ground);
- Sheds;
- Wood stoves;
- Excavations and fills;
- Ponds;
- Towers;
- Signs (temporary and permanent);
- Demolitions;
- Foundations; and
- Conversions.

(City of Aurora, New York 2014)

In its Quick Facts, Aurora further outlines other requirements:

- "Permits are needed for any structural work;
- "Permits are good for one (1) year;
- "Certificate of Occupancy/Compliance is required upon completion of all building permits;
- "Roof shingles cannot be more than two (2) layers;
- "No permit needed for fencing (call for height regulations); and
- "A fence is required when installing an in-ground pool or a pool less than 48" above grade."

(City of Aurora, New York 2014)

Throughout the life of a building and community, code enforcement is conducted. Code enforcement includes responding to complaints from citizens of violations of codes and zoning regulations as well as inspectors monitoring neighborhoods to check for those violations themselves. Common complaints include graffiti, litter, noise, abandoned vehicles, weeds, rodent infestations, defective fences, roofs, windows, or doors, construction work done without a permit, electrical hazards, or dilapidated buildings. As discussed earlier, in cities with 311 systems, many of these complaints can be made through the 311 phone, web, or mobile systems. Many city code enforcement websites now have online complaint forms for code complaints, enabling citizens to submit these online.

BOX 10.3 PLANNING STRATEGIES FROM CITY SUSTAINABILITY PLANS

Planning

- "Discourage development that reduces transit, bike, and pedestrian activity." St. Louis, Missouri, p. 41.
- "Maintain density requirements set forth in General Plan." Avondale, Arizona, p. 52.
- "Provide development incentives to encourage transit-oriented development." St. Louis, Missouri, p. 38.
- "Design public spaces and neighborhood streets as gathering spaces for people." St. Louis, Missouri, p. 44.
- "Preserve existing neighborhoods and direct and accommodate growth, at a range of neighborhood types, where facilities and infrastructure exists or is planned." Virginia Beach, Virginia, p. 133.
- "Support and promote centers with multiple uses where appropriate." Virginia Beach, Virginia, p. 39.
- "Design for and encourage a sense of place in our centers with unique features that distinguish one place from another." Virginia Beach, Virginia, p. 39.

Sustainability

- "Recognize three examples of exceptional sustainable development by 2017." Avondale, Arizona, p. 52.
- "Remove obstacles and barriers that discourage or prevent sustainable land use practices in Burnsville." Burnsville, Texas, p. 29.

- "Provide incentives to encourage sustainable land use practices." Burnsville, Texas, p. 29.
- "Expand inclusionary policies in order to create economically-integrated communities." St. Louis, Missouri, p. 62.
- "Eliminate food deserts and improve access to fresh produce." St. Louis, Missouri, p. 143.
- "Set lawn design standards to require restoration of soil permeability after construction activity." Burnsville, Texas, p. 100.
- "Amend city standards to allow native vegetation in residential, commercial, and public laws." Burnsville, Texas, p. 100.

Infill

- "5% of available infill sites by 2020." Avondale, Arizona, p. 54.
- "Infill 20% of existing subdivisions by 2018." Avondale, Arizona, p. 54.
- "Encourage infill development, redevelopment of brownfield sites, and combination of underutilized parcels." Burnsville, Texas, p. 34.

Building

- "Increase the number of environmental certified buildings in Longmont to greater than five." Longmont, Colorado, p. 6.
- "Revise City Design Standards and Construction Specifications to incorporate

Green Building Codes

Today's "green" building codes are likely to have requirements built into them that will allow buildings and communities to achieve higher degrees of sustainability. Residential building codes will incorporate features to ensure higher levels of energy conservation, such as requirements for energy efficient appliances, high levels of insulation, as well as water conservation elements, like drip irrigation systems for landscaping and low-flow toilets and faucets. Commercial codes will require exterior light reduction and water reduction with roofing products that meet EPA energy standards.

Also, green building codes are likely to require being eligible for a certain number of LEED points or full LEED certification. The Leadership in Energy and Environmental Design (LEED) program is a green building certification program. To be certified, a project must meet prerequisites and then achieve points in various categories of building and design. These categories are:

- Integrative process, incorporating team members from a variety of disciplines;
- Location and transportation, with projects receiving points for locating in denser areas rather than adding to urban sprawl and with access to a variety of different types of transportation rather than just cars;
- Materials and resources, with more points for reducing waste and using sustainable building materials;
- Water efficiency, emphasizing water conservation throughout the project;
- Energy and atmosphere features that promote energy conservation;
- Sustainable sites, giving more points for ways to reduce impact on the natural environment;
- Indoor environmental quality, rewarding builders for providing indoor air quality and natural daylight; and
- Innovation, promoting expertise in sustainable building methods and items not covered in other categories (U.S. Green Building Council 2014).

Other strategies for which points can be obtained include building projects in walkable neighborhoods with open space, mixed use communities, and areas with transportation options.

The number of points earned by a project determines whether it can be certified at all and, if it can be certified, whether it can earn Silver, Gold, or Platinum certification.

ISSUES AND CHALLENGES IN URBAN PLANNING

Among the many issues and challenges in urban planning, several need to be highlighted. The first of these are the constant struggle for environmental justice, the need to ensure equity in planning, and planning and building outcomes, not only by ensuring adequate housing but also in the location of facilities and equitable access to resources like open spaces, parks, and other public facilities. Often, those in minority and lower income neighborhoods live the closest to undesirable sites like toxic manufacturing plants, oil refineries, and highways and do not have access to desirable schools and other resources. Awareness of these struggles and the uneven consequences of location and allocation decisions is important.

The use of urban legal powers such as the power of eminent domain is another challenge in urban planning today. The U.S. Supreme Court long ago found that governments had the right of eminent domain, or the ability to take private property for public purposes, as long as there was just compensation, although those rights have been limited by more than half of all state legislatures. Government's transfer of property without such just compensation is called a "taking." However, many citizens still believe that government should not use eminent domain even if supported by the Supreme Court, and the practice remains quite controversial, conflicting at a very deep level with many Americans' beliefs about private property and their property rights.

Finally, another continuing issue is that of ensuring adequate citizen participation in urban planning and building decisions. These decisions are critical and long-standing in a community, and citizens should take part in their development. Obtaining that involvement can be a difficult and time-consuming process.

TECHNOLOGY TOOLS

Planning departments typically utilize a wide variety of technology tools, including those related to online mapping and GIS. The online mapping systems allow citizens to see proposed developments in real time as applications are submitted, as well as to see zoning and parcel maps, the location of city facilities, and real-time information about emergencies. Cities also have online maps with overlays of streets, utilities, natural features, and buildings—even trees throughout the city. These are invaluable for allowing citizens to become better informed about planning, zoning, and development issues.

MEASURING PERFORMANCE IN PLANNING AND BUILDING

Planning department performance measures begin with those measuring department standards for timely review of site plans, plan approvals, environmental reviews, and historical significance certificates. They also include zoning-related measures, like average processing time for zoning inquiries and percentage of zoning plans reviewed within

30 days. Building permit issuance is another area for performance standards, particularly given that this is a problem area in many cities; this standard could include percentage of building permits reviewed within five working days and percentage of building inspections completed within 24 hours (Ammons 2015).

CONCLUSIONS

This chapter reviewed basic concepts of planning and zoning. Inclusionary and exclusionary zoning have equity implications, with a great potential for making positive or negative differences in people's lives. Citizen engagement is also an important component of most city planning processes. Planning shapes the contours of the city; those contours impact transit patterns, energy usage, and where people live. Planning is often the place where new issues (like climate change) are discussed, so they may be incorporated into future plans. The planning process often lays out the parameters for other processes within the city, including for urban service delivery areas like transportation and public works (important in the NASPAA Urban Administration student learning goals).

SELECTED WEB RESOURCES

- American Planning Association www. planning.org/
- New Urbanism www.newurbanism.org/
- Walkability www.walkable.org/

EXERCISES AND DISCUSSION QUESTIONS

1. **Know Your City:** Planning
   - Does your city have a comprehensive plan? Does the plan have an economic development element? Does it have a sustainability element?
   - Does your city's planning department utilize a GIS system?
   - Are there maps on the planning department's website to help citizens understand the city's plan? Are the maps interactive?
   - Is the city planning for less growth, more growth, or no growth?
   - What environmental justice issues exist in your city?
   - Are there any Not in My Backyard (NIMBY) issues in your city? Are group homes sited throughout the community?
   - Does your community include buildings with LEED certification?
2. Are there facilities that might be controversial that are located in your city? Where are they located? How can your community ensure environmental justice and work to make sure that controversial facilities are not just located in the poorer parts of the city? What are the equity considerations of this?
3. A city's zoning ordinance has strict standards about placing signs near the freeway that goes through the city. A fast food restaurant chain applies for a variance to this law, stating it needs the sign to be much taller than allowed in the zoning ordinance so that cars will be able to see it in time to stop and visit the restaurant. It says it will have to locate the restaurant elsewhere if the city will not grant it the variance and argues the sign ordinance is costing the city jobs. Should the zoning board of adjustment give in to the restaurant chain because the restaurant will bring jobs, or should it say no and adhere to the city's zoning ordinance?
4. There is controversy in your city over whether or not to grow and approve new housing developments. What would be the sides to that question, and what would you recommend?

REFERENCES

Bento, Antonio, Lowe, Scott, Knaap, Gerrit-Jan, and Chakraborty, Arnab. 2009. "Housing Market Effects of Inclusionary Zoning." In *The Affordable Housing Reader*. Edited by J. Rosie Tighe and Elizabeth Mueller. New York: Routledge Press, 2013.

City of Albany, New York. Article 5. Accessed on June 11, 2014 from www.cityofalbany. net/images/stories/cd/planning/development_code/05-Article%205-Mixed%20Use%20Village%20Center%20Zoning%20Districts.pdf

City of Aurora, New York. 2014. *Building and Code Enforcement*. Accessed on July 8, 2014 from www.townofaurora.com/departments/building-code-enforcement/

City of Charlotte. 2010. *Subdivision Ordinance*. Accessed on June 6, 2014 from http://ww.charmeck.org/Planning/Subdivision/SubdivisionOrdinanceCity.pdf

City of Indianapolis. 2014. *Department of Code Enforcement Mission Statement*. Accessed on July 8, 2014 from www.indy.gov/eGov/city/DCE/Pages/home.aspx

Coyle, Stephen. 2011. *Sustainable and Resilient Communities: A Comprehensive Action Plan for Towns, Cities, and Regions*. Hoboken, NJ: John Wiley and Sons.

Duerksen, Christopher J., Dale, C. Gregory, and Elliott, Donald L. 2009. *Citizen's Guide to Urban Planning*. Washington, DC: American Planning Association.

Frey, William H. 2012. "Population Growth in Metro America since 1980: Putting the Volatile 2000s in Perspective." Brookings Institute. Accessed on June 30, 2014 from https://www.brookings.edu/~/media/research/files/papers/2012/3/20%20population%20frey/0320_population_frey

Levy, John M. 2013. *Contemporary Urban Planning*, 10th ed. Upper Saddle River, NJ: Pearson Education.

Mori, Koichiro, and Christodoulou, Aris. January 2012. "Review of Sustainability Indices and Indicators: Towards a New City Sustainability Index (CSI)." *Environmental Impact Assessment Review* 32 (1): pp. 94–106.

Shen, Li-Yin, Ochoa, J. Jorge, Shah, Mona N., and Zhang, Ziaoling. 2011. "The Application of Urban Sustainability Indicators—A Comparison between Various Practices." *Habitat International* 31 (2011): pp. 17–29.

U.S. Census Bureau. 2001. "Population Change and Distribution: 1990 to 2000." Accessed on June 30, 2014 from www.census.gov/prod/2001pubs/c2kbr01-2.pdf

U.S. Green Building Council. 2014. *LEED Overview*. Accessed on July 8, 2014 from www.usgbc.org/LEED/#overview

City Infrastructure and Transportation

This chapter covers public works (streets, stormwater, sewage treatment) and transportation in today's cities. To complete NASPAA's Urban Administration student learning goals concerning urban service functions, students should learn about these areas; they literally comprise the backbone of our cities.

PUBLIC WORKS

The infrastructure of a city—its streets, water lines, electrical lines, sewer and storm drainage, and transportation hubs and lanes—is its backbone. In this nation, our infrastructure is failing with a grade of D+ from the American Society of Civil Engineers (ASCE; 2013), a slight improvement from the last report in 2009.

This grade is made up of parts of the nation's infrastructure that are under stress. For instance, drinking water gets a grade of D (Box 11.1) due to the aging water mains (pipes) across the country, many of them more than 100 years old. ASCE estimates there are 240,000 breaks in water mains every year; it would require more than $1 trillion to fix all of them. The country's efforts at recycling have improved its grade for solid waste to B–; 34 percent of its trash is now being recycled, up from 14.5 percent in 1980. There are still 250 million tons of trash created every year. However, the amount of waste generated per person has been steady for a while and is now even slightly declining. Wastewater and stormwater systems garner a D and need a great deal of investment, also mostly due to the need for new pipes. The federal government, through the U.S. Environmental Protection Agency, has been requiring cities to build more than $15 billion of new pipes and other infrastructure to fix sewer overflows (ASCE 2013, p. 6).

Many remember the collapse of the I-35 West Mississippi bridge to Minneapolis in 2007, causing 13 deaths and $400,000 in damages per day to road users. Also, the loss of the bridge cost another $17 million in 2007 and $43 million in 2008 in damage to the local economy (State of Minnesota Department of Employment and Economic Development 2010). There were at least two other bridges that collapsed that same year without the same attention—the Harp Road Bridge in Greys Harbor County, Washington, which collapsed due to the weight of a truck carrying equipment, and

BOX 11.1   ASCE GRADES FOR NATION'S INFRASTRUCTURE

Type of Infrastructure	Grade from ASCE
Transit	D
Roads	D
Rail	C+
Ports	C
Inland Waterways	D–
Bridges	C+
Aviation	D
Wastewater and Stormwater	D
Solid Waste	B–
Levees	D–
Drinking Water	D
Dams	D

Source: American Society of Civil Engineers. 2013. *2013 Report Card for America's Infrastructure.*
Accessed on November 1, 2016 from www.infrastructurereportcard.org/grades/.

the MacArthur Maze in Oakland, California, which collapsed from a fire caused by a tanker truck crash (ThinkReliability n.d.). Estimates are that one in nine of the 607,380 bridges in the United States is deficient; their average age is 42 years. The necessary investment in bridges would require spending $20.5 billion annually until 2028 to catch up with overdue maintenance and repairs, a total cost of $76 billion. So, due to the number of structurally deficient bridges across the nation, bridges get a C+ (ASCE 2013, p. 7).

Roads are another area of infrastructure to receive a D from the civil engineers. They say 42 percent of urban highways are congested and that, while funds to repair and update have increased, there is still not enough. According to them, $170 billion is needed each year, while only $91 billion is available. Transit also received a D. Transit agency funding is going down as the number of riders is increasing and systems are getting older. Not everyone has access to transit systems; 45 percent still have no ability to connect to transit systems today (ASCE 2013, p. 8).

Organization of Public Works in City Government

There are many different ways in which city infrastructure and transportation departments are organized (Figure 11.1). The Public Works Department in Oxford, Mississippi (City of Oxford 2015) provides one common organizational structure for infrastructure. Its department includes:

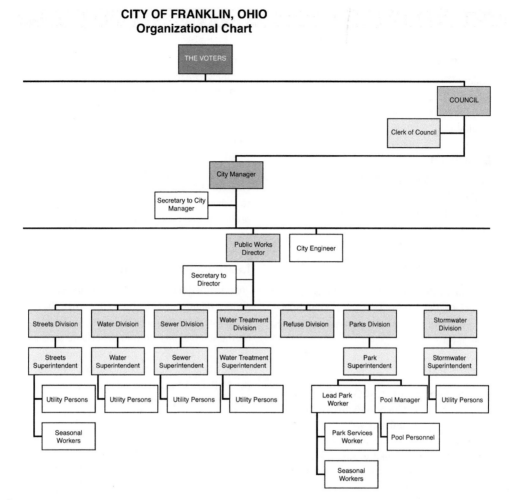

CITY OF FRANKLIN, OHIO
Organizational Chart

FIGURE 11.1
Organizational Chart of Franklin, Ohio Indicating Just the Department of Public Works

Source: Accessed in November 23 2015 from http://www.franklinohio.org/home/showdocument?id=162.

- Engineering. This division reviews development projects and monitors physical improvements within the city. It also conducts traffic counts and mapping projects.
- Streets. The Streets Division maintains City streets and sidewalks plus stormwater drainage and signage.
- Water and Waste Water Treatment Plant. These units provide water service, including 205 miles of water lines. The Waste Water Treatment Plant handles more than 3.5 million gallons of sewerage every day.
- Sewer. The Sewer Department provide sewerage service to residents, including 130 miles of sewer lines.
- Sanitation. The Sanitation Department collects and disposes of trash for the city and its residences.

▶ BOX 11.2   CAREER PATHWAYS IN PUBLIC WORKS

Current Position

County Director of Department of Public Works, a Registered Civil Engineer and Registered Traffic Engineer and "at-will" employee

Education

Bachelor of Science in Civil Engineering
M.P.A.
Harvard Executive Program, Kennedy School of Government—Local and State Senior Executive Seminar
Various training courses in civil engineering over the years
Regularly attendance at County Engineers Association of California (CEAC) conferences and events to stay current on legislation at the state level

Career Pathway

John began his career working for a large private sector engineering/construction firm that had a contract with the federal Nuclear Regulatory Commission remediating abandoned uranium mill tailing sites in the western United States. His primary duties were hydraulic design, roadway design, and grading/site layout design.

From there, he joined the staff of a mid-sized city, where he held positions from Junior Engineer to Senior Civil Engineer. There, he learned traffic engineering, water and sanitary sewer system design, roadway design, and more drainage design, and then began managing major capital projects.

He then moved on to another city, where he held the positions of Assistant Director and then Director of Public Works, where he was responsible for all aspects of public works, including maintenance functions. There, he honed his public speaking and meeting facilitation skills, as well as his general management skills.

He left that city to become the Director of Public Works for a large county, to manage a much larger department in a large organization. During an organizational restructuring and recession, he was also the county Parks Director for two years.

The County position that he currently occupies involves working in a highly political environment, which enhanced his skills related to strategic thinking and successfully delivering programs and projects in an environment of competing interests.

Learning about the Job

John learned the basics of civil engineering in undergraduate school, and then learned the details of public works engineering through on-the-job training, both in the private sector as a design engineer and later working for public agencies. About public administration, the M.P.A. education provided an overview of public management skills that he needed to leverage as he was promoted to Assistant Director and Director positions. In particular, the classes on budgeting as well as the written work necessary to complete the program were beneficial to him, since these skills were not part of civil engineering undergraduate training. All the political training he received came through on-the-job experience.

Finding His Way to Public Works

When John was a design engineer at the private firm, he focused on grading roads and drainage designs but also worked on dam design and construction projects. He left that position to work in municipal public works because of its proximity to home (at the time) and to avoid prolonged construction engineering assignments in the western United States. The projects that he was working on for the private firm were winding down, and the company was sending engineers to construction sites to manage projects he designed. He had a small child at the time and preferred to stay home with his family rather than being out of town on long assignments in other states.

A Typical Day

As a departmental director, John spends most of his time in meetings (his calendar is typically filled three weeks in advance). The meetings involve both internal and external agencies as well as members of the Board of Supervisors, community members, and staff from other cities in his county. Meeting topics range from construction of high-rise buildings to requests for traffic control devices to Sea Level Rise mitigation or County airport operations. When he is not in meetings, he is reviewing Board of Supervisors reports, signing construction contracts and progress payments, and making sure the work that the Department of Public Works is responsible for is completed on schedule and within budget.

One of John's very important duties is to manage information and work requests from elected officials that impact the Department, which operates as a cost-recovery department—it does not receive general funds but has to raise its operating funds through its operations. All of the business units for which he is responsible must be "self-supporting," and staff must remain productive and "billable" to minimize overhead. Board members are somewhat aware of the Department's funding structure, and, as Director, John's job is to tactfully make sure that Board member requests are addressed consistently with County and Department policies, and that a funding source is identified before he spends staff time on requested work.

Professional Associations and Networking

John is a member of quite a few professional associations, matching the spread of responsibilities in public works.

- County Engineer's Association;
- California County Public Works Directors;

- Local Chapter of the American Public Works Association;
- County City/County Engineers Association (CCEA);
- State Association of Counties;
- International City Manager's Association (ICMA);
- Local Stormwater Management Agencies Association;
- Stormwater Quality Association; and
- Moreover, a few other state and national associations for potable water and sanitary sewer professionals.

Of these, John's primary focus is the County Engineers Association involved in developing and advising on State legislation affecting the public works profession, and also ancillary legislation that impacts transportation funding and contracting practices in the State.

John has also become active in addressing local Sea Level Rise (SLR) impact through participation in a local Coastal Hazards Adaptation Resiliency Group (CHARG), a group of technical professionals and academics planning for SLR.

He knows his counterparts from other counties through these associations along with those in the major civil engineering consulting firms in the state. He attends events sponsored by these organizations and has gotten to know a lot of public works professionals over the years.

John also has good relationships with the state legislative members representing his county, as well as members of the U.S. Congress.

Most Helpful to His Career

John believes that taking on challenges outside of his area of expertise and learning how to get the work done has been most helpful to him. "It is sometimes scary, but taking on new things has broadened my knowledge base and my problem-solving skills. I've learned from my mistakes, and taken (or at least weighed) the advice of my peers to solve a variety of challenges."

He also believes that "being open and honest has also been an asset as I progressed to the Director level. I have been told that I have a reputation as a 'straight shooter' and am approachable by the public, elected officials, and staff. I operate under the DWYSYWD principle: do what you say you will do."

John has also developed an ability to explain complicated public works issues in a way that the public, elected officials, and non-technical staff can understand. He tries to use examples of issues similar to the topic at hand when he presents items in meetings that people can intuitively visualize and understand. When people are nodding their heads, he knows he is on the right track.

Finally, he has come to understand that most problems with which he deals do not have a right or wrong answer. The solution is what fits best for the community and budget available. The challenge is getting to that "sweet spot" where the majority is pleased with the results, or at least understands and acknowledges what led you to the result. Many times, the process is more important than the result.

Challenges

John finds there are several challenges in his job.

1. "Delivering projects that are sound from an engineering perspective, cost effective, and also address the needs and desires of the community. As we proceed through project development and design, we typically get requests from the community or elected officials to add enhancements that may not be necessary but are desired by the community. Depending on the budget and schedule, we try to accommodate as many requests as possible, but there are typically disappointed individuals at the end.

The key is finding the balance between addressing the desires of the community while moving a project forward that achieves our goals at a reasonable cost."

2. "Tactfully advising elected officials that DPW is funded through restricted funded sources that can only be used for the purposes collected. DPW does not receive unrestricted General Funds, and as such we are very careful in allocating our funds for eligible purposes. For instance, an elected official asked that Flood Control District Funds be used for sediment removal in a channel that is not within the jurisdiction of the Flood Control District. There is an art to saying 'no' that includes an explanation of budgeting principles and California legal restrictions regarding the use of funds."

3. "Every year, we get requests to do work that is either not in our work plan or is low on our priority list. Given the limited funds and staffing available to public agencies, it is necessary to prioritize work and adhere to our work plan to deliver the amount of work promised. When we receive unscheduled work, I explain that we can do it, but something else will not get completed. Although everyone acknowledges this fact early on, when the unscheduled work is completed, the same people that acknowledged other work will not be completed, then ask why we have not completed all of our other projects. I've tried various strategies to avoid this problem, including tracking priorities and unscheduled work and providing the information to the affected parties, but I've not yet been successful in addressing this challenge. My latest plan that we are carrying out is to track all unscheduled project costs, including staff time and present this to Board members in one-on-one meetings, and explain the actual expense and opportunity costs (for the uncompleted work) that mount by continuing this practice."

How He Deals with Challenges

John believes the best way to overcome these challenges is through educating elected officials and the public on what he does, how his agency is funded, and what they can and cannot do. He meets regularly with elected officials to update them on items of interest. In these meetings, he reminds them of his operating structure and what can and cannot be done. He does the same in community meetings. Once people understand the limitations and restrictions, they at least understand his position, although they may not agree with it.

Finally, he believes there is always a solution to a problem that is acceptable to the majority of the public. Typically, it involves accurately determining what the problem is and then finding the best solution. For instance, a pedestrian gets hit by a car or bicycle at an uncontrolled intersection, and he immediately gets requests to install stop signs or traffic signals. There are other, less costly, but equally effective ways to improve pedestrian safety at intersections, so they evaluate all possible solutions, listen to the community and get their feedback, and propose the solution that is both effective and affordable. It may be a traffic signal, but it is most often a different solution such as improving sight distance for vehicles or installing warning signs.

John believes that "you do not know what you do not know." He does not expect the public or elected officials to be experts in engineering and to educate interested parties on the available options, seek input, and recommend a favorable solution that meets the needs of the community and is acceptable from an engineering perspective. However, this assumes that people behave rationally, which is not always the case.

Most Rewarding Part of the Job

John says the most rewarding part of his job is that the work that he does has an impact on people's lives and the lives of future generations. He tells the staff that the work they do will be here long after they are gone. Think about how the work will perform over the next 50 years. The buildings they construct will be around long after they are gone. "Create a legacy of which you will be proud."

As he travels around the area, he can point to projects in which he has been involved: bridges, buildings, roadways, etc. "I am proud of the work that I do and hope that the influence that I have had will be well regarded by future generations and the next generation of public works professionals."

Also, there is nothing more rewarding than seeing a project in which you were involved in being constructed. "I love going to construction sites and watching contractors build what we envisioned on paper. It is very satisfying."

"The last point I would like to make is that my job is about solving problems. I've been doing this for 30 years now, and I'm constantly amazed how many different problems I encounter and how many ways things can go wrong. However, I also know that there are no public works problems that I cannot solve, or at least find a work-around to an acceptable compromise solution. You'll find that seasoned public works professionals never get very excited when problems arise. It comes with confidence in knowing you'll find a way to get through it, just like you have with every other problem that occurred in the past."

Recommendations for Students

John says that students do not have to be engineers to work in public works, but they do have to be motivated and ready to take on challenges outside of their comfort zone. If they are bright and willing to learn, they can be trained to be effective in whatever specialty they might like to try.

Most importantly, he advises being willing to take control of issues, exhibit leadership qualities, take calculated risks, and be open to other people's opinions.

Water Treatment and Public Drinking Systems

Overall, there are practically 170,000 public water systems, including 54,000 community systems, in the United States today. The existence of water systems goes back to the days of the Romans, who built reservoirs to store water and aqueducts to move it; some of those piping systems still exist today. These early systems have been upgraded by the development of pumping stations to move water uphill and by filtration and treatment systems to clean the water. The processes for cleaning water developed slowly over time, as science's understanding of disease, illness, and the roles of germs developed. By the late 1800s, Pasteur showed the importance of germs, and many cities filtered their water with sand filters. At the beginning of the 20th century, other processes were gradually added to remove minerals from the water (i.e., to "soften" the "hard" water) and to clean the water, with chlorine. By the mid-1970s, the federal government started taking more control over the quality of water, through the Safe Drinking Act of 1974, so now the U.S. Environmental Protection Agency regulates the contents of water even though the water treatment plants are operated by state and local governments (Coe 2009).

Water can go through four stages: untreated, treated, waste, or recycled. Today's water systems take advantage of the natural water cycle. Water is taken from the original source like a reservoir, a well to pull water from an aquifer, or a river. In typical water treatment cycles, the water then moves to a treatment plant (either through gravity or by being pumped), where impurities are removed. The now clean water is sent via distribution mains (pipes) to service lines, which connect directly to building plumbing systems, to be used. After use, the wastewater then goes to sewage treatment plants, where it undergoes a multi-step process of cleaning. Finally, it goes back into the water cycle by being used for irrigation or other purposes (American Water Works Association 2015) and, so, gets back into rivers or into the ground.

BOX 11.3   PUBLIC WORKS STRATEGIES FROM CITY SUSTAINABILITY PLANS

Infrastructure

- "Decrease the utility cost burden for low-income households through conservation measures." Longmont, Colorado, p. 7.
- "Maintain high performance infrastructure systems city-wide by retrofitting, designing for adaptability, and investing in new technologies." Virginia Beach, Virginia, p. 75.

Water Source

- "Ensure safe drinking water for all households in water service areas by developing a plan addressing consecutive systems by 2018." Longmont, Colorado, p. 7.
- "Increase water supply to 100% local." Santa Monica, California, p. 8.
- "Increase non-potable water use." Santa Monica, California, p. 8.
- "Reduce customer and City raw water demands by 10% by community buildout through water conservation efforts." Longmont, Colorado, p. 7.
- "Establish a comprehensive baseline of water quality conditions by 2020." Longmont, Colorado, p. 7.
- "Create an active Watershed Management Program by 2020." Longmont, Colorado, p. 7.

- "Implement continuous groundwater monitoring and educational programs to promote conservation and protection against aquifer depletion." Virginia Beach, Virginia, p. 111.
- "Continue restoration of Philadelphia's historic streams to improve surface water quality." Philadelphia, Pennsylvania, p. 25.

Stormwater

- "Increase stormwater quality upstream of beach outfalls." Virginia Beach, Virginia, p. 101.
- "Increase the number of green stormwater infrastructure projects on publicly owned lands and in the public right-of-way to meet federal regulatory obligations." Philadelphia, Pennsylvania, p. 25.

Sewage System

- "Maintain high-quality sanitary sewer service." Virginia Beach, Virginia, p. 101.

Waste and Recycling

- "Use waste diversion as a source of revenue." St. Louis, Missouri, p. 177.
- "Decrease household trash landfilled to less than 2 pounds per capita per day by 2018." Longmont, Colorado, p. 7.
- "Increase community-wide waste diversion to 50% by 2025." Longmont, Colorado, p. 7.
- "Increase internal waste diversion for all City operations." Longmont, Colorado, p. 7.
- "Reduce virgin paper use and increase use of paper with recycled content." St. Louis, Missouri, p. 178.

- "Replace Styrofoam cups with reusable cups and a dishwasher." Burnsville, Texas, p. 79.
- "Provide environmental responsible waste management services and operations for all of the community that are reliable and cost-effective." Virginia Beach, Virginia, p. 135.
- "Conduct a progressive educational program to reduce waste and promote reuse and recycling by both residents and businesses." Virginia Beach, Virginia, p. 135.
- "Work with institutional food procurement partners to identify opportunities for food composting and waste reduction." Philadelphia, Pennsylvania, p. 32.
- "Reduce marine debris to zero trash (cigarettes, plastic packaging, single-use bags, lids and straws)." Santa Monica, California, p. 10.

Sources: City of Burnsville, Minnesota. 2008. Sustainability Guide Plan. Accessed on February 22, 2017 from www.ci.burnsville.mn.us/DocumentCenter/Home/View/1287.

City of Longmont, Colorado. 2016. Sustainability Plan. November 2016. Accessed on February 22, 2017 from www.longmontcolorado.gov/home/showdocument?id=16700.

City of Santa Monica, California. 2014. Sustainable City Plan: City of Santa Monica. Accessed on February 22, 2017 from www.smgov.net/uploadedFiles/Departments/OSE/Categories/Sustainability/Sustainable-City-Plan.pdf.

City of St. Louis, Missouri. 2013. City of St. Louis Sustainability Plan. Accessed on February 22, 2017 from www.stlouis-mo.gov/government/departments/planning/documents/city-of-st-louis-sustainability-plan.cfm.

City of Virginia Beach, Virginia. 2013. A Community Plan for a Sustainable Future. City of VA Beach Environment and Sustainability Office. March 12, 2013. Accessed on February 22, 2017 from www.vbgov.com/government/offices/eso/sustainability-plan/Documents/vb-sustainability-plan-web.pdf.

The age of water system infrastructure, including pipes, is often quite high in our oldest cities, and the infrastructure needs to be replaced. Challenges in water system infrastructure can include broken water mains, the need to replace old pipes before they break, and the need to adhere to new water safety standards set by the U.S. Environmental Protection Agency. The water quality and old pipes challenges faced by Flint, Michigan are discussed later in this chapter. New pump stations are expensive but are often what is required to fix the system.

BOX 11.4 SELECTED TYPES OF ECOSYSTEM SERVICES

- Drinking water protection;
- Stormwater mitigation;
- Mitigating flood risk;
- Coastal protection;
- Air purification;
- Shade and heat wave mitigation;

- Biodiversity;
- Recreation and tourism; and
- Mental health.

Source: Based upon McDonald 2015: Table 1.1: Ecosystem Services of Greatest Relevance to Cities.

Conservationists sometimes call these traditional systems of pipes and water mains gray infrastructure—and believe that they can be supplemented or replaced by investments in green infrastructure, which would create more sustainable cities. They support replacing water pipes and concrete streams, then draining water and sewage with wetlands and natural streams used as natural filters. As stated by Robert McDonald, "Cities are centers of activity on the landscape, and there are strong bonds between cities and nature, whether inside the city's walls or far away. More and more, conservation biologists, urban planners, and landscape architects are being asked to craft plans that maintain or strengthen these bonds while also allowing for continued urban growth. As the urban century continues, the maintenance of these bonds will become more crucial, both because more people will depend on them and because rapid urban growth . . . risks severing them" (McDonald 2015, location 145). McDonald believes that natural infrastructure can be used to meet some urban challenges today, particularly in the area of water, using ecosystem services.

Ecosystem services are "'the components of nature, directly enjoyed, consumed, or used to yield human well-being.' An ecosystem service occurs when an ecosystem is supplying something that people are demanding" (McDonald 2015, location 201). Ecosystem services (Box 11.4) include using natural processes like trees and natural streambeds to help clean the water, rather than only traditional treatment plants.

Flint, Michigan and the Water Scandal

A recent scandal in Flint, Michigan has aptly illustrated the importance of effective water treatment—and the problems with old infrastructure. In the State of Michigan, a city's elected officials may be replaced by emergency managers appointed by the Governor. That happened in Flint, Michigan, and in the summer of 2014 when the emergency managers were trying to save money, they switched from using water from Lake Huron to water from their own local Flint River. What they did not do was arrange to have the water treated with necessary anti-corrosive chemicals. Since more than 50 percent of Flint's water pipes were lead, the water immediately began to corrode the pipes, which allowed hazardous levels of lead into the water supply of the city (Lazarus 2016).

Michigan Department of Environmental Quality (MDEQ) tests indicated the water was safe, with the MDEQ spokesperson even telling residents in October 2015, "Anyone who is concerned about lead in the drinking water in Flint can relax" (CBS/AP 2015).

However, independent experts from Virginia Tech, the Coalition for Clean Water, and the ACLU of Michigan found very different results. PRI reports, "At least 25 percent of homes in Flint had levels of lead that were well above the federal level, which is 15 ppb (parts per billion). In some homes, it was 13,200 ppb. Moreover, nearly every home had water that was distasteful or discolored" (Lazarus 2016). In just one year, children in Flint were showing signs of lead poisoning, with more accidents due to weaker bones, compromised immune systems, and memory problems in school.

Outside experts even suggested State tests had been skewed so that they would find no problems. Subsequently, emails from the Governor's office staff indicated there was private concern over what was happening, but, publicly, the Governor and MDEQ still maintained there was no problem. It is clear that, while Flint was under the control of State emergency managers, State officials did not follow federal water testing procedures, nor did they follow guidelines about necessary treatments for the water.

Only on January 5, 2016, after concerned experts, citizens and citizen groups, and the national media got involved, and the extent of the water crisis became obvious, did Governor Snyder declare a state of emergency in Flint. Fallout continues from the crisis, with the State now paying for water filters for Flint residents and the director of MDEQ resigning at the end of 2015. In early January 2016, the situation in Flint also became the subject of a U.S. Department of Justice investigation (Egan 2016).

Still, it took almost ten days after the declaration of the emergency for the State to start getting drinking water in any real amount to the public. By then, it became apparent that other problems were occurring, too—there had been eight deaths from Legionnaire's disease, which could also be attributed to the toxic water.

By the end of 2016, four individuals had been indicted (two from the City and two from the State), and, by January 24, 2017, the lead limits had fallen below the federal level of toxicity. However, by January 21, 2017, Flint residents had experienced 1,000 days of toxic drinking water. The City was making slow progress in replacing the pipes, but residents were distrusting of federal statements about the water being safe to drink. On February 1, 2017, residents sued the U.S. Environmental Protection Agency, stating the agency had failed to warn Flint or take necessary steps to protect them (Flint Water Class Action 2017).

Wastewater and Stormwater Systems

Wastewater and stormwater systems are one part of this overall water cycle. Until the late 1880s, people used outhouses or cesspools, or just poured waste into rivers or the streets. Once industrialization began, cities grew more extensively, scientists realized disease was connected to waste and bacteria, and treatment systems and methods were developed. Wastewater became not just sewerage but also water from showers, washing machines, and dishwashers as the sewerage systems connected to pipes coming from residences and businesses. Combined treatment plants also included water coming from stormwater systems.

The treatment of this mostly liquid waste is set up in stages. The primary stage removes large materials through screening, but, over time, other chemical treatment stages have been added. The secondary stage involves biological or chemical removal of waste from the water. Tertiary stage treatment plants provide even higher levels of water treatment. As manufacturing and technology have developed new chemicals and other materials, wastewater treatments have had to keep up ways to remove newer materials, as well. Funding for wastewater treatment plants is provided by the U.S. Environmental Protection Agency under the Clean Water Act and other legislation (Coe 2009).

A stormwater system, infrastructure to drain water from rain storms, is part of an overall urban drainage system. It must be designed with full knowledge of the local watershed area, complete with information about local flood patterns. One component of these local patterns are estimates of flooding and how often floods have occurred in the past, and how likely they are to occur in the future, at various locations throughout the city. These are now organized on maps called Flood Insurance Rate Maps (FIRMs). Planners map out 100-year flood zones, or areas that are likely to have heavy floods only every 100 years, and then plan a system of pipes, gutters, and drains from all areas of the city. Around homes and businesses, gutters and drain pipes serve to drain stormwater down to stormwater pipes; the stormwater piping system then drains the water to local streams or rivers. Ideally, the system then becomes part of the overall water cycle, in which this water is used for irrigation or other purposes within the city.

Natural streams filled with plants, rocks, and soils can serve an important role in a stormwater management system as they can enhance water quality as well as reduce water flow speed and flooding. Ecosystem services composed of trees on hills and natural vegetation on stream banks can also help by reducing erosion and, therefore, reducing sedimentation in water flows. Cities have also used permeable pavement (sometimes called green pavement) rather than traditional concrete, which does not allow water to seep back down into the ground. If the water does not settle back into the ground, it runs off down the surface of streets or gets into the stormwater system and then more rapidly moves down those pipes. Together, ecosystem services and permeable pavement can aid in reducing sediment erosion, natural water filtration, water yield, water retention, and increased infiltration of water back into the groundwater. Other methods protect vegetation and reduce water pollution, like fencing to keep livestock away from water resources, and changing agricultural methods. Forest and tree covering also have some effect on water quality in a watershed. It is far better to have stormwater seep back into the ground than to have it continue running down concrete streams and streets, where it picks up oil, gas, and other pollutants.

Some cities (Quito, Ecuador, for instance) have at least partially solved their erosion and water quality problems by investing in green infrastructure as well as gray (traditional pipes). Rather than expanding their treatment plant facilities, they invested in restoring watersheds and the natural terrain around them. These steps reduced water flows and erosion and helped improve their water quality. New York City also avoided having to build new treatment and filter plants through natural green infrastructure.

In Washington, D.C., gray infrastructure was replaced by green wetlands, trees, and other vegetation as concrete waterways were torn up so that water from storms could be slowed down enough that it could infiltrate and return below the soil. Allowing water to return to the land not only reduces the amount flowing through gray stormwater infrastructure to lower peak flows, it also helps to clean the water.

▶ BOX 11.5 CONNECTIONS UNDER THE GROUND

To illustrate the complexity of the physical infrastructure of cities, we can just examine the kinds of connections—pipes, wires, and other connections to utilities—that exist underground in cities. All of these pipes, drains, ducts, and wiring run beneath our feet, to keep cities running. These physical connections include:

- Electrical ducts with electrical wires;
- Telephone ducts with telephone wires;

- Fiber optic cable for the Internet;
- Gas mains;
- Water pipes;
- Sometimes, steam pipes;
- Sewerage pipes; and
- Storm drains.

Source: Based upon Macaulay, David. 1983. *Underground.* Figure: Ideal Utility Layout, p. 46.

Streets

At one time, streets and roads were made of gravel or stone, then wood planks, and, later, asphalt. Roads were first built in this country by voluntary labor; when traffic increased, roads became toll roads so that they could pay for themselves. Only later did the creation and maintenance of streets and roads become public goods and, so, the province of governments.

Streets and roads can be categorized into several groups: expressways (limited access roads); arterial roads (allowing more traffic); collector roads to connect arterial and local roads; local roads to directly connect businesses and homes; and rural roads. They can also be characterized as commercial, residential, and industrial, based upon their land use (Tumlin 2012).

Road maintenance is critical, as a road deteriorates "by 40 percent during the first 60 percent of its life, but by 40 percent more during the next 15 percent" of its life cycle (Coe 2009, p. 148). Maintenance includes tasks like sealing cracks or patching holes in the asphalt, filling potholes, replacing the sealant that goes over the asphalt, or replacing the overlay that covers that, as well.

Tumlin (2012) highlights important design elements for streets, including avoiding environmentally sensitive areas, incorporating the natural topography of the land, the sun, and the wind for shade and breezes into the street design and aesthetic views. He also suggests mixed use neighborhood centers, short blocks to enhance walkability, and locating successful businesses close to or within neighborhoods.

▶ BOX 11.6 "COMPLETE STREETS"

"Complete streets" is a term suggesting the ideal design of city streets, including a range of features that allow mobility and transit for all. Desired features in complete streets include:

- Street lanes for travel only;
- Designated parking areas;
- Lanes (separate) for safe bicycling travel;

- Sidewalks, including landscaping, places to sit, and lighting;
- Loading zones;
- Wheelchair ramps and accommodations, including safe curb-cuts;
- Transit stops; and
- Traffic signal improvements.

(*Tumlin* 2012, pp. 46–47)

Solid Waste Collection

In 2013, about 254 million tons of trash were created in the United States. According to the U.S. Environmental Protection Agency, 52.8 percent of what we throw away was discarded, only 34.3 percent was recycled or composted, and 12.9 percent was burned for energy (U.S. EPA 2016). Of the 4.4 pounds of garbage we generate each day, only 1.51 pounds is currently recycled. Figure 11.2 illustrates the composition of that municipal solid waste in 2013. The largest type was paper, followed by food and yard trimmings. Sixty-seven percent of newspapers were recycled in 2013, the highest rate of recycling for everything but lead-acid batteries (99.0 percent recycled) and steel cans (70.6 percent recycled). Still, only 55.1 percent of aluminum cans, 34.0 percent of glass containers, and 40.5 percent of tires were recycled in 2013, so progress is still needed.

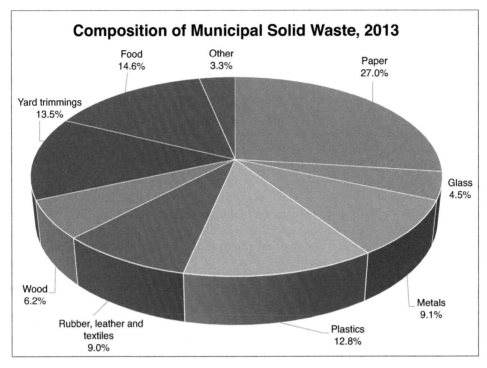

FIGURE 11.2
Composition of Municipal Solid Waste, 2013

Source: U.S. Environmental Protection Agency. Materials and Waste Management in the United States Key Facts and Figures. Retrieved on January 25, 2016, from www.epa.gov/smm/advancing-sustainable-materials-management-facts-and-figures#Materials.

These levels of recycling are after years of positive progress in increasing recycling rates, from 5.6 million tons in 1960 to 87.2 million tons in 2013, an increase from 6.4 percent recycled in 1960 to 34.3 in 2013 (U.S. Environmental Protection Agency 2016).

Trash and waste removal is an important function of local public works departments. Materials are trucked away and taken to transfer stations, landfills, recycling facilities, or incinerators. Transfer stations are locations where waste is moved to larger trucks for shipment to other facilities. Waste collection is one of the services most often contracted out by local governments to private firms, primarily due to its capital-intensive nature (requiring large numbers of trucks and other equipment). This function is accomplished occasionally by publicly owned trucks and other equipment, but, more often, today, it is done by private companies contracting with local governments. Landfills are locations where materials are dumped and left, creating large mounds of waste. They are required to be built in suitable areas away from wetlands, earthquake faults, or other hazardous areas and away from groundwater locations. They are lined at the bottom, then covered with waste, which is compacted and covered itself with soil to reduce smell and protect public health. Once the land is filled, the surface is often redone and reused for other purposes. Today, hazardous wastes are collected in other areas, not in regular landfills. The more material that is recycled, the less is sent to landfills, which prevents the release of tons of carbon dioxide into the air (186 million metric tons in 2013, the equivalent of 39 million cars on the road).

BOX 11.7 MEANS OF WASTE REDUCTION

- Swap shop, where unwanted items are dropped off, to be used by others;
- Paint exchange program, where unused paint is left, to be used by others;
- Grasscycling—instead of grass clippings being bagged and removed, they can be left on the lawn to enrich the soil;

- Xeriscaping—removing grass lawns altogether and replacing them with native plants needing less water;
- Buying more recyclable products, like refillable containers, rather than products that go into waste bins;
- Reducing use of toxic substances; and
- Composting yard and kitchen waste for use in the garden.

Source: Based upon Coe 2009.

Another method of waste disposal is burning it in high-temperature incinerators. In some communities, the heat generated from this process is converted to steam, which in turn is converted into electricity for usage by the public; this process is termed cogeneration and adds to the sustainability of the community, in that waste is turned into a positive substance, electricity.

Besides recycling, another sustainable process would be to reduce waste at its source. There are many possible methods of waste reduction (see Box 11.7).

Performance Measures

Like planning departments, engineering and public works departments review plans, so one performance measure used is the percentage of engineering plans reviewed on time. Due to the capital improvements projects under their department, they also could use the percentage of capital improvement project contracts completed on schedule and on budget to measure their performance. With their other responsibilities like trash collection and street sweeping, measures like percent of residential streets swept every four weeks, tons of trash collected per gutter mile, or curb-miles swept per operator-hour could also be used. Street lighting could be measured as a percentage of streetlight malfunctions completed within 48 hours. Graffiti is a big problem in many cities; its removal could be measured by the percentage of graffiti removed within one working day or 48 hours of reporting. Trash collection measurement is relatively straight-forward: the percentage of scheduled garbage routes completed on schedule, the percentage of missed collections per 100,000 households, complaints per year per 1,000 households, or tons collected per worker-hour are good measures. Recycling managers can use measures like the percentage of households participating in a recycling program, pounds of recycling collected per year, or pounds of solid waste diverted to recycling (Ammons 2015).

TRANSPORTATION AND THE CITY

Much of the reality of urban transportation lies in the history of each city, which at least partly determined its physical layout. Cities that developed and grew in the 1800s grew along the lines determined by how far people could walk or ride on horses or in horsecars;

this became the Walking-Horsecar Era (1800–1890), which produced condensed cities. From 1890 to 1920 was the Electric Streetcar Era, when suburbs started growing around streetcar lines, where the middle class could live and still easily get into the city. Cities themselves remained very dense with buildings close together, but they started stretching out along those streetcar lines. The Recreational Automobile Era moved the city boundaries and growth out even further (Muller 2004) and expanded city boundaries further, which was further accentuated with the Freeway Era (1945–present), when neighborhoods were torn down to make way for freeways. Freeways allowed further sprawl away from city centers, as well as a means of easily getting back to the city for work from suburbs built along the highways. With freeways came urban sprawl as growth could jump out to freeway exits far from the city center.

Cities took on the spatial character of the era in which they grew. Cities in the Northeast and Midwest were more densely populated and built closely together around the central business district, as they were developed before the development of cars. Cities in the Sunbelt, created after cars were developed and used widely, show more sprawl and are less densely populated over a wider area, as they were built to accommodate cars and freeways.

These sprawled-out patterns of development have enormous implications for the kinds of transportation and mass transit that are effective in those communities. In turn, the availability and effectiveness of mass transit have implications for energy usage and sustainability in those cities. Transportation has immense impact on the urban environment, affecting its sustainability in several ways: air pollution (including carbon monoxide [60 percent of all pollution generated in the United States], nitrogen oxide, and ozone), water pollution from runoff and leaks of fuel and oil, and greenhouse gasses (methane, nitrous oxide, hydrofluorocarbons, and carbon dioxide). Because of this, there are immense opportunities to increase sustainability in cities through changing modes of transportation and transit-oriented development (Tumlin 2012).

In 2009, the types of household-based vehicle miles showed three types of travel, almost equally split. Of all types of household-based vehicle miles, 23.7 percent were trips for visits and recreation, 30.7 were for shopping and errands, and 26.7 were for commuting to and from work (Federal Highway Administration, U.S. Department of Transportation 2010, pp. ES-1). These patterns have changed over time, driven by demographic changes such as the growth in the number of older drivers (who drive less) and the number of new immigrant families, who are less likely to own a car and so shift more trips to walking and carpooling. Further, shifts in the population as a whole from the Northeast and Midwest to the Sunbelt move people away from cities with more mass transit and into cities more dependent upon cars.

Figure 11.3 illustrates the transit modes by urban passenger miles (in millions of miles). Most of those miles (39.5 percent) are spent on motor buses, followed by heavy rail (31.4 percent), commuter rail (20.5 percent) and then, a sharp decline to only 3.9 percent moving on light rail. Vanpools, ferries, trolleys, demand response (like taxicabs and other, newer, means like Lyft and Uber) share very small percentages of total millions of passenger miles. Of these, the use of vanpools has grown the most since 2000 (an increase of 143.7 percent), followed by light rail (increased by 55.3 percent) and demand response (an increase of 43.5 percent).

Examining trips to work is important since they are fully one-third of all transportation trips made by individuals. As Figure 11.4 indicates, in 2013 just more than three-quarters (76.4 percent) of workers got to their jobs by driving alone. Practically 10 percent

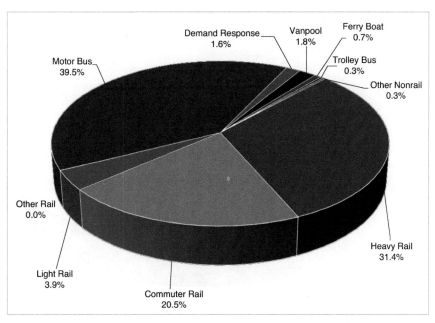

FIGURE 11.3
Modes of Transit, Urban Passenger Miles, 2008

Source: Based upon Federal Highway Administration, Chapter 2. Federal Highway Administration, U.S. Department of Transportation. 2010. *2010 Status of the Nation's Highways, Bridges, and Transit: Conditions and Performance. Report to Congress.* Accessed on January 29, 2016, from https://www.fhwa.dot.gov/policy/2010cpr/execsum.cfm#c2t.

BOX 11.8   DEFINITIONS OF TYPES OF TRANSIT

- Commuter rail: Passenger services that typically operate between cities and suburbs, serving commuters to work as well as other passengers.
- Demand responsive vehicle: A vehicle that comes when called in some way by a potential passenger. This could include paratransit vehicles attending persons with disabilities, taxicabs, or, today, cars from companies like Lyft or Uber.
- Ferry boat: Like a bus on land, a boat that conveys passengers on a fixed route, but across bodies of water.
- Heavy rail: Electric railway that runs on dedicated track with many cars per train; can run at high speeds. These can be subways, elevated railways, or metros.
- Light rail: A streetcar vehicle that runs on tracks built exclusively for the vehicle.

Runs in several, if not many, American urban downtowns.
- Motor bus: A bus that operates within a city as part of a mass transit system, school buses, or buses that carries passengers from city to city.
- Trolley bus: A vehicle steered by a driver but propelled by a motor receiving current from electrical lines, typically overhead.
- Vanpool: Commuter services that operate in vans with up to 18 passengers and that typically take riders on a pre-arranged schedule to one work location, and then back again to drop-off points. Some companies and government agencies operate these services for their employees.

Source: Federal Highway Administration. 2016. Planning Glossary. Accessed on February 2, 2016 from www.fhwa.dot.gov/planning/glossary/.

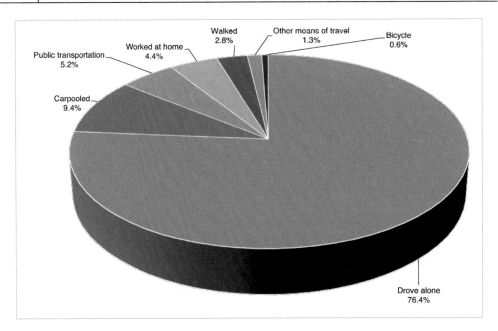

FIGURE 11.4
Means of Travel to Work (Percentages)

Source: Based on U.S. Census Bureau 2013. American Community Survey. Table S0801. In McKenzie, Brian. 2013. Who Drives to Work? Commuting by Automobile in the United States, 2013. American Community Survey Reports.

(9.4 percent) carpooled, 2.8 percent walked, and 0.6 percent rode a bicycle. Various types of public transportation (bus, subway, ferry, streetcar, or trolley) accounted for only 5.2 percent of worker travel. Another 4.4 percent of workers stayed at home to work. These figures are averages across the entire country, and there are enormous differences by city (McKenzie 2015).

In New York City, for instance, 56 percent of workers use public transit to get to work, and only 23 percent use their cars (New York State Department of Transportation 2012), but that is the lowest rate of car usage for work in the country.

Strategies for Reducing Transit

There are many strategies used today to reduce the use of transit, particularly private car usage, and to shift users to other means and, so, make cities more sustainable. Reducing private car usage and shifting users to other modes are critical to reducing energy usage and greenhouse gas emissions, reducing the need for additional highways and parking, and reducing urban sprawl.

Performance measures for public transportation start with the percentage of the population (or dwelling units) within one-quarter mile of a public transit route; this is a basic measure of equity, to ensure that public transit is available to all. Adherence to the route schedule is typically desired as zero minutes early to five minutes late, so the percentage of buses on time or adhering to that measure is a basic measure. The benchmark, or acceptable rate, of operating costs and revenues for a public transit system is that fares as a percentage of operating expenditures should be anywhere from 20 to 50 percent;

the remainder is typically subsidized by the city. Moreover, the level of demand (passengers per vehicle-mile) should be at least 1.5 passengers per vehicle-mile. Service frequency should be at least 30 minutes during peak periods and at least hourly during off-peak periods. Other possible measures include accidents per 100,000 bus miles, ridership complaints per 100,000 riders, and percentage of mobility challenged customers reaching their destination within 90 minutes (Ammons 2015).

Transit-Oriented Development

At the intersection of transit, planning, and sustainability lies transit-oriented development (TOD). TOD is a response to the need to reduce the amounts of energy and greenhouse gas emissions generated by transportation in cities; to do this, planners try to locate housing, retail, and offices directly around transit hubs in cities. By increasing the population density around these sites and also providing employment and retail opportunities nearby, private car usage is reduced and, therefore, greenhouse gas emissions and energy usage decrease, as well. Also, walkability can be increased so that people around the development subsequently walk more. If designed correctly, this can also enhance the neighborhood feel of an area (Dodman 2009). TODs can also be seen as an economic development strategy, since new retail and offices are established in the area, although the mix of retail must be carefully selected by taking possible customers into account.

Most TOD developments are sited near heavy rail locations (37.4 percent), followed by light rail (31.3 percent) and commuter rail (21.8) (Cervero 2004, p. 17). Many of the TOD projects in the United States are also joint developments—offices, housing, retail, and civic buildings are jointly built by cities, private sector developers, and the transit agencies themselves.

Cervero (2004) reports that in two-thirds of American cases, cities took the lead in planning and organizing the land use portions of transit-oriented developments, while, in another one-fifth, the land use responsibility is shared between partner agencies. Several states have also gotten involved by passing legislation that provides incentives or policy frameworks for TOD. The federal government has also passed rules or has programs that help support this trend, including saying that land purchased with federal dollars may be used for TODs.

Overall, results of studies indicate that TODs, in general, raise mass transit ridership, increase residential density, reduce car ownership, and move employment accessibility from highway-based to mass transit-based systems (Cervero 2004)—all critical trends for increasing the sustainability of cities.

Carsharing Services

Carsharing, or short-term vehicle access, is another program being used in many cities today to reduce traffic, need for parking, greenhouse gas emissions, and energy usage. Carsharing began in the United States in the late 1990s and grew rapidly in the mid-2000s. By January 2014, 1.23 million members were sharing 17,179 cars from 24 carsharing programs in the United States (Transportation Sustainability Research Center 2016). It is most successful in dense cities with high proportions of residents without cars. Only when there are enough residents without cars will there be enough demand for a carsharing service (Tumlin 2012).

Three types of services exist: a nonprofit providing carsharing as an environmental benefit, carsharing as a sustainable business, and carsharing as a private sector business;

the type determines how much local government support is required or requested (Shaheen, Rodier, Murray, Cohen and Martin 2010). However, in general, the process works as follows.

A carsharing service or company buys cars, and then the cars are left available in parking lots around the city, in small groups. Interested consumers join the carsharing service; they can then reserve a car at a particular location. Service members or users pick up the reserved car only when they need a car and return the car to the same location when they are finished. Service members or users pay a fee only for the use of the car when they are using it. Some services require users to be monthly dues paying members; others do not.

BOX 11.9   CAREER PATHWAYS OF A TRANSPORTATION PROFESSIONAL

Current Position

Transportation Demand Management (TDM) Program Manager. Transportation demand management refers to policies and strategies to reduce demand for transit. Donna began this exempt position in 2014.

Education

B.A., Public Administration
M.P.A.

Career Pathway

Donna got into this field through exposure to programs and policy that were related to greenhouse gas reduction and clean air quality.

Then she worked in these positions:

- Senior Assistant, Taxi Commission;
- Compliance and Training Coordinator, Municipal Transportation Agency;
- Safe Routes to School Assistant Program Manager, County Transportation Authority; and
- Commute Consultant II, County Transportation Authority.

Learning about the Job

Donna learned about her field through work experience, education, training, and workshops.

A Typical Day

As TDM Program Manager, Donna manages several transportation programs that require day-to-day follow-up. For example, if she is working on a transit-related program in partnership with a community college, she checks the database for results mainly related to trip reduction. She does this by analyzing the mileage and trips provided by participants of the program. She is interested in these data for what they say about program and cost effectiveness. She also works closely with employers and the community on transportation alternatives education and on-site visits to assist in reducing an organization's overall carbon footprint. She attends coordination meetings for events such as bike to work day, real-time rideshare, and other alternative transportation-related options. She attends regional TDM outreach working group meetings to discuss/share outcomes from pilots or programs. She also attends a monthly Program Managers' meeting where she meets with Program Managers from her county on cohesive TDM-related programs and policies that may impact her programs and sub-regions.

Professional Associations and Networking

Donna is a member of the Association for Commuter Transportation (ACT). She has attended and presented at international conferences. She also participates in team building and networking opportunities offered through the Association plus travels around the country to learn about other programs and how they are organized.

To network, she goes to meetings, conferences, and workshops.

Most Helpful to Her Career

Donna believes that meeting with others in her field and learning best practices have been the most help in her career, along with the relationships she built along the way and the leadership skills she developed from past positions.

Challenges

Coming to a position with little to no knowledge and having to engage stakeholders was a big challenge for Donna, as was understanding each organization's culture and mores. Additionally, creating partnerships to bring plans or programs to fruition and having to develop innovations were also challenges.

Overcoming These Challenges

To overcome these challenges, Donna had to learn to maximize the resources provided to her, such as public officials and transit demand management professionals with a wealth of knowledge, and to review and research past performance/program history. Relationships are important, and being educated on current issues in the field is critical.

Most Rewarding Part of the Job

For Donna, the rewards lie in being able to offer transit alternatives that can improve the quality of life of commuters who spend much of their day traveling to and from work. The contribution of the programs in which she works is a small but important piece to a larger puzzle in improving air quality. Also, she values having the opportunity to educate and work with the community.

Recommendations to Students

Donna recommends being open, and taking any opportunity to learn more about your field of interest. Also, research the policies that impact the field. If you end up in the transit field, always think outside of the box in your approach to change.

Carsharing operates at the intersection of public transit, taxis, car rentals, public transit, and bicycles. People without cars, because they normally go to work on public transit, might still have times when they might like a car—to go to the grocery store or specialty stores some distance away, to go on vacations, or for special events or entertainment.

Evidence already exists that carsharing can be successful in reducing car ownership, reducing some vehicle miles traveled, and increasing the use of public transportation (Shaheen et al. 2010). Also, Martin and Shaheen (2010) found that users participating in carsharing programs generated significantly less greenhouse gas emissions in households using the programs.

However, the growth of this program has declined as it has been more difficult to find spaces to park carshare cars available for usage in some cities. Cities' and special district/transit agencies' parking policies and programs used to accommodate carsharing vary widely across the country. In general, the number of spaces allocated to service is capped with carsharing agencies paying fees for the spaces. These spaces are clearly marked for carsharing cars, and anyone else parking there is ticketed. For instance, in 2010, 100 metered spaces and 66 on-street parking spaces in Portland, Oregon were set aside for carsharing, out of 14,500 total spaces (Shaheen et al. 2010, p. 22). In most cities, policies surrounding carsharing are laid out in formal city ordinances.

Bicycling in Cities

Bicycling is a relatively common activity within our cities and on our city streets; in a 2012 survey, 18 percent of the adult population (older than 16) said they rode a bicycle at least once during the summer (U.S. National Highway Safety Administration 2012). In 2009, there were nine million bicycle trips every day in the United States. Forty-one percent of those biking did so for health reasons, 37 percent for recreation, and 5 percent for commuting to work. Bicyclists used paved roads 48.1 percent of the time, sidewalks 13.6 percent, bike paths 13.1 percent, and bicycle lanes on paved roads 5.2 percent of the time. Most trips (42 percent) were no more than 30 minutes; another 36 percent were between 31 and 60 minutes (Pedestrian and Bicycle Information Center 2016).

There are several important aspects of increased cycling: safe, comfortable, and sociable bikeways, and places to go within bikeable distances (roughly 3 miles) (Tumlin 2012). The more people participate in biking and walking, the more additional people will bike and walk—and the safer biking and walking will be. The most comfortable bikeways have safe and level surfaces with space or barriers between bicycles and cars.

Bicycling can be thought of as for recreation or commuting, either vehicular (driving along with cars) or non-vehicular (riding on separate bikeways or bike lanes). Designing for bicycling, as opposed to just letting it happen, can lead to more, and safer, biking. Bike facilities include:

- Pathways, or shared-use pathways, with pedestrians and bicycles on the same paths. These should be at least 10 feet wide so that bicycles can pass safely.
- Separated bike lanes, or cycle tracks. These can be only 6–7 feet so two bicycles can ride together and are one-way only.
- Bike lanes with traffic lanes for bicycles placed between parking and travel lanes. These are usually only 4–6 feet wide; any wider and cars would start driving in them.
- Narrow lanes in narrow streets, generally placed so that cars have to slow down to pass slowly.

(Tumlin 2012)

Intersections and turns are where, in fact, most accidents involving bicycles occur and should be carefully planned in any bike network. Markings, barriers, and signs (including "sharrows" showing shared lanes) help to let drivers and bicyclists know where to go and how to turn safely. Planning for bicycle networks should also include bike parking facilities, including racks or lockers.

Many cities today are beginning to utilize bicycle sharing programs. These programs have some bicycles in racks around the city, and people can check out a bike to go to work, do errands, or just bike around. The Capital Bikeshare program, for instance, in Washington, D.C. (www.capitalbikeshare.com/), has 3,000 bicycles at 350 stations in the greater D.C. area. After people become a member, they can then check out a bike at any station and ride for 30 minutes for free and pay an additional fee for longer than 30 minutes. The program is also testing a Single Trip Fare by offering tickets for $2 for a single 30-minute trip.

In 2014, Capital Bikeshare had 27,600 members. Members at that time reported that 64 percent of at least one of their trips during a month started or ended at a Metrorail station, indicating the bike system was being used to extend the transit system. However,

BOX 11.10 TRANSPORTATION STRATEGIES FROM CITY SUSTAINABILITY PLANS

Equity

- "Increase to 100% households with high quality transit service within ½ mile." Santa Monica, California, p. 12.
- "Achieve more equitable access to transportation infrastructure for all segments of the community." Longmont, Colorado, p. 6.
- "Address service and infrastructure gaps to increase transit and active transportation options, with a focus on underserved communities." Longmont, Colorado, p. 7.

Comprehensiveness

- "Develop an efficient and convenient public transit system, connecting major centers and gathering places, and offering residents and visitors with comparative alternatives to the automobile." Virginia Beach, Virginia, p. 77.
- "Create active transportation routes, such as bikeways and trails, that are safe, connect our centers, and are widely used by our citizens and visitors." Virginia Beach, Virginia, p. 77.

Walking

- "Annual increase in pedestrian facilities: complete sidewalks, public/private pathways, crosswalk enhancements, and signal timing enhancements." Santa Monica, California, p. 12.
- "Maximize walkability in our places and reduce the amount of surface parking by promoting alternative parking strategies." Virginia Beach, Virginia, p. 39.

Biking

- "Continue to incorporate equity and neighborhood access as core values as Indego bike shares expands." Philadelphia, Pennsylvania, p. 28.

Using Fewer Car Miles

- "Downward trend in vehicle miles traveled." Santa Monica, California, p. 12.

- "Reduce drive alone trips." Burnsville, Texas, p. 34.
- "Increase shared-vehicle programs and opportunities." St. Louis, Missouri, p. 163.
- "Increase staff alternative commuting 5% by 2017, 20% by 2020, 20% by 2023." Avondale, Arizona, p. 52.

Sustainability

- "Pursue transit oriented development at MetroLink stations and major bus nodes to encourage more walking and fewer carbon emissions." St. Louis, Missouri, p. 228.
- "Upward trend in use of sustainable (bus, bike, pedestrian, rail) modes of trans. Drive alone max 60%, bike + walk + transit minimum: 25%, Bike + walk 15%." Santa Monica, California, p. 12.
- "Support low-carbon and high resource-efficiency transportation options through the development of supporting infrastructure, fuel purchasing and local fuel production." Dover, New Hampshire, p. 3.
- "Reduce transportation-related GHG." Longmont, Colorado, p. 7.

Sources: City of Burnsville, Minnesota. 2008. Sustainability Guide Plan. Accessed on February 22, 2017 from www.ci.burnsville.mn.us/DocumentCenter/Home/View/1287.
City of Longmont, Colorado. 2016. Sustainability Plan. November 2016. Accessed on February 22, 2017 from www.longmontcolorado.gov/home/showdocument?id=16700.
City of Santa Monica, California. 2014. Sustainable City Plan: City of Santa Monica. Accessed on February 22, 2017 from www.smgov.net/uploadedFiles/Departments/OSE/Categories/Sustainability/Sustainable-City-Plan.pdf.
City of St. Louis, Missouri. 2013. City of St. Louis Sustainability Plan. Accessed on February 22, 2017 from www.stlouis-mo.gov/government/departments/planning/documents/city-of-st-louis-sustainability-plan.cfm.
City of Virginia Beach, Virginia. 2013. A Community Plan for a Sustainable Future. City of VA Beach Environment and Sustainability Office. March 12, 2013. Accessed on February 22, 2017 from www.vbgov.com/government/offices/eso/sustainability-plan/Documents/vb-sustainability-plan-web.pdf.

85 percent also said they occasionally used the bikes for social trips or entertainment. Forty percent of members did not own cars. Bikeshare members tended to be younger, more male, Caucasian, and slightly less affluent that the commuting population in Washington, D.C. in general (Capital Bikeshare 2014).

Other systems do not require users to be members.

CONCLUSIONS

This chapter contained a great deal of material on city government processes that are often taken for granted and are sometimes invisible to most of us—streets, trash collection, sewer and stormwater management, infrastructure, and transit. As we have seen, much of our public infrastructure is in need of repair, and city governments are struggling as much as other levels of government to find the money to make those repairs. With transit, we are becoming more aware of the relationship between transit, land use, and energy usage. We are seeing a great deal of innovations in the transit area, as we have increased incentives to alter our patterns of high energy usage through traditional automobiles. Understanding the basics of these services is crucial to understanding the management of cities, as illustrated by NASPAA's inclusion of urban service areas in its Urban Administration student learning standards.

SELECTED WEB RESOURCES

- Alliance for Water Efficiency www.allianceforwaterefficiency.org/
- American Association of State Highway and Transportation Officials (AASHTO) www.transportation.org/
- American Society of Civil Engineers www.asce.org/
- American Water Works Association (AWWA) www.awwa.org/

- Association for Commuter Transportation (ACT). http://actweb.org/
- Federal Highway Administration www.fhwa.dot.gov/
- National Committee on Levee Safety www.leveesafety.org/
- Transportation Planning Division, American Planning Association www.planning.org/

EXERCISES AND DISCUSSION QUESTIONS

1. **Know Your City:** Public Works and Transportation
   - Does your city have a public works department? Does it maintain local roads?
   - What kind of recycling services does your city offer?
   - Is trash collection done by the city itself, or by a vendor through contracting out?
   - What kind of transit opportunities does your city provide? Are there regional systems, as well?
   - What is the ridership of the fastest mass transit system in your city?
   - Does your city have car- or bicycle-sharing services?

2. How successful do you think a bike-sharing service would be in your city? Why or why not?

3. How should cities decide which infrastructure project, in which neighborhoods, should be fixed first?

4. To what extent should cities subsidize public transit systems?

5. Is subsidizing public transit systems enhancing equity in your community? Why or why not?

REFERENCES

American Society of Civil Engineers. 2013. *2013 Report Card for America's Infrastructure*. Accessed on November 30, 2015 from www.infrastructurereportcard.org/

American Water Works Association. 2014. *2014 Water Shortage Preparedness Survey Results*. Accessed on December 20, 2015 from www.awwa.org/Portals/0/files/resources/water%20knowledge/rc%20drought/2014-AWWA-Water-Shortage-Preparedness-Survey-Results.pdf

American Water Works Association. 2015. *A Typical Water System: From Source to Tap and Back*. Accessed on December 28, 2015 from www.awwa.org/Portals/0/files/resources/water%20knowledge/how%20water%20works/ATypicalWaterSystemFromSourcetoTapandBack.pdf

Ammons, David N. 2015. *Municipal Benchmarks: Assessing Local Performance and Establishing Community Standards*, 3rd ed. London: Routledge.

Capital Bikeshare. 2014. *2014 Capital Bikeshare Member Survey Report*. Washington, DC: Capital Bikeshare. Accessed on July 19, 2016 from www.capitalbikeshare.com/assets/pdf/cabi-2014surveyreport.pdf

CBSNews. 2015. "Water Crisis in Flint Declared Public Health Emergency." Accessed on October 2, 2015 from www.cbsnews.com/news/water-crisis-in-flint-michigan-declared-public-health-emergency/

Cervero, Robert. 2004. "Transit-oriented Development in the United States." *Transportation Research Board*.

City of Oxford. 2015. *Public Works Department*. Accessed on November 21, 2015 from www.oxfordms.net/departments/public-works

Coe, Charles K. 2009. *Handbook of Urban Services: A Basic Guide for Local Governments*. Armonk, NY: M. E. Sharpe.

Dodman, David. 2009. "Blaming Cities for Climate Change? An Analysis of Urban Greenhouse Gas Emissions Inventories." *Environment and Urbanization* 21 (1): pp. 185–201.

Egan, Paul. 2016. "Snyder Declares Emergency as Feds Probe Flint Water." *Detroit Free Press*, January 6, 2016. Accessed from www.freep.com/story/news/local/michigan/2016/01/05/us-attorneys-office-investigating-lead-flint-water/78303960/

Flint Water Class Action. 2017. *News*. Accessed on February 8, 2017 from www.flintwaterclassaction.com/news/

Lazarus, Oliver. 2016. "In Flint, Michigan, a Crisis Over Lead Levels in Tap Water." *PRI*, January 7, 2016. Accessed from www.pri.org/stories/2016-01-07/flint-michigan-crisis-over-lead-levels-tap-water

Macaulay, David. 1983. *Underground*. New York: Houghton Mifflin Harcourt.

Martin, Elliot W., and Shaheen, Susan A. 2010. *Greenhouse Gas Emission Impacts of Carsharing in North America*. San Jose: Mineta Transportation Institute, San Jose State University.

McDonald, Robert I. 2015. *Conservation for Cities: How to Plan and Build Natural Infrastructure*. Washington, D.C.: Island Press.

McKenzie, Brian. 2015. *Who Drives to Work? Commuting by Automobile in the United State: 2013*. U.S. Census Bureau.

Muller, Peter O. 2004. "Transportation and Urban Form: Stages in the Spatial Evolution of the American Metropolis." pp. 59–85 in *The Geography of Urban Transportation*. Edited by Susan Hanson and Genevieve Giuliano. New York: Guilford Press.

New York State Department of Transportation. 2012. *Transportation Statistics at a Glance*. Accessed on February 2, 2016 from www.dot.ny.gov/divisions/policy-and-strategy/darb/dai-unit/ttss/repository/Table1_TranspStatsGlance_Update.pdf

Pedestrian and Bicycle Information Center, University of North Carolina Highway Safety Research. 2016. *Who's Walking and Bicycling Face Sheet*. Accessed on July 18, 2016 from www.pedbikeinfo.org/data/factsheet_general.cfm

Shaheen, Susan A., Rodier, Caroline, Murray, Gail, Cohen, Adam, and Martin, Elliot. 2010. *Carsharing and Public Parking Policies: Assessing Benefits, Costs and Best Practices in North America*. San Jose: Mineta Transportation Institute, San Jose State University.

State of Minnesota Department of Employment and Economic Development. 2010. *Economic Impacts of the I-35W Bridge Collapse*. Accessed on November 30, 2015 from www.dot.state.mn.us/i35wbridge/rebuild/pdfs/economic-impacts-from-deed.pdf

ThinkReliability. Undated. *Root Cause Analysis of the I-35 Bridge Collapse*. Accessed on November 30, 2015 from www.thinkreliability.com/cm-I35.aspx

Transportation Sustainability Research Center. 2016. *Carsharing*. Transportation Sustainability Research Center, University of California, Berkeley. Accessed on July 13, 2016 from http://tsrc.berkeley.edu/carsharing

Tumlin, Jeffrey. 2012. *Sustainable Transportation Planning: Tools for Creating Vibrant, Healthy and Resilient Communities*. New York: John Wiley and Sons.

U.S. Environmental Protection Agency. 2016. *Advancing Sustainable Materials Management: Facts and Figures*. Accessed on January 25, 2016 from www.epa.gov/smm/advancing-sustainable-materials-management-facts-and-figures#Materials

U.S. Federal Highway Administration, U.S. Department of Transportation. 2010. *2010 Status of the Nation's Highways, Bridges, and Transit: Conditions and Performance: Report to Congress*. Accessed on January 29, 2016 from www.fhwa.dot.gov/policy/2010cpr/pdfs.cfm

U.S. National Highway Traffic Safety Administration, U.S. Department of Transportation. 2012. *2012 National Survey of Bicyclist and Pedestrian Attitudes and Behavior*. Washington, DC: U.S. Department of Transportation.

Housing and Community/ Economic Development

This chapter covers housing, a basic human need, and community/economic development. These topics are all about neighborhoods and physical surroundings plus having adequate jobs and a good enough economy for families to be able to live. The NASPAA Urban Administration standard on core services and functions covers the importance of learning about this area as well as others in this section.

HOUSING

Adequate housing is a central, basic human need in cities and elsewhere, and the lack of adequate housing is one of the most critical problems in cities today. Paying for housing takes up such a large part of any family's budget that policies keeping anyone from getting housing have wide-ranging impacts, including keeping them from advancing economically and educationally (Eggers and Moumen 2013).

In general, the housing problem in the United States is one of cost, not one of poor physical quality (Hays 2012); a sample taken by the U.S. Census Bureau showed that, in 2009, only 1.7 percent of American housing units were severely inadequate (U.S. Census Bureau 2015). For many years, the federal government has supported a benchmark that, to be affordable, an individual household should not be paying any more than 30 percent of its income for housing costs. Still, the proportion of households that exceed this level has been increasing (from 26.2 percent in 1997 to 33.2 percent in 2007) (Hays 2012), with most believing this is an income rather than housing problem (Hays 2012) since housing costs have risen more than household incomes have risen. Most housing in the United States today is owner-occupied (57 percent) rather than rental (30.3 percent), but renters have a higher burden than owners due to renters' lower income. Also, African-American and Latino households have higher housing cost burdens, also due to their lower income.

Federal Housing Programs

The Housing Act of 1949 set out a goal to "provide a decent home and living environment for every American family"; this goal, yet to be achieved, has been periodically restated in legislation ever since. The federal government began to try to assist Americans with housing during the Great Depression. Over time, the feds have intervened in the quantity or quality of housing produced, in the cost of housing programs, and through regulating equity in housing. They have accomplished this by building new housing, helping the private sector build housing through incentives and subsidies, building and operating public housing, providing insurance to back up mortgages, and providing supplements to renters (Hays 2012).

The federal government has never built enough or helped to build enough new housing units to meet the actual demand for housing. Authorization for more units has been consistently given, but adequate funds to produce the housing have never been appropriated by the Congress. The importance of interest groups in the housing area cannot be overstated. Over the years, realtors and homebuilders have been active lobbyists and major influences upon federal housing policy. Realtors tended to support subsidy programs, which families could use to rent housing, while, of course, the homebuilders supported programs that directly increased the supply of new housing through building or subsidies.

Today's major federal housing programs falling into one or more of these categories are the FHA's Section 235 and 236 programs, public housing, Section 8 housing vouchers, and HOPE VI. They also include the Federal National Mortgage Association (FNMA, or "Fannie Mae") and Government National Mortgage Association ("Ginnie Mae"), which help those who need mortgage assistance to buy housing. The Section 235 program was originally part of the Housing Act of 1968 and was intended to provide federal subsidies to moderate-income individuals so they could pay mortgages on their homes. Section 236 of the Housing Act of 1968, on the other hand, attempted to encourage the building of rental housing.

Public housing programs, apartment units built and managed by government housing authorities for low-income individuals, began in 1937. Throughout its history, public housing has been plagued by NIMBYism (Not In My BackYard) politics over where the housing units should be located, who should be living in them, how much they should cost, and how they should be designed and administered (Hays 2012). For programs to be designed effectively, it would be better for low-income families to have housing dispersed through other neighborhoods; however, neighborhood groups and realtor associations loudly complained and won these arguments, and public housing units were placed in low-income areas. Given that these neighborhoods were typically in central cities, early public housing projects were typically high rises, or "vertical ghettos," and were already in so-called slum areas. This had the result of stigmatizing residents and furthering problems of crime and poor housing. Later public housing project designers learned from these mistakes and built human scale, low-rise projects complete with so-called private space with room for playgrounds, gardens, and community activities.

Today, more than 1.2 million households live in public housing projects (U.S. Department of Housing and Urban Development 2016a). Rules include income limits to determine who can live in units. Rent is determined by a formula, including 30 percent of monthly adjusted income or 10 percent of monthly income or welfare rent.

However, federal efforts since 1993 have been moving away from just public housing to new programs, like HOPE VI, or the Urban Revitalization Demonstration (URD). This program tries to encourage Public Housing Authorities (PHAs) to work with private companies to create mixed income affordable housing with mixed public-private funding. There has been no new funding for this strategy to decentralize public housing away from poor areas, HOPE VI, since 2010 (U.S. Department of Housing and Urban Development 2016b).

Another effort to decentralize the poor away from poor areas has been offering housing allowances or vouchers, largely the Section 8 vouchers, now called Housing Choice Vouchers, which have continued the earlier concept of housing allowances. To date, these have replaced both low- and moderate-income subsidy programs. At the beginning of the program in the 1970s, about one-half were for the elderly, and some were for families. Vouchers, or IOUs for a specific amount of money that are fulfilled by local public housing authorities, are used to assist very low-income families, the elderly, and the disabled to afford decent housing in the existing market. These individuals are free to live anywhere they choose as long as the housing meets the Section 8 requirements and the owner agrees to rent under the program. Congress determines the number of Section 8 units given out across the country; it has never been an entitlement program (U.S. Department of Housing and Urban Development 2017c).

Creating affordable housing opportunities in cities is one of today's central challenges for cities. Further, new housing for low- and moderate-income households is hardly ever produced without government assistance of some sort (Hays 2012). According to HUD, "Families who pay more than 30 percent of their income for housing are considered cost burdened and may have difficulty affording necessities such as food, clothing, transportation and medical care. An estimated 12 million renter and homeowner households now pay more than 50 percent of their annual incomes for housing. A family with one full-time worker earning the minimum wage cannot afford the local fair-market rent for a two-bedroom apartment anywhere in the United States" (U.S. Department of Housing and Urban Development 2017a, b).

HUD supports affordable housing through grants to state and local governments in the HOME Investments Partnerships Program (HOME) and the National Housing Trust Fund (HTF). Locally, some cities have their own programs for aiding affordable housing. Some cities have set-aside requirements for all new housing developments; developers have to ensure a certain proportion of the development is affordable. Other cities have directly supported the building of affordable units and set them aside for teachers and other middle-class individuals; some have a lottery program with accompanying classes for new homeowners to learn about the process of home buying.

Community Development

The early federal role in community development was largely urban renewal—the tearing down of slums and the building of new housing and neighborhoods. In the 1960s, Community Action Agencies (CAAs) were funded under the 1964 Economic Opportunity Act to reduce poverty; they were also required to engage citizens in their activities through "maximum feasible participation." These agencies then became the home of a great deal of community organizing. While many of these agencies still exist today and the threads of that participation are still around, forces uncomfortable with the resulting level of citizen power-sharing brought changes to these agencies that significantly changed their structure and effectiveness.

By the early 1970s, the Housing and Community Development Act of 1974 created a block grant out of what had previously been a series of categorical grants and moved away from housing and slum clearance to housing rehabilitation in doing community development. Some of these programs were a balance between housing and economic development. In 1974, block grants from the Community Development Block Grant (CDBG) program emerged from categorical grants: urban renewal, sidewalks, neighborhood facilities, open spaces, water and sewers, and Model Cities. The CDBG block grants, however, were distributed by formula; the formula has changed over the years. With categorical grants, cities had to write grant proposals to develop specific projects in order to receive the funds.

Under the block grant system begun under the Nixon Administration, cities were granted more discretion over how money would be spent. They also received the funds based upon a formula; the formula included factors like extent of poverty, population and population growth, overcrowded housing, and age of housing. The CDBG program emerging from this legislation still exists today. Through it, Entitlement Communities provide grants to large cities and counties "to develop viable communities by providing decent housing, a suitable living environment, and opportunities to expand economic opportunities, principally for low- and moderate-income persons" (U.S. Department of Housing and Urban Development 2017b). Other programs under the CDBG umbrella provide funds to smaller communities. Over a period of three years, at least 70 percent of CDBG funds have to be used for low- and moderate-income individuals.

Housing Discrimination

Early federal housing programs like FHA mortgages routinely discriminated against poor and minority households and neighborhoods, so minority families were kept from housing opportunities provided to other families. Due to the large share of housing costs for a family, this had a disproportionate impact on a family's economic well-being over time (Hays 2012).

Neighborhoods were "red-lined"; redlining means lines drawn around certain neighborhoods indicating they were considered poor lending risks for homeownership. These were generally, but not always, minority neighborhoods, which meant that minorities could not get loans to buy houses if they lived in these particular areas. Red-lining is illegal.

Blockbusting was another means of housing discrimination; it was a strategy of realtors to begin the transition of a neighborhood from white to black by encouraging one African-American family to buy on a block. The belief was that, once one black family bought and stayed, others would follow. Then, white families would become nervous about their housing values and move out, increasing the shift from a white to a black block. Of course, realtors would get lots of business with the entire block tipping over and people moving in then moving out. This was also referred to as racial tipping.

In many cities through the 1970s and beyond, this process took place through gentrification—a more class-based shift in neighborhoods. Gentrification occurs when a block or neighborhood that is working class gains a new business or new neighbor who upgrades their new home or new business. This first new occupant to upgrade is then followed by others who upgrade. Eventually, the character of the entire block or neighborhood changes and is upgraded as the new area becomes trendy. This forces out the original occupants, many of whom are renters, as they can no longer afford to live there; the owners go for the opportunity and money offered by the new group. Thus, the entire area changes, and the old occupants have to seek housing elsewhere.

The Fair Housing Act of 1968 attempted to deal with the racial discrimination in sale and rental of housing in the United States by dealing with the behavior of landlords, realtors, and buyers and sellers themselves, but these tactics still survive today.

Homelessness

While the number of homeless is decreasing slightly (by 2 percent from 2014 to 2015), there were still 564,708 people (roughly 18 people per 10,000 in our population) either sleeping

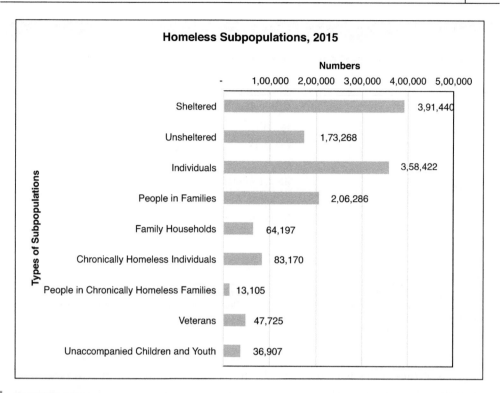

FIGURE 12.1
Homeless Subpopulations, 2015

Source: Based on National Alliance to End Homelessness. 2016. *The State of Homelessness in America 2016.* Accessed on October 14, 2016 from http://endhomelessness.org/wp-content/uploads/2016/10/2016-soh.pdf. p. 7.

outside, in an emergency shelter, or in transitional housing in 2015 (National Alliance to End Homelessness 2016). Figure 12.1 illustrates the numbers in each of the major subgroups of homeless: those who are sheltered, or left unsheltered; individuals, people in families, and family households; chronically homeless individuals or people in chronically homeless families; veterans; and unaccompanied children and youth. At the 2015 snapshot, 69.3 percent of the population were sheltered and 30.7 were unsheltered (National Alliance to End Homelessness 2016, p. 15). An individual or family is counted as chronically homeless if they have a disabling condition, have been continually homeless for one or more years, or have at least four episodes of homelessness in the past three years (National Alliance to End Homelessness 2016, p. 7). Individuals who are not chronically homeless are the largest group, at 48.7 percent, while those in non-chronically homeless families comprise another 34.2 percent of the population.

The numbers of homeless have steadily declined across each of these subgroups since 2007. And, there have been major decreases in the numbers of homeless veterans (35 percent since 2009), people living unsheltered (32 percent since 2007), and the chronic homeless (31 percent since 2007) (National Alliance to End Homelessness 2016, p. 9). This has meant the national rate of homelessness has declined from 21.5 per 10,000 in 2007 to 17.7 in 2015 (National Alliance to End Homelessness 2016, p. 11).

| TABLE 12.1 |

States with Ten Highest Rates of Homelessness, 2015

Ranking	State	Rate Per 10,000
1	Washington, D.C.	110.8
2	Hawaii	53.7
3	New York	44.7
4	Oregon	33.3
5	Massachusetts	31.3
6	Nevada	30.8
7	California	29.8
8	Washington	27.5
9	Alaska	26.5
10	Vermont	24.3

Source: National Alliance to End Homelessness. 2016. *The State of Homelessness in America 2016.* Accessed on October 14, 2016 from www.endhomelessness.org/page/-/files/2016%20State%20of%20Homelessness.pdf, pp. 13–14.

However, these rates vary dramatically from state to state and city to city, and, in some states (Alaska, California, Delaware, Hawaii, Illinois, Maryland, Nevada, New Hampshire, New York, North Dakota, Oregon, Pennsylvania, South Carolina, South Dakota, Washington, and Wyoming), homelessness has actually increased from 2014 to 2015 (National Alliance to End Homelessness 2016, p. 15). Table 12.1 indicates which states have the highest rates of homelessness, providing some indicator of the levels in their cities, since cities have the services and transit needed by individuals who are homeless. All of these states have homeless rates significantly above the national rate of 17.7 per 10,000.

Danger signs point to possible increases in homelessness; the poverty rate has not declined (steady at 15.5 percent), the number of low-income renters paying more than 50 percent of their income in housing has increased, and rents have continued to climb. The number of the poor living with family and friends has increased, which may suggest the increase of alternatives like shelters and transitional housing (National Alliance to End Homelessness 2016, pp. 37, 42). But, the unemployment rate has been declining since the end of the recession, although this varies widely.

Various types of housing assistance exist in cities across the country. Over the time of the homelessness crisis, services shifted away from a focus on purely emergency shelter to longer-term housing. Emergency housing began as the most basic type of service, followed by transitional housing as a step between emergency and permanent housing. Typically accompanying transitional housing were wrap-around services (meaning a wide variety of needed services), counseling, and other types of support for residents. Permanent supportive housing is the next step in services, with housing without time limits combined with services like counseling. The newest type of strategy developed has been rapid re-housing. Under this service model, homeless people are moved to permanent housing within 30 days of seeking services. Early program evaluation results indicate some successes (fewer families returning to homelessness). In addition, evidence suggests that rapid re-housing is

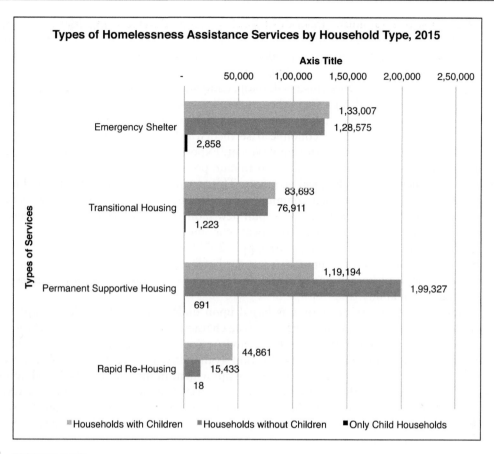

FIGURE 12.2
Types of Homeless Assistance Services, 2015

Source: Based on National Alliance to End Homelessness. 2016. *The State of Homelessness in America 2016.* Accessed on October 14, 2016 from http://endhomelessness.org/wp-content/uploads/2016/10/2016-soh.pdf, p. 52.

less expensive than transitional housing (National Alliance to End Homelessness 2014). Figure 12.2 illustrates the numbers of homeless in each of these types of services on the population count day in 2015.

ECONOMIC DEVELOPMENT

In addition to containing the most people in most of the states, metropolitan areas also house the most economic activity (Berube and Nadeau 2011) in 47 out of the 50 states. The only exceptions are Montana, Vermont, and Wyoming. In four states (Arizona, California, Maryland, and New York), cities create 95 or more percent of the state's gross domestic product.

And why is this? To quote Berube and Nadeau (2011, p. 1), "the most innovative and educated workers in states cluster in metro areas." The majority of scientists and engineers live in cities in 48 states.

According to economists' theories of local economic development, cities grow and thrive economically when they have clusters of successful companies located in their communities that can sell their goods or products outside of the community and bring money into the community. They need a quality, sustainable environment complete with an educated, skilled workforce. Once clusters develop, companies that supply those clusters with goods and services will also locate in the community, and innovation and new industries can develop from ideas generated by people networking and talking together.

According to the popular economic base theory, urban economies are made up of local (non-basic) and export (basic) employment. Export activities come from outside the local community and, so, have a disproportionate positive impact on each city, as their impact multiplies through the local economy. This is why cities try to attract new businesses to come and locate in their community. Local, non-basic employment supports the city, but it is those outside activities that pull new money into the community, add more support to local businesses, and help the local economy grow.

According to Leigh and Blakely (2013, pp. 72–73), sustainable local economic development is "achieved when a community's standard of living can be preserved and increased through a process of human and physical development that is based upon principles of equity and sustainability."

Understanding a city's economy is based upon understanding local demographics, the types of businesses operating in the area, characteristics of the area's workforce, education levels, transportation, tax base, environmental regulation and other regulations on business, utilities, and transportation availability. Box 12.1 provides an overview of the process of examining the types of employment in the community, based upon location quotients from the North American Industrial Classification System (NAICS). Table 12.2 provides a listing of the NAICS codes for major industries in the United States. Table 12.3 provides additional examples of location quotients calculated for other industries in several cities.

BOX 12.1 CALCULATING LOCATION QUOTIENTS FOR CITIES FROM INDUSTRY DATA

The basis of a location quotient is to first start with how large the employment in a given industry is nationwide, compared to total national employment. So a ratio is calculated:

1. In 2012 in the Mining, Quarrying, and Oil and Gas Extraction Industry (NAICS Code 21) nationwide, there were 758,971 employed, out of a total national employment of 121,079,879. The ratio for that is .00627 (or 0.63 percent). This means that only 0.63 percent of the population in the United States is employed in this industry—not even 1 percent.

2. In the Anchorage, Alaska MSA, however, there are 7,388 individuals employed in this particular sector—out of a total of 164,797. The ratio here of 7,388 divided by 164,797 is 0.04483, or 4.5 percent. Comparatively speaking, this is still small, but it is much, much larger than the proportion of the employment in the sector nationwide.

3. Finally, we explicitly compare the two ratios by dividing one by the other: divide the ratio of Mining employment to total employment in Anchorage by the ratio of Mining employment nationwide to total employment nationwide:

(7,388 employed in Anchorage MSA in Mining / 164,797 total employed in Anchorage)
Divided by
(758,971 employed nationwide in Mining / 121,079,879 total employed)
Location Quotient for Anchorage in Mining = 0.04483 / .00627 = 7.15

4. This location quotient is quite high, indicating that the Mining industry is quite important for the Anchorage area. Comparing it to the location quotients for Mining for the Los Angeles MSA (.20732) and Washington, D.C. (.03128) shows how much more important mining is to Anchorage's economy, as opposed to the economies of Los Angeles or Washington, D.C.

A location quotient higher than 1.0 indicates that the employment in that industry in that community is an export, or basic, industry, since the employment there is proportionately higher than in the nation as a whole.

TABLE 12.2

NAICS Codes for Major Categories of American Industries

Sector/NAICS Code	Industry Description
11	Agriculture, Forestry, Fishing and Hunting
21	Mining, Quarrying, and Oil and Gas Extraction
22	Utilities
23	Construction
31–33	Manufacturing
42	Wholesale Trade
44–45	Retail Trade
48–49	Transportation and Warehousing
51	Information
52	Finance and Insurance
53	Real Estate and Rental and Leasing
54	Professional, Scientific, and Technical Services
55	Management of Companies and Enterprises
56	Administrative and Support and Waste Management and Remediation Services
61	Educational Services
62	Health Care and Social Assistance
71	Arts, Entertainment, and Recreation
72	Accommodation and Food Services
81	Other Services (except Public Administration)
92	Public Administration

Source: U.S. Census Bureau. 2012. 2012 NAICS. Accessed on October 25, 2016 from www.census.gov/cgi-bin/sssd/naics/naicsrch?chart=2012.

TABLE 12.3

Example of Calculating Location Quotients for Selected Cities

		U.S. Employment in Industry	Washington, D.C. Employment in Industry	Washington, D.C. Location Quotient (Ratio of Local to National)	Los Angeles Employment in Industry	Los Angeles Location Quotient (Ratio of Local to National)	Anchorage Employment in Industry	Anchorage Location Quotient (Ratio of Local to National)
0	Total Employment	121,079,879	2,545,212		3,932,904		164,797	
11	Agriculture, Forestry, Fishing and Hunting	156,363	479	0.14573	455	0.08959	109	0.512171
21	Mining, Quarrying, and Oil and Gas Extraction	758,971	499	0.03128	5,111	0.20732	7,388	**7.151949**
22	Utilities	637,840	8,801	0.65640	824	0.949157		
23	Construction	5,705,146	142,419	**1.18754**	115,901	0.62543	13,064	**1.682411**
31–33	Manufacturing	11,424,251	47,741	0.19880	353,716	0.95320	2,037	0.131004
42	Wholesale Trade	5,966,747	58,066	0.46295	252,113	**1.30082**	6,696	0.824519
44–45	Retail Trade	15,372,632	273,215	0.84548	411,962	0.82503	18,836	0.90025
48–49	Transportation and Warehousing	4,406,767	54,107	0.58409	159,278	**1.11274**	11,197	**1.866828**
51	Information	3,364,530	104,062	**1.47135**	274,204	**2.50904**	5,140	**1.122435**
52	Finance and Insurance	6,078,713	101,233	0.79224	153,681	0.77834	5,392	0.65172
53	Real Estate and Rental and Leasing	2,021,372	53,501	**1.25911**	82,628	**1.25846**	2,636	0.958124
54	Professional, Scientific, and Technical Services	8,619,574	532,039	**2.93634**	393,437	**1.40523**	15,597	**1.329468**

55	Management of Companies and Enterprises	3,235,958	57,880	0.85089	77,180	0.73428	5,818	**1.320972**
56	Administrative and Support and Waste Management and Remediation Services	10,579,324	8,881	0.03993	334,418	0.97317	13,595	0.944156
61	Educational Services	3,562,364	2,865	0.03826	142,575	**1.23215**	1,672	0.344842
62	Health Care and Social Assistance	18,861,973	15,700	0.03960	510,223	0.83278	28,252	**1.100487**
71	Arts, Entertainment, and Recreation	2,170,121	2,056	0.04507	88,018	**1.24867**	3,150	**1.066472**
72	Accommodation and Food Services	12,791,928	12,644	0.04702	401,743	0.96688	17,369	0.997612
81	Other Services (except Public Administration)	5,347,121	16,500	0.14680	160,327	0.92309	6,001	0.824568

Source: Data used from U.S. Census Bureau. 2012. 2012 NAICS. Accessed on October 25, 2016 from www.census.gov/cgi-bin/sssd/naics/naicsrch?chart=2012.

Note: Numbers in larger font and bolded represent basic industries for the city in question.

For example, a city like Birmingham, Alabama had steel as its source of export employment until the 1960s, when those steel industries dried up. Today, Birmingham has successfully recreated itself into a thriving economy based upon health and high-tech employment. People and money come into the community, no longer to buy steel, but to seek medical care and education.

There can be many goals for a city's economic development strategy. Leigh and Blakely (2013) identify four possibilities:

1. Provide jobs for residents;
2. Ensure the stability of the local economy;
3. Work to create a diverse economy, with a wide variety of types of industries and companies; and
4. Build a sustainable community.

Ensuring diversity among the economic base of a community is particularly important, as few events can destabilize a city like losing a large industry or military base, upon which the community is dependent. Overreliance upon one company or industry can be dangerous, as cities like Birmingham (steel) and Las Vegas (entertainment) have found out in the past. Ensuring sustainability in a community's economy means relying upon multiple export industries, not just one, and the use of a variety of economic development strategies.

Economic Development Strategies

Economic development strategies fall into one of several categories: business attraction, business development, job training and development, site development, community development, and specific project development.

BOX 12.2 CAREER PATHWAYS IN HOMELESSNESS SERVICES

Current Position

Coordinated Entry System Manager in a large city's Department of Homelessness

Education

B.A., Politics
M.P.A.

Career Pathway

Marie started in the field working at a small advocacy and technical assistance firm as an intern, then was hired on there as an entry-level employee in undergrad. In that role she did writing, research, and support for projects led by others. She then worked for six years at a community-based agency providing housing, services, and shelter to homeless and formerly homeless families. She started there as a Case Manager assisting families with their needs, served in a variety of roles, and finished her work there as the organization-wide Data System Manager. In her final role there, she supervised a team of ten and managed a budget of about $2 million.

Then, she moved to local government, again working as an analyst on homelessness. She wrote grants and facilitated a competitive process for $35 million per year in federal funds, facilitated public meetings on issues related to homelessness, and led a local team working with the federal government to end veteran homelessness. In the portion of her role dedicated to homeless veterans, she managed contractual relationships with a variety of nonprofit agencies totaling $5 million.

Her current role (begun in July 2016) is a new position on the management team of her city's new Department of Homelessness. She is responsible for implementing a new data system and reforming all of its service programs to improve coordination. To do this, she supervises a team of seven civil service employees who manage contracts with nonprofit agencies and for-profit technology companies.

Learning about the Job

Marie began learning about the field of homelessness and housing during an excellent internship at a nonprofit firm that focused on grant writing and technical assistance in the homeless and housing field. Since then, she has received a critical grounding in the experience of homeless people from providing direct services as a Case Manager and later serving as a Program Manager at a community-based agency responding to homelessness.

Later, as an analyst and, now, as a manager, she keeps current on the latest developments in the field at conferences, in conversation with her colleagues locally and in other jurisdictions, and from newsletters disseminated by the National Alliance to End Homelessness (national advocacy and professional services firm) and the U.S. Interagency Council on Homelessness (a federal convening group on homelessness).

Finding Her Way to the Homelessness Field

Homelessness has always been Marie's passion. She became interested in the systemic response to homelessness as a young volunteer in high school and college. While she wondered about being a public interest lawyer or social worker earlier in her career, she settled on the community development aspect of the response to homelessness. She learned that the questions on which she wanted to work were not legal or personal; they had to do with the priorities and systems that address homelessness.

A Typical Day

As she is helping to develop the norms and culture of a new city department, she divides her time between her team, working with colleagues from other city agencies, working with other managers and leaders in her agency, working with the individuals she supervises, and working with nonprofit partners and for-profit vendors.

Her work centers on system development and change management within the agency and its network of partner nonprofits. She writes and edits guidance documents, gives presentations, and spends a tremendous amount of time hiring and training new staff—mostly new senior analysts who will work closely with her on the rollout of their new systems. As her department moves from pre-implementation planning and hiring up to implementation, she will be more outward-facing in her daily tasks. However, for now, daily tasks vary a lot.

Networks and Professional Associations

Marie works a great deal with the National Alliance to End Homelessness; she has been recognized for her work by the National Coalition for Homeless Veterans.

She networks with local colleagues extensively and does her best to think carefully about maintaining strong working and professional relationships as her work responsibilities evolve. Her best friends to this day are the folks she worked with in her first full-time job in the field and whom she continues to see.

She also networks at conferences and among interagency groups. She makes a habit of saying yes to opportunities to give presentations at conferences and other gatherings; this provides lots of networking opportunities.

Most Helpful to Her Career

A career working with homelessness can be stressful; there are many competing priorities, the topic can be controversial, and the work exposes staff to many big injustices, especially related to economic justice and racial justice. It has been critical for Marie to have a strong support system of friends and family and to balance and prioritize self-care.

Challenges

Much of the work around homelessness is bound up in the politics of scarcity; it can be challenging to be creative and highly motivated when concerns about scarcity frame the work and the attitude of stakeholders and potential partners.

Overcoming These Challenges

Expertise in group facilitation and gathering new perspectives are very important. Marie has also found that working with executive leaders who are bold and frank is tremendously important—as they clear a path for their team to be successful. Often, people will move off fixation with scarcity and change to a problem-solving perspective when reminded of a larger advocacy need. Finding a way to praise and give personal compliments to difficult stakeholders is also a valuable strategy to help people think more creatively and help people listen to new ideas.

Most Rewarding Part of the Job

Marie says, "The problem-solving approach and the diverse wisdom of the stakeholders in the field of homelessness never ceases to amaze me. Homelessness is a complex issue caused by racism, poverty, injustice at the systems level and experienced by a very vulnerable population. I am fortunate to be part of a group of professionals locally, and nationally that takes a problem-solving approach, embraces the complexity and seeks solutions. This is a field with a tremendous diversity of professional skill sets, from social work and clinical psychology to economics and business administration—that diversity can make decision making and agenda setting complex, but it is also part of the wisdom that creates flexible and effective solutions."

Recommendations for Students

The best advice that Marie says she ever received was from a former mayor, who said, "I have never interviewed anyone for a job who did not already agree with your passions. Stop telling me what you care about and tell me what you can do. When I was mayor, I needed to lead the police force and a fire department, I needed to make a plan for disaster management, I needed to build housing, and I needed to communicate with the citizens of the community about all of my work. What I needed then was people who can do something, and what I was looking for in hiring was people who could tell me what they can do." In the hiring she has done in her career so far, she has seen this happen—smart people in an interview telling her what interested them, when she was trying to figure out what they could do to help homeless people. So figure out what you can do to help the agency, and describe that.

Many cities, along with their community partners like the local chamber of commerce, seek to attract businesses to move to their community. To do this, they often use combinations of their own tax incentives along with incentives that might be provided by their individual states. City leaders might bring company leaders to their community to show them around and attempt to convince them of their supportive business atmosphere, as well. These efforts from cities often turn quite competitive, with cities working against each other to attract businesses, manufacturing facilities, or warehouses. One vehicle used by cities to attract new businesses is tax increment financing, in which a district is created around the new business; any increase in taxes obtained from that district is reasoned to come from the new business and would be used specifically to pay off the bonds or whatever other means of financing had funded the project (Zimbalist 2013).

Cities' competitive efforts often become very public, as when one city is attempting to lure a sports team from its current home in another city. Prominent examples in National Football League (NFL) football are the Colts moving from Baltimore to Indianapolis, the Rams moving from Los Angeles to St. Louis, and the San Francisco 49ers moving from a stadium in San Francisco to one nearby in Santa Clara (still retaining their name). A very recent example is the Raiders moving from Oakland to Los Angeles, back to Oakland—and, now (Fall 2016), supposedly moving to Las Vegas with the Nevada State Legislature and Las Vegas officials putting together a package to lure them to that state.

In fact, so many cities have believed that sports teams are the way to successful economic development that only 3 of the then (2012) 31 NFL stadiums did not use public money for their construction and development. Moreover, two of those three later did use public money to further develop the stadium or surrounding area. Garofalo and Waldron (2012) report that only MetLife Stadium, shared by both the New York Giants and the New York Jets, received no public money (Garofalo and Waldron 2012).

Often, cities will try to attract these teams or appeal to the governing bodies of other sports for an expansion team by putting public funds into building new sports arenas. The story of the Phoenix Coyotes, an ice hockey team that located itself in Glendale, Arizona, a suburb of Phoenix, is a cautionary tale. Glendale built an arena for the team, and the city council also agreed to give the Coyotes owner $15 million each year for more than 20 years, even while the city was in the midst of a financial crisis. The City believed the team would bring in new money from outside Glendale, but all it ended up receiving was $2.2 million per year from rent, ticket surcharges, sales taxes, and other sources (Garofalo and Waldron 2012).

In fact, most sports economists believe that sports stadiums are not effective economic development tools because they do not have a positive impact on income, employment, or tax collections in the local economy (Coates 2015; Coates and Humphreys 1999). One of the main reasons is that, by definition, sports seasons are not long, so the facility frequently is empty most of the year; even when the plan is to bring in outside entertainment, this rarely works except for a very few venues like the Staples Center in Los Angeles. Another reason is that much of the revenue that does come from the arenas is not from the outside (not export, or basic, revenue); it is still from locals (Garofalo and Waldron 2012). Other reasons are that households' entertainment budgets for sports events often substitute for other kinds of entertainment—it is not new money. Also, not all of a sports team's revenues are spent within the confines and boundaries of the city with the arena, so the city spending funds (and often creating a funding gap for itself) does not reap all the benefits of the arena (Zimbalist 2013).

There are some exceptions to the general finding that sports arenas are often not successful. Columbus, Ohio's Arena District is one considered successful. It is not just an arena; developers there created an entire mixed use arena district, complete with office space, housing, pedestrian retail, hotels, restaurants, and other entertainment—in addition to the arena for a hockey (Columbus Blue Jackets) and AAA level baseball team, the

Columbus Clippers (affiliated with the Cleveland Indians). They believed the combination of this wide variety of activities created a critical mass of activities and, so, is attracting 2.75 million visitors each year. Because the district is connected to the city's central business district (CBD), the CBD has also been revitalized (Kirk 2015). Developers of the Columbus project believe that, to be successful, these projects need some upfront public funding (Pennington-Cross 2015).

BOX 12.3 HOUSING AND ECONOMIC DEVELOPMENT STRATEGIES FROM CITY SUSTAINABILITY PLANS

Housing

- "Increase the amount of housing for families in serious need (defined by those who make less than 40% of the median income and pay more than 40% of their income for rent)." Grand Rapids, Michigan, p. 7.
- "Increase the number of participants in the owner-occupied Housing Rehabilitation Program." Longmont, Colorado, p. 6.
- "Increase the amount of dedicated funding to the Affordable Housing Fund to $1 million per year." Longmont, Colorado, p. 6.

Economic Development

- "Expand beyond traditional business sectors by fostering opportunities for investment in alternative energy, marine sciences, and environmental research." Virginia Beach, Virginia, p. 61.
- "Continue to grow VA Beach into the most livable city in America to attract the best and brightest workforce." Virginia Beach, Virginia, p. 65.
- "Help businesses reduce operating costs through pollution prevention, energy efficiency, or other sustainability related activities." Longmont, Colorado, p. 6.
- "Increase number of green/clean tech industries." Longmont, Colorado, p. 6.

- "Increase number of recognized sustainable businesses beyond . . . current." Longmont, Colorado, p. 6.
- "Expand business opportunities for minority-owned and disadvantaged businesses." Longmont, Colorado, p. 6.
- "Create incentives for development of socially responsible B-corporations by June 30, 2021." Grand Rapids, Michigan, p. 6
- "Ensure that 80% of jobs created or retained with incentives will be permanent, full-time employment with benefits annually." Grand Rapids, Michigan, p. 6.
- "Increase private business investment by $500 million between July 1, 2017 and June 30, 2021." Grand Rapids, Michigan, p. 6.
- "Ensure that SmartZone continues to cultivate innovation and entrepreneurship progress in biotech, health services, and other knowledge-based industries through contracts with Start Garden and other service providers by June 30, 2021." Grand Rapids, Michigan, p. 6.
- "Enhance traditional business retention, expansion and attraction activities to work with individual businesses of a range of sizes and types to increase overall economic environmental and human health, and social responsibility of business enterprises." Dover, New Hampshire, p. 3.
- "Strengthen and diversify local economies by developing localized networks for

economic exchange and increase the total number and market share of locally owned, socio-culturally diverse and neighborhood- and community-based businesses." Dover, New Hampshire, p. 3.

- "Grow our ecotourism potential by developing, marketing, and investing to enhance our existing natural resources." Virginia Beach, Virginia, p. 43.
- "Transform our hospitality and restaurant industry into a nationwide leader in sustainable practices." Virginia Beach, Virginia, p. 43.
- "Pursue public-private partnerships that can broaden the array of facilities and attractions." Virginia Beach, Virginia, p. 43.

Agriculture and Farming

- "Increase percent of fresh, local, organic produce served at city facilities to 14% of total." Santa Monica, California, p. 11.
- "Increase percent of fresh, local, organic produce served at community institutions." Santa Monica, California, p. 11.
- "100% of City food purchases should comply with Santa Monica Sustainable Food Commitment." Santa Monica, California, p. 9.
- "Pursue an annual increase in total sales of Farmers' Markets." Santa Monica, California, p. 9.
- "Pursue an annual increase in percent organic of Farmers' Markets." Santa Monica, California, p. 9.
- "Pursue an annual increase in percent low chemical of Farmers' Markets." Santa Monica, California, p. 11.
- "Strengthen local and regional food systems and support and encourage an economically viable, environmentally sound and socially equitable system." Dover, New Hampshire, p. 3.
- "Support our local fishing community and promote the sale and consumption of local harvested sustainable seafood." Virginia Beach, Virginia, p. 105.

- "Support our local farmers to ensure the preservation of our previous agricultural land and to increase demand for our locally grown crops." Virginia Beach, Virginia, p. 133.

Jobs

- "Expand the partnering of our public schools with technical/vocational training, higher learning institutions and local businesses to coordinate our workforce skills with current and project future job base." Virginia Beach, Virginia, p. 53.
- "Develop a green jobs program for youth." St. Louis, Missouri, p. 120.

Neighborhoods

- "Expand existing neighborhood programs to address neighborhood sustainability by 2017." Longmont, Colorado, p. 6.
- "Increase diversity of neighborhood business districts by ensuring 20 new businesses are established annually." Grand Rapids, Michigan, p. 6.

Sources: City of Dover, New Hampshire. Not Dated. City of Dover Sustainability Goals with Purpose Statements. Accessed on February 22, 2017 from www.dover.nh.gov/Assets/government/city-operations/2document/planning/outreach/sustainabilitygoals.pdf.

City of Grand Rapids, Michigan. 2016. Sustainability Plan FY 2017–2021. Accessed on February 22, 2017 from http://grcity.us/Documents/2016-07-22%20Sustainability%20Plan.pdf.

City of Longmont, Colorado. 2016. Sustainability Plan. November 2016. Accessed on February 22, 2017 from www.longmontcolorado.gov/home/showdocument?id=16700.

City of Santa Monica, California. 2014. Sustainable City Plan: City of Santa Monica. Accessed on February 22, 2017 from www.smgov.net/uploadedFiles/Departments/OSE/Categories/Sustainability/Sustainable-City-Plan.pdf.

City of St. Louis, Missouri. 2013. City of St. Louis Sustainability Plan. Accessed on February 22, 2017 from www.stlouis-mo.gov/government/departments/planning/documents/city-of-st-louis-sustainability-plan.cfm.

City of Virginia Beach, Virginia. 2013. A Community Plan for a Sustainable Future. City of VA Beach Environment and Sustainability Office. March 12, 2013. Accessed on February 22, 2017 from www.vbgov.com/government/offices/eso/sustainability-plan/Documents/vb-sustainability-plan-web.pdf.

Today, other projects are attempting to follow this model, as opposed to the outdated one of a sports arena surrounded by nothing but parking. These include the Ark project in Irvine, Texas, the Banks on Cincinnati's waterfront, and Los Angeles's AEG project surrounding the Staples Center. Financing for these projects often includes tax increment financing, sales tax rebates to businesses locating in the districts, and use of local property tax revenues.

Site and community development strategies are those that utilize existing planning and zoning tools plus other strategies to create the necessary infrastructure to attract businesses and provide for business needs once they are residing in the city. They can include the zoning and planning controls discussed elsewhere in this book, the development of infrastructure for transportation and utilities, and the physical improvement of business districts and commercial areas. Also, many states and the federal government have enterprise and economic zone programs of tax relief or tax incentives to offer businesses operating within certain areas of a city. Community-based nonprofit organizations are also options, as another avenue for efforts to improve community access to jobs, as are affordable housing groups (Leigh and Blakely 2013).

Finally, communities can use funds from the U.S. Department of Housing and Urban Development like the Community Development Block Grant program or other federal funds. Providing funds to communities by a funding formula, the program can fund physical infrastructure development, housing, and neighborhood revitalization projects.

There are even more options available for business development. Many cities have business and technology parks already provided with the infrastructure and amenities needed by a business. Some have created small business development centers or one-stop permitting centers to help businesses more easily comply with laws and regulations. Some also have created micro-financing programs to provide small loans for businesses, or other programs to aid women- and minority-owned businesses.

Job training and development strategies can include customized training, welfare, or school to work programs, targeted placement programs to give certain benefits to employers that employ disadvantaged individuals.

Other cities have attempted to develop specific projects in their communities, in the hope that they will attract business. Many of these projects are convention centers; as is the case for sports stadiums, many city leaders believe that convention centers will bring in business, visitors, and revenues to their areas but are often disappointed with the results. Table 12.4 provides an idea of the number of attendees and exhibitors attending the top ten trade shows in the United States last year, as an illustration of the potential revenue that can be made from conventions. However, there is a great deal of competition between cities for these trade shows and conventions. If all cities built hundreds of thousands of square feet of convention space, they still would not all succeed because there would be too many venues available (Sanders 2014).

Performance measurement for economic development programs is difficult since there are many factors beyond the control of the city. Some measures include the dollar amount of investment created through efforts, the number of new jobs created, and the number of business licenses in the community. Other measures include the growth in appraised value of downtown hotel rooms and office space vacancy rate (Ammons 2015).

TABLE 12.4

Top Ten Trade Shows in the United States, 2015

Rank	Event	Venue	# Exhibitors	# Attendees	Net Square Feet (NSF)
1	International Consumer Electronics Show (CES)	Las Vegas Convention Center, NV, and other venues	3,631	109,507	2,235,936
2	Atlanta International Gift & Home Furnishings Market, July	AmericasMart, Atlanta, GA	2,482	88,023	1,259,967
3	Atlanta International Gift & Home Furnishings Market, January	AmericasMart, Atlanta, GA	2,675	91,134	1,219,440
4	International Construction and Utility Equipment Exposition (ICUEE)	Kentucky Exposition Center, Louisville, KY	972	10,963	1,206,046
5	Specialty Equipment Market Association (SEMA)	Las Vegas Convention Center, NV	2,400	159,700	1,181,000
6	MAGIC Market Week—apparel, accessories	Las Vegas Convention Center, NV, and other hotel convention centers	5,864	74,328	1,159,450
7	International Plastics Showcase	Orange County Convention Center, Orlando, FL	2,023	43,478	1,128,242
8	National Business Aviation Convention (NBAA)	Las Vegas Convention Center, NV, and airport facilities	1,142	27,888	1,080,600
9	America's RV Show	Giant Center, Hershey, PA	197	3,382	1,069,078
10	Florida RV SuperShow	Florida State Fairgrounds, Tampa, FL	337	800	1,018,926

Source: Developed from 2016. 2015 Top 250 U.S. Trade Shows. Trade Show News Network. Retrieved on October 31, 2016 from www.tsnn.com/toplists-us.

CONCLUSIONS

Housing and economic/community development are among the very basic needs of individuals and communities and are covered in NASPAA's Urban Administration standards under core services and functions. In this chapter, we have focused upon federal programs, but states and cities often have their own programs to enhance local efforts in these areas. University-community partnerships also exist in many cities that have developed projects and try out new ideas and innovations. Many more ideas and efforts are needed across the country to try to solve the problems of affordable housing, homelessness, poverty, the need to more jobs, and the sustainability of our communities.

SELECTED WEB RESOURCES

- National Alliance to End Homelessness www.endhomelessness.org/
- National Coalition for Homeless Veterans www.nchv.org/
- U.S. Department of Housing and Urban Development https://hud.gov/
- U.S. Interagency Council on Homelessness www.usich.gov/

EXERCISES AND DISCUSSION QUESTIONS

1. **Know Your City**: Housing, Economics, and Community Development
   - What kind of homelessness program does your selected city provide? What kind of policies and programs are provided?
   - Does your city have public housing projects? Where are they located?
   - How does your city help provide affordable housing to its residents?
   - Does your city have programs to create jobs, or to provide assistance for businesses to locate there? What kind of programs are these?
   - Does your city have a professional or semi-professional sports team? Did it have city assistance in building its stadium?

2. What are the arguments for and against the use of public money to help build sports stadiums in communities?
3. Programs in cities to sweep up homeless people and move them out of very visible areas are quite controversial. What are the pros and cons of these strategies? What else could be done?
4. What are the equity issues with cities providing tax breaks for businesses to relocate from their current cities? Why should cities have these programs, or why should they not participate in those efforts?
5. Should cities with high housing costs spend public funds to help their teachers, police officers, and firefighters live in their communities? Why or why not?

REFERENCES

Ammons, David N. 2015. *Municipal Benchmarks: Assessing Local Performance and Establishing Community Standards*, 3rd ed. London: Routledge.

Berube, Alan and Nadeau, Carey Anne. 2011. *Metropolitan Areas and the Next Economy: A 50-State Analysis. Brookings*. Accessed on October 13 2016 from https://www.brookings.edu/research/metropolitan-areas-and-the-next-economy-a-50-state-analysis/

Coates, Dennis. 2015. *Growth Effects of Sports Franchises, Stadiums, and Arenas: 15 Years Later. Mercatus Center, George Mason University*. Accessed on October 26, 2016 from www.mercatus.org/system/files/Coates-Sports-Franchises.pdf

Coates, Dennis, and Humphreys, B. R. 1999. "The Growth Effects of Sports Franchises, Stadia, and Arenas." *Journal of Policy Analysis and Management* 18 (4): pp. 601–624.

Eggers, Frederick J., and Moumen, Fouad. 2013. *American Housing Survey: Housing Adequacy and Quality as Measured by the AHS*. Washington, DC: U.S. Department of

Housing and Urban Development Office of Policy Development and Research.

Garofalo, Pat, and Waldron, Travis. 2012. "If You Build It, They Might Not Come: The Risky Economics of Sports Stadiums." *The Atlantic*, September 7, 2012.

Hays, R. Allen. 2012. *The Federal Government and Urban Housing*. Albany, NY: SUNY Press.

Kirk, Patricia. 2015. "Making Sports-Oriented Mixed Use Work." *Urban Land*, April 29, 2015.

Leigh, Nancy Green, and Blakely, Edward J. 2013. *Planning and Local Economic Development: Theory and Practice*, 5th ed. Los Angeles: Sage.

National Alliance to End Homelessness. 2014. *Rapid Re-Housing: A History and Core Components*. Accessed on October 18, 2016 from www.endhomelessness.org/library/entry/rapid-re-housing-a-history-and-core-components

National Alliance to End Homelessness. 2016. *The State of Homelessness in America 2016*. Accessed on October 14, 2016 from http://endhomelessness.org/wp-content/uploads/2016/10/2016-soh.pdf

Pennington-Cross, Anthony. 2015. *Cities, Sports Arenas, and Redevelopment: The Case of Milwaukee and the Arena District Redevelopment Plan*. Accessed on October 26, 2016 from www.thewheelerreport.com/wheeler_docs/files/0601mmacpaper.pdf

Sanders, Heywood T. 2014. *Convention Center Follies: Politics, Power, and Public Investment in American Cities*. Philadelphia: University of Pennsylvania Press.

U.S. Census Bureau. 2015. *2013 Housing Profile: United States*. U.S. Census Bureau. May 2015.

U.S. Department of Housing and Urban Development. 2016a. *About HOPE VI*. Accessed on October 14, 2016 from http://portal.hud.gov/hudportal/HUD?src=/program_offices/public_indian_housing/programs/ph/hope6/about

U.S. Department of Housing and Urban Development. 2016b. *HUD's Public Housing Program*. Accessed on October 14, 2016 from http://portal.hud.gov/hudportal/HUD?src=/topics/rental_assistance/phprog

U.S. Department of Housing and Urban Development. 2017a. *Affordable Housing*. Accessed on January 30, 2017 from https://portal.hud.gov/hudportal/HUD?src=/program_offices/comm_planning/affordablehousing/

U.S. Department of Housing and Urban Development. 2017b. *Housing Choice Vouchers Fact Sheet*. Accessed on January 24, 2017 from https://portal.hud.gov/hudportal/HUD?src=/topics/housing_choice_voucher_program_section_8

U.S. Department of Housing and Urban Development. 2017c. *Community Development Block Grant Program- CDBG*. HUD.gov. Accessed on January 24, 2017 from https://portal.hud.gov/hudportal/HUD?src=/program_offices/comm_planning/communitydevelopment/programs

Zimbalist, Andrew. 2013. "Sports Facilities and Economic Development." *Government Finance Review*. Government Finance Officers Association: August 2013, pp. 94–96.

Parks, Recreation, and Libraries

One more core function and set of services covered by NASPAA's Urban Administration standards, parks, recreation, and libraries, contribute to the public's health, education, and quality of life within cities. Services in these areas have all expanded and changed enormously recently, and all make a difference in the quality of any given city.

PARKS

Parks have been enhancing the quality of life in cities in the United States since some of the very earliest cities were established. The Boston Common (Boston, Massachusetts) was established in 1634; Newark, New Jersey had two parks created in the 1660s; Philadelphia and its four squares were established in 1682; and Battery Park and City Hall Park in New York City were developed in 1691 (The Trust for Public Land 2016, Table 14, p. 29).

Parks are part of many city dwellers' and city visitors' daily lives. Estimates are that New York City's Central Park has 42 million visitors every year, Washington D.C.'s National Mall and Memorial Parks have close to 30 million, Chicago's Lincoln Park has 20 million, and San Diego's Mission Bay Park has 16.6 million visitors (The Trust for Public Land 2016, Table 15, p. 30).

Park usage is positively linked to improved health outcomes, reduced stress, and better social integration. Parks provide not just individual-level benefits but also environmental benefits for the community at large. Trees filter air pollutants, they cool increasingly hot city neighborhoods and store water, and thereby assist stormwater drainage systems (Ussery, Yngve, Whitfield, Foster, Wendel and Boehmer 2016).

Figure 13.1 shows one example of the organizational structure of a small city's parks and recreation department—that of Clayton, Missouri, a suburb of St. Louis. This figure illustrates very well the different components of what a parks and recreation department does—the department is separated into Parks and Recreation, two separate areas, with administration personnel supporting both. The Parks component includes a Horticulturist and Field Technicians and other workers who take care of the plants and grass within the parks in the city. The Recreation side contains personnel to oversee the pools, fitness facilities, and athletics programs and facilities. Also included are a Museum and

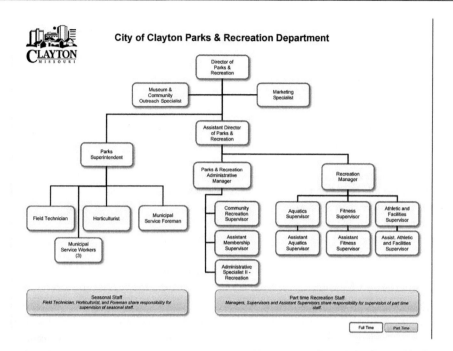

FIGURE 13.1
Organizational Chart of Clayton, Missouri Parks and Recreation Department

Source: Parks and Recreation Department, City of Clayton, MO. 2016. Organizational Chart. Accessed on September 13, 2016 from http://www.claytonmo.gov/Assets/Parks+And+Recreation/PDF+Files/Parks+and+Rec+Org+Chart.pdf.

Community Outreach Specialist and a Marketing Specialist to ensure the public knows about the activities and facilities sponsored by the city. The chart also indicates the existence of seasonal staff to help take care of parks during peak times like the summers, and part-time recreation staff, who might work on summer camps or supervise pools during extra summer hours.

Box 13.1 containing the vision and mission statement for the Parks and Recreation Department of the City of Trenton, Michigan further explains the functions of these departments—providing parks, open space, and recreation programs that enhance residents' lives.

BOX 13.1 CITY OF TRENTON, MICHIGAN PARKS AND RECREATION VISION AND MISSION STATEMENT

Parks and Recreation Vision and Mission

Parks and Recreation Vision Statement

We Create Community through People, Parks and Programs' articulates the vision of Trenton Parks & Recreation Department. Through parks and recreation services, we take an active role in creating community through people; our staff and volunteers who make connections with our residents to improve lives. It is this person-to-person contact that relieves the loneliness of senior citizens, reduces the stress and isolation of working adults and inspires and teaches youth to become productive community members. Through our parks, open space and facilities, we provide relief from urban development, preserve the environment and provide opportunities for recreation through facilities to meet the needs of the community. Our programs and services produce specific benefits for our residents, as well as, being an important means of connecting with residents.

Our vision is therefore based on the belief that through high-quality recreation programs, facilities and people, an economically vibrant and dynamic community are created and enhanced.

Parks and Recreation Mission

The mission or 'business' of the department is to provide all citizens of Trenton the highest level of programs, facilities, and services that will positively affect our vision of creating community. To effectively 'Create Community through People, Parks and Programs' we have broken the Department mission into specific areas. These areas are designed to provide our department staff with direction and guidance for developing and evaluating programs,

facilities, and services. These mission areas include:

- Provide Diversified Recreational and Educational Experiences
- Foster Human Development
- Promote Health and Wellness
- Strengthen Community Image and Sense of Place
- Efficiently utilize resources and demonstrate fiscal responsibility
- Develop and Cultivate Partnerships
- Support Economic Development
- Protect environmental resources
- Develop and empower staff
- Increase cultural unity
- Be good stewards of public resources

By taking a customer-driven, outcome oriented and collaborative approach, the Department will continue to play a critical role in maintaining and improving the quality of life for our residents.

Source: City of Trenton, Michigan Parks, and Recreation Department. Vision and Mission Statement. Downloaded from www.trentonmi.org/index-Page.asp?Page_ID=13&SubPage_ID=54 on September 14, 2016.

Access

Access to parks is a function of safety, quality, and amenities plus proximity; people are more likely to use parks to exercise if they are nearby. The question of whether parks, libraries, and other amenities are equitably sited in cities, so they can be used by everyone, is an old one (Levy, Meltsner and Wildavsky 1975).

Access to parks and recreation facilities varies widely across cities; the median for all cities is 8.8 percent of total acreage devoted to parkland. Table 13.1 reports on how widely the number of acres and parkland's percent of total city acreage varies in just high-density cities. Washington, D.C. has the most acreage devoted to parkland at 21.9 percent of its total land area. Arlington, Virginia is 10th on the list with 11.2 percent of its total acreage. Among low-density cities, Anchorage, Alaska has the most acreage devoted to parkland, at 84.2 percent of its more than one million acres; Anchorage also is first for the highest total acreage (914,121 acres) devoted to parkland. In fact, the Chugach National Forest is partly within the boundaries of the City of Anchorage. Of high-density cities, Oakland, California has the highest number of park acres per 1,000 city residents (14.7 acres). Anchorage, on the other hand, has 3,036.8 acres per

TABLE 13.1		
Ten High-Density Cities with Largest Percent Parkland		
City	Parkland (Acres)	Percent Parkland
Washington, D.C.	8,525 Acres	21.9% of total city area
New York, NY	39,615	21.1
San Francisco, CA	5,693	19.1
Oakland, CA	6,063	18.3
Jersey City, NJ	1,660	17.9
Boston, MA	4,956	17.0
Los Angeles, CA	38,822	13.2
Philadelphia, PA	10,830	13.1
Seattle, WA	6,590	12.5
Arlington, VA	1,786	11.2

Source: Based upon The Trust for Public Land. 2016. 2016 City Park Facts. Available at www.tpl.org/sites/default/files/2016%20City%20Park%20Facts_0.pdf, page 9.

1,000 residents. The median for all cities is 13.1 acres per resident (The Trust for Public Land 2016).

Parkland is separated into two categories—designed parkland (like playgrounds) and natural parkland (natural forests or meadows). Only 0.26 percent of Anchorage, Alaska's parkland is designed parkland—the other 911,721 acres are all natural parkland. At the other extreme, Hialeah, Florida; Newark, New Jersey; and Richmond, California each has zero natural parklands as part of their parks (The Trust for Public Lands 2016).

The U.S. Centers for Disease Control (CDC) developed the National Environmental Public Health Tracking Network Access to Parks Indicator (API); this is measured as the number of residents living within one-half mile around a park boundary. The population within a park buffer was then measured at the census block level for each census block; the population within each park buffer was aggregated to the county level, and then the proportion of each county's population living within the half-mile buffer of a park was calculated. Based on these calculations, the CDC estimates that 39.2 percent of the U.S. population lives within one-half mile of a park. For cities, the proportion increases to 43.4 percent. Larger cities have more access; 48.7 percent of citizens in cities with more than one million residents are in the buffer zone, while only 27.3 percent have that level of access in much smaller cities (less than 250,000) (Ussery, Yngve, Whitfield, Foster, Wendel and Boehmer 2016).

There are also differences in access by race and ethnicity (Table 13.2). However, it is important to note that the researchers cannot tell if these differences have statistical significance due to complications with the GIS analysis.

The researchers also note extreme differences by state. Hawaii and the District of Columbia have very high levels of access (67 and 88 percent, respectively), but others in the South and Appalachia (West Virginia at 9 percent, Louisiana at 11 percent) have comparatively very low levels.

TABLE 13.2

Ethnic and Racial Differences in Access to Parks, 2010

	Percent of Population within One-Half Mile of a Park
Non-Hispanic White	39.2%
Hispanic	49.4
Non-Hispanic Black	44.5
Non-Hispanic Other	52.0
Non-Hispanic Multi-Race	45.3

Source: Ussery et al. 2016. Based upon Table 1: Number and Percentage of U.S. Population Living within a Half-Mile of a Park, by Race/Ethnicity and by Rural/Urban Status; United States; 2010.

Parkifying Cities

In today's cities, parks are not just those that have been developed by the city itself; planners, designers, and architects are working to make urban spaces more park-like—more open and welcoming to residents. One way to accomplish that goal is to make cities walkable—or to reclaim parts of a city that were once walkable. To be considered walkable, an area needs to have useful features, be safe and comfortable, and be interesting to pedestrians. The extent to which a portion of a city is walkable is the extent to which these conditions are met. Features like shade, restaurants, public spaces, shops, and interesting environments like a mixed use environment, complete streets, and pedestrian design elements can help make areas walkable. Walkable cities improve the health of residents, enhance social interactions and recreation, and, in general, improve the quality of life in cities and can reduce the need for transit (Future Cities Laboratory 2016).

Table 13.3 lists the ten cities (among those with more than 300,000 population) with the highest Walk Score, as scored by a proprietary scoring system from Walk Score

TABLE 13.3

Ten Most Walkable Cities (among Cities with More than 300,000 Population), 2016 (Walk Score)

Rank	City	Walk Score
1	New York, NY	88.9
2	San Francisco, CA	85.7
3	Boston, MA	80.1
4	Philadelphia, PA	78.3
5	Miami, FL	78.2
6	Chicago, IL	77.5
7	Washington, D.C.	77.0
8	Seattle, WA	72.9
9	Oakland, CA	71.5
10	Long Beach CA	69.0

Source: Musser, Amy. 2016. The Nation's Most-Walkable Cities Got Even More Walkable in 2016. Downloaded on September 20, 2016 from www.redfin.com/blog/2016/04/the-most-walkable-us-cities-of-2016.html.

(Walkscore 2016). It is not a coincidence that these cities are among those most enjoyed by tourists and other visitors. Also of note is that Baltimore dropped out of the top ten in 2016 to be replaced by Long Beach, California; the City of Long Beach has worked hard in redeveloping its downtown, with new and renovated buildings, improved pedestrian lighting, and event programming to bring people to the area. Projects like Long Beach's are underway across the country to create more mixed use residential and commercial areas, renew older areas, and make cities more livable (Musser 2016).

Another new(ish) trend in American cities are parklets, very small parks created from very small spaces, often a single parking space. Initiated by then Mayor Gavin Newsom in San Francisco after he went to a conference and learned of the idea being implemented elsewhere, now cities across the country are implementing them. In San Francisco, business owners or regular citizens can apply to the City to design a parklet. In it, the Pavement to Parks Program is described as "part of the City of San Francisco's overall strategy for creating safe, complete streets and new open space for the public. Complete streets balance the needs of people walking, riding bicycles, taking transit, or moving around in private automobiles. New open spaces created through *Pavement to Parks* are made up of small Parklets and Street Plazas which add to the City's larger City parks and playgrounds" (Pavement to Parks Program, Department of Public Works, City of San Francisco 2016a, p. 2). The City further describes the creation of parklets as intended to "repurpose part of the street next to the sidewalk into a public space for people. These small parks provide amenities like seating, planting, bicycle parking, and art" (Pavement to Parks Program, Department of Public Works, City of San Francisco 2016a, p. 3; Patton 2012).

The goals of the program are to:

1. Encourage safe walking and walkability;
2. Create more social interaction;
3. Recreate the potential of city streets;
4. Encourage alternative means of transit; and
5. Support local businesses.

(Pavement to Parks Program, Department of Public Works, City of San Francisco 2016a, pp. 4–5)

In San Francisco, parklets are funded by businesses or neighborhood associations but become public spaces. By 2015, San Francisco had more than 50 parklets throughout the city. One example of a San Francisco parklet is a mobile parklet (currently inside a public library but seen here in Figure 13.2 outside as the Ocean Avenue Mobile Parklet). This parklet was designed by public high school students working with a community group, the Youth Art Exchange, and was funded by a combination of foundation and city neighborhood investment funds with the neighborhood community benefit district and Youth Art Exchange as its community partners (Pavement to Parks 2016b).

An example of a neighborhood association sponsored parklet is shown in Figure 13.3, the Noe Valley Parklet. This parklet includes landscaping, tables, and chairs and is sponsored and maintained by the Noe Valley Association, a community benefit district.

Another way that cities are creating parks and park-like environments is through the use of biophilic design. Biophilia was defined by biologist E. O. Wilson as "the innately emotional affiliation of human beings to other living organisms. Innate means hereditary and hence part of ultimate human nature" (BiophilicCities.org 2016). Biophilic design means to incorporate living, growing plants into urban design—through gardens, green or living walls, green rooftops, and other deliberate means of incorporating living organisms

FIGURE 13.2
Ocean Avenue Mobile Parklet, San Francisco, California

Source: Youth Art Exchange Accessed on September 20, 2016 from https://youthartexchange.org/seen-in-san-francisco/designbuild/parklet/.

FIGURE 13.3
Noe Valley Parklet, San Francisco, California

Source: Pavement to Parks. 2016. Retrieved on September 20, 2016 from http://pavementtoparks.org/parklets/featured-parklet-projects/noe-valley-parklets/.

in our immediate surroundings. Green or brown roofs are roofs covered with living plants that can be used to reduce air pollution, while green or living walls are covered with plants (groundcovers, ferns, edible plants, or others). Green facades include plants trained to cover areas of a wall, but living or green walls are vertical gardens since they are covered with plant containers and growing media so that plants grow on the wall. Some buildings could have small planted edible or other kinds of gardens. Not only does this provide

FIGURE 13.4
Living Wall at One Bligh Street, Sydney, Australia

Source: Green Roofs Australia. 2016. Living Walls Improving Air Quality. Accessed on September 20, 2016, from https://greenroofsaustralasia.com.au/living-walls-improving-air-quality.

potential benefits for the reduction of air pollution, urban heat, and noise, but the biophilic movement believes that taking care of living things enhances our ability to care for others and fulfills our innate need for nature in our lives.

Cities in other countries, particularly Singapore, but also Australia and in Asia and Europe, have already made progress in greening their cities with biophilic roofs and walls. American cities have not yet progressed far with this strategy, however. Figure 13.4 shows a living wall in Sydney, Australia.

Another way cities are providing parks to residents is through repurposing older spaces previously used in other ways. Probably the most famous is New York City's elevated parkway, called the High Line, developed over years of design and work from unused railway tracks and trestle. The trains themselves ran from 1934 until 1980. Some wanted to demolish the trestle, but local activists fought back. Over years of advocacy work, local groups worked on trying to maintain the trestle as public open space. In 2005, the property was turned over to New York City, and, by 2009, sections began to be opened to the public. A nonprofit group, the Friends of the High Line, raised 98 percent of the budget for the ongoing project. As a previously industrial space, the High Line is now maintained using sustainable practices, mostly with native plants, and as closely as possible to a "wild" state with native grasses and plants throughout. Benches, chairs, semi-enclosed spaces for art and other programs, water features, food carts, open air cafés, and urban "forests" are some of the features found along the parkway (Friends of the High Line 2016). Friends of the High Line also organizes weekly meditation groups, education sessions, and tours as well as special events (art exhibits, cultural events) for all ages.

Atlanta's Beltline project is another project creating public open space out of a former rail line. The idea, creating a greenway with parks and connections to transit opportunities that encircle the city, developed from a Master's student thesis. Even though the project is far from complete, people are already using the completed areas, walking, bicycling, and using them to get to transit (Parksify 2016).

Moreover, then, some cities are making parks out of their city streets. Inspired by the Ciclovia in Bogotá, Columbia; San Francisco; and, now, Berkeley are doing City Streets events. Called Sunday Streets SF in San Francisco, the event involves blocking off one to four miles of city streets and making them car-free for a day. City managers work with community groups, and the atmosphere becomes like a street fair—food vendors, games, and people walking and biking down the streets. The event occurs all over the city—it is not on the same street every time, and, in San Francisco, it occurs eight times a year (Sunday Streets SF 2017). These have become very popular events in both cities. The mission of the event is to:

- Create temporary open space and recreational opportunities in neighborhoods most lacking;
- Encourage physical activity;
- Foster community building; and
- Inspire people to think differently about their streets as public spaces.

(Sunday Streets SF 2017: http://sundaystreetssf.com/about/)

RECREATION

Adequate recreation opportunities for residents are also important in cities. Within cities, it would be the parks and recreation departments that would create and maintain most of those opportunities. The median number of playgrounds per 10,000 residents in a city was 2.3 in 2015, but there were wide variations across cities. Madison, Wisconsin had 7.1 playgrounds per 10,000 residents; Cincinnati, Ohio had 5.1; and Detroit, Michigan had 4.5. However, many large cities had far fewer than the median (Los Angeles had only 1.1, Miami had 1.4, and Honolulu only 1.3).

Recreation and senior citizen centers are important facilities in most cities because community events like classes and community organization meetings can be held there. Chicago, for instance, has 242 recreation and senior centers (1.8 per 20,000 residents). Baton Rouge has 33, but that is 2.9 per 20,000 residents in that much smaller city.

Many other recreation facilities are offered in cities today: baseball diamonds, basketball hoops/courts, soccer fields, tennis courts, off-leash dog parks, skateboard parks, swimming pools, beaches, disc golf courses, nature centers, and community garden plots. Table 13.4 show how frequently these recreation facilities are seen in their most frequent locations. Table 13.5 indicates the cities with the largest number of environmental recreation facilities, like beaches and community garden plots.

Today's cities have many more recreation opportunities to offer than picnicking and swimming in their parks. One reason is the increased number of partnerships with outside groups, like school districts and schools themselves and local nonprofits. Newer features include climbing walls, bike trails, ice rinks, golf courses, mini golf, and water parks.

The nature of the direct connection with local users, including many children, means that recreation units often require certifications for their full-time or part-time employees. Practically 90 percent of all recreation facilities require a CPR/First Aid certification, and 84 percent require background checks. Most cities with swimming pools require lifeguard certifications (59.9 percent), and about a third (35.9 percent) require certifications for aquatic management and pool operations. Other types of possible certificates include personal fitness training, food service, pesticide application, playground safety, child care, grounds management, and climbing (Tipping 2016).

Programming among recreation units varies from city to city, largely dependent upon the number of staff and the type of facilities. However, typical programming includes summer and holiday camps, educational programs, recreational sports leagues, exercise programs, water sports, and sports training. Newer types of programming include mind-body/balance programs (Tipping 2016).

TABLE 13.4

Cities with Largest Per Capita Recreation Facilities (Number/Ratio of Number to 10 or 100 Thousand)

Baseball Diamonds	Basketball Hoops	Tennis Courts	Skateboard Parks	Swimming Pools	Disc Golf Courses
St. Paul, MN (159 / 5.3 per 10,000)	Madison, WI (259 / 10.5 per 10,000)	Richmond, VA (136 / 6.2 per 10,000)	Chula Vista, CA (8 / 3.1 per 100,000)	Cleveland, OH (42 / 10.8 per 100,000)	Tulsa, OK (7 / 1.8 per 100,000)
Minneapolis, MN (195 / 4.8)	Norfolk, VA (203 / 8.3)	Norfolk, VA (143 / 5.8)	Sacramento, CA (13 / 2.7)	Cincinnati, OH (25 / 8.4)	Durham, NC (4 / 1.6)
Pittsburgh, PA (128 / 4.2)	Minneapolis, MN (299 / 7.3)	Winston-Salem, NC (108 / 4.5)	Henderson, NV (7 / 2.5)	Pittsburgh, PA (19 / 6.2)	Charlotte, NC (14 / 1.4)
Cincinnati, OH (121 / 4.1)	Richmond, VA (146 / 6.7)	Omaha, NE (197 / 4.4)	Las Vegas, NV (11 / 1.8)	Washington, D.C. (35 / 5.3)	Lexington, KY (4 / 1.3)
Cleveland, OH (141 / 3.6)	Cleveland, OH (230 / 5.9)	Greensboro, NC (111 / 3.9)	Long Beach, CA (8 / 1.7)	Atlanta, GA (23 / 5.0)	Fort Wayne, IN (3 / 1.2)

Source: Based upon The Trust for Public Land. 2016. 2016 City Park Facts. Available at www.tpl.org/sites/default/files/2016%20City%20Park%20Facts_0.pdf, pp. 26–27.

TABLE 13.5

Cities with Largest Per Capita Environmental Recreation Facilities (Number/Ratio of Number to 10 or 100 Thousand)

Off-Leash Dog Parks	Beaches	Nature Centers	Community Garden Plots
Henderson, NV 15 (5.4 per 100,000)	Madison, WI 12 (4.9 per 100,000)	Cincinnati, OH 6 (2.0 per 100,000)	Portland, OR 2,174 (35.1 per 10,000)
Portland, OR 33 (5.3 per 100,000)	Virginia Beach, VA 14 (3.1 per 100,000)	Fremont, CA 4 (1.7 per 100,000)	Washington, D.C. 2,113 (32.1 per 10,000)
Norfolk, VA 11 (4.5 per 100,000)	Minneapolis, MN 12 (2.9 per 100,000)	Colorado Springs, CO 6 (1.3 per 100,000)	Madison, WI 699 (28.5 per 10,000)
Las Vegas, NV 25 (4.1 per 100,000)	Corpus Christi, TX 7 (2.2 per 100,000)	Arlington, VA 3 (1.3 per 100,000)	Seattle, WA 1,113 (16.7 per 10,000)
Madison, WI 10 (4.1 per 100,000)	St. Petersburg, FL 5 (2.0 per 100,000)	Long Beach, CA 6 (1.3 per 100,000)	San Francisco, CA 1,334 (15.6 per 10,000)

Source: Based upon The Trust for Public Land. 2016. 2016 City Park Facts. Available at www.tpl.org/sites/default/files/2016%20City%20Park%20Facts_0.pdf, page 26–27.

BOX 13.2   CAREER PATHWAYS OF A PARKS AND RECREATION PROFESSIONAL

Current Position

Director of Parks, Beaches, and Recreation in a small city

Education

B.A. in Psychology (psychological services)
Minor in Recreation and Leisure Studies
M.P.A.

Career Pathway

A combination of opportunity, interest, and timing led Martin to the parks and recreation field. Martin first got involved with parks and recreation when he volunteered as an outdoor education camp counselor as a high school senior. This volunteer job led to a paying job as a counselor at a summer camp, followed by another job with its transportation company that brought special needs children to school.

For three summers while he was in college, he worked at his current city's summer recreation program, where he found he enjoyed working with children. It became a great way to earn a part-time living while he was

going to school. He thought that he would eventually work with children, and he settled on Psychology as his undergraduate college major. He then wanted to be a Recreation Major; however, it would have taken him an extra year in school that he did not have— so he instead minored in the field. His final semester of college included an internship with the City's Child Care Division.

However, even those recreation classes in his minor inspired him to apply for, and be accepted to, a Recreation Therapy graduate program. He then had to turn down the grad school offer because he was working two jobs and had a young child. The day after he received his B.A., he began full-time hours with the City's Child Care Division, where he was a Child Care Assistant Teacher, a Child Care Activity Programmer, and a Child Care Site Coordinator.

From there, he moved to the recreation department, where he had started at the beginning of his career, and became a Recreation Supervisor. He worked in the

Department of Parks, Beaches, and Recreation and became its director in 2009, while he was still in his M.P.A. program. He remains its director, today.

Learning about the Job

"Experiential learning has probably been the most important—from early internships to all of the jobs/positions I have held over the years. Every stop along the way was an opportunity to learn more about this field. I was able to learn from supervisors, co-workers and clients over the years, which has also contributed greatly to my understanding of parks and recreation. Classes during school helped lay a foundation, and even though I did not major in recreation, they have all played a part in my career. I enrolled in graduate school 16 years after receiving my BA. The public administration graduate program not only gave me new knowledge and skills, but a way to practically apply them to my current job and the profession of parks and rec, and more specifically local government.

"I would also say that my peers, not just my co-workers, but those working for other agencies, have been a great source of education and knowledge. I have learned quite a bit from those who have either experienced or are experiencing similar situations."

A Typical Day

As an agency director, during a typical day, Martin attends various meetings, sets up future meetings, signs invoices and requisitions, approves vacation requests, and receives and responds to sometimes 100+ emails, and phone calls. In addition, he works on various projects (short and long term), writes a few letters, checks in on various programs, sites, and staff members, and attends to any situations that require his immediate attention: someone getting hurt, a resident issue that has risen to his level, or requests for assistance from other departments.

However, there is not a typical day, and to better describe his "day," it is probably easier to look at a typical week.

During a typical week, Martin attends various weekly, bi-monthly, and monthly meetings. Those involve city staff members, members of the public, Commissioners, and outside groups. He is part of various groupings in the city, and each group has its set of meetings.

The Executive Team is composed of all the department heads and executive positions in the city. Part of their job is to help the City Manager "run" the city. There is a weekly meeting of the Executive Team, attended by the City Manager, Assistant City Manager, Fire Chief, Police Chief, Martin (Parks, Beaches, and Recreation Director), City Clerk, Planning Director, City Attorney, and Public Works Director. These meetings focus on the business of the city, what will and has gone before the City Council, upcoming projects, events, the budget, and various items happening in each department that are relevant to this group and the City.

With regard to Martin's departmental staff, this group meets weekly, one-on-one. These include the two Division Supervisors/Managers in his department, as well as their main administrative staff members. This group discusses staffing, upcoming events, programs, projects, budget/finance, goals, calendar/timelines, issues, concerns, etc.

The Parks, Beaches, and Recreation Commission meets one to two times per month. This group is a City Council-appointed advisory commission for things related to Parks, Beaches, and Recreation. Martin is the liaison for this group, and so he prepares the agendas, coordinates and prepares all staff reports, meets monthly with the Commission chair, and coordinates all correspondence with members.

Also, there are other groups on which he serves that meet monthly:

- The steering committee for the city's Prevention Partnership, which works to reduce youth substance abuse by addressing factors to help minimize access and abuse;

- City Collaborative, a partnership of local organizations sharing resources to collaborate better; and
- City School Volunteers, which places volunteers in the local school district.

Martin's customer service philosophy includes being responsive to the public. On a daily basis, he receives emails, phone calls, or visits from citizens as well as staff. Whether he can answer them or help with their inquiry right away or not, he always makes sure to respond as soon as possible. This usually includes a quick "got your message" and an estimate of when to expect a more thorough response. If he can respond sooner, he does. However, he feels it is important that he does respond and set a realistic expectation. Receiving these inquiries also requires prioritizing; something is done on a daily, weekly, monthly, and yearly basis.

With a large department such as Parks, Recreation, and Beaches, Martin interacts with Human Resources at least weekly. This may include basic paperwork for employees relating to raises, hiring, and separation. More complicated interactions may include employee discipline and workplace injuries.

With regard to budget/finance, Martin's department has 20 expenditure accounts and 40+ revenue accounts. Martin usually takes time during his week to see "where we are at" regarding their financial picture. Then, there are monthly reports to be checked. Mid-year and annual budget work is required (and usually requires a lot of prep time prior, as well as work during and after the information is delivered).

In terms of staff reports, any item on the City Council or Parks, Beaches, and Recreation agenda requires an Agenda Summary Report; City Council meetings are two times per month. The Commission meets one to two times per month. Depending on the agenda, Martin also needs to be working on this written report.

Professional Associations and Networking

Martin is a member of his State's parks and recreation association and also participates in public administration conferences and training. Locally, Martin networks at special events put on by his department, and local community events put on by various local organizations. These are fundraisers, lunch socials, ribbon cuttings, and other special events.

When there is an opportunity to meet someone new in town who can become, or already may be, a partner with his department, he makes sure that he meets the newcomer, who could be the new school superintendent, the incoming president of a local service club, or even someone in another City department like a public works manager.

He meets bi-monthly with all the parks and recreation directors of his county, which is a wonderful opportunity to connect with his fellow park and recreation directors, to talk about issues relating to their profession. This is a great way to give and receive feedback and support for everything.

There are lots of listservs on which he can keep in touch with people in his particular field. Moreover, he also "cold calls" or "cold emails" someone who may have some important information.

Most Helpful to His Career

Martin believes that the ability to build relationships has been extremely important to his career. As a Director in a relatively small town (less than 40,000), or at least a town that operates like a small town, the relationships he has made over the years have benefited his work immensely. Many of the people he meets and works with in town often "wear several hats." Understanding this can be very helpful. For example, he might be working with a business owner who also serves on a nonprofit board and is a member of a service club. Relationships with employees and customers/citizens are also very important. Having people skills is required to be successful.

A willingness to learn has been critical. Things are changing, and if a leader is not open to learning a new skill or trying something different, they will not be equipped to deal with the reality of our world, necessary tools, employees, and customers.

Having, or learning, patience is also important. Not just for yourself, but leaders also need to help others—employees and customers/ citizens. Understand that government is not built for speed, but for stability (a borrowed phrase). We cannot always react in the timeliest of manner, but that does not mean we cannot try. However, it is always good to set realistic expectations for folks.

Challenges

With regard to staffing and budget, during the recession and at the beginning of a budgetary crisis, staff pulled together, and unique situations and collaborations were created to solve short-term problems. However, doing more with less support and resources is unrealistic in the long-run. It is a workable short-term strategy but has the potential for long-term consequences.

In addition to 21 full-time employees, Martin's department has approximately 110–130 part-time employees. Dealing with the sheer numbers of staff with a minimal supervisory/management team has been very challenging. Employee retention has been hard. Being able to provide incentives for great staff to stay can also be challenging. If the opportunities to advance are limited within the organization, the department loses employees to other agencies. They try to emphasize training to the best of their abilities, and offering opportunities to take on new assignments and investing in employee training are good ways to keep folks interested and maintain higher morale.

When Martin was a new director, there were decisions made that, if they were to be made today, he feels he would have advocated for a different solution. Being

new in the job at the time, he did not assert his point of view—partially because he was new and partially because he did not quite have an understanding of his ability to voice his opinion more assertively and the role it should play in impacting important decisions/ outcomes.

How He Dealt with Challenges

The budget and staffing will always be an issue in a department like parks and recreation. Solving one situation does not always mean it is taken care of forever. The economy has gotten much better since he became a director, which has helped the budgeting process. The challenge of balancing that budget will always be there, but the degree of difficulty can vary.

Regarding his decision-making and confidence level, he feels more confident asserting his thoughts and opinions than when he was a new director. Now, he believes it is important to take the opportunity to voice his opinions, concerns, criticisms, and suggestions whenever he has them.

Most Rewarding Part of the Job

Martin enjoys working with people who also enjoy working with people. He says, "It is a pleasure to be able to serve my community alongside people who feel the same. I enjoy watching folks grow in our programs. We will see young people start as a participant in our programs, move into a volunteer teen program, apply to be a staff member, and succeed here."

Recommendations to Students

Martin's recommendation for students is to learn how to write. Many people, whether coming out of college or not, do not have the writing skills he, as an employer, would want to see. One of the problems he has noticed is a lack of proofing and editing. People do not read what they write. This may come from the more casual texts and email communications. "It is so very important to read your work and have someone else proof it as well."

Recreation departments have challenges not necessarily faced by other departments within city governments. They have high needs for equipment and facility maintenance and staffing issues that include issues involved with volunteers and part-time staff who work with children and the elderly. Further, they are required to develop and implement innovative programming and have the marketing skills to bring in residents to attend those programs—skills not necessarily needed in other city offices (Tipping 2016).

Zoos and Aquariums

Another element of parks in many larger cities are zoos and aquariums on city land, owned and operated either by the cities themselves, by nonprofit organizations typically set up to manage the facilities, or through public-private partnerships. The American Zoo Association lists 215 accredited zoos or aquariums in 45 states and the District of Columbia (American Association of Zoos and Aquariums 2016).

The modern zoo has evolved enormously from the model of menageries of animals in small cages of even a few decades ago. Today, the role of zoos is seen as conservation of animal species (which includes breeding programs across zoos to preserve species), education about nature and the environment, and research (European Association of Zoos and Aquaria 2013, p. 6). Credible zoos are expected to be accredited and, so, adhere to standards of professionalism and animal care that are internationally accepted. Still, zoos are increasingly controversial among many, and some activists are calling for them to be shut down altogether.

BOX 13.3 PARKS AND RECREATION STRATEGIES FROM CITY SUSTAINABILITY PLANS

Parks and Open Space

- "Increase the Urban Tree Canopy to 40% by June 30, 2021." Grand Rapids, Michigan, p. 7.
- "Have 18% or more or the Longmont Planning Area covered by, regionally appropriate, tree canopy or vegetation by 2025." Longmont, Colorado, p. 7.
- "Increase the ratio of overstory trees to smaller trees in city parks." Burnsville, Texas, p. 87.
- "Evaluate and track carbon storage capacity of city's forests." Burnsville, Texas, p. 87.
- "(To reduce tree loss), Reduce the use of heavy machinery that overly compacts soil." Burnsville, Texas, p. 88.

- "Distribute information on water-wise landscaping and integrated pest management practices to all neighborhood groups by 2017." Longmont, Colorado, p. 7.
- "Increase number of people participating in community gardens." Santa Monica, California, p. 11.
- "Continue to work with the Philadelphia School District on greening schoolyards." Philadelphia, Pennsylvania, p. 25.
- "Promote inclusion of native plants and habitats on public and private land." St. Louis, Missouri, p. 54.
- "Natural habitat must be identified, preserved and potentially enhanced." El Paso, Texas, p. 53.

- "Promote the long-term preservation and conservation of our open spaces and natural areas throughout the city." Virginia Beach, Virginia, p. 133.

Community Gardening and Urban Farming

- "Decrease average wait time for community garden plot." Santa Monica, California, p. 11.
- "Increase number of community gardens connected." Santa Monica, California, p. 11.
- "Broaden the definition of acceptable forms of urban farming." St. Louis, Missouri, p. 70.
- "Continue creating and maintaining urban agriculture projects on Parks and Recreation land and using the gardens to educate Philadelphians about the food system. (Farm Philly)." Philadelphia, Pennsylvania, p. 9.
- "Evaluate opportunities to increase access and availability of local good including backyard urban gardens, backyard urban chickens and food cooperatives." Denton, Texas, p. 8.

Arts and Culture

- "Use our centers and gathering places for cultural, recreational, and educational events and activities." Virginia Beach, Virginia, p. 41.
- "Incorporate and invest in public art throughout the city to foster community pride and create community identity." Virginia Beach, Virginia, p. 41.

- "Designate pedestrian-friendly Arts and Cultural Districts and encourage the establishment of art galleries, arts-related businesses, and creative industries within the districts." Virginia Beach, Virginia, p. 41.

Sources: City of Burnsville, Minnesota. 2008. Sustainability Guide Plan. Accessed on February 22, 2017 from http://www.ci.burnsville.mn.us/DocumentCenter/Home/View/1287

City of Denton, Texas. 2012. Simply Sustainable Plan. Accessed on February 22, 2017 from www.cityofdenton.com/CoD/media/City-of-Denton/Simply_Sustainable_Plan_2012.pdf.

City of El Paso, Texas. 2009. Livable City Sustainability Plan. Accessed on February 22, 2017 from www.elpasotexas.gov/~/media/files/coep/sustainability/el%20paso%20tx%20%20livable%20city%20sustainability%20plan.ashx?la=en.

City of Grand Rapids, Michigan. 2016. Sustainability Plan FY 2017–2021. Accessed on February 22, 2017 from http://grcity.us/Documents/2016-07-22%20Sustainability%20Plan.pdf.

City of Longmont, Colorado. 2016. Sustainability Plan. November 2016. Accessed on February 22, 2017 from www.longmontcolorado.gov/home/showdocument?id=16700.

City of Philadelphia, Pennsylvania. 2016. Greenworks: A Vision for a Sustainable Philadelphia. Accessed on February 22, 2017 from https://beta.phila.gov/documents/greenworks-a-vision-for-a-sustainable-philadelphia/.

City of Santa Monica, California. 2014. Sustainable City Plan: City of Santa Monica. Accessed on February 22, 2017 from www.smgov.net/uploadedFiles/Departments/OSE/Categories/Sustainability/Sustainable-City-Plan.pdf.

City of St. Louis, Missouri. 2013. City of St. Louis Sustainability Plan. Accessed on February 22, 2017 from www.stlouis-mo.gov/government/departments/planning/documents/city-of-st-louis-sustainability-plan.cfm.

City of Virginia Beach, Virginia. 2013. A Community Plan for a Sustainable Future. City of VA Beach Environment and Sustainability Office. March 12, 2013. Accessed on February 22, 2017 from www.vbgov.com/government/offices/eso/sustainability-plan/Documents/vb-sustainability-plan-web.pdf.

LIBRARIES

The Aspen Institute project on public libraries recently reported that 69 percent of Americans 16 years old or older had either high or medium levels of engagement with their public libraries. Only 14 percent reported no library usage at all (Garner 2014, p. 13).

The mission of today's libraries has changed enormously from earlier models. Libraries today are not just storage places for books; they have become community centers and sites for meaningful engagement and conflict resolution (ALA 2016). With these changes in the role of libraries have also come changes in the role of librarians—from gatekeepers to navigators. They are responsible for understanding and translating traditional and digital content to all kinds of users as well as becoming media mentors in introducing new technologies and media.

In fact, public libraries are one of the central institutions in today's societies in the struggle for digital inclusion and to reduce the digital divide, particularly for teenagers. They are often the first place young children are exposed to reading and books, have become central places for summer learning when schools are out, and have become centers of adult lifelong learning. For example, the Cazenovia (New York) Public Library works with the city's food pantry to provide low-income residents with help completing applications for government services and adult literacy as well as early literacy programs for their children. The Pueblo of Santa Clara (New Mexico) Community Library hosts Technology Access Nights for children and their families and works together to connect youth with children in the Every Child Ready to Read program (Sheketoff, Visser and Clark 2016).

While many institutions expect students and adults to have Internet access at home today, 62 percent of public libraries say they are their community's only source of free Internet access (Garner 2014, p. 16). All public libraries provide access to databases, more than 90 percent provide online homework assistance and employment resources, and close to 90 percent provide e-books and digital references (Garner 2014, p. 25).

The Aspen Institute's *Rising to the Challenge: Re-Envisioning Public Libraries* report suggests, "Public libraries can be at the center of these changes: a trusted community resource and an essential platform for learning, creativity, and innovation in the community. Public libraries have the DNA needed to thrive in this new information-rich, knowledge-based society" (Garner 2014, p. iv). It suggests that libraries have three important benefits to offer the public: people, place, and platform and suggests libraries align their goals with those of their communities, provide access to all in all formats, and cultivate their leadership work toward their sustainability (Garner 2014, p. x).

Among the challenges for public libraries today is the need to develop more competencies in using digital media, change old rules about the use of library space, provide mobile devices and high-speed broadband for users, create wireless hotspots throughout, and work to brand libraries as a community place with the potential to aid in the economic development of the community (Garner 2014, pp. 50–52).

Further, libraries can be the centers of controversy within our community, as they have been the targets of community outrage over their provision of books controversial to some. Box 13.4 provides a list of the library books that were most challenged by community members in 2015.

CONCLUSIONS

This chapter covered parks, recreation, and libraries. All three of these areas are important to city quality of life and resident health, wealth, and education. Libraries are critical sources of learning today and often provide a means of Internet access to those without computers at home, thus providing an enormous contribution to reducing the

BOX 13.4   MOST CHALLENGED BOOKS IN PUBLIC LIBRARIES, 2015

Among the many challenges of public libraries are the controversies over the content of particular books, often leading to attempts to have these books removed from the shelves. Here we see the ten books in public libraries that were the most challenged in 2015.

Rank	Name of Book	Author	Among Reasons Challenged
1	*Looking for Alaska*	John Green	Offensive language; sexually explicit; wrong for age group
2	*Fifty Shades of Grey*	E. L. James	Sexually explicit; wrong for age group
3	*I Am Jazz*	Jessica Herthel and Jazz Jennings	Homosexuality; religious viewpoint; wrong for age group
4	*Beyond Magenta: Transgender Teens Speak Out*	Susan Kuklin	Homosexuality; offensive language; political and religious viewpoint; wrong for age group
5	*The Curious Incident of the Dog in the Night-Time*	Mark Haddon	Offensive language; religious viewpoint; wrong for age group
6	The Holy Bible		Religious viewpoint
7	*Fun Home*	Alison Bechdel	Violence
8	*Habibi*	Craig Thompson	Nudity; sexually explicit; wrong for age group
9	*Nasreen's Secret School: A True Story from Afghanistan*	Jeanette Winter	Wrong for age group; religious viewpoint; violence
10	*Two Boys Kissing*	David Levithan	Homosexuality

Source: American Library Association. 2016. Intellectual Freedom in State of America's Libraries. Retrieved from www.ala.org/news/state-americas-libraries-report-2016/issues-and-trends on September 20, 2016.

gap in this country's digital access. Parks need to have a variety of features to appeal to the diverse populations in cities today. And recreation services need to provide activities for children, adults, and seniors. All need to have their facilities and activities equally available to all citizens and to provide those services equitably across the city. For all three areas, this means keeping up with new trends but still maintaining their traditional services.

BOX 13.5 PERFORMANCE MEASURES FOR PARKS, RECREATION, AND LIBRARIES

Libraries

- Minimum number of items in all formats in the library's collection—3 per capita for high-quality library in large city, 5 per capita in small city;
- Returned materials should be promptly reshelved within 24 hours;
- Circulating materials from last 5 years should be at least 25 percent of circulating collection;
- Minimum number of public access computers/Public computers per 1,000;
- Percentage of on-site library users who find the materials they want at the time (93%); and

- Registered library users as a percentage of population.

Parks and Recreation

- Park acres per 1,000 population;
- Miles of trails per 1,000 population;
- Percentage of residents who live within a quarter mile of developed open space; and
- Number of residents per 1,000 for tennis courts, swimming pools, family picnic areas, playgrounds, off-leash dog parks, ball diamonds, senior centers.

Source: (Ammons 2015)

EXERCISES AND DISCUSSION QUESTIONS

1. **Know Your City:** Parks, Recreation, and Libraries
   - What kinds of parks and recreation opportunities are available in your city?
   - Does the city have senior centers and other opportunities for senior citizens? Where are these located?
   - Are these opportunities equitably spread across the city, or are some centered in particular neighborhoods?
   - Are there libraries all around the city? What is the number of books per population in the city? Does the library provide Internet access?
2. How can cities make sure there are equal opportunities for parks and recreation in their communities?

3. Some experts say they would recommend more soccer fields for communities with large Latino communities and more basketball courts for communities with large African-American communities. What is your opinion on this view? Would you agree or disagree, and why?
4. Say you are the city manager in your city. A newly organized group of parents is concerned about the books now available in the city's library. They want a certain group of books to be banned from the library and not be available to anyone for check-out. As city manager, how would you respond to their concerns?

REFERENCES

American Association of Zoos and Aquariums (AZA). 2016. *Zoo and Aquarium Statistics.* Accessed on September 19, 2016 from www.aza.org/zoo-and-aquarium-statistics

American Library Association. 2016. 2016: The State of America's Libraries. Accessed on January 29, 2017 from http://www.ala.org/news/sites/ala.org.news/files/content/state-of-americas-libraries-2016-final.pdf

Ammons, David N. 2015. *Municipal Benchmarks: Assessing Local Performance and Establishing Community Standards*, 3rd ed. London: Routledge.

Biophilic Cities.org. 2016. *Biophilic Cities: What are They?* Accessed on September 20, 2016 from http://biophiliccities.org/what-are-biophilic-cities/

European Association of Zoos and Aquaria (EAZA). 2013. *The Modern Zoo: Foundations for Management and Development.* Accessed on September 14, 2016 from www.eaza.net/assets/Uploads/images/

Membership-docs-and-images/Zoo-Management-Manual-compressed.pdf

Friends of the High Line. 2016. *About*. Accessed on September 21, 2016 from www.thehighline.org/about

Future Cities Laboratory. 2016. *Embracing Walkability (Video)*. Accessed on September 20, 2016 from https://parksify.com/embracing-walkability-176534997164#.2awp3v7u9

Garner, Amy. 2014. *Rising to the Challenge: Re-Envisioning Public Libraries*. The Aspen Institute. Accessed on September 20, 2016 from http://csreports.aspeninstitute.org/documents/AspenLibrariesReport.pdf

Levy, Frank S., Meltsner, Arnold J., and Wildavsky, Aaron. 1975. *Urban Outcomes: Schools Streets, and Libraries*. Berkeley: University of California Press.

Musser, Amy. 2016. *The Nation's Most-Walkable Cities Got Even More Walkable in 2016*. Accessed on September 20, 2016 from www.redfin.com/blog/2016/04/the-most-walkable-us-cities-of-2016.html

Parksify. 2016. *How Atlanta's Beltline Is Transforming the City*. Accessed on September 22, 2016 from https://parksify.com/how-atlantas-beltline-is-transforming-the-city-db4414dc5ef4#.pu2mawtmr

Patton, Zach. 2012. "Parklets: The Next Big Tiny Idea in Urban Planning." *Governing*. Accessed on September 20, 2016 from www.governing.com/topics/energy-env/gov-parklets-next-big-idea-in-urban-planning.html

Pavement to Parks, City of San Francisco Public Works Department. 2016a. *Pavement to Parks Website*. Accessed on September 20, 2016 from http://pavementtoparks.org/

Pavement to Parks, City of San Francisco Public Works Department. 2016b. *San Francisco Parklet Manual Version 2.2*. Accessed on September 20, 2016 from http://pavementtoparks.org/wpcontent/uploads//2015/12/SF_P2P_Parklet_Manual_2.2_FULL1.pdf

Sheketoff, Emily, Visser, Marijke, and Clark, Larra. 2016. *01–04–16 ALA Comments on HHS DoE Draft Policy Statement*.

Sunday Streets SF. 2017. *Sunday Streets SF*. Accessed on January 30, 2017 from http://sundaystreetssf.com/

Tipping, Emily. 2016. "2016 State of the Industry: A Look at What's Happening in Recreation, Sports and Fitness Facilities." *Recreation Management*. Accessed on September 22, 2016 from http://recmanagement.com/feature/201606FE01/1

The Trust for Public Land. 2016. *2016 City Park Facts*, pp. 26–27. Accessed on September 16, 2016 from www.tpl.org/sites/default/files/2016%20City%20Park%20Facts_0.pdf

Ussery, Emily Neusel, Yngve, Leah, Whitfield, Geoffrey, Foster, Stephanie, Wendel, Arthur, and Boehmer, Tegan. 2016. "The National Environmental Public Health Tracking Network Access to Parks Indicator: A National County-Level Measure of Park Proximity." *Journal of Park and Recreation Administration* 34 (3): pp. 52–63.

Walkscore. 2016. *What Makes a Neighborhood Walkable?* Accessed on September 20, 2016 from www.walkscore.com/walkable-neighborhoods.shtml

Sustainable Cities

STATE OF THE ENVIRONMENT IN CITIES TODAY

Our cities today experience a great deal, but not all, of the environmental problems we see today, as they are the location of most of our population. This chapter will discuss air and water pollution, climate change, and their impact on cities, and will highlight what cities are doing today to fight these environmental issues—and to make our cities more sustainable. To sustain our cities, we must reduce pollution and provide healthy, clean neighborhoods for all residents. Making cities sustainable should be considered a core function of city management today and should be covered under NASPAA Urban Administration standards.

Water Pollution

Water pollution is from outside elements being released into the water; the main cause of this nutrient pollution is too much nitrogen and phosphorus in the water. A delicate balance exists—these elements are needed, but if there are too many of them, there is pollution. Sources can include stormwater, wastewater, agriculture, and household products (U.S. Environmental Protection Agency 2016a).

Water pollution can be reduced through protecting waterways from pollution, ensuring that manufacturing plants and other facilities do not release their refuse or chemicals into nearby streams, protecting groundwater sources, keeping household wastes from flowing into streams, creeks, or bays, and improving how we manage water within our communities (Natural Resource Defense Council 2016).

Air Quality

Since cities are, by definition, the agglomeration of the most people in a dense environment, they would also be expected to have many environmental problems. This is certainly true of air pollution, although air quality (regarding the two most common types of air pollution today—ozone and particle pollution) has been improving for years. Still, nearly 44 percent of the U.S. population live in areas that still have unhealthy ozone or particle pollution, and some cities have worse air pollution than they had previously (American Lung Association 2016, p. 6).

Air pollution can create lots of problems for humans, animals, and plants and is particularly damaging to the lungs. There are several different components of air pollution: ozone, one common component, is a gas composed of a three oxygen molecule, often called smog. Ozone attacks tissue in the lungs. Particle pollution is pollution from tiny pieces in the air that become smoke and exhaust. The increase in diseases for people in these areas is from adult and pediatric asthma, chronic obstructive pulmonary disease (COPD), cardiovascular (CV) disease, and poverty.

The four cities with the cleanest air in terms of ozone levels and particle pollution in 2011–2013 were Burlington-South Burlington, Vermont; Elmira-Corning, New York; Honolulu, Hawaii; and Salinas, California (American Lung Association 2016, p. 7). As Table 14.1 indicates, most of the most polluted cities are in California, particularly in that state's Central Valley, the agricultural center of the state.

▶ TABLE 14.1

Most Polluted Cities from Air Pollution, 2011–2013

Rank	From Ozone	Rank	From Year-Round Particle Pollution	Rank	From Short-Term Particle Pollution
1	Los Angeles-Long Beach, CA	1	Bakersfield, CA	1	Fresno-Madera, CA
2	Bakersfield, CA	2	Visalia-Porterville-Hanford, CA	2	Bakersfield, CA
3	Visalia-Porterville-Hanford, CA	3	Fresno-Madera, CA	3	Visalia-Porterville-Hanford, CA
4	Fresno-Madera, CA	4	Los Angeles-Long Beach, CA	4	Modesto-Merced, CA
5	Phoenix-Mesa-Scottsdale, AZ	5	El Centro, CA	5	Los Angeles-Long Beach, CA
6	Sacramento-Roseville, CA	6	San Jose-San Francisco-Oakland, CA	6	San Jose-San Francisco-Oakland, CA
7	Modesto-Merced, CA	6	Modesto-Merced, CA	7	Salt Lake City-Provo-Orem, UT
8	Denver-Aurora, CO	8	Pittsburgh-New Castle-Weirton, PA-OH-WV	8	Logan, UT-ID
9	Las Vegas-Henderson, NV	9	Harrisburg-York-Lebanon, PA	9	Fairbanks, AK
10	Fort Collins, CO	10	Louisville-Jefferson County, KY	10	Pittsburgh-New Castle-Weirton, PA-OH-WV

Source: American Lung Association. 2015. Most Polluted Cities. *State of the Air 2015.* Accessed on December 15, 2016 from www.stateoftheair.org/2015/city-rankings/most-polluted-cities.html.

Greenhouse Gasses

Greenhouse gasses (typically written as GHG) are one of the most important causes of global warming and the climate change we see today. GHG are those that contain heat in the atmosphere in a kind of bubble, resulting in an increase in warming in the atmosphere. GHG include carbon dioxide (CO_2), methane (CH_4), nitrous oxide (N_2O), and fluorinated gasses like hydrofluorocarbons. Carbon dioxide is the GHG most frequently found (81 percent), followed by methane (11 percent). When the concentration of these gasses stays in the atmosphere for a long time so that they are present all over the globe, they can trap heat inside the atmosphere, and the climate warms up. These are the main source of global warming today (U.S. Environmental Protection Agency 2016a).

Some estimate that 75–80 percent of global CO_2 emerges from the world's cities, with their high number of people, vehicles, businesses, energy usage, and waste products, but Dodman (2016) argues that cities are not the primary source of the site of industrialization (Dodman 2016; Zahran, Grover, Brody and Vedlitz 2008). In truth, there are lots of variations of GHG emissions per city, due to the density of the city and, therefore, how reliant residents are on individual cars versus mass transit, how much manufacturing is in the city, and the kinds of development patterns that exist. An analysis of greenhouse gas emissions across the world in global cities includes only the District of Columbia and New York City for 2004 (Dodman 2016). In these two cases, New York City's per capita GHG emissions are much lower than that of the District of Columbia because New York is a great deal denser, and residents typically do not own cars, and instead rely on mass

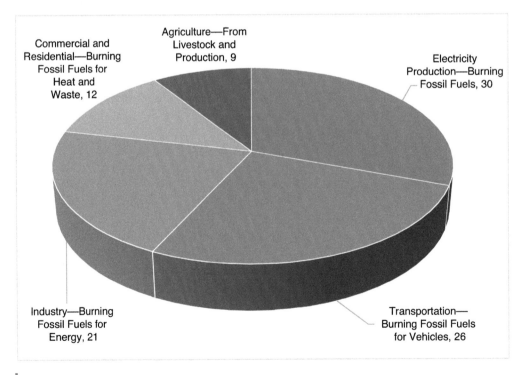

FIGURE 14.1
Sources of Greenhouse Gasses by Sector (Percent of Total), 2014

Source: U.S. Environmental Protection Agency. 2016b. Sources of Greenhouse Gas Emissions. Accessed on December 15, 2016 from www.epa.gov/ghgemissions/sources-greenhouse-gas-emissions.

BOX 14.1   U.S. ENVIRONMENTAL PROTECTION AGENCY HOUSEHOLD CARBON FOOTPRINT CALCULATOR

Every person, household, office, city, state, and nation has a carbon footprint or amount of greenhouse gasses they are responsible for emitting. These can be calculated and then used to reduce those emissions.

The U.S. Environmental Protection Agency Household Carbon Footprint

Calculator can be found at www.epa. gov/ghgemissions/household-carbon-footprint-calculator. The types of appliances, heat source, transportation, and garbage collection employed by a household will all contribute to the level of GHG emitted.

transit. For even this limited study, there are methodological issues with assessing GHG emissions for the District of Columbia since only the District itself was included, rather than the entire metropolitan area.

What is clear, however, is that cities can be the source of much of the world's solutions for climate change and GHG emissions.

Climate Change

Credible science has shown that, while some climate change can be attributed to nature itself, the vast increase in human activities over the past 150 years is responsible for most of the increases in greenhouse gasses during that time (U.S. Environmental Protection Agency 2016b). Just in the period from 1990 to 2014, GHG have increased by 7 percent. Figure 14.2 illustrates the increase in average of land and ocean temperatures since 1880.

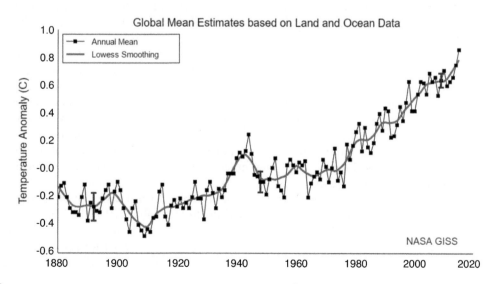

FIGURE 14.2
NASA Global Mean Estimates of Temperature Based upon Land and Ocean Data, 2016

Source: National Aeronautics and Space Administration. 2016. Goddard Institute for Space Studies (GISS) Surface Temperature Analysis/Analyses Graphs and Plots Graph: Global Mean Estimates Based on Land and Ocean Data. Accessed on December 26, 2016 from http://data.giss.nasa.gov/gistemp/graphs/.

The line with the boxes indicates the annual mean of land and sea temperature, and the smoother line provides an indication of the general direction of the trend. Thus, one can see that from year to year, the temperature fluctuates to some extent, but, overall, the mean temperature has been increasing since the early 1900s; this indicates the impact of the Industrial Age with its increased reliance on fossil fuels for energy for urbanization and manufacturing.

Signs of climate change were noted as early as the 1950s and started getting scientific attention in the 1970s. The concerns increased when the ozone hole over the Antarctic was discovered in 1985, leading to the creation of the Intergovernmental Panel on Climate Change (IPCC) as a coordinator and interpreter of the science around the growing phenomena (Henson 2014).

Action at the United Nations began in 1983 with the United Nations World Commission on Environment and Development, or the Brundtland Commission. Its report introduced many critical concepts into the field, including that of sustainable development. The IPCC's first report, highlighting what was then known about the risks of global warming and climate change, was released in 1990. The field continued to develop with collaboration from many sectors, with conferences like the 1992 Rio de Janeiro United Nations Conference on Environment and Development (Earth Summit), attended by scientists, activists, diplomats, and journalists. The Rio meeting introduced the UN Framework Convention on Climate Change (UNFCCC), which led to negotiations resulting in the Kyoto Protocol in 1997. The core of the Kyoto Protocol was reduction targets for CO_2, nitrogen oxides, methane, sulfur hexafluoride, hydrofluorocarbons, and perfluorocarbons in developed nations; individual nations had different targets. The United States, objecting to mandatory targets (the U.S. target was a 7 percent reduction), did not sign the Kyoto Protocol (Henson 2014).

Public awareness grew in the mid-2000s with former Vice President and Presidential candidate Al Gore's series of presentations on climate change. The presentation developed into an Oscar-winning documentary, *An Inconvenient Truth*. For their actions and leadership on global warming and climate change, Gore and the IPCC shared the 2007 Nobel Peace Prize.

The definitive documents on climate change are from the IPCC; the latest available at this writing is from 2014 and is part of the Panel's Fifth Assessment Report. This Panel is composed of scientists from around the world who weigh the evidence of global warming from a multitude of sources and derive conclusions. Over its five assessment reports, the Panel's conclusions have become more and more certain about the causes of climate change, as well as how immediate its impacts will be. Box 14.2 highlights the most important conclusions from the latest of the Panel's reports, showing the seriousness of the challenges that face the world today. Note how much the Panel attributes climate change to anthropogenic, or human, causes.

At the international level, work is always continuing with a series of conferences, negotiations and the implementation of action steps. In December 2015, the UN Climate Change Conference in Paris developed new agreements to limit temperature increases to below 2 degrees, a critical threshold for the world. A total of 188 nations, representing almost 100 percent of all global emissions, have submitted their individual plans and national goals (United Nations 2016).

For cities, alternate institutions were created to help their efforts to face climate change. In 1993, an ICLEI Cities for Climate Protection project, the Local Agenda 21 Model Communities Programme, began (Boswell, Greve and Seale 2010). The Sierra Club also assisted cities, with its Cool Cities project in 2005 (Wheeler 2008). The agenda for

BOX 14.2 IPCC CLIMATE CHANGE CONCLUSIONS, 2014

"1. Observed changes and their causes. Human influence on the climate system is clear, and recent anthropogenic emissions of greenhouse gasses are the highest in history. Recent climate changes have had widespread impacts on human and natural systems." (Intergovernmental Panel on Climate Change 2014, pg. 2)

"1.1 Observed changes in the climate system. Warming of the climate system is unequivocal, and since the 1950s, many of the observed changes are unprecedented over decades to millennia. The atmosphere and ocean have warmed, the amounts of snow and ice have diminished, and sea level has risen." (p. 2)

"1.2 Causes of climate change. Anthropogenic greenhouse gas emissions have increased since the pre-industrial era, driven largely by economic and population growth, and are now higher than ever. This has led to atmospheric concentrations of carbon dioxide, methane and nitrous oxide that are unprecedented in at least the last 800,000 years. Their effects, together with those of other anthropogenic drivers, have been detected throughout the climate system and are extremely likely to have been the dominant cause of the observed warming since the mid-20th century." (p. 4)

"1.3 Impacts of climate change. In recent decades, changes in climate have caused impacts on natural and human systems on all continents and across the oceans. Impacts are due to observed climate change, irrespective of its cause, indicating the sensitivity of natural and human systems to changing the climate." (p. 6)

"1.4 Extreme events. Changes in many extreme weather and climate events have been observed since about 1950. Some of these changes have been linked to human influences, including a decrease in cold temperature extremes, an increase in warm temperature extremes, an increase in extreme high sea levels and an increase in the number of heavy precipitation events in some regions." (p. 7)

"2. Future Climate Changes, Risks, and Impacts. Continued emission of greenhouse gasses will cause further warming and long-lasting changes in all components of the climate system, increasing the likelihood of severe, pervasive and irreversible impacts for people and ecosystems. Limiting climate change would require substantial and sustained reductions in greenhouse gas emissions which, together with adaptation, can limit climate change risks." (p. 8)

"2.1 Key drivers of future climate. Cumulative emissions of CO_2 largely determine global mean surface warming by the late 21st century and beyond. Projections of greenhouse gas emissions vary over a wide range, depending on both socio-economic development and climate policy." (p. 8)

"2.2 Projected changes in the climate system. Surface temperature is projected to rise over the 21st century under all assessed emission scenarios. It is *very likely* that heat waves will occur more often and last longer, and that extreme precipitation events will become more intense and frequent in many regions. The ocean will continue to warm and acidify, and global mean sea level to rise." (p. 10)

"2.3 Future risks and impacts caused by a changing climate. Climate change will amplify existing risks and create new risks for natural and human systems. Risks are unevenly distributed and are greater for disadvantaged people and communities in countries at all levels of development." (p. 13)

"2.4 Climate change beyond 2100, irreversibility and abrupt changes. Many aspects of climate change and associated impacts will continue for centuries, even if anthropogenic emissions of greenhouse gasses are stopped. The risks of abrupt or irreversible changes increase as the magnitude of the warming increases." (p. 16)

"3. Future pathways for adaptation, mitigation, and sustainable development. Adaptation and mitigation are complementary strategies for reducing and managing the risks of climate change. Substantial emissions reductions over the new few decades can reduce climate risks in the 21st century and beyond, increase prospects for effective adaptation, reduce the costs and challenges of mitigation in the longer term and contribute to climate-resilient pathways for sustainable development." (p. 17)

local action began, and many communities started developing plans for reducing greenhouse and carbon dioxide gasses.

The threat of climate change is a critical and, to many cities, an immediate one. "The effects of urbanization and climate change are converging in dangerous ways. Cities are major contributors to climate change: although they cover less than 2 percent of the earth's surface, cities consume 78 percent of the world's energy and produce more than 60% of all carbon dioxide and significant amounts of other greenhouse gas emissions, mainly through energy generation, vehicles, industry, and biomass use. At the same time, cities and towns are heavily vulnerable to climate change. Hundreds of millions of people in urban areas across the world will be affected by rising sea levels, increased precipitation, inland floods, more frequent and stronger cyclones and storms, and periods of more extreme heat and cold" (United Nations Habitat for a Better Urban Future 2016).

▶ BOX 14.3   CAREER PATHWAYS IN SUSTAINABILITY I

Current Position

Part-time Sustainability Associate in a small city

Education

B.A. in Psychology, Minor in Philosophy
M.P.A., Emphasis in Urban Administration

Career Pathway/Finding Her Way to Sustainability

Andrea was always interested in environmental issues and read a lot on the topic. Andrea started her career as an AmeriCorps Community Outreach and Volunteer Coordinator for a National Park Service Recreation Area. She then worked as a Legislative Aide and intern for a city council then as an intern transportation planner, then as a contract transportation planner for both a large city and then for a national consulting firm. She became a researcher, Board member, and Executive Director of a pedestrian advocacy group. Her interests in and experience with transportation issues transferred nicely to the field of sustainability planning.

Andrea has continually done volunteer work in her community—as a volunteer-appointed official on many different citizens' advisory boards for cities, all related to transportation. Moreover, she has also run for office twice in her community.

After moving to a smaller city for family reasons, she applied for and became a Sustainability Associate, a temporary part-time job that she began in 2015.

Learning about the Job

Andrea was a non-motorized transportation (bicycle and walking) advocate for many years and was mostly self-taught in transportation planning, which led to work in sustainability.

A Typical Day

On a typical day, Andrea:

- Answers emails from the public;
- Looks for interesting news and grant opportunities to share with her team members;
- Drafts proposed policy memos;
- Conducts research on all kinds of sustainability-related issues; and
- Sits in and sometimes leads inter- and multi-agency meetings many times a week.

Professional Associations and Networking

- Air and Waste Management Association
- Institute of Transportation Engineers
- Urban Sustainability Directors Network

Through her job, she has access to usdn.org, an amazing resource for new ideas of how to do sustainable projects in cities. She also works with employees from several local nonprofits and different departments in her City.

Most Helpful to Her Career

Keeping a sense of curiosity and a desire to learn new things have been most helpful to her career.

Challenges

The lack of current funding means that her job is a temporary and part-time one. Our climate is in peril, and yet city positions to work on climate mitigation or adaptation are only slowly coming online. Her department is currently working on a $1.25 million "ask" for City Council to step up and fund climate works seriously. She believes it has been a challenge but also a privilege to work hard on funding issues.

Most Rewarding Part of the Job

Andrea considers learning new things all the time to be the most rewarding part of her job. "It is my job to read the news re everything from solar industry trends to electric car charging protocols."

Recommendations for Students

1. Do not be afraid to be an intern if you can swing it financially.
2. Keep passionate about the topic but also be careful to know where "advocacy" must stop so you can remain somewhat impartial as a researcher—this is a very hard line to find. Moreover, with something as important as the looming climate catastrophe, it can be hard to remain objective (whatever that is).
3. Go to national conferences and attend sessions you are interested in but know nothing about. Meet people there even if you are shy.
4. Your research can take you a long way professionally—do not squander the chance to use your college or grad school projects on topics that matter to people in the "real world."
5. Good luck!

Sustainability

How can cities survive these environmental problems, as well as climate change? How can they become sustainable? The concept of sustainability can mean various things to different people. In fact, one researcher (Zeemering 2009) did research just on how planners defined the term. It is crucial to note the importance of the three E's in sustainability: environment, economy, and equity, which all need to be considered—and achieved—together. Portney (2015) offers further several definitions:

> Environmental sustainability focuses on preserving and protecting ecosystems and natural resources that are essential to human health. Sustainable development places a priority on engaging in economic-development activities that avoid depleting natural resources and damaging ecosystems. The equity elements of sustainability emphasize achieving a more equitable distribution of environmental impacts, natural resources, goods and services, and income and wealth. Regardless of which of the three elements or which combination of elements is considered paramount, sustainability adds an important time dimension. It is a dynamic concept, prescribing actions for the future.
>
> (Portney 2015, location 2027–2028)

Portney (2015) also identifies six roots of sustainability: ecological/carrying capacity, resource/environment, biosphere, a critique of technology, no growth to slow growth, and eco-development. The concept of carrying capacity adds to sustainability in that it refers to the ability of the environment to handle the press of population and its requirement for resources. It assumes that different environments have different carrying capacities, some (like wetlands) able to sustain many fewer people than others. Resource/environment refers to the fact that the use of resources depletes the environment and, so, is an important component of sustainability; a sustainable environment is one that does not deplete resources at such a rate that the environment suffers. The biosphere component adds the notion of the entire earth as a self-contained vehicle, where every action could have an effect on other residents of the biosphere. The critique of technology implies a focus on the damage that dependence on technology can do to the environment, particularly on an inaccurate assumption that technology can always save us from problems. The no-growth-slow-growth thread contributing to sustainability contributes the sense that we can no longer afford the assumption that growth is always the goal in society. This string of thought is pulled together in the eco-development thread, illustrating that our economic, political, and other goals need to take the environment into account.

▶ BOX 14.4   CAREER PATHWAYS IN SUSTAINABILITY II

Current Position

Sustainability Analyst, mid-sized city

Education

B.A., Environmental Sciences, and Policy
M.P.A.
Other graduate coursework in environmental sciences

Besides Education, How Maria Learned about Sustainability

Maria learned on the job. She benefited greatly from learning from and working with the leaders in the field of sustainability. She also read as much as she could—books like *The Big Pivot: Radically Practical Strategies for a Hotter, Scarcer, and More Open World*—and subscribed to sustainability newsletters from groups like Sustainable Brands and Rocky Mountain Institute.

Career Pathway

Maria has held her current position as a Sustainability Analyst since September 2016. Before that, she worked in a series of environmental policy positions. She began by working at the Environmental Protection Agency on indoor air quality issues in schools. Then she worked at the National Education Association (NEA), providing environmental education for teachers. Before moving to her current position, Maria worked for the Natural Resources Defense Council, an environmental advocacy and conservation nonprofit, where she worked directly with sustainable businesses and business leaders.

A Typical Day

Maria does not have a typical day. Depending on the issue on which she is working, she will spend part of the day in meetings with key stakeholders either in other departments or in the community. She also spends time with the Office of Sustainability team to make sure they are all aligned with their projects. The tasks can include but are not limited to analyzing data, reporting on sustainability efforts, marketing, and communications.

Professional Associations and Networking

Maria is active in Women in Cleantech and Sustainability, which is launching a mentoring program, in which she wants to participate. She makes connections through LinkedIn, conferences, and existing organizational relationships.

Most Helpful

To Maria, what has been most helpful has been having a female mentor who not only understands the sustainability field but also understands the challenges of gender inequality.

Most Challenging

Maria believes there are two major challenges in her career in sustainability—1) the

misconception that incorporating sustainability initiatives comes with a high price tag that requires extra staffing and 2) the lack of diversity in staff in the clean energy economy, especially in upper management.

To overcome these challenges, she is working to reach out to the community to educate it about the sustainability work being done. At a previous job, she was a member of the Diversity, Equity, and Inclusion (DEI) Committee, which made recommendations on how to improve DEI at all levels—from the hiring process to employee retention to Board Member recruitment.

Most Rewarding

"I am working at the intersection of environment, economics, and social and cultural issues—the 'triple bottom line' of people, profits, and the planet. The work that I'm doing can make a huge impact on leaving a better planet for future generations."

Recommendations to Students

Maria has several recommendations for students interested in working in the field of sustainability:

- "Sustainability is a growing field with job opportunities in diverse areas like clean energy, technology, education, management, political science, business, science, and engineering. The degree and certification requirements vary greatly, so do your research to figure out the best path for your interests. Look at senior-level job listings for jobs that interest you. Look at the job requirements and figure out a path to gain the skills and education you need to one day be able to apply for your 'dream' job.
- "Do your research—learn as much as you can, ask for informational interviews, network.
- "Find a mentor.
- "Read the U.S. Department of Labor report, 'Why Green Is Your Color: A Woman's Guide to a Sustainable Career.'"

Sustainability Strategies

Sustainability is composed of concerns for the environment, the economy, and people. Much like emergency management, the sustainability movement focuses on three broad areas: mitigation, adaptation, and resiliency. Mitigation efforts are those that try to reduce climate change, misuse of energy resources, and pollution—and attempt to reduce the effects of these trends. Adaptation is the next stage; adaptation strategies are those that already accept the reality of climate change and other environmental problems but attempt to manage the consequences. Resiliency efforts are those that try to protect people from the consequences of these events and to help them recover.

For instance, if a city were by the ocean, part of its adaptation efforts might be to mitigate climate change by reducing its carbon footprint and trying to shore up coastal barriers and low-lying locations around the city. For resiliency, city officials would also be working with neighborhood groups to help them survive floods and to encourage preparation and assistance of their neighbors during crises.

Cities are most vulnerable to climate change when they are close to coastal areas, have a great deal of wetlands and forest cover surrounding them, or are susceptible to extreme weather events (Zahran et al. 2008). However, cities also have the ability to make significant changes to many of the most important elements affecting climate change: transit, land use policy, waste management, and urban forests (Hawkins, Krause, Feiock and Curley 2016). As Zeemering (2009) points out, to prepare for climate change, cities could be required to alter their land use, zoning, and planning decisions, and to change their transportation and housing orientation, their construction codes, or their waste and water management practices. Cities may also have different priorities for their climate change policies—some are more traditional in their development interests, some have very participatory cultures and so will have plans focused more on citizen engagement, and some aspire to be innovative and lead in the area (Zeemering 2014).

Cities Respond to Climate Change and Environmental Problems

By the early 1990s, cities in Canada and the United States were organizing to reduce their carbon dioxide emissions, under the auspices of the Urban CO_2 Reduction Project (UCRP) from ICLEI—Local Governments for Sustainability. Those efforts were then broadened into the Cities for Climate Change program (Zahran et al. 2008). In 2005, the U.S. Conference of Mayors created the Climate Protection Agreement, and more than 500 mayors signed the Agreement, which promised to work toward greenhouse gas reduction, to further move action to the local level. The action kept coming at both the state and local levels since the federal government was providing no leadership on the issue at that time. By 2016, more than 1,000 cities had signed the Mayors Climate Protection Agreement (MCPA), and more than 500 joined the ICLEI (Hawkins et al. 2016).

However, by 2010, only 80 cities had created climate action plans to reduce greenhouse gas emissions (Boswell et al. 2010). The earliest city climate change plans dealt primarily with reducing emissions (mitigation), rather than adaptation. Many of these plans were developed utilizing ICLEI's five-step planning process: determining the level of greenhouse gas emissions, setting targets for reduction, developing policies to reduce those emissions, implementing those policies, and measuring the results. For those earliest

BOX 14.5   THE U.S. MAYORS CLIMATE PROTECTION AGREEMENT, 2005

(Endorsed by the 73th Annual U.S. Conference of Mayors meeting, Chicago, 2005)

A. We urge the federal government and state governments to enact policies and programs to meet or beat the target of reducing global warming pollution levels to 7 percent below 1990 levels by 2012, including efforts to: reduce the United States' dependence on fossil fuels and accelerate the development of clean, economical energy resources and fuel-efficient technologies such as conservation, methane recovery for energy generation, waste to energy, wind and solar energy, fuel cells, efficient motor vehicles, and biofuels;

B. We urge the U.S. Congress to pass bipartisan greenhouse gas reduction legislation that 1) includes clear timetables and emissions limits and 2) a flexible, market-based system of tradable allowances among emitting industries; and

C. We will strive to meet or exceed Kyoto Protocol targets for reducing global warming pollution by taking actions in our own operations and communities such as:

1. Inventory global warming emissions in City operations and in the community, set reduction targets and create an action plan;

2. Adopt and enforce land-use policies that reduce sprawl, preserve open space, and create compact, walkable urban communities;

3. Promote transportation options such as bicycle trails, commute trip reduction programs, incentives for carpooling and public transit;

4. Increase the use of clean, alternative energy by, for example, investing in 'green tags', advocating for the development of renewable energy resources, recovering landfill methane for energy production, and supporting the use of waste to energy technology;

5. Make energy efficiency a priority through building code improvements, retrofitting city facilities with energy efficient lighting and urging employees to conserve energy and save money;

6. Purchase only Energy Star equipment and appliances for City use;

7. Practice and promote sustainable building practices using the U.S. Green Building Council's LEED program or a similar system;

8. Increase the average fuel efficiency of municipal fleet vehicles; launch an employee education program including anti-idling messages; convert diesel vehicles to biodiesel;

9. Evaluate opportunities to increase pump efficiency in water and wastewater systems; recover wastewater treatment methane for energy production;

10. Increase recycling rates in City operations and in the community;

11. Maintain healthy urban forests; promote tree planting to increase shading and to absorb CO_2; and

12. Help educate the public, schools, other jurisdictions, professional association, business and industry about reducing global warming pollution.

Source: U.S. Conference of Mayors. 2005. *The U.S. Conference of Mayors Climate Protection Agreement.* Accessed on February 26, 2017 from www.cityofsignalhill.org/DocumentCenter/View/225.

efforts, implementation was difficult, and the results were not adequate to address the issue (Wheeler 2008).

Wang, Hawkins, Lebredo and Berman (2012) reported on city environmental and sustainability activities based on a survey of American cities (Table 14.2). By 2012, more than half of the cities responding to their survey had implemented some tree conservation program, purchased vehicles using alternative fuels or used those fuels for the city itself, joined a sustainability group, built a new building using LEED standards, or had a website focusing on green programs.

While none of the listed economic sustainability practices were implemented by even 50 percent of the cities responding to the survey, two of them were implemented by 49 percent: implementing buy local campaigns and building partnerships with local businesses to achieve sustainability. Others included creating demand for green products through their cities' purchasing power, developing a green building list for local residential projects, developing green workforce training programs, or creating fee waiver programs to provide incentives to build using LEED criteria (Wang et al. 2012).

Acknowledging that climate and global warming have spillover effects and reach beyond their urban boundaries, cities also are typically engaged in collaborative partnerships with other governments in their region (Hawkins et al. 2016; Zeemering 2014,

---

TABLE 14.2

Most Frequent Environmental and Sustainability Practices by Cities, 2012

Activity Area	Percent of Responding Cities
Used tree planting or conserving program	78.0
Bought alternative fuel vehicles	77.7
Joined sustainability organization	61.1
Built new building using LEED standards	59.5
Developed a website for city's green programs	53.4
Used renewable energy for city	51.9
Bought and protected sensitive lands	49.6
Adopted standards for green cleaning and maintenance	44.7
Offered energy audits to residents and businesses	36.7
Adopted green standard for new city buildings	35.6
Offered green tech classes to community	34.1
Developed green purchasing program	31.8
Used green standards to renovate buildings	29.9
Offered green tech classes to employees	29.9
Posted air and water quality results on the city website	29.5
Adopted green landscaping ordinance for city	24.2
Offered renewable energy to citizens	18.6

Source: Based upon Table 1: Sustainability in U.S. Cities. In Wang, XiaoHu, Hawkins, Christopher V., Lebredo, Nick, and Berman, Evan M. 2012. "Capacity to Sustain Sustainability: A Study of U.S. Cities." *Public Administration Review* 72(6): p. 844.

TABLE 14.3

Examples of Possible Climate Action and Sustainability Strategies for Cities

	City Government
Transportation	• Incentives for employees to use mass transit rather than drive own vehicles • Buying alternative fuel cars • Buying energy efficient cars
Solid Waste and Recycling	• Including recycling and locally sourced materials in city procurement priorities
Energy Efficiency	• Weatherizing city buildings • Renovating city buildings to reduce energy usage • Building new city buildings with LEED standards • Using energy efficient streetlights
Renewable Energy	• Using solar and other renewable energy for city buildings • Having city buy renewable power for its use
Forestry	• Planting trees in median strips, parks, and other city land
Land Use Planning	• Planning for transit villages, mixed use developments, and more dense use of housing

Source: Based upon Feiock, Richard C., Francis, Nathan, and Kassekert, Tony. 2010. "Explaining the Adoption of Climate Change Policies in Local Government." Pathways to Low Carbon Cities Workshop. Hong Kong, China. December 13–14, 2010. Also based upon Zeemering, Eric. 2012. "Recognizing Interdependence and Defining Multi-Level Governance in City Sustainability Plans" *Local Environment* 17 (4), April 2012: pp. 409–424. Available at www.seattle.gov/Documents/Departments/OSE/2013_CAP_20130612.pdf.

2012), leading to the development of support networks across regions and even more implementation strategies.

There are several different ways of considering the many different sustainability strategies that can be adopted by cities. Some strategies focus on what cities can do with their agencies, buildings, and personnel, while others apply to actions taken within the broader community (Feiock, Francis and Kassekert 2010). Some cities follow the environment, economy, and equity structure, while others follow the mitigation and adaptation structure (Svara, Watt, and Jang 2013; Sharp, Daley, and Lynch 2011; Fitzgerald 2010).

A 2010 study found that all plans (100 percent) from a stratified random sample of 30 plans included GHG reduction targets and mitigation policies; 97 percent also included a GHG emissions inventory. Seventy-three percent included a basic description of climate science, and 77 percent incorporated information about climate change impacts on the local environment. Seventy percent included a forecast of GHG emissions, but only 27 percent included adaptation policies and actions (Boswell et al. 2010).

Developing a Climate Action Plan

Table 14.3 provides examples of specific items that can be included in city sustainability plans. Other examples are included throughout this book in almost every chapter. There are six general principles to keep in mind when developing climate action or sustainability plans (Francis and Feiock 2011):

1. Formulate specific targets and benchmarks;
2. Include citizen participation in the design process;

3. Actively engage in climate and sustainability networks;
4. Create a dedicated sustainability office complete with funding;
5. Coordinate sustainability and energy strategies with other, existing services; and
6. First practice sustainability strategies on city government offices and buildings, before expanding them to the broader community.

One of the most important of these steps is finding resources to dedicate to sustainability and climate change programs. As it is a relatively new issue, many cities are attempting to plan and manage climate change with just existing resources. In 2016, Hawkins et al. (2016) found that only 34 percent of cities with more than 50,000 residents have dedicated funding for sustainability, 56 percent have dedicated staff, but only 31 percent have both. However, having these resources makes a difference in the progress made in the sustainability planning process—along with joining sustainability networks.

Excellent models of existing climate action plans already exist, such as those from Seattle, Washington and those sustainability plan strategies from cities across the country highlighted in each chapter of this book.

> *Seattle, Washington's Climate Action Plan.* Seattle was one of the very first, if not the first, cities to start addressing climate change when it developed a climate action plan, led 1,000 mayors in 2005 to commit to reducing their emissions by 2012, and agreed to become a carbon neutral city. Today, it has an updated (2016) plan in draft form from its Office of Sustainability and Environment (OSE).

For Seattle, the rationale for urgency are the rising temperatures, rainier winters, and drier summers, increasing the risk of coastal floods and rising sea levels since the city is on the Pacific West Coast. Its priorities are listed as:

- Equity: Prioritize actions that reduce risk and enhance resilience in frontline communities (e.g., communities of color, lower income communities, immigrant and refugee communities, disabled residents and seniors), as they are at greater risk from the impacts of climate change and often have the fewest resources to respond to changing conditions.
- Co-Benefits: Design and implement resilience strategies that advance community goals by enhancing physical spaces and services in ways that support quality/livable urban environments, health, and social cohesion.
- Natural Systems: Use nature-based solutions that leverage ecosystem services and foster natural systems resilience.

(City of Seattle 2016, p. 3)

Seattle's earlier plan focused upon three outcomes: reducing GHG intense travel, increasing building and energy efficiency, and moving to lower carbon energy sources; however, its new draft 2016 plan is instead organized by strategies within sectors.

It begins the 2016 draft plan by discussing the impacts of climate change, then talking about the connection with equity and focusing on a series of sector-specific actions: transportation, land use and buildings, city buildings, parks, drainage and water supply, electricity system, and community preparedness. Lastly, there is a section titled "What You Can Do."

The section on equity goes further in highlighting the important vulnerability factors for various populations. The first of these is income; low-income residents are most

BOX 14.6   ENVIRONMENT AND SUSTAINABILITY STRATEGIES FROM CITY SUSTAINABILITY PLANS

Air and GHG

- "Update and implement the Green Ports Initiative to reduce emissions from cranes, diesel vehicles, and other sources." Philadelphia, Pennsylvania, p. 12.
- "Train and educate city employees on anti-idling policies to reduce air pollution." Philadelphia, Pennsylvania, p. 12.
- "Get to zero days ambient air quality standards exceeded." Santa Monica, California, p. 10.
- "Reduce city vehicle emissions 10% by 2017, 20% by 2020 and 15% by 2025." Avondale, Arizona, p. 52.
- "Provide more oversight of emissions from oil and gas operations." Longmont, Colorado, p. 6.
- "Monitor and reduce average annual fourth-highest daily maximum ozone emissions to less than 70 parts per billion." Longmont, Colorado, p. 6.
- "Increase public access to local air quality information and information on actions the public can take to improve air quality." Longmont, Colorado, p. 6.
- "Create baseline information for GHG emissions by 2018 and maintain ongoing reporting." Longmont, Colorado, p. 6.
- "Increase citizen awareness of potential air quality problems and solutions to the problems." Longmont, Colorado, p. 6.

Water

- "Applicable City facilities use Integrated Pest Management by 2016." Avondale, Arizona, p. 45.
- "Promote potable water conservation and the use of non-potable water, such as rainwater capture and ground water well, for non-potable activities." Virginia Beach, Virginia, p. 99.
- "Increase biofiltration habitat (oysters, wetlands, submerged aquatic vegetation,

living shorelines)." Virginia Beach, Virginia, p. 101.

Energy

- "Increase percentage of biodiesel in fuel used by city vehicles." Philadelphia, Pennsylvania, p. 12.
- "Reduce building energy use 2% by 2016, 5% by 2020, and 10% by 2025." Avondale, Arizona, p. 53.
- "Achieve 100% of energy use for City-owned buildings from renewable sources such as solar, wind, and geothermal by June 30, 2025." Grand Rapids, Michigan, p. 7.
- "Decrease the utility cost burden for low-income households through energy efficiency measures." Longmont, Colorado, p. 6.
- "Increase participation in renewable energy options." Longmont, Colorado, p. 6.
- "Explore viability of a community solar garden with Platte River Power Authority by 2020." Longmont, Colorado, p. 7.
- "Achieve electric energy savings of 1% annually through energy efficiency measures by 2020." Longmont, Colorado, p. 7.
- "Explore the incorporation of geothermal systems into City facilities." Burnsville, Texas, p. 34.

Climate Change

- "Investigate the extent of impacts and develop strategies to address sea level rise and land subsidence and educate the community regarding these issues." Virginia Beach, Virginia, p. 137.

Sustainability

- "Improve the response and resiliency of all communities to climate change impacts on the built, natural and social environments with an emphasis on public health and historically underserved populations." Dover, New Hampshire, p. 2.

Environmental Justice

• "Environmental Justice: Develop and enforce government policies and practices that not only contribute to reducing polluted and toxic environments for all residents but also lead to an equitable distribution of the positive and negative environmental effects on the health and wellbeing of communities." Dover, New Hampshire, p. 5.

Sources: City of Avondale, Arizona. 2014. Municipal Sustainability Plan. June 16, 2014. Accessed on February 22, 2017 from www.avondale.org/DocumentCenter/View/34278 Arizona.

City of Dover, New Hampshire. Not Dated. City of Dover Sustainability Goals with Purpose Statements. Accessed on February 22, 2017 from www.dover.nh.gov/Assets/government/city-operations/2document/planning/outreach/sustainabilitygoals.pdf.

City of Grand Rapids, Michigan. 2016. Sustainability Plan FY 2017–2021. Accessed on February 22, 2017 from http://grcity.us/Documents/2016-07-22%20Sustainability%20Plan.pdf.

City of Longmont, Colorado. 2016. Sustainability Plan. November 2016. Accessed on February 22, 2017 from www.longmontcolorado.gov/home/showdocument?id=16700.

City of Philadelphia, Pennsylvania. 2016. Greenworks: A Vision for a Sustainable Philadelphia. Accessed on February 22, 2017 from https://beta.phila.gov/documents/greenworks-a-vision-for-a-sustainable-philadelphia/.

City of Virginia Beach, Virginia. 2013. A Community Plan for a Sustainable Future. City of VA Beach Environment and Sustainability Office. March 12, 2013. Accessed on February 22, 2017 from www.vbgov.com/government/offices/eso/sustainability-plan/Documents/vb-sustainability-plan-web.pdf.

vulnerable to increased temperatures because they are less likely to have air conditioning, and because they are less likely to have a vehicle in which to evacuate, should the need arise from sudden flooding, among other reasons. Individuals with language barriers could have problems understanding cautionary information and emergency preparedness information. People of color dealing with racism could find dealing with institutional barriers even more difficult during emergency situations arising from extreme weather events and are also more likely to be lower income. Those with health conditions or disabilities like asthma are going to be affected by increased ozone in the air and increased smoke from fires, while those with other disabilities will find it more difficult to evacuate during extreme weather events. The elderly will also have many of the same issues. Various living conditions and locations could lead to problems evacuating or dealing with poor air quality or even geographic isolation. Finally, occupation can make a difference for those with jobs that require them to work outdoors, where they would be more impacted by increased temperature (City of Seattle 2016, p. 18).

CONCLUSIONS

Sustainability is a broader term than we normally believe; in a holistic sense, it can mean not just environmental sustainability but also sustaining an organization fiscally and keeping it moving forward. This chapter has focused upon environmental sustainability—reducing pollution in our cities and trying to reduce impacts of climate change while simultaneously preparing for climate change to happen. We no longer have a choice; we must ensure our cities, particularly our vulnerable cities, are prepared. Cities close to wetlands or the coast must have physical infrastructure set up to handle flooding, and all cities should be prepared for extreme weather events. Many other areas of city management can contribute to these efforts: public works can address the issue through its stormwater and drainage systems, parks can be set up as absorption areas for excess water, police and fire personnel need to be trained to protect the public and deal with extreme weather events, and service delivery mechanisms should be responsive to disruptions of service.

The ability to sustain our cities through new crises, with all of our means at hand, is going to require the ability to innovate and change, come up with new solutions, and abandon those no longer working.

SELECTED WEB RESOURCES

- Air and Waste Management Assn www.awma.org/
- ICLEI Local Governments for Sustainability www.iclei.org/
- Institute for Sustainable Communities www.iscvt.org
- Institute for Sustainable Communities— American Society for Adaptation

- Professionals www.iscvt.org/program/american-society-adaptation-professionals-asap/
- Resilient Cities www.100resilientcities.org
- Rocky Mountain Institute www.rmi.org/
- Urban Sustainability Directors Network http://usdn.org

EXERCISES AND DISCUSSION QUESTIONS

1. **Know Your City:** Sustainability and the Environment
   - What kind of environmental problems does your city have? What is the air and water quality?
   - What is your city doing about environmental problems?
   - Does your city have a sustainability coordinator, or office?
   - Does your city have a sustainability or climate action plan?
   - Is your city preparing for potential impacts of climate change, or is it organizing strategies to try to reduce climate change impacts?
   - Are there any signs of environmental justice problems; do poorer communities experience less quality in air or water?
2. Say you are the new city manager of a city that discovers the same problems that developed in Flint, Michigan—the pipes are

corroding and residents are being exposed to lead poisoning. As the city manager, what steps would you take to resolve the situation?

3. While 97 percent of climate scientists believe that climate change is real and results from human involvement, there are a few who do not agree. You are the city manager in a city on the coast and are concerned about the growing number of times your city has been flooded after heavy rains. You want to plan for more extreme weather events and other impacts of climate change, but some in your community complain it is not necessary because climate change is not real. What do you do?

4. You are the city manager again. The landfill and hazardous waste disposal facilities are both located on the poor side of your city. You know this creates an environmental justice problem. What do you do?

REFERENCES

American Lung Association. 2016. *State of the Air 2016.* American Lung Association.

Boswell, Michael R., Greve, Adrienne, and Seale, Tammy L. Autumn 2010. "An Assessment of the Link between Greenhouse Gas Emissions Inventories and Climate Action Plans." *Journal of the American Planning Association* 76 (4): pp. 451–462.

City of Seattle. 2016. *Preparing for Climate Change.* Accessed on December 29, 2016 from www.seattle.gov/Documents/Departments/OSE/ClimateDocs/SEAClimatePreparedness_Draft_Oct2016.pdf

Dodman, David. 2016. "Blaming Cities for Climate Change? An Analysis of Urban Greenhouse Gas Emissions Inventories." *Environment and Urbanization* 21 (1): pp. 185–201.

Feiock, Richard C., Francis, Nathan, and Kassekert, Tony. 2010. *Explaining the Adoption of Climate Change Policies in Local Government.* Pathways to Low Carbon Cities Workshop, Hong Kong, China. December 13–14 2010.

Fitzgerald, Joan. 2010. *Emerald Cities: Urban Sustainability and Economic Development.* New York: Oxford Press.

Francis, Nathan, and Feiock, Richard C. 2011. *A Guide for Local Government Executives on Energy Efficiency and Sustainability.* Alexandria, VA: IBM Center for The Business of Government.

Hawkins, Christopher V., Krause, Rachel M., Feiock, Richard C., and Curley, Cali. 2016. "Making Meaningful Commitments: Accounting for Variation in Cities' Investments of Staff and Fiscal Resources to Sustainability." *Urban Studies* 53 (9): pp. 1902–1924.

Henson, Robert. 2014. *A Thinking Person's Guide to Climate Change.* Boston: American Meteorological Society.

Intergovernmental Panel on Climate Change. 2014. *Climate Change 2014: Synthesis Report.* Accessed on December 20, 2016 from www.ipcc.ch/report/ar5/syr/

Natural Resource Defense Council. 2016. *Water Pollution.* Accessed on December 20, 2016 from www.nrdc.org/issues/water-pollution

Portney, Kent E. 2015. *Sustainability.* Cambridge, MA: The MIT Press.

Seattle Office of Sustainability. 2013. Seattle Climate Action Plan. Accessed on September 20, 2016 from www.seattle.gov/Documents/Departments/OSE/2013_CAP_20130612.pdf

Sharp, Elaine B., Daley, Dorothy M., and Lynch, Michael S. 2011. "Understanding Local Adoption and Implementation of Climate Change Mitigation Policy." *Urban Affairs Review* 47 (3): pp. 433–457.

Svara, James H., Watt, Tanya C., and Jang, Hee Soun. 2013. "How Are U.S. Cities Doing Sustainability? Who Is Getting on the Sustainability Train, and Why?" *Cityscape: A Journal of Policy Development and Research* 15 (1): pp. 9–44.

United Nations. 2016. *The Paris Agreement: Frequently Asked Questions.* Accessed on December 27, 2016 from www.un.org/sustainabledevelopment/blog/2016/09/the-paris-agreement-faqs/

United Nations Habitat for a Better Urban Future. 2016. *Climate Change.* Accessed on December 20, 2016 from http://unhabitat.org/urban-themes/climate-change/

U.S. Environmental Protection Agency. 2016a. *Nutrient Pollution.* Accessed on December 20, 2016 from www.epa.gov/nutrientpollution

U.S. Environmental Protection Agency. 2016b. *Overview of Greenhouse Gases.* Accessed on December 16, 2016 from www.epa.gov/ghgemissions/overview-greenhouse-gases

Wang, XiaoHu, Hawkins, Christopher V., Lebredo, Nick, and Berman, Evan M. 2012. "Capacity to Sustain Sustainability: A Study of U.S. Cities." *Public Administration Review* 72 (6): pp. 841–853.

Wheeler, Stephen M. Autumn 2008. "State and Municipal Climate Change Plans." *Journal of the American Planning Association* 74 (4): pp. 481–496.

Zahran, Sammy, Grover, Himanshu, Brody, Samuel, and Vedlitz, Arnold. March 2008. "Risk, Stress, and Capacity: Commitment to Climate Protection." *Urban Affairs Review* 43 (4): pp. 447–474.

Zeemering, Eric. November 2009. "What Does Sustainability Mean to City Officials?" *Urban Affairs Review* 45 (2): pp. 247–273.

Zeemering, Eric. April 2012. "Recognizing Interdependence and Defining Multi-Level Governance in City Sustainability Plans." *Local Environment* 17 (4): pp. 409–424.

Zeemering, Eric. 2014. *Collaborative Strategies for Sustainable Cities: Economy, Environment, and Community in Baltimore.* New York: Routledge.

AFTERWORD

Cities, with their dense mixtures of people and economic activity, have long been fonts of innovation. To start, density spurs innovation by pushing people and ideas together, enabling them to combine and recombine in new ways. And advances in transportation—from railroads to subways to automobiles, planes, and high-speed rail—increase the circulation not only of goods and people, but of ideas as well.

(Florida 2015)

Many innovative new trends are emerging right now in our cities—civic technology and the data movement, resiliency to climate change, the development of more strategies towards sustainability, more citizens getting directly engaged in their communities, and lots of new partnerships.

For those who work in city government, there are enormous opportunities to work at the crux of innovative attempts to solve urban problems. Cities offer the prime laboratory for new ideas and innovations. And there are many organizations working hard at urban problems, partnering with city governments, universities, nonprofits, foundations, and others. To provide just an idea of the brain power and energy behind many new efforts, here are just a few of these organizations:

- Living Cities (www.livingcities.org/). "Founded in 1991, Living Cities harnesses the collective power of the world's largest foundations and financial institutions to build a new type of urban practice that gets dramatically better results for low-income people, faster." (Living Cities 2017, www.livingcities.org/about).
- Meeting of the Minds (http://cityminded.org/). "Meeting of the Minds is a global leadership network and knowledge sharing platform based in the San Francisco Bay Area. Since it was founded, Meeting of the Minds has been dedicated to a singular proposition: bring together a carefully chosen set of key urban sustainability and technology stakeholders and gather them around a common platform in ways that help build lasting alliances. . . . Meeting of the Minds focuses on the innovators and initiatives at the bleeding edge of urban sustainability and connected technology." (Meeting of the Minds 2017, http://cityminded.org/about)
- Code for America (www.codeforamerica.org/). "The two biggest levers for improving people's lives at scale are technology and government. We put them together." (Code for America 2017, www.codeforamerica.org/)
- Urban Innovation Fund (www.urbaninnovationfund.com/). "We provide seed capital and regulatory expertise to entrepreneurs solving our toughest urban challenges—helping them grow into tomorrow's most valued companies." (Urban Innovation Fund 2017, www.urbaninnovationfund.com/#mission)
- MetroLab Network (http://metrolab.heinz.cmu.edu/). "MetroLab Network includes 38 cities, 4 counties, and 51 universities, organized in more than 35 regional city-university partnerships. Partners focus on research, development and deployment (RD&D) projects that offer technological and analytically-based solutions to challenges facing urban areas including: inequality in income, health, mobility, security and opportunity; aging infrastructure; and environmental sustainability and resiliency." (MetroLab Network 2017, http://metrolab.heinz.cmu.edu/)

- Aspen Institute Center for Urban Innovation (www.aspeninstitute.org/programs/center-for-urban-innovation/). "The Aspen Institute Center for Urban Innovation will identify, connect, and support urban innovators, with a special emphasis on people who come from or work in underserved neighborhoods. The Center will also help leaders from government, business, and philanthropy better understand the needs of urban innovators so that their powerful ideas can spread rapidly from place to place." (Aspen Institute Center for Urban Innovation 2017, www.aspeninstitute.org/programs/center-for-urban-innovation/)

Some of the many new ideas and innovations emerging also provide just a taste of what is possible, in the future.

- Alameda County, California is partnering with Google on a variety of projects under the Google Gov Lab name, including online one-stop permitting and service contracts, and a 211 app to help guide residents to social services.

(Shueh 2015)

- New York City is known for its High Line Park, built on an old train trestle. But it is now adding to its assets by building a one-acre park underground in a former subway trolley tunnel. To try out the concept, it built an underground park in a warehouse, where it grew strawberries and other plants.

(Hester 2016)

- The Spring Hill Tennessee Public Library has developed a new way to increase access to the Internet and reduce the digital divide; it now offers portable WiFi hotspot technology for check-out so users can take their WiFi home with them.

(Eidam 2016)

- Sunrise City in Broward County, Florida is creating walkable pathways while simultaneously ensuring rainwater can still permeate down the water aquifer below. It is using material made from old tires and stone to create permeable pathways in City parks.

(Public Works 2015)

- In Las Vegas, new streetlights are being tested that are not just powered by solar energy, but are also powered by the energy (kinetic energy) of people walking by the area.

(Public Works 2017)

- Along with Chief Financial Officers (CFOs), Chief Information Officers (CIOs), and now Chief Data Officers (CDOs) and Chief Innovation Officers (CIOs), there is now at least one Chief Strategy Officer (CSO)—in Nashville/Davidson County. The new CSO will work to better align the city budget with its strategic priorities, and enhance transparency and accountability.
- Burlington, Vermont has become the first American city to receive 100 percent of its power from renewable sources. It sustainably harvests wood slash (small branches and leaves) from the surrounding areas, draws hydroelectric power from a nearby plant, and has wind turbines and solar panels at its airport. It is now working toward being a new zero consumer of energy in ten years.

(Woodard 2016)

Of course, these are just a few of the many new ideas emerging from cities today, and just a few of the partners available with whom cities can work. But they illustrate what can happen when the energy to try new ideas is available.

Guided by the NASPAA student learning goals in Urban Administration, students interested in working in city management can participate in this innovative environment and join in the search for solutions to urban problems. Using a context of public service values and ethics, students can combine their knowledge of cities and their governments, public policy, and how to engage residents and effectively provide urban services with their skills in public management, communication, critical thinking, and analysis in a meaningful way to make a difference in city management.

REFERENCES

Code for America. 2017. Code for America. Accessed on January 20, 2017 from https://www.codeforamerica.org/

Eidam, Eyragon. 2016. "WiFi Hot Spots for Rent: How Public Libraries are Changing With The Times." *Digital Communities*. Accessed on January 15, 2017 from www.govtech.com/dc/articles/Wi-Fi-Hot-Spots-for-Rent-How-Public-Libraries-Are-Changing-with-the-Times.html?utm_term=Wi-Fi%20Hot%20Spots%20for%20Rent%3A%20How%20Public%20Libraries%20Are%20Changing%20with%20the%20Times&utm_campaign=Libraries%20Lend%20Wi-Fi%20Hot%20Spots%20to%20Patrons%2C%20How%20Tech%20Chiefs%20Work%20Together&utm_content=email&utm_source=Act-On+Software&utm_medium=email

Florida, Richard. 2015. "The Historic Link between Cities and Innovation." *CityLab*, December 30, 2015. Accessed on February 26, 2017 from www.citylab.com/design/2015/12/the-historic-link-between-cities-and-innovation/422226/?utm_source=nl__link3_123015

Hester, Jessica Leigh. 2016. "A Park beneath New York City's Sidewalks." *CityLab*, July 14, 2016. www.citylab.com/navigator/2016/07/low-line-nyc-city-approval/491378/?utm_source=nl__link5_071516

Living Cities. Who We Are. Accessed on January 20, 2017 from https://www.livingcities.org/about

Meeting of the Minds. 2017. Meeting of the Minds. Accessed on January 20, 2017 from http://meetingoftheminds.org

MetroLab Network. 2017. A City-University Collaborative for Urban Innovation. Accessed on January 20, 2017 from https://metrolabnetwork.org/

Public Works. 2015. "Porous Pathways Perk Up Public Parks." *Public Works*, November 23, 2015. Accessed on January 15, 2017 from www.pwmag.com/roadways/porous-pathways-perk-up-public-parks-slideshow_o

Public Works. 2017. "These Are the Coolest Streetlights EVER." *Public Works*. Accessed on January 15, 2017 from www.pwmag.com/roadways/traffic-control-lighting/these-are-the-coolest-streetlightsever_c?utm_source=newsletter&utm_content=Article&utm_medium=email&utm_campaign=PW_012517%20(1)&he=

Shueh, Jason. 2015. "Alameda County, Calif., Announces 7 Google Gov Lab Prototypes." *Digital Communities*, October 13, 2015. Accessed on January 15, 2017 from www.govtech.com/dc/articles/Alameda-County-Calif-Announces-7-Google-Gov-Lab Prototypes.html?utm_term=seven%20projects%20launched%20in%20partnership%20with%20the%20Google%20Government%20Innovation%20Lab&utm_campaign=GovTech%27s%20Best%20of%20the%20Week&utm_content=email&utm_source=Act-On+Software&utm_medium=email

Urban Innovation Fund. 2017. Urban Innovation Fund. Accessed on January 20, 2017 from http://www.urbaninnovationfund.com/

Woodard, Colin. 2016. "America's First All-Renewable-Energy City." *Politico Magazine*. Accessed on January 15, 2017 from www.politico.com/magazine/story/2016/11/burlington-what-works-green-energy-214463

INDEX

Note: Page numbers followed by *t, f,* or *b* indicate a table, figure, or box respectively.

cogeneration 215
Cold War civil defense 177
Collaborate.org 56
collaboration: defined 35; of technology and
    performance measurement in regionalism 55–59
collaborative management, in city structure 35–36
collective bargaining and labor relations 105,
    116–118, 121
Columbus, Ohio, mixed use arena district 241–242
"The Coming Decade of Local Government"
    (O'Neill) 54
commercial building codes 197
commission form of government structure 19, 22, 23*t*
communications: smart cities 134–136;
    telecommunications and WiFi networks 134;
    working with the media 136–140; *see also*
    information
Community Action Agencies (CAAs) 229
community development, and housing 229–230
Community Development Block Grant (CDBG)
    program 229–230, 244
community policing 158–159
complete streets 213*b*
complex network type of regional governance 49
comprehensive plan, in urban planning 185–186
CompStat 164–165
concurrency regulations, in urban planning 190
Consolidated Metropolitan Statistical Area,
    defined 3*b*
consolidationist regions 49
contracting: for civil services 107, 108; for service
    delivery 146–151; for waste collection 214
conventional/high carbon (CHC) land use 187–188
convention centers 244, 245*t*
conversation cafes, to engage the public 70
cooperative (marble cake) federalism 42
coordinating regionalism 48
core public service values 31, 33
council-manager form of government structure 19,
    22–23
counties: and civil service workforce 110, 111*t*, 112;
    in intergovernmental relations 42, 49–50; types of
    regional governance 50
*County Manager's Guide to Shared Services in Local
    Government* 151
court challenges: for civil service workforce 117–118;
    pension retrenchment 120–122
Crawford, John III 162
crime rates 157, 165
crowdsourcing: in emergency management 180;
    social media for civic engagement 66, 78
cultures, diversity in cities 10

data 126–133; big data 126–127; civic technology 130;
    measuring amounts of 127*t*; open data 128–129;
    storage of 127; sustainability plans 135*b*;
    see also information
data centers 127

data journalism 130
data mining 127
data scientists 128
data visualizations 130–133; considerations 133*b*
data warehouses 127
defined benefits plans 119*b*
defined contributions plans 119*b*
deliberative polling, to engage the public 70
demographics *see* diversity of cities
Detroit, Michigan, bankruptcy 97–98
dialogue circles, to engage the public 70
Dillon, John Forrest 25
Dillon's Rule 25–26, 43
dimensional standards, in urban planning 191
disaster planning and recovery: in Arkansas 46–47;
    emergency management of 174–175, 179–181; GIS
    technology in Miami-Dade, Florida 56, 57
Disaster Relief Acts (1966, 1970) 179
disasters 173–175, 177–179*t*
discrimination in housing 230
discussion forums, to consult the public 66
Dispatch Magazine On-Line 153
diversity: in civil service workforce 114–116; in fire
    departments 171; in police departments 158
diversity of cities 1–17; age of citizens 10–12;
    immigration 10, 11; income 12–15; lesbian/gay
    households 12, 13*t*; populations 1–9, 109*t*, 110,
    113*t*; poverty 14–15; race and ethnicity 6–10;
    sustainability plans 9*b*
drinking water systems 201, 208–211
dual (layer cake) federalism 42
Duggan, Mike 97

earthquakes *see* disasters
economic development 233–245; convention centers
    244, 245*t*; industry codes 234, 235*t*; location
    quotients 234–235*b*, 236–237*t*; performance
    measurement 244; sports arenas 241–242, 244;
    strategies 238, 240–244; sustainability plans
    242–243*b*
Economic Opportunity Act (1964) 229
e-consultation, to consult the public 66
ecosystem services 210, 212
e-deliberation, to engage the public 70
e-government service delivery 152
elections, local and urban and city structure 19,
    28–30
elite model of public policy 27
Emanuel, Rahm 52, 129
emergency management 173–182; disasters 173–175;
    history of 175, 177, 179–180; Hurricane Katrina
    181; Joplin, Missouri tornadoes 181; major
    disasters in America 177–179*t*; natural hazards
    173–174; performance measurement 182*b*;
    technological hazards 174; technology in 180;
    terrorism 174
Emergency Management Reform Act (2006) 180
emergency medical services, by fire departments 173

eminent domain 189, 198
employees, governmental *see* civil service workforce
employees per citizen (EPC) 113–114
energy, sustainability plans 283*b*
enterprise districts 45
environmental issues, coalition-based regionalism 51*b*
environmental recreation facilities 256
environmental status of cities 268–286; air quality 268–269; climate change 271–274, 278–284; *see also* climate change; greenhouse gasses 270–271; sustainability 276–284; *see also* sustainability; sustainability plans 283–284*b*; water pollution 268
e-service delivery 151–153
ethics: in city management and public administration 33–35; regionalism barrier 54
ethnicity *see* race and ethnicity
exclusionary zoning, urban planning 191–192
expenditures of local government 86

Facebook, social media for civic engagement 73, 74
Fair Housing Act (1968) 230
families with children, demographics in cities 10–11
Fatal Encounters website 161–162
Federal Communications Commission 153
Federal Emergency Management Agency (FEMA) 180
federal government, characteristics of 53*b*
Federal Housing Administration (FHA) 187, 228
federal housing programs 227–229
federal system/federalism 41–42
Ferguson, Missouri, diversity in civil service workforce 114–115
financial management 84–85, 98–100; *see also* budget and financial management
financial statements 98–99, 100
Financial Trend Monitoring System (FTMS) 95*b*
fire departments 166–173; emergency medical services 173; hiring process 171; history of fire service 166–167; organization 167–169; performance measurement 182*b*; perspective on regionalism and localism 55*b*; response time to calls 171, 172*t*; revenue for 172–173; risk assessment 171, 172*t*; standard operating procedures (SOPs) 169–170
fires, major disasters 166, 177*t*
fiscal regionalism 50
fiscal stress, in budget and financial management 94–98
Fishkin, James 70
Fitch's 94
Flint, Michigan, water scandal 210–211
Flood Insurance Rate Maps (FIRMs) 212
floods *see* disasters
Florida, bankruptcies of cities 96
Florida, Richard 11
Florida Interoperable Picture Processing for Emergency Response (FLIPPER) 56
food systems, regional 48*b*

Ford, Ezell 162
form-based standards, in urban planning 191
fragmentation: and civil service workforce 110–111; in intergovernmental relations 44–46
Franklin, Ohio, public works department 203*f*
freedom of information, in social media 80
Freedom of Information Act 140
free rider problem 118
fuzzy boundaries 144, 147

G2G Cloud Solutions 58
Gableman, Michael J. 118
Gainsville, Florida, Police Department 159
game theory 27
garden city concept 185
Garner, Eric 162
gender occupational segregation 116
gentrification in housing 230
geographic information technology (GIS) 56–57, 153
global warming 270, 271–272
Goldstein, Brett 129
Gore, Al 272
government, as hollow state 144, 147, 149
governmental employees *see* civil service workforce
government structures: and city structure 19–23; *see also* intergovernmental relations (IGR)
graphic displays 130
gray infrastructure 210, 212
Great Recession of 2007, and bankruptcy of Stockton 96
green building codes 197–198
greenhouse gasses (GHG) 270–271, 283*b*
green infrastructure 210
Grodzins, Morton 42
growth management, in urban planning 192–193

hacking, and city data 130
Hanover Park, Illinois, fire department organizational chart 168*f*
Hawaii, Collaborate.org technology 56
hazards 173
health care costs, of pension obligations 91
Hispanics: elections and city council in Anaheim, California 29; population and diversity in cities 7–10; in urban workforce 116
hollow state, government as 144, 147, 149
Homeland Security Act (2002) 179*t*, 180
homelessness 230–233, 238–240*b*
home rule authority 25
home voters 28
HOPE VI 228
housing 227–233; coalition-based regionalism 51*b*; community development 229–230; federal housing programs 227–229; Great Recession of 2007 and market collapse 96; homelessness 230–233; housing discrimination 230; sustainability plans 242*b*
Housing Acts (1949, 1968) 227, 228